300 CHOCOLATE DESSERTS AND TREATS

300 CHOCOLATE DESSERTS AND TREATS

RICH RECIPES FOR HOT AND COLD DESSERTS, ICE CREAMS, TARTS, PIES, CANDIES, BARS, TRUFFLES AND DRINKS, WITH OVER 300 MOUTHWATERING PHOTOGRAPHS

EDITED BY FELICITY FORSTER

southwater

This edition is published by Southwater,
an imprint of Anness Publishing Ltd,
Hermes House,
88–89 Blackfriars Road,
London SE1 8HA;
tel. 020 7401 2077; fax 020 7633 9499

www.southwaterbooks.com; www.annesspublishing.com

If you like the images in this book and would like to investigate using them for publishing, promotions or advertising, please visit our website www.practicalpictures.com for more information.

UK agent: The Manning Partnership Ltd;
tel. 01225 478444; fax 01225 478440;
sales@manning-partnership.co.uk
UK distributor: Book Trade Services;
tel. 0116 2759086; fax 0116 2759090;
uksales@booktradeservices.com;
exportsales@booktradeservices.com
North American agent/distributor: National Book Network;
tel. 301 459 3366; fax 301 429 5746; www.nbnbooks.com
Australian agent/distributor: Pan Macmillan Australia;
tel. 1300 135 113; fax 1300 135 103;
customer.service@macmillan.com.au
New Zealand agent/distributor: David Bateman Ltd;
tel. (09) 415 7664; fax (09) 415 8892

Publisher: Joanna Lorenz
Senior Editor: Felicity Forster
Recipes: Christine France, Christine McFadden and Elizabeth Wolf-Cohen
Photography: Karl Adamson, Edward Allwright, David Armstrong, Steve Baxter, James Duncan, Michelle Garrett, Amanda Heywood, Tim Hill and Don Last
Jacket Design: Nigel Partridge
Production Controller: Helen Wang

Previously published as part of a larger volume, *500 Chocolate Recipes*

Main front cover image shows Steamed Chocolate and Fruit Pudding with Chocolate Syrup – for recipe, see page 12.

ETHICAL TRADING POLICY

At Anness Publishing we believe that business should be conducted in an ethical and ecologically sustainable way, with respect for the environment and a proper regard to the replacement of the natural resources we employ.

As a publisher, we use a lot of wood pulp to make high-quality paper for printing, and that wood commonly comes from spruce trees. We are therefore currently growing more than 750,000 trees in three Scottish forest plantations: Berrymoss (130 hectares/320 acres), West Touxhill (125 hectares/305 acres) and Deveron Forest (75 hectares/185 acres). The forests we manage contain more than 3.5 times the number of trees employed each year in making paper for the books we manufacture.

Because of this ongoing ecological investment programme, you, as our customer, can have the pleasure and reassurance of knowing that a tree is being cultivated on your behalf to naturally replace the materials used to make the book you are holding.

Our forestry programme is run in accordance with the UK Woodland Assurance Scheme (UKWAS) and will be certified by the internationally recognized Forest Stewardship Council (FSC). The FSC is a non-government organization dedicated to promoting responsible management of the world's forests. Certification ensures forests are managed in an environmentally sustainable and socially responsible way. For further information about this scheme, go to www.annesspublishing.com/trees

NOTES

Bracketed terms are intended for American readers.
For all recipes, quantities are given in both metric and imperial measures and, where appropriate, in standard cups and spoons. Follow one set, but not a mixture, because they are not interchangeable.
Standard spoon and cup measures are level.
1 tsp = 5ml, 1 tbsp = 15ml, 1 cup = 250ml/8fl oz.
Australian standard tablespoons are 20ml. Australian readers should use 3 tsp in place of 1 tbsp for measuring small quantities of gelatine, flour, salt etc.
Medium (US large) eggs are used unless otherwise stated.

The nutritional analysis given for each recipe is calculated per portion (i.e. serving or item), unless otherwise stated. If the recipe gives a range, such as Serves 4–6, then the nutritional analysis will be for the smaller portion size, i.e. 6 servings.

PUBLISHER'S NOTE

Although the advice and information in this book are believed to be accurate and true at the time of going to press, neither the authors nor the publisher can accept any legal responsibility or liability for any errors or omissions that may be made nor for any inaccuracies nor for any harm or injury that comes about from following instructions or advice in this book.

Contents

Introduction

One of the greatest treasures ever discovered was the bean from the tree *Theobroma cacao*, the original source of chocolate. Smooth in texture, intense in taste, subtly perfumed and elegant to behold, chocolate is a rich source of sensory pleasure, adored by almost everyone. Divine it really is – the name *Theobroma* is a Greek word meaning 'food of the gods'. The ultimate decadent treat, it is hardly surprising that in the past chocolate has been credited with being an aphrodisiac. Chocolates are traditional lovers' gifts, and special events, such as Easter and Christmas, are celebrated with chocolate eggs or the traditional yuletide log.

Once the preserve of Aztec emperors, highly prized and coveted, chocolate was unknown in Europe until the middle of the 16th century, when it was introduced as a rare and wonderful beverage. It took almost 200 years before the sweetened chocolate bar made its appearance, and the rest, as they say, is history. Although chocolate is now accessible to all, familiarity has done nothing to dim its huge popularity. Consumption of all types of chocolate continues to rise. In recent years there has been an increased demand for the pure product with more than 50 per cent cocoa solids, and aficionados scout out new varieties of chocolate with all the enthusiasm and energy of the ardent wine buff or truffle fancier.

For the cook, the fascination with chocolate goes even deeper. It is a sensitive ingredient that needs careful handling, but which offers remarkable rewards. The velvety texture and rich flavour add a touch of luxury to desserts, puddings, cakes, mousses, terrines, ice creams, sorbets, tarts, pies, brownies, truffles and drinks, and it is equally good in hot or cold dishes. As an added bonus, chocolate can be piped, shaped and moulded to make a variety of exciting decorations.

This book is for serious chocolate lovers. As you would expect, we've included classic after-dinner desserts and treats such as Sachertorte, Belgian Chocolate Mousse, American Chocolate Brownies and Chocolate Truffles, but – and this is the mark of the true chocoholic – we've also investigated every conceivable way of introducing our favourite ingredient into familiar and much-loved dishes. There is a rich chocolate trifle flavoured with mandarin oranges, a rare chocolate pavlova filled with the delectable zing of passion fruit cream, an unusual chocolate crème brûlée, a hot chocolate zabaglione and even fruit kebabs with chocolate and marshmallow fondue.

Also in the luscious line-up are gloriously gooey puddings, voluptuous gateaux with fudgy centres, light fairy cakes, muffins and profiteroles, and sweet chocolate treats for gifts and dinner-party delights. In honour of those ancient Aztecs, there is a recipe for Mexican hot chocolate and even an iced chocolate and peppermint drink.

The book is helpfully divided into eight differently themed sections so that you can easily find the recipes you want – there are Rich Cakes; Little Cakes, Slices and Bars; Tarts, Pies and Cheesecakes; Hot Desserts; Cold Desserts; Ice Creams and Sorbets; Candies and Truffles; and Drinks. All the classic desserts and treats are included, as well as many decadent dishes you may not have tried before. Once you get started, you'll soon want to begin experimenting with new ideas.

To help you make the most of these incredibly tempting recipes, there are cook's tips and variations scattered throughout the book, with suggestions for how to work with chocolate, the ingredients and equipment that will get the best results, and how to serve and decorate the finished dishes, as well as ideas for making alternative recipes by substituting other ingredients. Complete nutritional notes are provided for every dish, giving a useful breakdown of energy, carbohydrate and fibre so you can plan for individual diets and healthy eating, as well as knowing the fat and cholesterol content of special treats.

Whether you are planning a lavish dinner party or pampering yourself with an afternoon treat, this book has the perfect recipe. So go on, indulge yourself with every chocolate dish imaginable.

Chocolate Pecan Nut Torte

This torte uses finely ground nuts instead of flour. Toast and cool the nuts before grinding finely in a processor.

Makes one 20cm/8in round cake

200g/7oz plain (semisweet) chocolate, chopped
150g/5oz/10 tbsp unsalted (sweet) butter, diced
4 eggs
90g/3½oz/½ cup caster (superfine) sugar
10ml/2 tsp vanilla extract
115g/4oz/1 cup ground pecan nuts
10ml/2 tsp ground cinnamon
24 toasted pecan nut halves, to decorate (optional)

For the honey glaze
115g/4oz plain (semisweet) chocolate, chopped
60g/2oz/¼ cup unsalted (sweet) butter, cut into pieces
30ml/2 tbsp honey
a pinch of ground cinnamon

1 Preheat the oven to 180°C/350°F/Gas 4. Grease a 20cm/8in springform tin (pan), line with baking parchment, then grease the paper. Wrap the tin with foil.

2 Melt the chocolate and butter in a double boiler or in a heatproof bowl over a pan of simmering water, stirring until smooth. Set aside. Beat the eggs, sugar and vanilla extract until frothy. Stir in the melted chocolate and butter, ground nuts and cinnamon.

3 Pour into the tin. Place in a large roasting pan and pour boiling water into the roasting pan, to come 2cm/¾in up the side of the springform tin. Bake for 25–30 minutes, or until the edge of the cake is set, but the centre soft. Remove the foil and set on a wire rack.

4 To make the glaze, melt the chocolate, butter, honey and cinnamon as before, stirring until smooth. Remove from the heat. Dip the toasted pecan halves halfway into the glaze and place on baking parchment to set. Remove the cake from its tin and invert on to a wire rack. Remove the paper. Pour the glaze over the cake, tilting the rack to ensure it is evenly spread out. Use a metal spatula to smooth the sides. Arrange the pecan nut halves on top.

Walnut Coffee Gateau with Chocolate Frosting

This cake uses finely ground walnuts instead of flour.

Serves 8–10

150g/5oz/generous 1 cup walnuts
150g/5oz/¾ cup caster (superfine) sugar
5 eggs, separated
50g/2oz/scant 1 cup dry breadcrumbs
15ml/1 tbsp unsweetened cocoa powder
15ml/1 tbsp instant coffee
30ml/2 tbsp rum or lemon juice
1.5ml/¼ tsp salt
90ml/6 tbsp redcurrant jam
chopped walnuts, for decorating

For the frosting
225g/8oz plain (semisweet) chocolate
750ml/1¼ pint/3 cups whipping cream

1 To make the frosting, combine the chocolate and cream in the top of a double boiler until the chocolate melts. Cool, then cover and chill overnight, or until the mixture is firm.

2 Preheat the oven to 180°C/350°F/Gas 4. Line and grease a 23 × 5cm/9 × 2in cake tin (pan). Grind the nuts with 45ml/3 tbsp of the sugar in a food processor, blender or coffee grinder.

3 With an electric mixer, beat the egg yolks and remaining sugar until thick and pale. Fold in the walnuts. Stir in the breadcrumbs, cocoa, coffee and rum or lemon juice.

4 In another bowl, beat the egg whites and salt until they hold stiff peaks. Fold carefully into the walnut mixture. Pour the batter into the prepared tin and bake until the top of the cake springs back when touched, about 45 minutes. Leave in the tin for 5 minutes, then turn out and cool. Slice in half horizontally.

5 With an electric mixer, beat the frosting mixture on a low speed until it becomes lighter, about 30 seconds. Warm the redcurrant jam and brush some over the cut cake layer. Spread with some of the frosting, then sandwich with the remaining cake layer. Brush the top of the cake with some more jam, then cover the side and top with the remaining frosting. Make a starburst pattern with a knife and sprinkle the walnuts around the edge.

Torte Energy 4744kcal/19729kJ; Protein 53.2g; Carbohydrate 335.4g, of which sugars 330.8g; Fat 363.6g, of which saturates 175.2g; Cholesterol 1228mg; Calcium 380mg; Fibre 13.3g;Sodium 1582mg.
Walnut Gateau Energy 651kcal/2707kJ; Protein 9.5g; Carbohydrate 43.5g, of which sugars 38.5g; Fat 50.1g, of which saturates 24.9g; Cholesterol 175mg; Calcium 101mg; Fibre 1.8g; Sodium 149mg.

Luxurious Chocolate Cake

This attractive and delicious chocolate cake contains no flour and has a light mousse-like texture.

Makes one 20cm/8in round cake

225g/9oz plain (semisweet) chocolate, broken into squares
175g/6oz/¾ cup butter, softened
130g/4½oz/⅔ cup caster (superfine) sugar
225g/8oz/2 cups ground almonds
4 eggs, separated
115g/4oz squares white chocolate, melted, to decorate

1 Preheat the oven to 180°C/350°F/Gas 4. Grease and base-line a 20cm/8in springform cake tin (pan).

2 Melt the chocolate in a heatproof bowl over a pan of simmering water. Beat 115g/4oz/½ cup butter and all the sugar until light and fluffy in a large bowl. Add two-thirds of the plain chocolate, the almonds and egg yolks, and beat well.

3 Whisk the egg whites in another clean, dry bowl until stiff peaks form. Fold them into the chocolate mixture, then transfer to the tin and smooth the surface. Bake for 50–55 minutes, or until a skewer inserted into the centre comes out clean.

4 Cool in the tin for 5 minutes, then remove from the tin and transfer to a wire rack. Remove the lining paper and cool completely.

5 Place the remaining butter and remaining melted chocolate in a pan. Heat very gently, stirring constantly, until melted and smooth. Place a large sheet of baking parchment under the wire rack to catch any drips. Pour the chocolate topping over the cake, allowing the topping to coat the top and sides. Leave to set for at least 1 hour.

6 To decorate, fill a paper piping (pastry) bag with the melted white chocolate and snip the end. Drizzle the white chocolate around the edges. Use any remaining chocolate to pipe leaves on to baking parchment. Allow to set then place in the middle on top of the cake.

Torte Varazdin

This classic chocolate cake is a favourite worldwide, and appears in many guises.

Serves 8–12

225g/8oz/1 cup butter, at room temperature
225g/8oz/generous 1 cup caster (superfine) sugar
200g/7oz plain (semisweet) chocolate, melted
6 eggs, separated
130g/4½oz/generous 1 cup plain (all-purpose) flour, sifted
chocolate curls, to decorate

For the filling

250ml/8fl oz/1 cup double (heavy) cream, lightly whipped
450g/1lb/1¾ cups canned chestnut purée
115g/4oz/generous ½ cup caster (superfine) sugar

For the topping

150g/5oz/10 tbsp unsalted (sweet) butter
150g/5oz/1¼ cups icing (confectioners') sugar, sifted
115g/4oz plain (semisweet) chocolate, melted

1 Preheat the oven to 180°C/350°F/Gas 4. Grease and line the base and sides of a 20–23cm/8–9in round cake tin (pan). Cream the butter and sugar together in a bowl until pale and fluffy. Stir in the melted chocolate and egg yolks. Fold the flour carefully into the chocolate mixture.

2 In a grease-free bowl, whisk the egg whites until stiff. Add a spoonful of the egg white to the chocolate mixture to loosen it, then carefully fold in the remainder. Spoon the cake mixture into the prepared tin.

3 Bake the cake for 45–50 minutes, or until firm to the touch and a skewer inserted into the middle comes out clean. Cool on a wire rack. When cold, peel off the lining paper and slice the cake in half horizontally.

4 Meanwhile, gently mix the filling ingredients together in a bowl. Sandwich the two cake halves together firmly with the chestnut filling. In a mixing bowl, cream together the butter and sugar for the topping before stirring in the melted chocolate. Using a dampened knife, spread the chocolate topping over the sides and top of the cake. Chill for 60 minutes before serving if possible, decorated with chocolate curls.

Luxurious Energy 5823kcal/24249kJ; Protein 103.4g; Carbohydrate 426.5g, of which sugars 418.4g; Fat 424.1g, of which saturates 186.5g; Cholesterol 1148mg; Calcium 1436mg; Fibre 22.3g; Sodium 1641mg.
Varazdin Energy 731kcal/3055kJ; Protein 3.8g; Carbohydrate 82g, of which sugars 62.4g; Fat 45.4g, of which saturates 27.9g; Cholesterol 97mg; Calcium 79mg; Fibre 2.5g; Sodium 202mg.

French Chocolate Cake

This is typical of a French home-made cake – dense, dark and utterly delicious. Serve with cream or a fruit coulis.

Makes one 24cm/9½in round cake

150g/5oz/¾ cup caster (superfine) sugar
275g/10oz plain (semisweet) chocolate, chopped
175g/6oz/¾ cup unsalted (sweet) butter, cut into pieces
10ml/2 tsp vanilla extract
5 eggs, separated
40g/1½oz/⅓ cup plain (all-purpose) flour, sifted
a pinch of salt
icing (confectioners') sugar, for dusting

1 Preheat the oven to 160°C/325°F/Gas 3. Butter a 24cm/9½in round springform tin (pan), sprinkle with sugar and tap out excess.

2 Set aside 45ml/3 tbsp of the caster sugar. Place the chopped chocolate, butter and remaining sugar in a heavy pan and cook gently over a low heat until melted, stirring occasionally.

3 Remove the pan from the heat, stir in the vanilla extract and leave to cool slightly.

4 Beat the egg yolks, one at a time, into the chocolate mixture, then stir in the flour.

5 Beat the egg whites with the salt until soft peaks form. Sprinkle over the reserved sugar and beat until stiff and glossy. Beat one-third of the whites into the chocolate mixture to lighten it, then fold in the rest.

6 Pour the mixture into the tin and tap it gently to release any air bubbles.

7 Bake the cake for 35–45 minutes, or until well risen and the top springs back when touched lightly. Transfer to a wire rack, remove the sides of the tin and leave the cake to cool. Remove the tin base, dust the cake with icing sugar and transfer to a serving plate.

French Chocolate Cake with Brandy

A deliciously dense dessert with an attractive topping.

Serves 10

250g/9oz dark (bittersweet) chocolate, chopped into pieces
225g/8oz/1 cup unsalted (sweet) butter, cut into small pieces
90g/3½oz/scant ½ cup sugar
30ml/2 tbsp brandy or orange-flavoured liqueur
5 eggs
15ml/1 tbsp plain (all-purpose) flour
icing (confectioners') sugar, for dusting
whipped or sour cream, to serve

1 Preheat the oven to 180°C/350°F/Gas 4. Generously grease a 23 × 5cm/9 × 2in springform tin (pan). Line the base with baking parchment and grease. Wrap the bottom and sides of the tin in foil to prevent water from seeping into the cake.

2 In a pan, over a low heat, melt the chocolate, butter and sugar, stirring frequently until smooth. Remove from the heat, cool slightly and stir in the brandy or liqueur.

3 In a bowl, beat the eggs for 1 minute. Beat in the flour, then slowly blend in the chocolate mixture. Pour into the tin.

4 Place the springform tin in a large roasting pan. Add enough boiling water to come 2cm/¾in up the side of the springform tin. Bake for 25–30 minutes, until the edge of the cake is set but the centre is still soft. Remove the springform tin from the roasting pan and remove the foil. Cool on a wire rack. The cake will sink in the centre and become its classic slim shape as it cools. Don't worry if the surface cracks slightly.

5 Remove the side of the springform tin and turn the cake on to a wire rack. Lift off the tin base and then carefully peel back the paper, so the base of the cake is now the top. Leave the cake on the rack until it is quite cold.

6 Cut 6–8 strips of baking parchment 2.5cm/1in wide and place randomly over the cake. Dust the cake with icing sugar, then carefully remove the paper. Slide the cake on to a plate and serve with whipped or sour cream.

French Energy 3799kcal/15862kJ; Protein 50.6g; Carbohydrate 363.5g, of which sugars 330.6g; Fat 249.1g, of which saturates 145.2g; Cholesterol 1341mg; Calcium 400mg; Fibre 8.1g; Sodium 1437mg.
Brandy Energy 379kcal/1576kJ; Protein 4.7g; Carbohydrate 26.6g, of which sugars 25.2g; Fat 28.3g, of which saturates 16.7g; Cholesterol 145mg; Calcium 33mg; Fibre 0.7g; Sodium 173mg.

Chocolate and Almond Cake

This rich and sumptuous chocolate cake is filled with a sweet almond paste.

Serves 6

6 eggs, separated
115g/4oz/1 cup caster (superfine) sugar
150g/5oz/1 ¼ cups unsweetened cocoa powder
150g/5oz/1 ¼ cups ground almonds

For the almond paste

150g/5oz/1 ¼ cups caster (superfine) sugar
120ml/4fl oz/½ cup water
150g/5oz/1 ¼ cups ground almonds
15–30ml/1–2 tbsp lemon juice
½ vanilla pod (bean)

For the icing

115g/4oz dark (bittersweet) chocolate, chopped
25g/1oz/2 tbsp unsalted (sweet) butter, cubed
120ml/4fl oz/½ cup double (heavy) cream
50g/2oz/½ cup icing (confectioners') sugar, sifted

1 Preheat the oven to 200°C/400°F/Gas 6. Grease and line a 20cm/8in springform cake tin (pan). Beat the egg yolks in a large bowl, add the sugar and beat until the mixture is thick and creamy. Add the cocoa powder and almonds, and gently fold in.

2 Whisk the egg whites until stiff peaks form. Fold a spoonful of the whites into the yolk mixture, then mix in the remaining whites. Spoon into the tin and bake for 1 hour, or until a skewer inserted into the centre comes out clean. Cool in the tin.

3 Make the almond paste. Gently heat the sugar and water in a pan until the sugar has dissolved. Boil for 5 minutes, or until a thick syrup forms. Stir in the almonds and transfer to a bowl. Add the lemon juice and the seeds from the vanilla pod. Mix well.

4 Remove the cake from the tin and slice into two even layers. Sandwich the two halves together with the almond paste.

5 Make the icing. Melt the chocolate and butter in a heatproof bowl over a pan of simmering water. Remove from the heat and stir in the cream, then add the sugar and stir well. Cover the top of the cake with the chocolate icing. Leave to set.

Chocolate Gooey Cake

This is Sweden's favourite chocolate cake. For perfect results it is essential to undercook the cake so that it is really dense in the middle. It is made with ground almonds instead of flour so the cake is gluten-free and therefore the perfect tempting, self-indulgent treat for a coeliac dinner guest.

Serves 8

115g/4oz dark (bittersweet) chocolate with 75 per cent cocoa solids
5ml/1 tsp water
115g/4oz/½ cup unsalted (sweet) butter, plus extra to grease
2 eggs, separated
175g/6oz/1 ½ cups ground almonds
5ml/1 tsp vanilla sugar
whipped double (heavy) cream, to serve

1 Preheat the oven to 180°C/350°F/Gas 4. Grease a 20cm/8in shallow round cake tin (pan) with butter.

2 Break the dark chocolate into pieces and place in a pan. Add the water and heat gently, stirring constantly, until the chocolate has melted and the mixture is smooth. Remove from the heat and set aside.

3 Cut the butter into small pieces, add to the chocolate and stir until melted.

4 Add the egg yolks, ground almonds and vanilla sugar and stir together until the mixture is evenly blended. Transfer the mixture in a large bowl.

5 Whisk the egg whites until stiff, then carefully fold them into the chocolate mixture.

6 Spoon the mixture into the prepared tin and bake in the oven for 15–17 minutes, until just set. The mixture should still be soft in the centre.

7 Leave the cake to cool in the tin. When cold, serve with a spoonful of the whipped cream.

Almond Cake Energy 892kcal/3726kJ; Protein 23g; Carbohydrate 73.7g, of which sugars 69.3g; Fat 58.4g, of which saturates 19g; Cholesterol 228mg; Calcium 226mg; Fibre 7.2g; Sodium 349mg.
Gooey Cake Energy 311kcal/1288kJ; Protein 6.8g; Carbohydrate 10g, of which sugars 9.3g; Fat 27.4g, of which saturates 9.9g; Cholesterol 75mg; Calcium 66.2mg; Fibre 1.9g; Sodium 97mg.

Berry Chocolate Savarin

This exquisite cake is soaked in a wine and brandy syrup.

Serves 6–8

100ml/3½fl oz/scant ½ cup milk
4 eggs
225g/8oz/2 cups unbleached white bread flour
40g/1½oz/⅓ cup unsweetened cocoa powder
2.5ml/½ tsp salt
25g/1oz/¼ cup caster (superfine) sugar
90g/3½oz/7 tbsp butter, melted
5ml/1 tsp easy-blend (rapid-rise) dried yeast

For the syrup
115g/4oz/generous ½ cup sugar
75ml/2½fl oz/⅓ cup white wine
45ml/3 tbsp brandy

For the filling
150ml/¼ pint/⅔ cup double (heavy) cream, whipped, or crème fraîche

For the topping
225g/8oz/2 cups strawberries, halved
115g/4oz/1 cup raspberries
physalis and strawberry leaves

1 Pour the milk and eggs into a bread machine pan. If necessary for your machine, reverse the order in which you add the liquid and dry ingredients. Sprinkle the flour and cocoa powder over the liquid in the pan, until covered. Place the salt, sugar and butter in separate corners. Make an indent in the flour; add the yeast.

2 Start the machine on the dough setting (basic dough setting if available). Oil a 1.5 litre/2½ pint/6¼ cup savarin or ring mould. When the machine has finished mixing, leave on the dough setting for 20 minutes, then stop it. Put the dough into the mould, cover with oiled clear film (plastic wrap) and leave for 1 hour, or until the dough is near the top of the mould. Meanwhile, preheat the oven to 200°C/400°F/Gas 6. Bake for 25–30 minutes, or until golden and well risen. Cool on a wire rack.

3 Make the syrup. Place the sugar, wine and 75ml/2½fl oz/⅓ cup water in a pan. Heat gently, stirring until the sugar dissolves. Bring to the boil, then lower the heat and simmer for 2 minutes. Remove from the heat and stir in the brandy. Spoon over the savarin. Transfer to a serving plate and leave to cool. To serve, fill the centre with the cream or crème fraîche and top with the berries. Decorate with physalis and strawberry leaves.

Death by Chocolate

One of the richest chocolate cakes ever.

Serves 16–20

225g/8oz dark (bittersweet) chocolate, broken into squares
115g/4oz/½ cup unsalted (sweet) butter
150ml/¼ pint/⅔ cup milk
225g/8oz/1 cup light muscovado (brown) sugar
10ml/2 tsp vanilla extract
2 eggs, separated
150ml/¼ pint/⅔ cup sour cream
225g/8oz/2 cups self-raising (self-rising) flour
5ml/1 tsp baking powder

For the filling
60ml/4 tbsp seedless raspberry jam
60ml/4 tbsp brandy
400g/14oz dark (bittersweet) chocolate, broken into squares
200g/7oz/scant 1 cup unsalted (sweet) butter

For the topping
250ml/8fl oz/1 cup double (heavy) cream
225g/8oz dark (bittersweet) chocolate, broken into squares
plain (semisweet) and white chocolate curls, to decorate
chocolate-dipped physalis or raspberries, to serve (optional)

1 Preheat the oven to 180°C/350°F/Gas 4. Grease and base-line a deep 23cm/9in springform cake tin (pan). Place the chocolate, butter and milk in a pan. Heat gently until smooth. Remove from the heat, beat in the sugar and vanilla, then cool.

2 Beat the egg yolks and cream in a bowl, then beat into the chocolate mixture. Sift the flour and baking powder over the surface and fold in. Whisk the egg whites in a grease-free bowl until stiff; fold into the mixture.

3 Scrape into the prepared tin and bake for 45–55 minutes, or until firm. Cool in the tin for 15 minutes, then turn out and cool.

4 Slice the cold cake across the middle to make three even layers. In a small pan, warm the jam with 15ml/1 tbsp of the brandy, then brush over two of the layers. Heat the remaining brandy in a pan with the chocolate and butter, stirring, until smooth. Cool until beginning to thicken.

5 Spread the bottom layer of the cake with half the chocolate filling, taking care not to disturb the jam. Top with a second layer, jam side up, and spread with the remaining filling. Top with the final layer and press lightly. Leave to set.

6 Make the topping. Heat the cream and chocolate together in a pan over a low heat, stirring frequently until the chocolate has melted. Pour into a bowl, leave to cool, then whisk until the mixture begins to hold its shape.

7 Spread the top and sides of the cake with the chocolate topping. Decorate with chocolate curls and chocolate-dipped physalis or raspberries, if you like.

Cook's Tip

For chocolate-coated physalis, melt the chocolate in a bowl, then dip in the fruit, holding them by their tops. Leave to set completely before using.

Savarin Energy 335kcal/1396kJ; Protein 4.9g; Carbohydrate 25.6g, of which sugars 21.7g; Fat 22.4g, of which saturates 13.1g; Cholesterol 146mg; Calcium 66mg; Fibre 0.8g; Sodium 116mg.
Death by Chocolate Energy 432kcal/1809kJ; Protein 4.7g; Carbohydrate 49.9g, of which sugars 38.4g; Fat 24.7g, of which saturates 14.9g; Cholesterol 57mg; Calcium 99mg; Fibre 1.4g; Sodium 120mg.

Multi-layer Chocolate Cake

For a change, try sandwiching the layers with softened vanilla ice cream. Freeze the cake before serving.

Makes one 20cm/8in cake
115g/4oz plain (semisweet) chocolate
175g/6oz/¾ cup butter
450g/1lb/2¼ cups caster (superfine) sugar
3 eggs
5ml/1 tsp vanilla extract
175g/6oz/1½ cups plain (all-purpose) flour
5ml/1 tsp baking powder
115g/4oz/1 cup chopped walnuts

For the filling and topping
350ml/12fl oz/1½ cups whipping cream
225g/8oz plain (semisweet) chocolate
15ml/1 tbsp vegetable oil

1 Preheat the oven to 180°C/350°F/Gas 4. Line two 20cm/8in shallow round cake tins (pans) with baking parchment and grease the paper.

2 Melt the chocolate and butter together in the top of a double boiler or in a heatproof bowl over a pan of simmering water. Transfer to a bowl and stir in the sugar. Add the eggs and vanilla and mix well. Sift over the flour and baking powder. Stir in the chopped walnuts.

3 Pour the mixture into the prepared cake tins. Bake until a skewer inserted into the centre comes out clean, about 30 minutes. Leave to stand for 10 minutes, then unmould on to a wire rack to cool completely.

4 To make the filling and topping, whip the cream until firm. Slice the cakes in half horizontally. Sandwich them together with the cream and cover the cake with the remainder. Chill.

5 To make the chocolate curls, melt the chocolate and oil as before. Stir to combine well. Spread on to a non-porous surface. Just before it sets, hold the blade of a knife at an angle to the chocolate and scrape across the surface to make curls. Use to decorate the cake and add tiny curls made with the tip of a rounded knife as well, if you like.

Mississippi Mud Cake with Filling

A rich dark chocolate cake, reminiscent of the shores of the great Mississippi River.

Serves 8–10
150g/5oz unsweetened chocolate
225g/8oz/1 cup butter
300ml/¼ pint/1¼ cups strong coffee or espresso
pinch of salt
400g/14oz/2 cups sugar
60ml/4 tbsp bourbon or whisky
2 eggs, lightly beaten
10ml/2 tsp vanilla extract
275g/10oz/2½ cups plain (all-purpose) flour, sifted
130g/4½oz/1 cup sweetened desiccated (dry unsweetened shredded) coconut

For the filling and topping
250ml/8fl oz/1 cup evaporated milk
115g/4oz/½ cup soft light brown sugar
115g/4oz/½ cup butter
75g/3oz plain (semisweet) chocolate
3 egg yolks, lightly beaten
5ml/1 tsp vanilla extract
225g/8oz/2 cups pecans, chopped
75g/3oz/1 cup small marshmallows
350ml/12fl oz/1½ cups whipping or double (heavy) cream
5ml/1 tsp vanilla extract
fresh coconut for ruffles, to decorate

1 Preheat the oven to 180°C/350°F/Gas 4. Grease two 23cm/9in cake tins (pans). Melt the chocolate, butter, coffee, salt and sugar in a pan. Stir in the bourbon or whisky. Cool in a bowl slightly. Beat in the eggs and vanilla, then beat in the flour and coconut. Pour into the tins. Bake for 25–30 minutes. Cool in the tins for 10 minutes, then transfer to a wire rack.

2 For the filling, cook the milk, sugar, butter, chocolate, egg yolks and vanilla in a pan for 8–10 minutes. Remove from heat and stir in the nuts and marshmallows. Chill until thick enough to spread. Slice both cakes in half. Spread each bottom layer with half the chocolate nut filling and cover with the top layers.

3 Whip the cream and the vanilla until firm peaks form. Spread a filled cake with half the whipped cream. Top with the second filled cake and spread with the remaining cream. To make the coconut ruffles, draw a swivel-bladed peeler along the curved edge of a coconut piece to make thin wide curls with a brown edge.

Multi Energy 7850kcal/32796kJ; Protein 79.4g; Carbohydrate 836.4g, of which sugars 699.2g; Fat 488.8g, of which saturates 249.3g; Cholesterol 1332mg; Calcium 1024mg; Fibre 17.9g; Sodium 1419mg.
Mississippi Energy 1108kcal/4624kJ; Protein 13g; Carbohydrate 102.8g, of which sugars 79.9g; Fat 73.1g, of which saturates 40.7g; Cholesterol 181mg; Calcium 227mg; Fibre 4.3g; Sodium 294mg.

Sachertorte

This glorious gateau was created in Vienna in 1832 by Franz Sacher, a royal chef.

Serves 10–12
225g/8oz dark (bittersweet) chocolate, broken into squares
150g/5oz/10 tbsp unsalted (sweet) butter, softened
115g/4oz/generous ½ cup caster (superfine) sugar
8 eggs, separated
115g/4oz/1 cup plain (all-purpose) flour
chocolate curls, to decorate

For the glaze
225g/8oz/¾ cup apricot jam
15ml/1 tbsp lemon juice

For the icing
225g/8oz plain dark (bittersweet) chocolate, broken into squares
200g/7oz/1 cup caster (superfine) sugar
15ml/1 tbsp golden (light corn) syrup
250ml/8fl oz/1 cup double (heavy) cream
5ml/1 tsp vanilla extract

1 Preheat the oven to 180°C/350°F/Gas 4. Grease a 23cm/9in round springform tin (pan). Line with baking parchment. Melt the chocolate in a heatproof bowl over a pan of hot water.

2 Cream the butter and sugar in a bowl until pale and fluffy. Add the egg yolks, one at a time, beating after each addition. Beat in the melted chocolate. Sift the flour over the mixture and fold in.

3 Whisk the egg whites until stiff, then stir a quarter into the chocolate mixture to lighten it. Fold in the remaining whites. Turn the mixture into the cake tin and smooth level. Bake for 50–55 minutes, or until firm. Turn out on to a wire rack to cool.

4 Heat the apricot jam with the lemon juice in a small pan until melted, then strain. Slice the cake horizontally into two even layers. Brush the cut surfaces and sides of each layer with the apricot glaze, then sandwich together. Place on a wire rack.

5 Mix the icing ingredients in a heavy pan. Heat gently, stirring until thick. Simmer for 3–4 minutes, without stirring, until the mixture registers 95°C/200°F on a sugar thermometer. Pour over the cake and spread evenly. Decorate with the curls and leave to set before serving.

Chocolate and Fresh Cherry Gateau

Make this sophisticated cake for a special occasion.

Makes one 20in/8in round cake
115g/4oz/½ cup butter
150g/5oz/¾ cup caster (superfine) sugar
3 eggs, lightly beaten
175g/6oz/1 cup plain (semisweet) chocolate chips, melted
60ml/4 tbsp Kirsch
150g/5oz/1¼ cups self-raising (self-rising) flour
5ml/1 tsp ground cinnamon
2.5ml/½ tsp ground cloves
350g/12oz fresh cherries, pitted and halved
45ml/3 tbsp morello cherry jam, warmed
5ml/1 tsp lemon juice

For the frosting
115g/4oz/⅔ cup plain (semisweet) chocolate chips
50g/2oz/¼ cup unsalted (sweet) butter
60ml/4 tbsp double (heavy) cream

To decorate
18 fresh cherries dipped in 75g/3oz/½ cup white chocolate chips, melted, and a few rose leaves, washed and dried

1 Preheat the oven to 160°C/325°F/Gas 3. Grease, base-line and flour a 20cm/8in round springform tin (pan).

2 Cream the butter and 115g/4oz/½ cup of the sugar until pale. Beat in the eggs. Stir in the chocolate and half the Kirsch. Fold in the flour and spices. Transfer to the tin and bake for 55–60 minutes. Cool for 10 minutes, then transfer to a wire rack.

3 For the filling, bring the cherries, the remaining Kirsch and sugar to the boil, cover, and simmer for 10 minutes. Uncover for a further 10 minutes until syrupy. Leave to cool.

4 Halve the cake horizontally. Cut a 1cm/½in deep circle from the middle of the base, leaving a 1cm/½in edge. Crumble this cake into the filling mixture and fill the cut-away depression.

5 Strain the jam and lemon juice. Brush all over the cake. For the frosting, melt all the ingredients together and stir until combined. Cool, then pour over the cake. Decorate with chocolate-dipped cherries and rose leaves.

Sachertorte Energy 625kcal/2618kJ; Protein 7.6g; Carbohydrate 73.1g, of which sugars 65.5g; Fat 35.8g, of which saturates 20.8g; Cholesterol 184mg; Calcium 73mg; Fibre 1.2g; Sodium 143mg.
Cherry Energy 5172kcal/21630kJ; Protein 60.1g; Carbohydrate 587.6g, of which sugars 470.7g; Fat 287.9g, of which saturates 171.5g; Cholesterol 1022mg; Calcium 781mg; Fibre 16.6g; Sodium 1337mg.

Tia Maria and Walnut Gateau

Whipped cream and Tia Maria make a mouthwatering filling for this light chocolate and walnut cake.

Serves 6–8

150g/5oz/1 1/4 cups self-raising (self-rising) flour
25g/1oz/1/4 cup unsweetened cocoa powder
7.5ml/1 1/2 tsp baking powder
3 eggs, beaten
175g/6oz/3/4 cup unsalted (sweet) butter, softened
175g/6oz/scant 1 cup caster (superfine) sugar
50g/2oz/1/2 cup chopped walnuts
walnut brittle, to decorate

For the filling and coating

600ml/1 pint/2 1/2 cups double (heavy) cream
45ml/3 tbsp Tia Maria
50g/2oz/2/3 cup desiccated (dry unsweetened shredded) coconut, toasted

1 Preheat the oven to 160°C/325°F/Gas 3. Grease and base-line two 18cm/7in sandwich tins. Sift the flour, cocoa powder and baking powder into a large bowl. Add the beaten eggs, butter, sugar and chopped walnuts and mix together thoroughly.

2 Divide the mixture between the cake tins, level the surface and bake for 35–40 minutes, until risen and browned. Turn out the cakes and leave to cool on a wire rack.

3 For the filling, add the Tia Maria to the cream and whisk until the mixture forms soft peaks.

4 Slice each cake horizontally in half to give four layers. Sandwich the layers together, spreading some of the flavoured cream between each layer.

5 Coat the sides of the cake with cream. Spread out the toasted coconut on a sheet of non-stick baking parchment. Then, holding the top and bottom of the cake, roll the side in the coconut until evenly coated. Put the cake on a serving plate, spread more of the cream on top and pipe the remainder around the outside rim. Decorate inside the rim with walnut brittle.

Rich Chocolate Nut Cake

Use walnuts or pecan nuts for the cake sides, if you prefer.

Makes one 23cm/9in round cake

225g/8oz/1 cup butter
225g/8oz plain (semisweet) chocolate
115g/4oz/1 cup unsweetened cocoa powder
350g/12oz/1 3/4 cups caster (superfine) sugar
6 eggs
100ml/3 1/2fl oz/scant 1/2 cup brandy
225g/8oz/2 cups finely chopped hazelnuts

For the glaze

50g/2oz/1/4 cup butter
150g/5oz cooking (unsweetened) chocolate
30ml/2 tbsp milk
5ml/1 tsp vanilla extract

1 Preheat the oven to 180°C/350°F/Gas 4. Line a 23 × 5cm/9 × 2in round tin (pan) with baking parchment and grease the paper.

2 Melt the butter and chocolate in the top of a double boiler. Leave to cool.

3 Sift the cocoa powder into a bowl. Add the sugar and eggs, stirring until combined. Add the chocolate mixture and brandy.

4 Fold in three-quarters of the hazelnuts, then pour the mixture into the prepared cake tin.

5 Set the tin in a roasting pan and pour 2.5cm/1in hot water into the outer pan. Bake until the cake is firm to the touch, about 45 minutes. Leave for 15 minutes, then unmould on to a wire rack. When cool, wrap in baking parchment and chill for at least 6 hours.

6 To make the glaze, melt the butter and chocolate with the milk and vanilla extract as before.

7 Place the cake on a wire rack over a plate. Drizzle the glaze over, letting it drip down the sides. Cover the cake sides with the remaining nuts. Transfer to a serving plate when set.

Tia Maria Energy 815kcal/3380kJ; Protein 7.4g; Carbohydrate 39.8g, of which sugars 25.1g; Fat 69.4g, of which saturates 41.1g; Cholesterol 221mg; Calcium 101mg; Fibre 2g; Sodium 209mg.
Nut Energy 7802kcal/32523kJ; Protein 113.7g; Carbohydrate 633.7g, of which sugars 612.6g; Fat 532.7g, of which saturates 241.2g; Cholesterol 1752mg; Calcium 1030mg; Fibre 37.9g; Sodium 3249mg.

Chocolate Fudge Gateau

A glorious dessert that is sure to delight everyone.

Serves 8–10
275g/10oz/2½ cups self-raising wholemeal (self-rising whole-wheat) flour
50g/2oz/½ cup unsweetened cocoa powder
45ml/3 tbsp baking powder
225g/8oz/generous 1 cup caster (superfine) sugar
few drops of vanilla extract
135ml/9 tbsp sunflower oil
350ml/12fl oz/1½ cups water
sifted unsweetened cocoa powder, for sprinkling
25g/1oz/¼ cup chopped nuts

For the chocolate fudge
50g/2oz/¼ cup soya margarine
45ml/3 tbsp water
250g/9oz/2¼ cups icing (confectioners') sugar
30ml/2 tbsp unsweetened cocoa powder
15–30ml/1–2 tbsp hot water

1 Preheat the oven to 160°C/325°F/Gas 3. Grease a deep 20cm/8in round cake tin (pan), line with baking parchment and grease the paper lightly with a little sunflower oil.

2 Sift the flour, cocoa and baking powder into a mixing bowl. Add the sugar and vanilla extract, then gradually beat in the oil. Gradually add the water, beating constantly to produce a thick batter. Pour into the prepared tin and level the surface.

3 Bake the cake for about 45 minutes or until a fine metal skewer inserted in the centre comes out clean. Leave in the tin for about 5 minutes, before turning out on to a wire rack. Peel off the lining and cool. Cut in half to make two equal layers.

4 Make the chocolate fudge. Place the margarine and water in a pan and heat gently until the margarine has melted. Remove from the heat and sift in the icing sugar and cocoa powder, beating until shiny, adding more hot water if needed. Pour into a bowl and cool until firm enough to spread and pipe.

5 Sandwich the cake layers together with two-thirds of the chocolate fudge. Pipe the remaining fudge over the cake. Sprinkle with cocoa powder and decorate with the nuts.

Chocolate Potato Cake

Mashed potato makes this cake moist and delicious.

Makes one 23cm/9in cake
200g/7oz/1 cup sugar
250g/9oz/1 cup and 2 tbsp butter
4 eggs, separated
275g/10oz dark (bittersweet) chocolate
75g/3oz/¾ cup ground almonds
165g/5½oz mashed potato
225g/8oz/2 cups self-raising (self-rising) flour
5ml/1 tsp cinnamon
45ml/3 tbsp milk
white and dark (bittersweet) chocolate shavings, to garnish
whipped cream, to serve

1 Preheat the oven to 180°C/350°F/Gas 4. Grease and line a 23cm/9in round cake tin (pan) with baking parchment.

2 In a bowl, cream together the sugar and 225g/8oz/1 cup of the butter until light and fluffy. Then beat the egg yolks into the creamed mixture one at a time until it is smooth and creamy.

3 Finely chop or grate 175g/6oz of the chocolate and stir it into the creamed mixture with the ground almonds. Pass the mashed potato through a sieve (strainer) or ricer and stir it into the creamed chocolate mixture. Sift together the flour and cinnamon and fold into the mixture with the milk.

4 Whisk the egg whites until they hold stiff but not dry peaks, and fold into the cake mixture.

5 Spoon into the tin and smooth the top, but make a slight hollow in the middle to keep the surface of the cake level while cooking. Bake in the oven for 1¼ hours, until a skewer inserted in the centre comes out clean. Allow the cake to cool slightly in the tin, then turn out and cool on a wire rack.

6 Break up the remaining chocolate into a heatproof bowl over a pan of hot water. Add the remaining butter in small pieces and stir until the mixture is smooth and glossy.

7 Peel off the lining paper and trim the top of the cake so it is level. Smooth over the chocolate icing. When set, decorate with the chocolate shavings and serve with whipped cream.

Fudge Gateau Energy 446kcal/1878kJ; Protein 4.5g; Carbohydrate 71.5g, of which sugars 50.1g; Fat 17.8g, of which saturates 3.2g; Cholesterol 0mg; Calcium 134mg; Fibre 1.9g; Sodium 218mg.
Potato Energy 5749kcal/24,034kJ; Protein 87.1g; Carbohydrate 590.9g, of which sugars 391.8g; Fat 354.8g, of which saturates 188.1g; Cholesterol 1465mg; Calcium 1408mg; Fibre 21.5g; Sodium 2731mg.

Coffee Chocolate Mousse Cake

Serve this dense, dark chocolate cake in small portions as it is very rich.

Serves 6

175g/6oz plain (semisweet) chocolate
30ml/2 tbsp strong brewed coffee
150g/5oz/10 tbsp butter, cubed
50g/2oz/¼ cup caster (superfine) sugar
3 eggs
25g/1oz/¼ cup ground almonds
about 25ml/1½ tbsp icing (confectioners') sugar, for dusting

For the mascarpone and coffee cream

250g/9oz/generous 1 cup mascarpone
30ml/2 tbsp icing (confectioners') sugar, sifted
30ml/2 tbsp strong brewed coffee

1 Preheat the oven to 200°C/400°F/Gas 6. Grease and line the base of a 15cm/6in square tin (pan) with baking parchment.

2 Put the chocolate and coffee in a small heavy pan and heat very gently until melted, stirring occasionally.

3 Add the butter and sugar to the pan and stir until dissolved. Whisk the eggs until frothy and gently stir into the chocolate mixture with the ground almonds until blended.

4 Pour into the prepared tin, then put in a large roasting pan and pour in enough hot water to come two-thirds up the cake tin. Bake for 50 minutes, or until the top feels springy. Leave to cool in the tin for 5 minutes, then turn the cake out on to a board and leave to cool.

5 Meanwhile, beat the mascarpone with the icing sugar and coffee. Dust the cake generously with icing sugar, then cut into slices. Serve on individual plates with the mascarpone and coffee cream alongside.

Cook's Tip
The top of this flourless cake, with its moist mousse-like texture, will crack slightly as it cooks.

Caribbean Chocolate Ring with Rum Syrup

This delectable chocolate and rum cake brings you a taste of the Caribbean.

Serves 8–10

115g/4oz/½ cup unsalted (sweet) butter, plus extra for greasing
115g/4oz/scant ½ cup light muscovado (brown) sugar
2 eggs, beaten
2 ripe bananas, mashed
30ml/2 tbsp desiccated (dry unsweetened shredded) coconut
30ml/2 tbsp sour cream
115g/4oz/1 cup self-raising (self-rising) flour
45ml/3 tbsp unsweetened cocoa powder
2.5ml/½ tsp bicarbonate of soda (baking soda)

For the syrup

115g/4oz/generous ½ cup caster (superfine) sugar
60ml/4 tbsp water
30ml/2 tbsp dark rum
50g/2oz plain (semisweet) chocolate, chopped
mixture of tropical fruits and chocolate shapes or curls, to decorate

1 Preheat the oven to 180°C/350°F/Gas 4. Grease a 1.5 litre/2½ pint/6¼ cup ring tin (pan) with butter.

2 Cream the butter and sugar in a bowl until light and fluffy. Add the eggs gradually, beating well, then mix in the bananas, coconut and sour cream. Sift the flour, cocoa and bicarbonate of soda over the mixture and fold in thoroughly.

3 Transfer to the prepared tin and spread evenly. Bake for 45–50 minutes, until firm to the touch. Cool for 10 minutes in the tin, then turn out to finish cooling on a wire rack.

4 Make the syrup. Place the sugar in a small pan. Add the water and heat gently, stirring occasionally until dissolved. Bring to the boil and boil rapidly, without stirring, for 2 minutes. Remove from the heat.

5 Add the rum and chocolate to the syrup and stir until smooth, then spoon evenly over the top and sides of the cake. Decorate the ring with tropical fruits and chocolate shapes.

Coffee Cake Energy 524kcal/2180kJ; Protein 9.5g; Carbohydrate 34.2g, of which sugars 33.8g; Fat 39.9g, of which saturates 22.7g; Cholesterol 168mg; Calcium 46mg; Fibre 1g; Sodium 190mg.
Caribbean Ring Energy 315kcal/1319kJ; Protein 4g; Carbohydrate 40.5g, of which sugars 31g; Fat 15.6g, of which saturates 9.7g; Cholesterol 65mg; Calcium 72mg; Fibre 1.6g; Sodium 172mg.

Rich Chocolate Cake

This dark, fudgy cake is easy to make and is a chocolate lover's dream come true.

Serves 14–16

250g/9oz plain (semisweet) chocolate, chopped
225g/8oz/1 cup unsalted (sweet) butter, cut into pieces
5 eggs
100g/3½oz/½ cup caster (superfine) sugar, plus 15ml/1 tbsp and extra for sprinkling
15ml/1 tbsp unsweetened cocoa powder
10ml/2 tsp vanilla extract
unsweetened cocoa powder, for dusting
chocolate shavings, to decorate
icing (confectioners') sugar, for dusting

1 Preheat the oven to 170°C/325°F/Gas 3. Lightly butter a 23cm/9in springform tin (pan) and line the base with baking parchment. Butter the paper and sprinkle with a little sugar, then tip out the excess. The cake is baked in a *bain-marie*, so carefully wrap the base and sides of the tin with a double thickness of foil to prevent water leaking into the cake.

2 Melt the chocolate and butter in a pan over a low heat until smooth, stirring, then remove from the heat. Beat the eggs and 100g/3½oz/½ cup of the sugar with a mixer for 1 minute.

3 Mix together the cocoa and the remaining 15ml/1 tbsp sugar and beat into the egg mixture until well blended. Beat in the vanilla extract, then slowly beat in the melted chocolate until well blended. Pour the mixture into the prepared tin and tap gently to release any air bubbles.

4 Place the cake tin in a roasting pan and pour in boiling water to come 2cm/¾in up the sides of the wrapped tin. Bake for 45–50 minutes, until the edge of the cake is set and the centre still soft. Lift the tin out of the water and remove the foil. Place the cake on a wire rack, remove the sides of the tin and leave the cake to cool completely (the cake will sink in the centre).

5 Invert the cake on to the wire rack. Remove the base of the tin and the paper. Dust the cake with cocoa and arrange the shavings around the edge. Slide the cake on to a serving plate.

Chocolate Mousse Gateau

This special occasion dessert is a double batch of chocolate mousse, glazed with chocolate ganache and decorated with long, slim chocolate curls.

Serves 8–10

275g/10oz plain (semisweet) chocolate, chopped
115g/4oz/½ cup unsalted (sweet) butter, cut into pieces
8 eggs, separated
1.5ml/¼ tsp cream of tartar
45ml/3 tbsp brandy or rum (optional)
chocolate curls, to decorate

For the chocolate ganache
250ml/8fl oz/1 cup double (heavy) cream
225g/8oz plain (semisweet) chocolate, chopped
30ml/2 tbsp brandy or rum (optional)
25g/1oz/2 tbsp unsalted (sweet) butter, softened

1 Preheat the oven to 180°C/350°F/Gas 4. Grease two 20–23cm/8–9in springform tins (pans) and line the bases with buttered baking parchment.

2 In a pan, melt the chocolate and butter over a low heat until smooth, stirring frequently. Remove from the heat and whisk in the egg yolks until completely blended. Beat in the brandy or rum, if using, and pour into a bowl. Set aside.

3 In a clean, grease-free bowl, beat the egg whites slowly until frothy. Add the cream of tartar and continue beating until stiffer peaks form that just flop over a little at the top. Stir a large spoonful of whites into the chocolate mixture to lighten it, then fold in the remaining whites until they are just combined.

4 Divide about two-thirds of the mousse between the two prepared tins, smoothing the tops. Chill the remaining mousse. Bake for 30–35 minutes until puffed; the cakes will fall slightly. Cool in the tins for 15 minutes, then remove the sides and leave to cool completely. Invert the cakes on to a wire rack, remove the tin bases and peel off the paper. Wash the tins.

5 To assemble, place one layer, flat side down in one of the clean tins. Spread the remaining mousse over the surface, smoothing the top. Cover with the second cake layer, flat side up. Press down gently so the mousse is evenly distributed. Chill for 2–4 hours or overnight.

6 To make the ganache, bring the cream to the boil in a heavy pan over a medium heat. Remove the pan from the heat and add the chocolate all at once, stirring until melted and smooth. Stir in the brandy or rum, if using, and beat in the softened butter. Set the mixture aside for about 5 minutes to thicken slightly (ganache should be thick enough to coat the back of a spoon in a smooth layer).

7 Run a knife around the edge of the assembled cake to loosen it, then remove the sides of the tin. Invert the cake on to a wire rack, remove the base and place the rack over a baking tray. Pour the warm ganache over the cake all at once, tilting gently to help spread it evenly on all surfaces. Use a spatula to smooth the sides, decorate the top with chocolate curls, then leave to set.

Rich Chocolate Cake Energy 214kcal/888kJ; Protein 3g; Carbohydrate 11.1g, of which sugars 10.8g; Fat 17.9g, of which saturates 10.6g; Cholesterol 90mg; Calcium 18mg; Fibre 0.5g; Sodium 117mg.
Mousse Gateau Energy 542kcal/2252kJ; Protein 8g; Carbohydrate 32.3g, of which sugars 31.8g; Fat 43.4g, of which saturates 25.3g; Cholesterol 219mg; Calcium 54mg; Fibre 1.3g; Sodium 149mg.

Classic Chocolate Roulade

This rich, squidgy chocolate roll should be made at least eight hours before serving to allow it to soften. Expect the roulade to crack a little when you roll it up. Sprinkle with a little grated chocolate, if you like, as a final decoration.

Serves 8
200g/7oz plain (semisweet) chocolate
200g/7oz/1 cup caster (superfine) sugar, plus extra caster or icing (confectioners') sugar to dust
7 eggs, separated
300ml/½ pint/1¼ cups double (heavy) cream

1 Preheat the oven to 180°C/350°F/Gas 4. Grease a 33 × 23cm/13 × 9in Swiss roll tin (jelly roll pan) and line the tin with baking parchment.

2 Break the chocolate into squares and melt in a heatproof bowl over a pan of barely simmering water. Remove from the heat and leave to cool for about 5 minutes.

3 In a large bowl, whisk the sugar and egg yolks until light and fluffy. Stir in the melted chocolate.

4 Whisk the egg whites until stiff, but not dry, and then gently fold into the chocolate mixture.

5 Pour the chocolate mixture into the prepared tin, spreading it level with a metal spatula. Bake for about 25 minutes, or until firm. Leave the cake in the tin and cover with a cooling rack, making sure that it does not touch the cake. Cover the rack with a damp dish towel, then wrap in clear film (plastic wrap). Leave in a cool place for 8 hours, preferably overnight.

6 Dust a sheet of baking parchment with caster or icing sugar and turn out the roulade on to it. Peel off the lining paper.

7 Whip the cream until soft peaks form and spread it evenly over the roulade. Roll up the cake from a short end.

8 Place the roulade, seam side down, on to a serving plate and dust generously with more caster or icing sugar before serving.

Chocolate and Coffee Roulade

This version of the classic roll is flavoured with coffee and liqueur.

Serves 8
200g/7oz plain (semisweet) chocolate
200g/7oz/1 cup caster (superfine) sugar
7 eggs, separated

For the filling
300ml/½ pint/1¼ cups double (heavy) cream
30ml/2 tbsp cold brewed coffee
15ml/1 tbsp coffee liqueur, such as Tia Maria, Kahlúa or Toussaint
60ml/4 tbsp icing (confectioners') sugar, for dusting
little grated chocolate, for sprinkling

1 Preheat the oven to 180°C/350°F/Gas 4. Grease and line a 33 × 23cm/13 × 9in Swiss roll tin (jelly roll pan) with baking parchment. Break the chocolate into squares and melt in a heatproof bowl over a pan of barely simmering water. Remove from the heat and leave to cool for 5 minutes.

2 In a large bowl, whisk the sugar and egg yolks until light and fluffy. Stir in the melted chocolate.

3 Whisk the egg whites until stiff, but not dry, and then gently fold into the chocolate mixture.

4 Pour the chocolate mixture into the prepared tin, spreading it level with a metal spatula. Bake for about 25 minutes, or until firm. Leave the cake in the tin and cover with a cooling rack, making sure that it does not touch the cake. Cover the rack with a damp dish towel, then wrap in clear film (plastic wrap). Leave in a cool place for 8 hours, preferably overnight.

5 Dust a large sheet of baking parchment with icing sugar and turn out the roulade on to it. Peel off the lining.

6 Make the filling. Whip the double cream with the coffee and liqueur until soft peaks form and spread over the roulade. Carefully roll up the cake, using the paper to help.

7 Place the roulade, seam side down, on to a serving plate, dust with icing sugar and sprinkle with a little grated chocolate.

Classic Roulade Energy 476kcal/1988kJ; Protein 7.4g; Carbohydrate 42.6g, of which sugars 42.4g; Fat 32g, of which saturates 18.1g; Cholesterol 219mg; Calcium 65mg; Fibre 0.6g; Sodium 73mg.
Coffee Roulade Energy 511kcal/2134kJ; Protein 7.5g; Carbohydrate 51.1g, of which sugars 50.9g; Fat 32g, of which saturates 18.1g; Cholesterol 219mg; Calcium 69mg; Fibre 0.6g; Sodium 73mg.

Chocolate Fairy Cakes

Make these delightful butter-iced chocolate fairy cakes to serve for a children's party.

Makes 24

115g/4oz good-quality plain (semisweet) chocolate, cut into small pieces
15ml/1 tbsp water
300g/10oz/2½ cups plain (all-purpose) flour
5ml/1 tsp baking powder
2.5ml/½ tsp bicarbonate of soda (baking soda)
a pinch of salt
300g/11oz/generous 1½ cups caster (superfine) sugar
175g/6oz/¾ cup butter or margarine, at room temperature
150ml/¼ pint/⅔ cup milk
5ml/1 tsp vanilla extract
3 eggs
butter icing, flavoured to taste

1 Preheat the oven to 180°C/350°F/Gas 4. Grease and flour 24 deep bun cups, about 6.5cm/2¾in in diameter, or use paper cases in the tins (pans).

2 Put the chocolate and water in a bowl set over a pan of almost-simmering water. Heat until melted and smooth, stirring. Remove from the heat and leave to cool.

3 Sift the flour, baking powder, bicarbonate of soda, salt and sugar into a large bowl. Add the chocolate mixture, butter or margarine, milk and vanilla extract.

4 With an electric mixer on medium-low speed, beat until smoothly blended. Increase the speed to high and beat for 2 minutes. Add the eggs and beat for 2 more minutes.

5 Divide the mixture evenly among the prepared bun tins and bake for 20–25 minutes, or until a skewer inserted into the centre of a cake comes out clean.

6 Cool in the tins for 10 minutes, then turn out to cool completely on a wire rack.

7 Ice the top of each cake with butter icing, swirling it into a peak in the centre.

Chocolate Mint-filled Cupcakes

For extra mint flavour, chop eight thin cream-filled after-dinner mints and fold into the cake batter.

Makes 12

225g/8oz/2 cups plain (all-purpose) flour
5ml/1 tsp bicarbonate of soda (baking soda)
a pinch of salt
50g/2oz/½ cup unsweetened cocoa powder
150g/5oz/10 tbsp unsalted (sweet) butter, softened
300g/11oz/generous 1½ cups caster (superfine) sugar
3 eggs
5ml/1 tsp peppermint extract
250ml/8fl oz/1 cup milk

For the filling
300ml/½ pint/1¼ cups double (heavy) or whipping cream
5ml/1 tsp peppermint extract

For the glaze
175g/6oz plain (semisweet) chocolate
115g/4oz/½ cup unsalted (sweet) butter
5ml/1 tsp peppermint extract

1 Preheat the oven to 180°C/350°F/Gas 4. Line a 12-cup bun tray with paper cases. Sift together the dry ingredients.

2 In another bowl, beat the butter and sugar until light and creamy. Add the eggs, one at a time, beating well after each addition; beat in the peppermint. On low speed, beat in the flour mixture alternately with the milk, until just blended. Spoon into the paper cases.

3 Bake for 12–15 minutes. Transfer to a wire rack to cool. When cool, remove the paper cases.

4 To make the filling, whip the cream and peppermint extract until stiff. Spoon into a piping (pastry) bag fitted with a small plain nozzle. Pipe 15ml/1 tbsp of the mixture into each cake through the base.

5 To make the glaze, melt the chocolate and butter in a heatproof bowl over a pan of simmering water, stirring until smooth. Remove from the heat and stir in the peppermint extract. Cool, then spread on top of each cake.

Fairy Cakes Energy 228kcal/957kJ; Protein 2.5g; Carbohydrate 30.6g, of which sugars 21g; Fat 11.5g, of which saturates 3.3g; Cholesterol 33mg; Calcium 40mg; Fibre 0.5g; Sodium 95mg.
Cupcakes Energy 535kcal/2234kJ; Protein 6.3g; Carbohydrate 52g, of which sugars 37.1g; Fat 35.1g, of which saturates 21.4g; Cholesterol 123mg; Calcium 100mg; Fibre 1.4g; Sodium 209mg.

Chocolate Chip Muffins

These classic cakes are studded inside with plain chocolate chips.

Makes 10

115g/4oz/½ cup butter or margarine, softened
75g/3oz/scant ½ cup granulated (white) sugar
30ml/2 tbsp soft dark brown sugar
2 eggs
175g/6oz/1½ cups plain (all-purpose) flour,
5ml/1 tsp baking powder
120ml/4fl oz/½ cup milk
175g/6oz/1 cup plain (semisweet) chocolate chips

1 Preheat the oven to 190°C/375°F/Gas 5. Grease a ten-cup muffin tin (pan), or use paper cases in the tin.

2 In a bowl, beat the butter or margarine with the white and brown sugars until llight and creamy.

3 Add the eggs, one at a time. Beat the mixture well after each egg is added.

4 Sift together the flour and baking powder and then add into the mixture, alternating with the milk. Stir until the mixture is well combined.

5 Divide half the mixture among the muffin cups or cases, filling each one halfway to the top.

6 Sprinkle the chocolate chips on top, then cover with the remaining mixture.

7 Bake for 25 minutes until a skewer inserted in a muffin comes out clean but slightly sticky.

8 Leave the cakes in the tin for 5 minutes, then transfer to a rack to cool.

Variation
You can use milk, dark (bittersweet) or white chocolate chips.

Chunky Chocolate and Banana Muffins

Luxurious but not overly sweet, these muffins are simple and quick to make. Serve warm while the chocolate is still gooey.

Makes 12

90ml/6 tbsp semi-skimmed (low-fat) milk
2 eggs
150g/5oz/10 tbsp unsalted (sweet) butter, melted
225g/8oz/2 cups unbleached plain (all-purpose) flour
pinch of salt
5ml/1 tsp baking powder
150g/5oz/¾ cup golden caster (superfine) sugar
150g/5oz plain (semisweet) chocolate, cut into large chunks
2 small bananas

1 Place 12 large paper cases in a deep muffin tin (pan). Preheat the oven to 200°C/400°F/Gas 6.

2 Place the semi-skimmed milk, eggs and melted butter in a medium bowl and whisk until well combined.

3 Sift together the flour, salt and baking powder into a separate large bowl.

4 Add the sugar and chocolate to the flour mixture and then stir until well combined. Slowly stir in the milk mixture, but do not beat it.

5 Peel the bananas. Using a potato masher or fork, mash the bananas in a bowl. Fold into the batter mixture.

6 Spoon the mixture into the paper cases. Bake for 20 minutes until golden. Cool on a wire rack.

Cook's Tip
Bananas are rich in potassium, which is vital for muscle and nerve function. They are also a good source of energy.

Chip Muffins Energy 296kcal/1238kJ; Protein 4.3g; Carbohydrate 36.4g, of which sugars 22.9g; Fat 15.8g, of which saturates 3.4g; Cholesterol 40mg; Calcium 56mg; Fibre 1g; Sodium 113mg.
Chunky Muffins Energy 240kcal/1003kJ; Protein 3.7g; Carbohydrate 26.3g, of which sugars 11.6g; Fat 14.1g, of which saturates 8.4g; Cholesterol 59mg; Calcium 47mg; Fibre 1g; Sodium 92mg.

Chocolate Cinnamon Doughnuts

Delicious, light doughnuts have a hidden nugget of chocolate inside.

Makes 16

500g/1¼lb/5 cups strong plain (all-purpose) flour
30ml/2 tbsp unsweetened cocoa powder
2.5ml/½ tsp salt
1 sachet easy-blend (rapid-rise) dried yeast
300ml/½ pint/1¼ cups milk
40g/1½oz/3 tbsp butter, melted
1 egg, beaten
115g/4oz plain (semisweet) chocolate, broken into 16 pieces
sunflower oil, for deep frying

For the coating

45ml/3 tbsp caster (superfine) sugar
15ml/1 tbsp unsweetened cocoa powder
5ml/1 tsp ground cinnamon

1 Sift the flour, cocoa and salt into a large bowl. Stir in the yeast. Warm the milk in a pan, then add to a well in the centre of the flour mixture along with the melted butter and egg. Stir, incorporating the dry ingredients, to make a soft dough.

2 Knead the dough on a lightly floured surface for about 5 minutes, until smooth and elastic. Return to the clean bowl, cover with clear film (plastic wrap) or a clean dry dish towel and leave in a warm place until the dough has doubled in bulk.

3 Knead the dough lightly again, then divide into 16 pieces. Shape each into a round, press a piece of plain chocolate into the centre, then fold the dough over to enclose the filling, pressing firmly to make sure the edges are sealed. Re-shape the doughnuts when sealed, if necessary.

4 Heat the oil for frying to 180°C/350°F, or until a cube of dried bread browns in 30–45 seconds. Deep fry the doughnuts in batches. As each doughnut rises and turns golden brown, turn it over carefully to cook the other side. Drain the cooked doughnuts well on kitchen paper.

5 Mix the sugar, cocoa and cinnamon in a shallow bowl. Toss the doughnuts in the mixture to coat them evenly. Pile on a plate and serve warm.

Chocolate Orange Sponge Drops

Light and crispy, with a zesty marmalade filling, these sponge drops are truly delightful.

Makes 14–15

2 eggs
50g/2oz/¼ cup caster (superfine) sugar
2.5ml/½ tsp grated orange rind
50g/2oz/½ cup plain (all-purpose) flour
60ml/4 tbsp fine-shred orange marmalade
40g/1½oz plain (semisweet) chocolate

1 Preheat the oven to 200°C/400°F/Gas 6. Line three baking sheets with baking parchment.

2 Put the eggs and sugar in a heatproof bowl over a pan of simmering water. Whisk until the mixture becomes thick and pale. Remove from the heat and whisk until cool.

3 Whisk the orange rind into the egg mixture. Sift the flour over and fold it in gently until well combined.

4 Place 28–30 dessertspoonfuls of the mixture on to the prepared baking sheets. Bake for 8 minutes, or until golden.

5 Remove from the oven and leave to cool slightly on the baking sheets, then carefully transfer the cakes to a wire rack to cool completely.

6 Spread a cake with about 5ml/1 tsp of marmalade and sandwich another one on top. Repeat this process until all the cakes have been sandwiched together.

7 Melt the plain chocolate in a heatproof bowl over a pan of simmering water, stirring until smooth. Drizzle over the cakes.

Cook's Tip

If you have only thick-cut marmalade with large chunks inside, then simply push the marmalade through a sieve (strainer) to filter out the large pieces of orange.

Doughnuts Energy 235kcal/989kJ; Protein 5.1g; Carbohydrate 33.2g, of which sugars 9g; Fat 10.1g, of which saturates 2.7g; Cholesterol 14mg; Calcium 76mg; Fibre 1.5g; Sodium 48mg.
Sponge Drops Energy 58kcal/247kJ; Protein 1.3g; Carbohydrate 10.5g, of which sugars 8g; Fat 1.5g, of which saturates 0.7g; Cholesterol 26mg; Calcium 12mg; Fibre 0.2g; Sodium 12mg.

Fruity Chocolate Cookie-cakes

The combination of light spongy cookie, fruity preserve and dark chocolate makes irresistible eating for children of all ages. These cookie-cakes are ideal as a tea-time treat or for a kid's party. As cookies go, they are a little time-consuming to make, but that's all part of the fun.

Makes 18

90g/3½oz/½ cup caster (superfine) sugar
2 eggs
50g/2oz/½ cup plain (all-purpose) flour
75g/3oz/6 tbsp apricot-orange marmalade or apricot jam
125g/4¼oz plain (semisweet) chocolate

1 Preheat the oven to 190°C/375°F/Gas 5. Grease 18 patty tins (muffin pans), preferably non-stick. (If you don't have that many patty tins, you'll need to bake the cookies in batches.)

2 Stand a mixing bowl in very hot water for a couple of minutes to heat through, keeping the inside of the bowl dry. Place the sugar and eggs in the bowl and whisk with a hand-held electric mixer until light and frothy and the beaters leave a ribbon trail when lifted. Sift the flour over the mixture and stir in gently using a large metal spoon.

3 Divide the mixture among the patty tins. Bake for 10 minutes until just firm and pale golden around the edges. Using a metal spatula, lift from the tins and transfer to a wire rack to cool.

4 Press the marmalade or jam through a sieve (strainer) to remove any rind or fruit pieces. Spoon a little of the smooth jam on to the centre of each cookie.

5 Break the chocolate into pieces and place in a heatproof bowl set over a pan of gently simmering water. Heat, stirring frequently, until melted and smooth.

6 Spoon a little chocolate on to the top of each cookie and spread gently to the edges. Once the chocolate has just started to set, very gently press it with the back of a fork to give a textured surface. Leave to set for at least 1 hour.

Chocolate Eclairs

This tempting recipe is a delicious version of a popular French dessert.

Makes 12

300ml/½ pint/1¼ cups double (heavy) cream
10ml/2 tsp icing (confectioners') sugar, sifted
1.5ml/¼ tsp vanilla extract
115g/4oz plain (semisweet) chocolate
30ml/2 tbsp water
25g/1oz/2 tbsp butter

For the pastry

65g/2½oz/9 tbsp plain (all-purpose) flour
pinch of salt
50g/2oz/¼ cup butter, diced
150ml/¼ pint/⅔ cup water
2 eggs, lightly beaten

1 Preheat the oven to 200°C/400°F/Gas 6. Grease a large baking sheet and line with baking parchment. Make the pastry. Sift the flour and salt on to a sheet of parchment. Heat the butter and water in a pan until the butter melts. Increase the heat to a rolling boil. Remove from the heat and pour in the flour all at once. Return to a low heat, then beat with a wooden spoon until the mixture forms a ball. Set the pan aside and cool for 2–3 minutes.

2 Gradually beat in the beaten eggs until you have a smooth paste thick enough to hold its shape. Spoon the pastry into a piping (pastry) bag with a 2.5cm/1in plain nozzle. Pipe 10cm/4in lengths on to the prepared baking sheet. Bake for 25–30 minutes, until the pastries are well risen and golden brown. Remove from the oven and make a slit along the side of each to release steam. Lower the heat to 180°C/350°F/Gas 4 and bake for 5 minutes. Cool on a wire rack.

3 Make the filling. Whip the cream with the icing sugar and vanilla extract until it just holds its shape. Spoon into a piping bag fitted with a 1cm/½in plain nozzle and use to fill the éclairs.

4 Place the chocolate and water in a small heatproof bowl set over a pan of hot water. Melt, stirring until smooth. Remove from the heat and gradually stir in the butter. Dip the top of each éclair in the melted chocolate, place on a wire rack and leave in a cool place to set. Ideally, serve within 2 hours of making.

Fruity Cookie-cakes Energy 84kcal/353kJ; Protein 1.3g; Carbohydrate 14.7g, of which sugars 12.5g; Fat 2.6g, of which saturates 1.3g; Cholesterol 22mg; Calcium 12mg; Fibre 0.3g; Sodium 11mg.
Chocolate Eclairs Energy 253kcal/1050kJ; Protein 2.5g; Carbohydrate 11.6g, of which sugars 7.4g; Fat 22.2g, of which saturates 13.5g; Cholesterol 80mg; Calcium 29mg; Fibre 0.4g; Sodium 56mg.

Chocolate Profiteroles

These mouthwatering treats are served in cafés throughout France. Sometimes the profiteroles are filled with whipped cream instead of ice cream.

Makes 12

275g/10oz plain (semisweet) chocolate
120ml/4fl oz/½ cup warm water
750ml/1¼ pints/3 cups vanilla ice cream

For the profiteroles

100g/3¾oz/scant 1 cup plain (all-purpose) flour
1.5ml/¼ tsp salt
pinch of freshly grated nutmeg
75g/3oz/6 tbsp unsalted (sweet) butter, cut into 6 pieces, plus extra for greasing
175ml/6fl oz/¾ cup water
3 eggs

1 Preheat the oven to 200°C/400°F/Gas 6 and lightly butter a baking sheet.

2 Make the profiteroles. Sift together the flour, salt and nutmeg. In a medium pan, bring the butter and the water to the boil. Remove from the heat and add the dry ingredients all at once. Beat with a wooden spoon for about 1 minute until blended and the mixture starts to pull away from the sides of the pan, then set the pan over a low heat and cook the mixture for about 2 minutes, beating constantly. Remove from the heat.

3 Beat one egg in a small bowl and set aside. Add the remaining eggs, one at a time, to the flour mixture, beating well. Add the beaten egg gradually until the dough is smooth and shiny; it should fall slowly when dropped from a spoon.

4 Using a tablespoon, drop the dough on to the baking sheet in 12 mounds. Bake for 25–30 minutes until the pastry is well risen and browned. Turn off the oven and leave the puffs to cool with the oven door open.

5 Melt the chocolate and warm water in a bowl over a pan of hot water. Split the profiteroles in half and put a small scoop of ice cream in each. Pour the sauce over the top and serve.

Chocolate Cream Puffs

These light pastry puffs are filled with chocolate cream.

Makes 12 large puffs

115g/4oz/1 cup plain (all-purpose) flour
30ml/2 tbsp unsweetened cocoa powder
250ml/8fl oz/1 cup water
2.5ml/½ tsp salt
15ml/1 tbsp sugar
115g/4oz/½ cup unsalted (sweet) butter, diced
4 eggs

For the pastry cream

450ml/¾ pint/scant 2 cups milk
6 egg yolks
115g/4oz/generous ½ cup sugar
50g/2oz/½ cup plain (all-purpose) flour
150g/5oz plain (semisweet) chocolate, chopped into pieces
120ml/4fl oz/½ cup whipping cream

For the chocolate glaze

225g/8oz dark (bittersweet) or plain (semisweet) chocolate
300ml/½ pint/1¼ cups whipping cream
50g/2oz/¼ cup unsalted (sweet) butter, diced
15ml/1 tbsp golden (light corn) syrup
5ml/1 tsp vanilla extract

1 Preheat the oven to 220°C/425°F/Gas 7. Lightly grease two large baking sheets. Sift the flour and cocoa powder. In a pan, bring to the boil the water, salt, sugar and butter. Remove from the heat and add the flour and cocoa mixture in one go, stirring vigorously until smooth and it leaves the sides of the pan clean.

2 Return the pan to the heat to cook the choux pastry for 1 minute, beating constantly. Remove from the heat. With a hand-held electric mixer, beat in four of the eggs, one at a time, beating well after each addition, until well blended. The mixture should be thick and shiny. Spoon the mixture into a large piping (pastry) bag fitted with a plain nozzle. Pipe 12 mounds about 7.5cm/3in across at least 5cm/2in apart on the baking sheet.

3 Bake for 35–40 minutes until puffed and firm, then remove. With a knife, slice off and reserve the top third of each puff, then return the opened puffs to the oven for 5–10 minutes to dry out. Transfer to a wire rack to cool.

4 Prepare the pastry cream. Bring the milk to the boil in a small pan. In a bowl, heat the yolks and sugar until pale and thick. Stir in the flour. Slowly pour about 250ml/8fl oz/1 cup of the hot milk into the yolks, stirring constantly. Return the yolk mixture to the remaining milk in the pan and cook, stirring, until the sauce boils for a minute. Remove from the heat and stir in the chocolate until smooth.

5 Strain into a bowl and cover closely with clear film (plastic wrap). Cool to room temperature. In a bowl, whip the cream until stiff. Fold into the pastry cream.

6 Using a large piping bag, fill each puff bottom with pastry cream, then cover each puff with its top. Arrange the cream puffs on a large serving plate in a single layer, or as a pile.

7 Make the glaze. Break the chocolate and heat with the cream, butter, syrup and vanilla extract in a pan over a low heat until melted, stirring frequently. Cool for 30 minutes until thickened. Pour glaze over each of the cream puffs to serve.

Chocolate Profiteroles Energy 647kcal/2707kJ; Protein 11.7g; Carbohydrate 68.2g, of which sugars 52.4g; Fat 36.9g, of which saturates 22.7g; Cholesterol 155mg; Calcium 182mg; Fibre 1.7g; Sodium 189mg.
Cream Puffs Energy 527kcal/2196kJ; Protein 8.8g; Carbohydrate 44.7g, of which sugars 33.6g; Fat 36.1g, of which saturates 20.8g; Cholesterol 224mg; Calcium 121mg; Fibre 1.5g; Sodium 164mg.

Chocolate Puffs

These delicious cream-filled choux pastry puffs are an exquisite treat.

Serves 6

65g/2½oz/9 tbsp plain (all-purpose) flour
150ml/¼ pint/⅔ cup water
50g/2oz/¼ cup butter
2 eggs, beaten

For the filling and icing

150ml/¼ pint/⅔ cup double (heavy) cream
225g/8oz/1½ cups icing (confectioners') sugar
15ml/1 tbsp unsweetened cocoa powder
30–60ml/2–4 tbsp water

1 Preheat the oven to 220°C/425°F/Gas 7. Sift the flour into a bowl. Put the water in a pan over a medium heat, add the butter and heat gently until it melts. Increase the heat and bring to the boil, then remove from the heat. Add all the flour at once and beat quickly until the mixture sticks together and becomes thick and glossy, leaving the side of the pan clean. Leave the mixture to cool slightly.

2 Add the eggs, a little at a time, to the mixture and beat by hand with a wooden spoon or with an electric whisk, until the mixture (choux pastry) is thick and glossy and drops reluctantly from a spoon. (You may not need to use all of the egg.) Spoon the choux pastry into a piping (pastry) bag fitted with a 2cm/¾in nozzle. Dampen two baking sheets with cold water.

3 Pipe walnut-size spoonfuls of the choux pastry on to the dampened baking sheets. Leave some space for them to rise. Cook for 25–30 minutes, until they are golden brown and well risen. Use a metal spatula to lift the puffs on to a wire rack, and make a small hole in each one with the handle of a wooden spoon to allow the steam to escape. Leave to cool.

4 Make the filling and icing. Whip the cream until thick. Put it into a piping bag fitted with a plain or star nozzle. Push the nozzle into the hole in each puff and squirt a little cream inside. Put the icing sugar and cocoa in a small bowl and stir together. Add enough water to make a thick glossy icing. Spread a little icing on each puff and serve when set.

Coffee Profiteroles with White Chocolate Sauce

Irresistible coffee-flavoured choux puffs, with a liqueur-laced white chocolate sauce.

Makes 24

65g/2½oz/9 tbsp plain (all-purpose) flour
pinch of salt
50g/2oz/¼ cup butter, diced
150ml/¼ pint/⅔ cup freshly brewed coffee
2 eggs, lightly beaten
250ml/8fl oz/1 cup double (heavy) cream, whipped

For the sauce

50g/2oz/¼ cup sugar
120ml/4fl oz/½ cup water
150g/5oz white chocolate, broken into pieces
25g/1oz/2 tbsp unsalted (sweet) butter
45ml/3 tbsp double (heavy) cream
30ml/2 tbsp coffee liqueur

1 Preheat the oven to 220°C/425°F/Gas 7. Sift the flour and salt on to a piece of baking parchment.

2 Place the butter in a pan with the coffee. Bring to a rolling boil, then remove from the heat and pour in the sifted flour in one go. Beat hard until the mixture leaves the side of the pan, forming a ball of thick paste. Leave to cool for 5 minutes.

3 Gradually add the eggs, beating well after each addition, until the mixture forms a stiff dropping consistency. Spoon into a piping (pastry) bag fitted with a 1cm/½in plain nozzle. Pipe 24 small buns on a dampened baking sheet, leaving plenty of room between them. Bake for 20 minutes, until risen. Remove the buns from the oven and pierce the side of each one with a sharp knife to let out the steam.

4 Make the sauce. Put the sugar and water in a heavy pan, and heat gently until the sugar has completely dissolved. Bring to the boil and simmer for 3 minutes. Remove the pan from the heat, and add the white chocolate and butter, stirring constantly until smooth. Stir in the double cream and liqueur.

5 Spoon the whipped cream into a piping bag and fill the buns through the slits. Serve with the chocolate sauce poured over.

Chocolate Puffs Energy 403kcal/1687kJ; Protein 4.2g; Carbohydrate 48.4g, of which sugars 39.8g; Fat 22.8g, of which saturates 13.6g; Cholesterol 115mg; Calcium 62mg; Fibre 0.6g; Sodium 106mg.
Coffee Profiteroles Energy 577kcal/2393kJ; Protein 6g; Carbohydrate 34.3g, of which sugars 26g; Fat 46.4g, of which saturates 28.1g; Cholesterol 157mg; Calcium 123mg; Fibre 0.3g; Sodium 139mg.

Brioches au Chocolat

Serve for breakfast as a luxurious start to the day.

Makes 12

250g/9oz/2¼ cups strong white flour
pinch of salt
30ml/2 tbsp caster (superfine) sugar
1 sachet easy-blend (rapid-rise) dried yeast
3 eggs, beaten, plus extra beaten egg, for glazing
45ml/3 tbsp hand-hot milk
115g/4oz/½ cup unsalted (sweet) butter, diced
175g/6oz plain (semisweet) chocolate, broken into squares

1 Sift the flour and salt into a mixing bowl and stir in the sugar and yeast. Make a well in the centre and add the eggs and milk. Beat well, gradually incorporating the dry ingredients to make a fairly soft dough. Turn the dough on to a lightly floured surface and knead well for about 5 minutes, until smooth and elastic, adding a little more flour if necessary.

2 Add the butter to the dough, a few pieces at a time, kneading until each addition is absorbed before adding the next. When all the butter has been incorporated and small bubbles appear in the dough, wrap it in clear film (plastic wrap) and chill for at least 1 hour. If you intend serving the brioches for breakfast, the dough can be left overnight.

3 Grease 12 individual brioche tins (pan) set on a baking sheet or a 12-hole brioche or patty tin (muffin pan). Divide the dough into 12 pieces and shape into smooth rounds. Place a chocolate square in the centre of each. Bring up the sides of the dough and press the edges together to seal.

4 Place the brioches, join side down, in the prepared tins. Cover and leave them in a warm place for about 30 minutes or until doubled in size. Preheat the oven to 200°C/400°F/Gas 6.

5 Brush the brioches with beaten egg. Bake for 12–15 minutes, until well risen and golden brown. Place on wire racks and leave to cool slightly. They should be served warm and can be made in advance and reheated if necessary. Do not serve straight from the oven, as the chocolate will be very hot.

Sicilian Brioches with Hot Chocolate Fudge Sauce

For sheer indulgence, this dessert is unbeatable. Warm brioches filled with ice cream and topped with a glorious hot fudge sauce will make anyone's day.

Serves 2

2 individual brioches
2 large scoops of best vanilla or coffee ice cream

For the hot fudge sauce
50g/2oz best dark (bittersweet) chocolate with 70 per cent cocoa solids
15g/½oz/1 tbsp butter
75ml/5 tbsp boiling water
30ml/2 tbsp golden (light corn) syrup
150g/5oz/¾ cup soft light brown sugar, sifted
5ml/1 tsp vanilla extract

1 Preheat the oven to 200°C/400°F/Gas 6. Meanwhile, make the hot fudge sauce. Break up the chocolate into small pieces and place in a heatproof bowl set over a pan of barely simmering water. Leave, without stirring, for about 10 minutes until the chocolate has completely melted, then add the butter and stir to combine.

2 Add the boiling water to the melted chocolate and butter, stir well to blend, then stir in the syrup, sugar and vanilla extract. Pour and scrape the chocolate mixture into a pan and bring to the boil, then turn down the heat and allow to barely bubble for 5 minutes.

3 Meanwhile, put the brioches on a baking sheet and warm them in the oven for approximately 5 minutes – or until they are slightly crisp on the outside but are still soft, fluffy and warm on the inside.

4 Remove the pan of chocolate sauce from the heat. Immediately split the brioches open and gently pull out a little of the insides. Generously fill each brioche base with ice cream and gently press down on the tops.

5 Put the filled brioches into individual bowls or on to dessert plates, and pour over the hot fudge sauce. Serve immediately.

Brioches au Chocolat Energy 236kcal/988kJ; Protein 4.3g; Carbohydrate 27g, of which sugars 11g; Fat 13.1g, of which saturates 7.6g; Cholesterol 69mg; Calcium 48mg; Fibre 1g; Sodium 79mg.
Sicilian Brioches Energy 913kcal/3853kJ; Protein 13.8g; Carbohydrate 163.3g, of which sugars 121.5g; Fat 27.2g, of which saturates 15.4g; Cholesterol 18mg; Calcium 257mg; Fibre 3g; Sodium 674mg.

Pain au Chocolat

Buttery, flaky yet crisp pastry conceals a delectable chocolate filling.

Makes 9

250g/9oz/2¼ cups unbleached white bread flour
30ml/2 tbsp skimmed milk powder (non-fat dry milk)
15ml/1 tbsp caster (superfine) sugar
2.5ml/½ tsp salt
7.5ml/1½ tsp easy-blend (rapid-rise) dried yeast
150g/5oz/10 tbsp butter, softened
125ml/4½fl oz/generous ½ cup hand-hot water
225g/8oz plain (semisweet) chocolate, broken into pieces

For the glaze
1 egg yolk
15ml/1 tbsp milk

1 Mix the flour, milk powder, sugar and salt in a bowl. Stir in the yeast and make a well in the middle. Melt 25g/1oz/2 tbsp of the butter and pour it into the well in the middle of the mixture. Pour in the water and then mix to form a firm dough.

2 Turn the dough out on to a lightly floured surface and knead it for about 10 minutes, until smooth and elastic. When pressed on the surface it should spring back rather than retain the dent.

3 Dust the bowl with flour and return the dough to it. Cover with clear film (plastic wrap) and leave in a warm place until doubled in size. Meanwhile, shape the remaining softened butter into an oblong block, about 2cm/¾in thick.

4 Grease two baking sheets. When the dough has doubled, turn it out on to a floured surface. Knock back (punch down) and shape into a ball. Cut a cross halfway through the top. Roll out around the cross, leaving a risen centre. Place the butter in the centre. Fold the dough over the butter. Seal the edges.

5 Roll to a rectangle 2cm/¾in thick, twice as long as wide. Fold the bottom third up and the top down; seal the edges with a rolling pin. Wrap in lightly oiled clear film. Chill for 20 minutes. Do the same again twice more, giving a quarter turn and chilling each time. Chill again for 30 minutes.

6 Roll out the dough to a rectangle measuring 52 × 30cm/21 × 12in. Using a knife, cut into three strips lengthways and widthways to make nine 18 × 10cm/7 × 4in rectangles. Divide the chocolate among the three dough rectangles, placing the pieces lengthways at one short end.

7 Mix together the egg yolk and milk for the glaze. Brush the mixture over the edges of the dough. Roll up each piece of dough to completely enclose the chocolate, then press the edges together to seal.

8 Place the pastries seam side down on the prepared baking sheets. Cover with oiled clear film and leave to rise in a warm place for about 30 minutes or until doubled in size.

9 Meanwhile, preheat the oven to 200°C/400°F/Gas 6. Brush the pastries with the remaining glaze and bake for 15 minutes, or until golden. Turn out on to a wire rack to cool just slightly and serve warm.

Ice Cream Croissants with Chocolate Sauce

A deliciously easy-to-make croissant sandwich with a tempting filling of vanilla custard, ice cream and chocolate sauce melting inside the warmed bread.

Makes 4

75g/3oz plain (semisweet) chocolate, broken into pieces
15g/½oz/1 tbsp unsalted (sweet) butter
30ml/2 tbsp golden (light corn) syrup
4 croissants
90ml/6 tbsp good-quality ready-made vanilla custard
4 large scoops of vanilla ice cream
icing (confectioners') sugar, for dusting

1 Preheat the oven to 180°C/350°F/Gas 4. Put the chocolate in a small, heavy pan. Add the butter and syrup and heat very gently until smooth, stirring the mixture frequently.

2 Split each of the croissants in half horizontally and place the base halves on a baking sheet. Spoon over the ready-made custard so that it covers the croissant bases, cover with the lids and bake in the oven for approximately 5 minutes, or until warmed through.

3 Remove the lids and place a scoop of ice cream in each croissant. Spoon half the chocolate sauce over the ice cream and press the lids down gently. Put the croissants in the oven for 1 minute more.

4 Dust the filled croissants with icing sugar, spoon over the remaining chocolate sauce and serve immediately.

Variation
Add a dash of brandy to the chocolate sauce for a treat for adults. Experiment with different ice creams – try using some coffee-flavoured ice cream instead of vanilla.

Pain au Chocolat Energy 345kcal/1441kJ; Protein 4g; Carbohydrate 39.3g, of which sugars 17.9g; Fat 20.1g, of which saturates 12.4g; Cholesterol 35mg; Calcium 51mg; Fibre 1.5g; Sodium 206mg.
Ice Cream Croissants Energy 498kcal/2086kJ; Protein 8.7g; Carbohydrate 59.4g, of which sugars 35g; Fat 29.5g, of which saturates 14.6g; Cholesterol 55mg; Calcium 134mg; Fibre 1.5g; Sodium 341mg.

Puffy Chocolate Pears

These pear-shaped pastries will go down a treat with children – who will also love to help make them.

Makes 4

225g/8oz puff pastry, thawed if frozen
2 pears, peeled
2 squares plain (semisweet) chocolate, roughly chopped
15ml/1 tbsp lemon juice
1 egg, beaten
15ml/1 tbsp caster (superfine) sugar

1 Roll out the pastry into a 25cm/10in square on a lightly floured surface. Trim the edges, then cut it into four equal smaller squares. Cover the pastry with clear film (plastic wrap) and set aside.

2 Remove the core from each pear half and pack the gap with the chopped chocolate. Place a pear half, cut side down, on each piece of pastry and brush them with the lemon juice, to prevent them from going brown.

3 Preheat the oven to 190°C/375°F/Gas 5. Cut the pastry into a pear shape, by following the lines of the fruit, leaving a 2.5cm/1in border. Use the trimmings to make leaves and brush the pastry border with the beaten egg.

4 Arrange the pastry and pears on a baking sheet. Make deep cuts in the pears, taking care not to cut right through the fruit, and sprinkle them with the sugar. Cook for 20–25 minutes, until lightly browned. Serve hot or cold.

Variation

Try using apples instead of pears for this recipe, if preferred. Cut the puff pastry into 10cm/4in rounds. Slice 2 peeled and cored eating apples. Toss with a little lemon juice to avoid the fruit discolouring, drain and arrange on the pastry. Dot with 25g/1oz/2 tbsp butter and chopped milk chocolate. Bake as for Puffy Chocolate Pears. While still hot, brush the apple slices with warmed redcurrant jam.

Choux Pastries with Two Custards

These sweetly scented Italian pastry treats have two contrasting custards – chocolate and vanilla.

Makes about 48

200ml/7fl oz/scant 1 cup water
115g/4oz/½ cup butter
2cm/1in piece vanilla pod (bean)
pinch of salt
150g/5oz/1¼ cups plain (all-purpose) flour
5 eggs

For the custard fillings

50g/2oz cooking chocolate
300ml/½ pint/1¼ cups milk
4 egg yolks
65g/2½ oz/scant ⅓ cup sugar
40g/1½oz/⅓ cup plain (all-purpose) flour
5ml/1 tsp pure vanilla extract
300ml/½ pint/1¼ cups whipping cream
unsweetened cocoa powder and icing (confectioners') sugar, to garnish

1 Preheat the oven to 190°C/375°F/Gas 5. Heat the water with the butter, vanilla and salt. When melted, beat in the flour. Cook over low heat, stirring, for 10 minutes. Remove from the heat. Mix in the eggs one at a time. Remove the vanilla pod.

2 Butter a flat baking tray. Using a piping (pastry) bag fitted with a round nozzle, pipe walnut-size balls on to the tray. Bake for 20–25 minutes, or until golden brown. Cool before filling.

3 Prepare the custard fillings. Melt the chocolate in the top half of a double boiler, or in a bowl set over a pan of simmering water. Heat the milk in a small pan, taking care not to let it boil.

4 Whisk the egg yolks. Add the sugar, and beat until pale. Beat in the flour. Slowly pour in the hot milk, stirring until combined. Pour into a pan, and bring to a boil. Simmer for 5–6 minutes, stirring constantly. Remove from the heat and divide the custard between two bowls. Add the chocolate to one, and stir the vanilla extract into the other. Allow to cool completely.

5 Whip the cream. Fold half into each custard. Fill two pastry bags fitted with round nozzles with each custard. Fill half the pastries with chocolate custard, and the rest with vanilla custard, through a little hole in the side. Dust the chocolate pastries with cocoa powder, and the rest with sugar. Serve immediately.

Puffy Pears Energy 464kcal/1944kJ; Protein 6.9g; Carbohydrate 56.1g, of which sugars 35.6g; Fat 25.8g, of which saturates 6.7g; Cholesterol 50mg; Calcium 62mg; Fibre 2.6g; Sodium 197mg.
Choux Pastries Energy 79kcal/331kJ; Protein 1.8g; Carbohydrate 7.3g, of which sugars 3.3g; Fat 5g, of which saturates 3g; Cholesterol 44mg; Calcium 24mg; Fibre 0.2g; Sodium 32mg.

Chocolate Brownies

Traditional American brownies are usually rich in butter. This version uses sunflower oil in place of butter. It still tastes rich and gooey, but is best eaten on the day it is made.

Makes 20

120ml/4fl oz/½ cup sunflower oil
150g/5oz plain (semisweet) chocolate, chopped
2 eggs
115g/4oz/1 cup self-raising (self-rising) flour
115g/4oz/generous ½ cup caster (superfine) sugar
5ml/1 tsp vanilla extract
75g/3oz/¾ cup halved pecan nuts

1 Preheat the oven to 200°C/400°F/Gas 6. Use a little of the oil to grease a 23cm/9in square shallow cake tin (pan) and then line it with lightly oiled baking parchment.

2 Melt the chocolate with the remaining oil in a heatproof bowl set over a pan of barely simmering water, stirring constantly until smooth.

3 Beat the eggs lightly and add them to the melted chocolate, stirring vigorously. Beat in the flour, caster sugar and vanilla extract and pour the mixture into the prepared tin. Arrange the pecan nut halves over the top.

4 Bake for 10–15 minutes. If you like chewy brownies, take them out of the oven at this point. However, if you prefer a more cake-like finish, leave the brownies to bake for a further 5 minutes. Cut into squares and leave to cool before removing them from the tin.

Cook's Tip

Ingredients can be melted easily in a microwave oven. To soften chocolate, butter, sugar or syrup, microwave on high power for a few seconds, until soft. Remember that chocolate and butter may not look melted, so check them carefully by stirring before returning them to the microwave for a few seconds more.

American Chocolate Fudge Brownies

This is the classic American recipe. The delicious chocolate frosting makes the brownies taste decadently rich.

Makes 12

175g/6oz/¾ cup butter
40g/1½oz/⅓ cup unsweetened cocoa powder
2 eggs, lightly beaten
175g/6oz/¾ cup soft light brown sugar
2.5ml/½ tsp vanilla extract
115g/4oz/1 cup chopped pecan nuts
50g/2oz/½ cup self-raising (self-rising) flour

For the frosting

115g/4oz plain (semisweet) chocolate
25g/1oz/2 tbsp butter
15ml/1 tbsp sour cream

1 Preheat the oven to 180°C/350°F/Gas 4. Grease a 20cm/8in square shallow cake tin (pan) and line with baking parchment. Melt the butter in a pan and stir in the unsweetened cocoa powder. Set aside to cool.

2 Beat together the eggs, sugar and vanilla extract in a bowl, then stir in the cooled cocoa mixture with the nuts. Sift over the flour and fold into the mixture with a metal spoon.

3 Pour the mixture into the cake tin and bake in the oven for 30–35 minutes, or until risen. Remove from the oven (it will still be soft and wet, but firms while cooling). Cool in the tin.

4 To make the frosting, melt the chocolate and butter together in a pan and remove from the heat. Beat in the sour cream until smooth and glossy. Leave to cool slightly, and then spread over the top of the brownies. When set, cut into 12 pieces.

Cook's Tip

Brownies are firm family favourites and, once you find a recipe you like, you will want to make them regularly. For brownie enthusiasts you can now buy a special pan with a slide-out base, which makes removing the cooked brownies so much easier.

Chocolate Brownies Energy 152kcal/635kJ; Protein 1.9g; Carbohydrate 15.5g, of which sugars 11g; Fat 9.6g, of which saturates 2.2g; Cholesterol 19mg; Calcium 19mg; Fibre 0.5g; Sodium 8mg.
American Brownies Energy 335kcal/1396kJ; Protein 3.6g; Carbohydrate 25.6g, of which sugars 21.9g; Fat 25.1g, of which saturates 11.7g; Cholesterol 69mg; Calcium 45mg; Fibre 1.2g; Sodium 161mg.

Chocolate Chip Brownies

A double dose of chocolate is incorporated into these melt-in-the-mouth brownies.

Makes 24

115g/4oz plain (semisweet) chocolate
115g/4oz/½ cup butter
3 eggs
200g/7oz/1 cup caster (superfine) sugar
2.5ml/½ tsp vanilla extract
a pinch of salt
150g/5oz/1¼ cups plain (all-purpose) flour
175g/6oz/1 cup chocolate chips

1 Preheat the oven to 180°C/350°F/Gas 4. Line a 33 × 23cm/13 × 9in baking tin (pan) with baking parchment and grease the paper.

2 Melt the chocolate and butter together in the top of a double boiler, or in a heatproof bowl set over a pan of gently simmering water.

3 Beat together the eggs, sugar, vanilla extract and salt. Stir in the chocolate mixture. Sift over the flour and fold in. Add the chocolate chips.

4 Pour the mixture into the baking tin and spread evenly. Bake until just set, about 30 minutes. The brownies should be slightly moist inside. Leave to cool in the tin.

5 To turn out, run a knife all around the edge and invert on to a baking sheet. Remove the paper. Place another sheet on top and invert again. Cut into bars for serving.

Variations

Rich chocolate: *Use the best-quality chocolate (consisting of at least 70 per cent cocoa solids) cut into chunks to give the brownies a fantastic flavour.*
Chunky choc and nut: *Use 75g/3oz coarsely chopped white chocolate and 75g/3oz/¾ cup chopped walnuts.*
Almond: *Use almond extract, add 75g/3oz/¾ cup chopped almonds and reduce the chocolate chips to 75g/3oz/½ cup.*

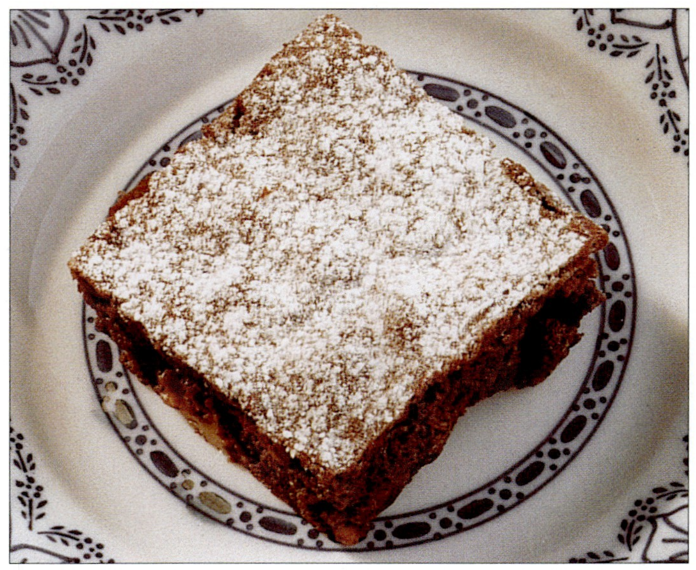

Raisin Chocolate Brownies

Cover these divine fruity brownies with a light chocolate frosting for a truly decadent treat.

Makes 16

115g/4oz/½ cup butter or margarine
50g/2oz/½ cup unsweetened cocoa powder
2 eggs
225g/8oz/generous 1 cup caster (superfine) sugar
5ml/1 tsp vanilla extract
40g/1½oz/⅓ cup plain (all-purpose) flour
75g/3oz/¾ cup finely chopped walnuts
75g/3oz/generous ½ cup raisins

1 Preheat the oven to 180°C/350°F/Gas 4. Line the base and sides of a 20cm/8in square baking tin (pan) with baking parchment and grease the paper.

2 Gently melt the butter or margarine in a small pan. Remove from the heat and stir in the cocoa powder.

3 With an electric mixer, beat the eggs, caster sugar and vanilla extract together until light. Add the cocoa and butter mixture and stir to blend.

4 Sift the flour over the cocoa mixture and gently fold in. Do not overmix.

5 Add the walnuts and raisins, and scrape the mixture into the prepared baking tin.

6 Bake in the centre of the oven for 30 minutes. Leave in the tin to cool before cutting into 5cm/2in squares and removing from the tin. The brownies should be soft and moist.

Cook's Tip

Adding dried fruit makes brownies a little more substantial and adds to their delicious flavour. Try to find Californian or Spanish raisins for the best flavour and texture.

Chip Brownies Energy 161kcal/674kJ; Protein 2g; Carbohydrate 21.3g, of which sugars 16.4g; Fat 8.1g, of which saturates 4.7g; Cholesterol 35mg; Calcium 22mg; Fibre 0.5g; Sodium 39mg.
Raisin Brownies Energy 181kcal/759kJ; Protein 2.5g; Carbohydrate 20.4g, of which sugars 18.1g; Fat 10.5g, of which saturates 4.6g; Cholesterol 39mg; Calcium 26mg; Fibre 0.7g; Sodium 86mg.

Maple and Pecan Nut Brownies

This recipe provides a delicious adaptation of the classic American chocolate brownie, using maple syrup and pecan nuts.

Makes 12

115g/4oz/½ cup butter, melted
75g/3oz/scant ½ cup soft light brown sugar
90ml/6 tbsp maple syrup
2 eggs
115g/4oz/1 cup self-raising (self-rising) flour
75g/3oz/¾ cup pecan nuts, chopped

For the topping
115g/4oz/⅔ cup plain (semisweet) chocolate chips
50g/2oz/¼ cup unsalted (sweet) butter
12 pecan nut halves, to decorate

1 Preheat the oven to 180°C/350°F/Gas 4. Line and grease a 25 × 18cm/10 × 7in cake tin (pan).

2 Beat together the melted butter, sugar, 60ml/4 tbsp of the maple syrup, the eggs and flour for 1 minute, or until smooth.

3 Stir in the nuts and transfer to the cake tin. Smooth the surface and bake for 30 minutes, or until risen and firm to the touch. Cool in the tin for 10 minutes, then transfer to a wire rack to cool completely.

4 Melt the chocolate chips, butter and remaining syrup over a low heat. Cool slightly, then spread over the cake. Press in the pecan nut halves, leave to set for about 5 minutes, then cut into squares or bars.

Cook's Tips

- *Maple syrup is a sweet sugar syrup made from the sap of the sugar maple tree. It has a distinctive flavour which is delightful in a variety of sweet recipes as well as when added to ice creams and waffles.*
- *Buy a good-quality maple syrup as blends are often disappointing.*
- *Store opened maple syrup in the refrigerator, as its delicate flavour will deteriorate once the bottle is opened.*

Banana Chocolate Brownies

Nuts traditionally give brownies their chewy texture. Here oat bran is used instead, creating a wonderful alternative.

Makes 9

75ml/5 tbsp unsweetened cocoa powder
15ml/1 tbsp caster (superfine) sugar
75ml/5 tbsp milk
3 large bananas, mashed
215g/7½oz/scant 1 cup soft light brown sugar
5ml/1 tsp vanilla extract
5 egg whites
75g/3oz/⅔ cup self-raising (self-rising) flour
75g/3oz/⅔ cup oat bran
icing (confectioners') sugar, for dusting

1 Preheat the oven to 180°C/350°F/Gas 4. Line a 20cm/8in square cake tin (pan) with baking parchment.

2 Blend the cocoa powder and caster sugar with the milk. Add the bananas, soft brown sugar and vanilla extract. Lightly beat the egg whites with a fork. Add the chocolate mixture and continue to beat well. Sift the flour over the mixture and fold in with the oat bran. Pour into the prepared tin.

3 Cook in the oven for 40 minutes, or until firm. Cool in the tin for 10 minutes, then turn out on to a wire rack. Cut into slices or squares and lightly dust with icing sugar before serving.

Cook's Tips

Win a few brownie points by getting to know what makes them great.

- *They should be moist and chewy with a sugary crust on the outside but squidgy on the inside.*
- *True versions contain a high proportion of sugar and fat and most contain nuts. Lighter versions often contain white chocolate and are often referred to as blondies.*
- *Brownies make superb individual cakes but the cooked slab can also be left whole and then served as a larger cake for dessert, decorated with cream and fruit.*

Maple Brownies Energy 285kcal/1189kJ; Protein 3.1g; Carbohydrate 26.2g, of which sugars 18.9g; Fat 19.4g, of which saturates 9.4g; Cholesterol 62mg; Calcium 52mg; Fibre 0.8g; Sodium 151mg.
Banana Brownies Energy 223kcal/947kJ; Protein 5.7g; Carbohydrate 46.4g, of which sugars 32.4g; Fat 2.9g, of which saturates 1.2g; Cholesterol 0mg; Calcium 70mg; Fibre 2.2g; Sodium 151mg.

Fudge-glazed Chocolate Brownies

These pecan nut-topped brownies are irresistible, so you may find that you have to hide them from your friends!

Makes 16

250g/9oz dark (bittersweet) chocolate, chopped
25g/1oz unsweetened chocolate, chopped
115g/4oz/½ cup unsalted (sweet) butter, cut into pieces
90g/3½oz/scant ½ cup soft light brown sugar
50g/2oz/¼ cup caster (superfine) sugar
2 eggs
15ml/1 tbsp vanilla extract
65g/2½oz/9 tbsp plain (all-purpose) flour
115g/4oz/1 cup pecan nuts or walnuts, toasted and chopped
150g/5oz white chocolate, chopped
pecan nut halves, to decorate (optional)

For the glaze
175g/6oz dark (bittersweet) chocolate, chopped
50g/2oz/¼ cup unsalted (sweet) butter, cut into pieces
30ml/2 tbsp golden (light corn) syrup
10ml/2 tsp vanilla extract
5ml/1 tsp instant coffee

1 Preheat the oven to 180°C/350°F/Gas 4. Line a 20cm/8in square baking tin (pan) with foil, then grease the foil.

2 Melt the dark chocolates and butter in a pan over a low heat. Off the heat, add the sugars and stir for 2 minutes. Beat in the eggs and vanilla extract, and then blend in the flour.

3 Stir in the pecan nuts or walnuts and the chopped white chocolate.

4 Pour into the tin. Bake for 20–25 minutes. Cool in the tin for 30 minutes then lift, using the foil, on to a wire rack to cool for 2 hours.

5 To make the glaze, melt the chocolate in a pan with the butter, golden syrup, vanilla extract and instant coffee. Stir until smooth. Chill the glaze for 1 hour, then spread over the brownies. Top with pecan nut halves, if you like. Chill until set, then cut into bars.

Nutty Chocolate Squares

These delicious squares are incredibly rich, so cut them smaller if you wish.

Makes 16

2 eggs
10ml/2 tsp vanilla extract
1.5ml/¼ tsp salt
175g/6oz/1½ cups pecan nuts, coarsely chopped
50g/2oz/½ cup plain (all-purpose) flour
50g/2oz/¼ cup caster (superfine) sugar
120ml/4fl oz/½ cup golden (light corn) syrup
75g/3oz plain (semisweet) chocolate, finely chopped
40g/1½oz/3 tbsp butter
16 pecan nut halves, to decorate

1 Preheat the oven to 160°C/325°F/Gas 3. Line the base and sides of a 20cm/8in square baking tin (pan) with baking parchment and lightly grease the paper.

2 Whisk together the eggs, vanilla extract and salt. In another bowl, mix together the chopped pecan nuts and flour. Set both aside until needed.

3 In a pan, bring the sugar and golden syrup to the boil. Watch it carefully and remove from the heat as soon as it comes to the boil. Stir in the chocolate and butter, and blend thoroughly with a wooden spoon. Mix in the beaten egg mixture, then fold in the pecan nut mixture.

4 Pour the mixture into the baking tin and bake until set, about 35 minutes. Cool in the tin for 10 minutes before unmoulding.

5 Cut into 5cm/2in squares and press pecan nut halves into the tops while warm. Cool on a wire rack.

Variation
Toasted hazelnuts also taste great in this recipe in place of the pecan nuts. Simply brown the hazelnuts under a hot grill (broiler), turning them every so often. When toasted all over, leave to cool, then rub them in a clean dish towel until the skins are removed.

Brownies Energy 382kcal/1595kJ; Protein 4.1g; Carbohydrate 37.6g, of which sugars 34.1g; Fat 25g, of which saturates 12.4g; Cholesterol 47mg; Calcium 55mg; Fibre 1.2g; Sodium 89mg.
Nutty Squares Energy 172kcal/719kJ; Protein 2.4g; Carbohydrate 15.2g, of which sugars 12.7g; Fat 11.8g, of which saturates 2.9g; Cholesterol 29mg; Calcium 19mg; Fibre 0.7g; Sodium 45mg.

Butterscotch and White Chocolate Brownies

These gorgeous treats are made with brown sugar, white chocolate chips and walnuts. Who could possibly have the willpower to resist? You might want to make two batches at a time.

Makes 12

450g/1lb white chocolate chips
75g/3oz/6 tbsp unsalted (sweet) butter
3 eggs
175g/6oz/¾ cup light muscovado (brown) sugar
175g/6oz/1½ cups self-raising (self-rising) flour
175g/6oz/1½ cups walnuts, chopped
5ml/1 tsp vanilla extract

1 Preheat the oven to 190°C/375°F/Gas 5. Line the base of a 28 × 18cm/11 × 7in shallow tin (pan) with baking parchment. Lightly grease the sides.

2 Melt 90g/3½oz of the chocolate chips with the butter in a heatproof bowl set over a pan of simmering water, stirring until smooth. Leave to cool slightly.

3 Put the eggs and light muscovado sugar into a large bowl and whisk well, then whisk in the melted chocolate mixture.

4 Sift the flour into the bowl and gently fold in along with the chopped walnuts, vanilla extract and the remaining chocolate chips. Mix until all the ingredients are combined, but be careful not to overmix.

5 Spread the mixture out in the prepared tin, pushing it to the edges, and bake for about 30 minutes.

6 When the mixture is risen and golden brown, remove from the oven. The centre of the brownie should still be quite firm to the touch but will be slightly soft. As it cools down it will become firmer.

7 Leave to cool slightly in the tin, then cut into 12 bars, or more if you prefer, when the brownie is completely cool.

Marbled Chocolate Brownies

These fancy chocolate brownies have an impressive flavour as well a pretty, marbled appearance.

Makes 24

225g/8oz plain (semisweet) chocolate
75g/3oz/6 tbsp butter
4 eggs
300g/11oz/1½ cups caster (superfine) sugar
150g/5oz/1¼ cups plain (all-purpose) flour
2.5ml/½ tsp salt
5ml/1 tsp baking powder
10ml/2 tsp vanilla extract
115g/4oz/1 cup chopped walnuts

For the plain mixture

50g/2oz/¼ cup butter, at room temperature
175g/6oz/¾ cup cream cheese
90g/3½oz/1½ cups caster (superfine) sugar
2 eggs
25g/1oz/¼ cup plain (all-purpose) flour
5ml/1 tsp vanilla extract

1 Preheat the oven to 180°C/350°F/Gas 4. Line a 33 × 23cm/13 × 9in baking tin (pan) with baking parchment and grease.

2 Melt the chocolate and butter in a small pan over a very low heat, stirring. Set aside to cool. Meanwhile, beat the eggs until light and fluffy. Gradually beat in the sugar. Sift over the flour, salt and baking powder, and fold to combine.

3 Stir in the cooled chocolate mixture. Add the vanilla extract and chopped walnuts. Measure and set aside 475ml/16fl oz/2 cups of the chocolate mixture.

4 For the plain mixture, cream the butter and cream cheese with an electric mixer. Add the sugar and continue beating until blended. Beat in the eggs, flour and vanilla extract.

5 Spread the unmeasured chocolate mixture in the tin. Pour over the plain mixture. Drop spoonfuls of the reserved chocolate mixture on top.

6 With a metal spatula, swirl the mixtures to marble them. Do not blend completely. Bake until just set, 35–40 minutes. Turn out when cool and cut into squares for serving.

Butterscotch Energy 469kcal/1961kJ; Protein 8.1g; Carbohydrate 48.7g, of which sugars 37.7g; Fat 28.3g, of which saturates 11.4g; Cholesterol 61mg; Calcium 182mg; Fibre 1g; Sodium 151mg.
Marbled Brownies Energy 259kcal/1083kJ; Protein 3.8g; Carbohydrate 28.8g, of which sugars 23.1g; Fat 15.1g, of which saturates 7.1g; Cholesterol 66mg; Calcium 42mg; Fibre 0.6g; Sodium 73mg.

Nutty Marshmallow and Chocolate Squares

Unashamedly sweet, with chocolate, marshmallows, cherries, nuts and coconut, this recipe is a favourite with children of all ages, and sweet-toothed adults too.

Makes 9

200g/7oz digestive biscuits (graham crackers)
90g/3½oz plain (semisweet) chocolate
200g/7oz mini coloured marshmallows
150g/5oz/1¼ cups chopped walnuts
90g/3½oz/scant ½ cup glacé (candied) cherries, halved
50g/2oz/⅔ cup desiccated (dry unsweetened shredded) coconut
350g/12oz milk chocolate

1 Put the digestive biscuits in a plastic bag and, using a rolling pin, crush them until they are fairly small. Place them in a bowl.

2 Melt the plain chocolate in the microwave or in a heatproof bowl set over a pan of hot water. Pour the melted plain chocolate over the broken biscuits and stir well. Spread the mixture in the base of a 20cm/8in square shallow cake tin (pan).

3 Put the marshmallows, walnuts, cherries and coconut in a large bowl. Melt the milk chocolate in the microwave or in a heatproof bowl set over a pan of hot water.

4 Pour the melted milk chocolate over the marshmallow and nut mixture and toss together until almost everything is coated.

5 Spread the mixture over the chocolate base, but leave in chunky lumps – do not spread flat. Chill until set, then cut into squares or bars.

Variation
A variety of nuts can be used in this recipe instead of the walnuts – the choice is yours.

Very Low-fat Chocolate Brownies

If you ever need proof that you can still enjoy sweet treats even when you are on a low-fat diet, here it is. These brownies are not only tasty, but also very quick and easy to make.

Makes 16

90g/3½oz/¾ cup plain (all-purpose) flour
2.5ml/½ tsp baking powder
45ml/3 tbsp unsweetened cocoa powder
200g/7oz/1 cup caster (superfine) sugar
100ml/3½fl oz/scant ½ cup natural (plain) low-fat yogurt
2 eggs, beaten
5ml/1 tsp vanilla extract
25ml/1½ tbsp vegetable oil

1 Preheat the oven to 180°C/350°F/Gas 4. Line a 20cm/8in square cake tin (pan) with baking parchment.

2 Sift the flour, baking powder and cocoa powder into a large mixing bowl.

3 Stir in the caster sugar to the flour mixture, then beat in the natural yogurt, eggs, vanilla extract and vegetable oil until thoroughly combined.

4 Spoon the mixture into the prepared tin, filling it to the edges. Bake for about 25 minutes.

5 Remove the tin from the oven when the cake is just firm to the touch. Leave in the tin until cooled completely.

6 Using a sharp knife, cut into 16 squares, then remove from the tin using a metal spatula.

Variation
Try adding some dried fruits to the brownies. They will keep the fat content down while adding a delicious succulent flavour to the brownie. Mix in 75g/3oz/generous ½ cup of raisins, sultanas (golden raisins) or a similar quantity of finely chopped prunes or dates, in step 3.

Nutty Squares Energy 603kcal/2523kJ; Protein 8.6g; Carbohydrate 69.7g, of which sugars 53.2g; Fat 34.1g, of which saturates 14.7g; Cholesterol 19mg; Calcium 133mg; Fibre 2.5g; Sodium 179mg.
Low-fat Brownies Energy 101kcal/426kJ; Protein 4.6g; Carbohydrate 16.6g, of which sugars 10.8g; Fat 2.2g, of which saturates 1.2g; Cholesterol 0mg; Calcium 31mg; Fibre 2.8g; Sodium 167mg.

Oat, Date and Chocolate Brownies

These brownies are marvellous as a break-time treat. The secret of chewy, moist brownies is not to overcook them.

Makes 16

150g/5oz plain (semisweet) chocolate
50g/2oz/¼ cup butter
75g/3oz/scant 1 cup rolled oats
25g/1oz/3 tbsp wheatgerm
25g/1oz/⅓ cup milk powder
2.5ml/½ tsp baking powder
2.5ml/½ tsp salt
50g/2oz/½ cup chopped walnuts
50g/2oz/⅓ cup finely chopped dates
50g/2oz/¼ cup muscovado (molasses) sugar
5ml/1 tsp vanilla extract
2 eggs, beaten

1 Break the chocolate into a heatproof bowl and add the butter. Place over a pan of simmering water and stir until completely melted.

2 Cool the chocolate, stirring occasionally. Preheat the oven to 180°C/350°F/Gas 4. Grease and line a 20cm/8in square cake tin (pan).

3 Combine the oats, wheatgerm, milk powder and baking powder together in a bowl. Add the salt, walnuts, chopped dates and sugar, and mix well. Beat in the melted chocolate, vanilla and beaten eggs.

4 Pour the mixture into the cake tin, level the surface and bake in the oven for 20–25 minutes, or until firm around the edges yet still soft in the centre.

5 Cool the brownies in the tin, then chill in the refrigerator. When they are more solid, turn them out of the tin and cut into 16 squares.

Cook's Tip

When melting chocolate always make sure that the water in the pan does not touch the bowl, or it might bubble up the side of the bowl and splash into the chocolate, changing its texture.

Chunky White Chocolate and Coffee Brownies

Brownies – unlike cakes – should have a gooey texture, so take care not to overcook them. When ready, the mixture should still be slightly soft under the crust, but it will become firm as it cools.

Makes 12

25ml/1½ tbsp ground coffee
45ml/3 tbsp near-boiling water
300g/11oz plain (semisweet) chocolate, broken into pieces
225g/8oz/1 cup butter
225g/8oz/1 cup caster (superfine) sugar
3 eggs
75g/3oz/⅔ cup self-raising (self-rising) flour, sifted
225g/8oz white chocolate, chopped

1 Preheat the oven to 190°C/375°F/Gas 5. Grease and line the base of a 18 × 28cm/7 × 11in square cake tin (pan) with baking parchment.

2 Put the ground coffee in a bowl and pour the hot water over. Leave to infuse (steep) for 4 minutes, then strain through a sieve (strainer).

3 Put the plain chocolate and butter in a heatproof bowl over a pan of simmering water and stir occasionally until melted. Remove from the heat and cool for 5 minutes.

4 Mix the sugar and eggs together. Stir in the chocolate and butter mixture and the coffee. Stir in the sifted flour.

5 Fold in the white chocolate pieces and mix until just combined. Pour the mixture into the prepared tin, ensuring it is spread to the edges.

6 Bake for 45–50 minutes, or until just firm to the touch and the top is crusty. Leave to cool in the tin.

7 When the cake is completely cold, cut into 12 squares and remove from the tin.

Oat Brownies Energy 138kcal/577kJ; Protein 2.8g; Carbohydrate 13.3g, of which sugars 9.3g; Fat 8.6g, of which saturates 3.6g; Cholesterol 31mg; Calcium 32mg; Fibre 1g; Sodium 36mg.
Chunky Energy 480kcal/2005kJ; Protein 5.1g; Carbohydrate 51.4g, of which sugars 46.4g; Fat 29.7g, of which saturates 17.8g; Cholesterol 89mg; Calcium 88mg; Fibre 0.8g; Sodium 155mg.

Chocolate Cheesecake Brownies

A very dense chocolate brownie mixture is swirled with creamy cheesecake mixture to give a marbled effect. Cut into tiny squares for little mouthfuls of absolute heaven.

Makes 16

For the cheesecake mixture

1 egg
225g/8oz/1 cup full-fat cream cheese
50g/2oz/¼ cup caster (superfine) sugar
5ml/1 tsp vanilla extract

For the brownie mixture

115g/4oz dark (bittersweet) chocolate (minimum 70 per cent cocoa solids)
115g/4oz/½ cup unsalted (sweet) butter
150g/5oz/⅔ cup light muscovado (brown) sugar
2 eggs, beaten
50g/2oz/½ cup plain (all-purpose) flour

1 Preheat the oven to 160°C/325°F/Gas 3. Line the base and sides of a 20cm/8in cake tin (pan) with baking parchment.

2 To make the cheesecake mixture, beat the egg in a mixing bowl, then add the cream cheese, caster sugar and vanilla extract. Beat together until smooth and creamy.

3 To make the brownie mixture, melt the chocolate and butter together in the microwave or in a heatproof bowl set over a pan of gently simmering water. When the mixture is melted, remove from the heat, stir well, then add the sugar. Gradually pour in the beaten eggs, a little at a time, and beat well until thoroughly combined. Gently stir in the flour.

4 Spread two-thirds of the brownie mixture over the base of the prepared tin. Spread the cheesecake mixture on top, then spoon on the remaining brownie mixture in heaps. Using a metal skewer, swirl the two mixtures together to achieve a marbled effect.

5 Bake for 30–35 minutes, or until just set in the centre. Leave to cool in the tin, then cut into squares.

White Chocolate Brownies

These irresistible brownies are packed full of creamy white chocolate and juicy dried fruit. They are best served cut into very small portions as they are incredibly rich.

Makes 18

75g/3oz/6 tbsp unsalted (sweet) butter, diced
400g/14oz white chocolate, chopped
3 eggs
90g/3½oz/½ cup golden caster (superfine) sugar
10ml/2 tsp vanilla extract
90g/3½oz/¾ cup sultanas (golden raisins)
coarsely grated rind of 1 lemon, plus 15ml/1 tbsp juice
200g/7oz/1¾ cups plain (all-purpose) flour

1 Preheat the oven to 190°C/375°F/ Gas 5. Grease and line a 28 × 20cm/ 11 × 8in shallow rectangular baking tin (pan) with baking parchment.

2 Put the butter and 300g/11oz of the white chocolate in a heatproof bowl and melt over a pan of gently simmering water, stirring frequently until smooth.

3 Remove from the heat and beat in the eggs and sugar, then add the vanilla extract, sultanas, lemon rind and juice, and stir well to combine all the ingredients.

4 Sift in the flour and fold in until well combined. Mix in the remaining chocolate.

5 Tip the mixture into the prepared tin, ensuring it is spread into the corners. Bake for about 20 minutes.

6 Remove from the oven when slightly risen and the surface is only just turning golden. The centre should still be slightly soft as the brownie mixture will firm up a little as it cools down. Leave to cool completely in the tin.

7 Cut the brownies into about 18 small squares and remove from the tin.

Cheesecake Brownies Energy 228kcal/952kJ; Protein 2.6g; Carbohydrate 20.1g, of which sugars 17.7g; Fat 15.9g, of which saturates 9.5g; Cholesterol 72mg; Calcium 35mg; Fibre 0.3g; Sodium 103mg.
White Chocolate Brownies Energy 235kcal/984kJ; Protein 4.3g; Carbohydrate 30.3g, of which sugars 21.8g; Fat 11.6g, of which saturates 6.6g; Cholesterol 47mg; Calcium 88mg; Fibre 0.4g; Sodium 65mg.

Chocolate Dominoes

A recipe for children to eat rather than make, these fun bars are ideal for birthday parties, when you can match the spots on the dominoes to the children's ages.

Makes 16

175g/6oz/¾ cup soft margarine
175g/6oz/generous ¾ cup caster (superfine) sugar
150g/5oz/1¼ cups self-raising (self-rising) flour
25g/1oz/¼ cup unsweetened cocoa powder, sifted
3 eggs

For the topping
175g/6oz/¾ cup butter
25g/1oz/¼ cup unsweetened cocoa powder
300g/11oz/2¾ cups icing (confectioners') sugar
a few liquorice strips and 115g/4oz packet candy-coated chocolate drops, to decorate

1 Preheat the oven to 180°C/350°F/Gas 4. Lightly brush an 18 × 28cm/7 × 11in rectangular baking tin (pan) with a little oil and line the base with baking parchment.

2 Put all the cake ingredients into a large mixing bowl and beat until smooth and creamy. Spoon the mixture evenly into the prepared cake tin, filling it to the edges and levelling the surface with a metal spatula.

3 Bake for 30 minutes, or until the cake springs back when pressed with the fingertips.

4 Cool in the tin for 5 minutes, then loosen the edges with a knife and transfer to a wire rack. Peel off the lining paper and leave the cake to cool completely. When cold, turn it out on to a chopping board.

5 To make the topping, place the butter in a bowl. Sift together the cocoa powder and the icing sugar into the bowl and beat until smooth. Spread the topping evenly over the cake with a metal spatula.

6 Cut the cake into 16 bars. Place a strip of liquorice across the middle of each bar, then decorate with candy-coated chocolate drops to make the domino spots.

Cranberry and Chocolate Squares

The flavour of the cranberries in these cake squares will add a pleasing tartness that perfectly complements the rich chocolate taste.

Makes 12

150g/5oz/1¼ cups self-raising (self-rising) flour, plus extra for dusting
115g/4oz/½ cup unsalted (sweet) butter
60ml/4 tbsp unsweetened cocoa powder
225g/8oz/1 cup light muscovado (brown) sugar
2 eggs, beaten
115g/4oz/1 cup fresh or thawed frozen cranberries
75ml/5 tbsp coarsely grated plain (semisweet) chocolate, for sprinkling

For the topping
150ml/¼ pint/⅔ cup sour cream
75g/3oz/ scant ½ cup caster (superfine) sugar
30ml/2 tbsp self-raising (self-rising) flour
50g/2oz/¼ cup soft margarine
1 egg, beaten
2.5ml/½ tsp vanilla extract

1 Preheat the oven to 180°C/350°F/Gas 4. Lightly grease a 27 × 18cm/10½ × 7in rectangular cake tin (pan) and dust lightly with flour.

2 Combine the butter, cocoa powder and sugar in a pan and stir over a low heat until melted and smooth.

3 Remove the melted mixture from the heat and stir in the flour and eggs, beating until thoroughly mixed.

4 Add in the cranberries, mixing until thoroughly combined. Spread the mixture in the prepared tin, ensuring it is filled to the corners.

5 Make the topping by mixing all the ingredients in a large bowl. Beat until smooth, then spread over the base.

6 Sprinkle with the grated chocolate and bake for 40–45 minutes, or until risen and firm. Cool in the tin for 10 minutes, then cut neatly into 12 squares. Remove from the tin and cool completely on a wire rack.

Dominoes Energy 335kcal/1400kJ; Protein 2.9g; Carbohydrate 38.8g, of which sugars 31.3g; Fat 19.8g, of which saturates 6.4g; Cholesterol 59mg; Calcium 41mg; Fibre 0.7g; Sodium 199mg.
Cranberry Squares Energy 343kcal/1439kJ; Protein 4.8g; Carbohydrate 42.9g, of which sugars 30.8g; Fat 18.2g, of which saturates 8.7g; Cholesterol 76mg; Calcium 63mg; Fibre 1.4g; Sodium 164mg.

White Chocolate Slices

If you wish, toasted and skinned hazelnuts can be substituted for the macadamia nuts in the topping for these white chocolate slices.

Serves 12

150g/5oz/1 ¼ cups plain (all-purpose) flour
2.5ml/½ tsp baking powder
a pinch of salt
175g/6oz fine-quality white chocolate, chopped
90g/3½oz/½ cup caster (superfine) sugar
115g/4oz/½ cup unsalted (sweet) butter, cut into pieces
2 eggs, lightly beaten
5ml/1 tsp vanilla extract
175g/6oz/1 cup plain (semisweet) chocolate chips

For the topping

200g/7oz milk chocolate, chopped
215g/7½oz/1⅓ cups unsalted macadamia nuts, chopped

1 Preheat the oven to 180°C/350°F/Gas 4. Grease a 23cm/9in springform tin (pan). Sift together the flour, baking powder and salt, and set aside.

2 In a medium pan over a medium heat, melt the white chocolate, sugar and butter until smooth, stirring frequently. Cool slightly, then beat in the eggs and vanilla. Stir in the chocolate chips. Spread evenly in the prepared tin, smoothing the top.

3 Bake for 20–25 minutes, or until a cocktail stick (toothpick) inserted 5cm/2in from the side of the tin comes out clean. Remove from the oven to a heatproof surface, sprinkle chopped milk chocolate over the surface (avoid touching the side of tin) and return to the oven for 1 minute.

4 Remove from the oven and, using the back of a spoon, gently spread out the softened chocolate. Sprinkle with the macadamia nuts and gently press into the chocolate. Cool on a wire rack for 30 minutes, and then chill for 1 hour.

5 Run a sharp knife around the side of the tin to loosen, then unclip and remove. Cut the brownies into thin wedges to serve.

Almond-scented Chocolate Cherry Wedges

These cookies are a chocoholic's dream, and use the very best-quality chocolate. Erratically shaped, they are packed with crunchy cookies, juicy raisins and munchy nuts.

Makes about 15

50g/2oz ratafia biscuits (almond macaroons) or small amaretti
90g/3½oz shortcake biscuits (cookies)
150g/5oz/1 cup jumbo raisins
50g/2oz/¼ cup undyed glacé (candied) cherries, quartered
450g/1lb dark (bittersweet) chocolate (minimum 70 per cent cocoa solids)
90g/3½oz/7 tbsp unsalted (sweet) butter, diced
30ml/2 tbsp amaretto liqueur (optional)
25g/1oz/¼ cup toasted flaked (sliced) almonds

1 Line a baking sheet with baking parchment. Put the ratafia biscuits or amaretti in a large bowl. Leave half whole and break the remainder into coarse pieces. Break each of the shortcake biscuits into three or four jagged pieces and add to the bowl. Add the raisins and cherries and toss lightly together.

2 Melt the chocolate and butter with the liqueur, if using, in a heatproof bowl over a pan of hot water. When melted, remove from the heat and stir until combined. Set aside to cool slightly.

3 Pour the chocolate over the biscuit mixture and stir together until combined. Spread out over the prepared baking sheet. Sprinkle over the almonds and push them in at angles so they stick well to the chocolate-coated biscuits.

4 When the mixture is cold and set, cut or break into crazy shapes, such as long thin triangles or short stumpy squares.

Cook's Tip

If you cannot find undyed glacé cherries in the supermarket, look for them in your local delicatessen instead.

White Slices Energy 526kcal/2190kJ; Protein 6.3g; Carbohydrate 43.8g, of which sugars 34g; Fat 37.4g, of which saturates 16.1g; Cholesterol 64mg; Calcium 82mg; Fibre 2.1g; Sodium 154mg.
Cherry Wedges Energy 288kcal/1206kJ; Protein 2.7g; Carbohydrate 34.6g, of which sugars 29.7g; Fat 16.4g, of which saturates 9.5g; Cholesterol 20mg; Calcium 31mg; Fibre 1.3g; Sodium 75mg.

Bitter Chocolate and Pistachio Wedges

These are rich and grainy in texture, with a delicious bitter chocolate flavour. They go well with vanilla ice cream and are good with bananas and custard.

Makes 16

200g/7oz/scant 1 cup unsalted (sweet) butter, at room temperature, diced
90g/3½oz/½ cup golden caster (superfine) sugar
250g/9oz/2¼ cups plain (all-purpose) flour
50g/2oz/½ cup unsweetened cocoa powder
25g/1oz/¼ cup shelled pistachio nuts, finely chopped
unsweetened cocoa powder, for dusting

1 Preheat the oven to 180°C/350°F/Gas 4 and line a 23cm/9in round sandwich tin (layer pan) with baking parchment.

2 Beat the butter and sugar until light and creamy. Sift the flour and cocoa powder, then add the flour mixture to the butter and work in with your hands until the mixture is smooth. Knead until soft and pliable, then press into the prepared tin.

3 Using the back of a tablespoon, spread the mixture evenly in the tin. Sprinkle the pistachio nuts over the top and press in gently. Prick with a fork, then mark into 16 segments using a round-bladed knife.

4 Bake for 15–20 minutes. Do not allow to brown at all or the wedges will taste bitter.

5 Remove the tin from the oven and dust the wedges with cocoa powder. Cut through the marked sections with a round-bladed knife and leave to cool completely before removing from the tin and serving.

Variation
Try using almonds or hazelnuts instead of pistachio nuts.

Rocky Road Wedges

This is a gluten-free recipe for chocolate and marshmallow treats. These crumbly chocolate wedges contain home-made popcorn in place of broken cookies, which are the main ingredient in no-bake cookies. This recipe uses an orange-flavoured bar, but any chocolate can be used.

Makes 8

15ml/1 tbsp vegetable oil
25g/1oz/2½ tbsp popping corn
150g/5oz orange-flavoured plain (semisweet) chocolate
25g/1oz/2 tbsp unsalted (sweet) butter, diced
75g/3oz soft vanilla fudge, diced
icing (confectioners') sugar, for dusting

1 Heat the oil in a heavy pan. Add the popping corn, cover with a lid and heat, shaking the pan once or twice, until the popping noises die down. (It is important not to lift the lid until the popping stops.)

2 Remove the pan from the heat and leave for about 30 seconds before removing the lid. Be careful, as there may be quite a lot of steam trapped inside. Transfer the popcorn to a bowl and leave to cool for about 5 minutes.

3 Meanwhile, line the base of an 18cm/7in sandwich tin (pan) with baking parchment.

4 Once cooled, tip the corn into a plastic bag and tap with a rolling pin to break up into small pieces.

5 Break the chocolate into a heatproof bowl. Add the butter and rest the bowl over a pan of gently simmering water. Stir frequently until melted. Remove the bowl from the heat and leave to cool for 2 minutes.

6 Stir the popcorn and fudge into the chocolate until well coated, then turn the mixture into the tin and press down firmly in an even layer. Leave to set for about 30 minutes.

7 Turn the cookie out on to a board and cut into eight wedges. Serve lightly dusted with sugar.

Pistachio Wedges Energy 188kcal/783kJ; Protein 2.4g; Carbohydrate 18.6g, of which sugars 6.3g; Fat 12g, of which saturates 7.1g; Cholesterol 27mg; Calcium 33mg; Fibre 1g; Sodium 115mg.
Rocky Road Energy 191kcal/798kJ; Protein 1.5g; Carbohydrate 21g, of which sugars 19.3g; Fat 11.8g, of which saturates 5.9g; Cholesterol 11mg; Calcium 19mg; Fibre 0.5g; Sodium 33mg.

Chocolate and Coconut Slices

These are easier to slice if they are chilled overnight.

Makes 24

175g/6oz digestive biscuits (graham crackers)
50g/2oz/¼ cup caster (superfine) sugar
a pinch of salt
115g/4oz/½ cup butter or margarine, melted
75g/3oz/1 cup desiccated (dry unsweetened shredded) coconut
250g/9oz plain (semisweet) chocolate chips
250ml/8fl oz/1 cup sweetened condensed milk
115g/4oz/1 cup chopped walnuts

1 Preheat the oven to 180°C/350°F/Gas 4. Put the digestive biscuits in a plastic bag and, using a rolling pin, crush them until they are fairly small.

2 In a bowl, combine the crushed digestive biscuits, sugar, salt and butter or margarine. Mix the ingredients until thoroughly combined. Press the mixture evenly over the base of an ungreased 33 × 23cm/13 × 9in baking tin (pan).

3 Sprinkle the desiccated coconut over the cookie base, then sprinkle over the chocolate chips.

4 Pour the condensed milk evenly over the chocolate chips, spreading to the edges of the tin with a metal spatula. Sprinkle the chopped walnuts on top.

5 Bake in the oven for 30 minutes, until just firm to the touch and golden brown.

6 Leave in the tin to cool slightly before turning out on to a board. Leave to cool completely before cutting into 24 slices.

Variations

- *Try substituting 75g/3oz ginger nut biscuits (gingersnaps) for half the digestive biscuits.*
- *Other nuts can be used in place of the walnuts, such as pecans, hazelnuts or almonds.*

White Chocolate Macadamia Slices

Nutty, fruity and chocolately slices – what more could anybody want?

Makes 16

150g/5oz/1¼ cups macadamia nuts, blanched almonds or hazelnuts
400g/14oz white chocolate, broken into squares
115g/4oz/½ cup ready-to-eat dried apricots
75g/3oz/6 tbsp unsalted (sweet) butter
5ml/1 tsp vanilla extract
3 eggs
150g/5oz/generous ½ cup light muscovado (brown) sugar
115g/4oz/1 cup self-raising (self-rising) flour

1 Preheat the oven to 190°C/375°F/Gas 5. Lightly grease two 20cm/8in round sandwich cake tins (layer pans) and line the base of each with baking parchment.

2 Roughly chop the nuts and half the white chocolate, making sure that the pieces are more or less the same size, then use scissors to cut the apricots to similar size pieces. Set aside.

3 In a heatproof bowl over a pan of barely simmering water, add the remaining white chocolate with the butter, stirring until melted and smooth. Remove from the heat and stir in the vanilla extract.

4 Whisk the eggs and sugar together in a mixing bowl until thick and pale. Pour in the melted chocolate mixture, whisking constantly until well combined.

5 Sift the flour over the mixture and fold it in evenly, ensuring that all the ingredients are well mixed.

6 Add the nuts, chopped white chocolate and chopped dried apricots to the mixture, stirring to combine.

7 Spoon the mixture into the tins, filling the corners. Level the tops of the mixtures with a metal spatula. Bake for 30–35 minutes, or until the top is firm to the touch, crusty and golden brown. Leave to cool in the tins before cutting each cake into eight slices.

Coconut Slices Energy 217kcal/907kJ; Protein 2.8g; Carbohydrate 20g, of which sugars 15.8g; Fat 14.6g, of which saturates 7.5g; Cholesterol 18mg; Calcium 48mg; Fibre 1g; Sodium 89mg.
Macadamia Slices Energy 317kcal/1326kJ; Protein 4.8g; Carbohydrate 31.6g, of which sugars 26g; Fat 20g, of which saturates 8.4g; Cholesterol 46mg; Calcium 95mg; Fibre 0.9g; Sodium 97mg.

Marbled Caramel Chocolate Slice

This classic recipe is made even more special here with a decorative marbled topping swirled into the chocolate.

Makes about 24

250g/9oz/2¼ cups plain (all-purpose) flour
75g/3oz/scant ½ cup caster (superfine) sugar
175g/6oz/¾ cup unsalted (sweet) butter, softened

For the filling

90g/3½oz/7 tbsp unsalted (sweet) butter, diced
90g/3½oz/scant ½ cup light muscovado (brown) sugar
2 x 400g/14oz cans evaporated milk

For the topping

90g/3½oz plain (semisweet) chocolate
90g/3½oz milk chocolate
50g/2oz white chocolate

1 Preheat the oven to 180°C/350°F/Gas 4. Lightly grease a 33 × 23cm/13 × 9in Swiss roll tin (jelly roll pan) and line with baking parchment. Put the flour and sugar in a bowl and rub in the butter until the mixture resembles breadcrumbs, then form into a soft dough.

2 Press the dough over the base of the tin. Prick all over with a fork and bake for about 20 minutes, or until firm to the touch and very light brown. Set aside and leave in the tin to cool.

3 Make the filling. Put the butter, muscovado sugar and milk in a pan and heat gently, stirring, until the sugar has dissolved. Simmer the mixture very gently, stirring constantly, for about 5–10 minutes, or until it has thickened and has turned a caramel colour. Remove from the heat.

4 Pour the filling mixture over the pastry base, spread evenly, then leave until cold.

5 Make the topping. Melt each type of chocolate separately in a microwave or in a heatproof bowl set over hot water. Spoon lines of plain and milk chocolate over the set caramel filling.

6 Add small spoonfuls of white chocolate. Use a skewer to form a marbled effect on the topping. Leave to cool until set.

Chocolate Salami

This after-dinner sweetmeat resembles a salami in shape, hence its curious name – although, of course, the flavour is somewhat different. It is very rich and will serve a lot of people. Slice it very thinly and serve with espresso coffee and amaretto liqueur.

Makes 10–12

24 Petit Beurre cookies, broken into pieces
350g/12oz dark (bittersweet) or plain (semisweet) chocolate, broken into squares
225g/8oz/1 cup unsalted (sweet) butter, softened
60ml/4 tbsp amaretto liqueur
2 egg yolks
50g/2oz/½ cup flaked (sliced) almonds, lightly toasted and thinly shredded lengthways
25g/1oz/¼ cup ground almonds

1 Place the cookies in a food processor and process until crushed into coarse crumbs. Place the chocolate in a large heatproof bowl over a pan of barely simmering water, add a small knob (pat) of the butter and all the liqueur, and heat, stirring, until the chocolate melts. Remove from the heat.

2 Leave the chocolate to cool for a minute, then stir in the egg yolks, followed by the remaining butter, a little at a time. Add in most of the crushed cookies, reserving a handful, and mix well. Stir in the almonds. Leave the mixture to cool for about 1 hour.

3 Process the remaining crushed cookies in the food processor until finely ground. Transfer to a bowl and mix with the ground almonds. Cover and set aside until you are ready to serve.

4 Turn the chocolate and cookie mixture on to a sheet of lightly oiled baking parchment, then shape into a 35cm/14in long sausage with a metal spatula, tapering the ends slightly so the roll resembles a salami. Wrap securely in the paper and freeze the roll for at least 4 hours, until solid.

5 Spread the finely ground cookies and almonds out on baking parchment and roll the 'salami' in them until coated. Leave to stand on a board for about 1 hour before serving in slices.

Marbled Slice Energy 305kcal/1279kJ; Protein 4.5g; Carbohydrate 39.8g, of which sugars 31.8g; Fat 15.3g, of which saturates 9.5g; Cholesterol 36mg; Calcium 125mg; Fibre 0.5g; Sodium 117mg.
Salami Energy 453kcal/1885kJ; Protein 4.5g; Carbohydrate 36.6g, of which sugars 26.9g; Fat 32.3g, of which saturates 16.8g; Cholesterol 96mg; Calcium 47mg; Fibre 1.4g; Sodium 173mg.

Rich Chocolate Cookie Slice

These rich, dark chocolate refrigerator cookies are perfect when served with strong coffee, either as a mid-morning treat or even in place of dessert. They are always very popular, so don't expect them to last for long.

Makes about 10

275g/10oz fruit and nut plain (semisweet) chocolate
130g/4½oz/½ cup unsalted (sweet) butter, diced
90g/3½oz digestive biscuits (graham crackers)
90g/3½oz white chocolate

1 Grease and line the base and sides of a 450g/1lb loaf tin (pan) with baking parchment.

2 Break the fruit and nut chocolate into even pieces and place them in a heatproof bowl along with the butter.

3 Set the bowl over a pan of simmering water and stir gently until melted. Remove the bowl from the heat and leave to cool for 20 minutes.

4 Break the digestive biscuits into small pieces with your fingers. Finely chop the white chocolate.

5 Stir the broken biscuits and white chocolate into the cooled, melted fruit and nut chocolate until combined.

6 Turn the mixture into the prepared tin and pack down gently. Chill for 2 hours, or until set.

7 To serve, turn out the mixture and remove the lining paper. Cut into slices with a sharp knife.

Variation

You can use this simple basic recipe to create all kinds of variations. Try different kinds of chocolate, such as ginger, hazelnut, honey and almond, peanut or mocha. You can also experiment with different kinds of biscuits or cookies.

Chocolate Nut Slice

Children of all ages will love this combination of broken cookies, chocolate and nuts. Although the unsliced bar looks small, it's very rich so is best sliced very thinly. If you have any other plain cookies in the cupboard, you can use them instead of the rich tea, with equally good results.

Makes 10

225g/8oz milk chocolate
40g/1½oz/3 tbsp unsalted (sweet) butter, diced
75g/3oz rich tea biscuits (cookies)
50g/2oz/½ cup flaked (sliced) almonds
75g/3oz plain (semisweet) or white chocolate, roughly chopped
icing (confectioners') sugar, for dusting

1 Break the milk chocolate into pieces and place in a heatproof bowl with the butter. Rest the bowl over a pan of simmering water and stir frequently until melted.

2 Meanwhile, dampen a 450g/1lb loaf tin (pan) and line the base and sides with clear film (plastic wrap). Don't worry about smoothing out the creases in the film.

3 When the chocolate has melted, remove it from the heat and leave for 5 minutes until slightly cooled.

4 Break the biscuits into small pieces, then stir into the melted chocolate with the almonds. Add the chopped chocolate to the bowl and fold in quickly and lightly.

5 Turn the mixture into the tin and pack down with a fork. Tap the base of the tin gently on the work surface. Chill for 2 hours until set.

6 To serve, turn the chocolate loaf on to a board and peel away the clear film. Dust lightly with icing sugar and slice thinly.

Variation

Use whatever biscuits or cookies you have available. To add a ginger taste, use ginger nut biscuits (gingersnaps).

Cookie Slice Energy 326kcal/1361kJ; Protein 2.7g; Carbohydrate 29g, of which sugars 23.8g; Fat 23g, of which saturates 13.9g; Cholesterol 33mg; Calcium 44mg; Fibre 0.9g; Sodium 144mg.
Nut Slice Energy 248kcal/1034kJ; Protein 3.7g; Carbohydrate 23.5g, of which sugars 19.4g; Fat 16.1g, of which saturates 8.2g; Cholesterol 16mg; Calcium 74mg; Fibre 0.9g; Sodium 75mg.

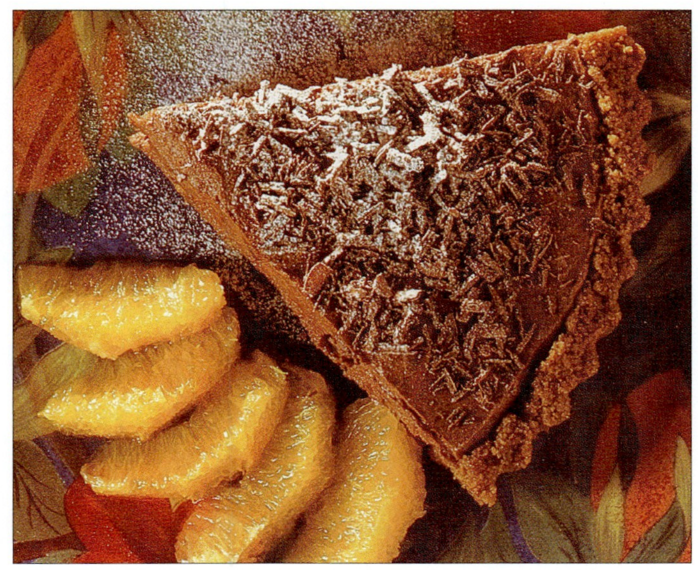

Chilled Chocolate and Date Slice

This richly flavoured chocolate and date dessert is wonderful served in wedges, accompanied by fresh orange segments.

Serves 6–8

115g/4oz/½ cup unsalted (sweet) butter, melted
225g/8oz ginger nut biscuits (gingersnaps) finely crushed
50g/2oz/⅔ cup stale sponge cake crumbs
75ml/5 tbsp orange juice
115g/4oz/⅔ cup stoned (pitted) dates
25g/1oz/¼ cup finely chopped nuts
175g/6oz dark (bittersweet) chocolate
300ml/½ pint/1¼ cups whipping cream
grated chocolate and icing (confectioners') sugar, to decorate
single (light) cream, to serve (optional)

1 Mix the butter and ginger biscuit crumbs in a bowl, then press the mixture on to the sides and base of an 18cm/7in loose-based flan tin (pan). Chill while making the filling.

2 Put the cake crumbs in a bowl. Pour over 60ml/4 tbsp of the orange juice, stir well with a wooden spoon and leave to soak. Put the dates in a pan and add the remaining orange juice. Warm the mixture over a low heat. Mash the warm dates thoroughly and stir in the cake crumbs, with the chopped nuts.

3 Mix the chocolate with 60ml/4 tbsp of the cream in a heatproof bowl. Place the bowl over a pan of barely simmering water and stir occasionally until melted. In a separate bowl, whip the rest of the cream to soft peaks, then fold in the melted chocolate.

4 Add the cooled date, crumb and nut mixture to the cream and chocolate and mix lightly but thoroughly. Pour into the tin. Using a spatula, level the mixture. Chill until just set, then mark the tart into portions, using a sharp knife dipped in hot water. Return the tart to the refrigerator and chill until firm.

5 To decorate, sprinkle the grated chocolate over the surface and dust with icing sugar. Serve with cream, if you wish.

Double Chocolate Slices

These delicious gluten-free cookies have a smooth chocolate base, topped with a mint-flavoured cream and drizzles of melted chocolate. Perfect for a tea-time treat – or at any time of day.

Makes 12

200g/7oz/1¾ cups gluten-free flour
25g/1oz/¼ cup unsweetened cocoa powder
150g/5oz/10 tbsp unsalted (sweet) butter, cut into small pieces
75g/3oz/⅔ cup icing (confectioners') sugar

For the topping

75g/3oz white chocolate mint crisps
50g/2oz/¼ cup unsalted (sweet) butter, softened
90g/3½oz/scant 1 cup icing (confectioners') sugar
50g/2oz milk chocolate

1 Preheat the oven to 180°C/350°F/Gas 4. Grease an 18cm/7in square shallow baking tin (pan) and line with a strip of baking parchment that comes up over two opposite sides. This will make it easier to remove the cookie base from the tin after baking.

2 Put the flour and cocoa powder into a food processor and add the pieces of butter. Process briefly until the mixture resembles fine breadcrumbs. Add the icing sugar and mix briefly again to form a smooth soft dough.

3 Turn the flour mixture into the prepared tin and gently press out to the edges with your fingers to make an even layer. Bake for 25 minutes, then remove from the oven and leave the base to cool completely in the tin.

4 To make the topping, put the chocolate mint crisps in a plastic bag and tap firmly with a rolling pin until crushed. Beat the butter and sugar together until creamy, then beat in the crushed chocolate mint crisps. Spread the mixture over the cookie base.

5 Melt the milk chocolate in a small heatproof bowl set over a pan of hot water. Lift the cookie base out of the tin; remove the paper. Using a teaspoon, drizzle the melted chocolate over the topping. Leave to set, then cut into squares.

Date Slice Energy 575kcal/2394kJ; Protein 5.1g; Carbohydrate 51.3g, of which sugars 37.5g; Fat 40.2g, of which saturates 22.8g; Cholesterol 78mg; Calcium 87mg; Fibre 1.8g; Sodium 214mg.
Double Slices Energy 299kcal/1248kJ; Protein 2.3g; Carbohydrate 34.4g, of which sugars 20.8g; Fat 17.3g, of which saturates 10.8g; Cholesterol 37mg; Calcium 28mg; Fibre 0.8g; Sodium 126mg.

Fudge-nut Chocolate Bars

Although your kids will be desperate to tuck into these fudgy treats, it's well worth chilling them for a few hours before slicing so that they can be easily cut into neat pieces.

Makes 16

150g/5oz/10 tbsp unsalted (sweet) butter, chilled and diced
250g/9oz/2¼ cups plain (all-purpose) flour
75g/3oz/scant ½ cup caster (superfine) sugar

For the topping
150g/5oz milk chocolate, broken into pieces
40g/1½oz/3 tbsp unsalted (sweet) butter
400g/14oz can sweetened condensed milk
50g/2oz/½ cup chopped nuts

1 Preheat the oven to 160°C/325°F/Gas 3. Lightly grease a 28 × 18cm/11 × 7in shallow baking tin (pan).

2 Put the butter and flour in a food processor and process until the mixture resembles fine breadcrumbs.

3 Add the sugar to the flour mixture and process again until the mixture starts to cling together.

4 Tip the mixture into the baking tin and spread out with the back of a wooden spoon to fill the base in an even layer.

5 Bake for 35–40 minutes, or until the surface of the cookie base is very lightly coloured.

6 To make the topping, put the chocolate in a heavy pan with the butter and the condensed milk. Heat gently, stirring occasionally, until the chocolate and butter have melted, then increase the heat and cook, stirring, for 3–5 minutes until the mixture starts to thicken.

7 Add the chopped nuts to the pan and pour the mixture over the cookie base, spreading it in an even layer with a metal spatula. Leave to cool, then chill for at least 2 hours until firm. Serve cut into bars.

Chocolate-topped Date Crunch

A tasty mixture of dried fruit, syrup and chocolate is guaranteed to be a success with the younger members of the family – and they will need to keep an eye on the adults, too.

Makes 24

225g/8oz digestive biscuits (graham crackers)
75g/3oz/⅓ cup butter
30ml/2 tbsp golden (light corn) syrup
75g/3oz/½ cup finely chopped pitted dried dates
75g/3oz/⅔ cup sultanas (golden raisins)
150g/5oz milk or plain (semisweet) chocolate, chopped into small pieces

1 Line an 18cm/7in square shallow cake tin (pan) with foil. Put the biscuits in a plastic bag, keep the opening sealed and crush coarsely with a rolling pin.

2 Gently heat the butter and syrup together in a small pan until the butter has melted.

3 Stir the crushed biscuits, dates and sultanas into the butter and syrup mixture and mix well with a wooden spoon until evenly combined.

4 Spoon into the prepared tin, spreading it out evenly, press flat with the back of the spoon and chill for 1 hour.

5 Melt the chocolate in a heatproof bowl set over a pan of simmering water, stirring until smooth. Remove from the heat and spoon over the cookie mixture, spreading evenly with a metal spatula. Chill until set.

6 Lift the foil out of the cake tin and peel away. Cut the crunch into 24 pieces to serve.

Variation
You could drizzle 75g/3oz each melted white and dark (bittersweet) chocolate over the topping.

Fudge Bars Energy 315kcal/1317kJ; Protein 4.9g; Carbohydrate 36.6g, of which sugars 24.7g; Fat 17.5g, of which saturates 9.7g; Cholesterol 37mg; Calcium 123mg; Fibre 0.7g; Sodium 116mg.
Date Crunch Energy 120kcal/503kJ; Protein 1.3g; Carbohydrate 15.3g, of which sugars 10.1g; Fat 6.4g, of which saturates 3.6g; Cholesterol 12mg; Calcium 27mg; Fibre 0.4g; Sodium 85mg.

Chocolate and Toffee Bars

The irresistible combination of chocolate, toffee and nuts will ensure that these bars go down a treat at any time of day or night. It is possible to use white chocolate instead of plain, if you prefer.

Makes 32

350g/12oz/2 cups soft light brown sugar
450g/1lb/2 cups butter or margarine, softened
2 egg yolks
7.5ml/1½ tsp vanilla extract
450g/1lb/4 cups plain (all-purpose) or wholemeal (whole-wheat) flour
2.5ml/½ tsp salt
175g/6oz plain (semisweet) chocolate, broken into squares
115g/4oz/1 cup walnuts or pecan nuts, chopped

1 Preheat the oven to 180°C/350°F/Gas 4. Lightly grease a 33 × 23 × 5cm/13 × 9 × 2in baking tin (pan).

2 Beat the sugar and butter or margarine in a large mixing bowl until light and fluffy. Beat in the egg yolks and vanilla extract, then stir in the flour and salt to make a soft dough.

3 Spread the dough evenly into the prepared tin. Level the surface. Bake for 25–30 minutes, until lightly browned. The texture will be soft.

4 Remove the bake from the oven and immediately place the broken chocolate on top. Set aside until the chocolate is soft, then spread it out with a metal spatula. Sprinkle with the chopped nuts.

5 While the bake is still warm, cut it into 5 × 4cm/2 × 1½in bars. Remove from the tin and leave to cool completely on a wire rack.

Cook's Tip

If you find that the chocolate isn't softening enough to be easily spread over the base, then put the tin back in the oven for a minute or two to melt the chocolate a little.

Chocolate Raspberry Macaroon Bars

Any seedless preserve, such as strawberry or apricot, can be substituted for the raspberry in this fruity macaroon recipe.

Makes 16–18

115g/4oz/½ cup unsalted (sweet) butter, softened
50g/2oz/½ cup icing (confectioners') sugar
25g/1oz/¼ cup unsweetened cocoa powder
a pinch of salt
5ml/1 tsp almond extract
115g/4oz/1 cup plain (all-purpose) flour

For the topping
150g/5oz/½ cup seedless raspberry preserve
15ml/1 tbsp raspberry-flavoured liqueur
175g/6oz/1 cup milk chocolate chips
175g/6oz/1½ cups finely ground almonds
4 egg whites
a pinch of salt
200g/7oz/1 cup caster (superfine) sugar
2.5ml/½ tsp almond extract
50g/2oz/½ cup flaked (sliced) almonds

1 Preheat the oven to 160°C/325°F/Gas 3. Line a 23 × 33cm/9 × 13in baking tin (pan) with foil and then grease the foil. Beat together the butter, sugar, cocoa and salt until blended. Beat in the almond extract and flour to make a crumbly dough.

2 Turn the dough into the tin and smooth the surface. Prick all over with a fork. Bake for 20 minutes, or until just set. Remove the tin from the oven and increase the temperature to 190°C/375°F/Gas 5.

3 To make the topping, combine the raspberry preserve and liqueur. Spread over the cooked crust, then sprinkle with the chocolate chips.

4 In a food processor fitted with a metal blade, process the almonds, egg whites, salt, caster sugar and almond extract. Pour this mixture over the jam layer, spreading evenly. Sprinkle with almonds.

5 Bake for 20–25 minutes, or until the top is golden and puffed. Cool in the tin for 20 minutes. Carefully remove from the tin and cool completely. Peel off the foil and cut into bars.

Toffee Bars Energy 252kcal/1053kJ; Protein 2.4g; Carbohydrate 26g, of which sugars 15.2g; Fat 16.1g, of which saturates 8.6g; Cholesterol 43mg; Calcium 35mg; Fibre 0.7g; Sodium 87mg.
Macaroon Bars Energy 266kcal/1115kJ; Protein 4.5g; Carbohydrate 32.1g, of which sugars 26.6g; Fat 14.1g, of which saturates 5.7g; Cholesterol 16mg; Calcium 66mg; Fibre 1.2g; Sodium 79mg.

Chocolate Walnut Bars

These delicious double-decker bars should be stored in the refrigerator in an airtight container.

Makes 24

50g/2oz/⅓ cup walnuts
55g/2¼oz/generous ¼ cup caster (superfine) sugar
100g/3¾oz/scant 1 cup plain (all-purpose) flour, sifted
90g/3½oz/7 tbsp cold unsalted (sweet) butter, cut into pieces

For the topping

25g/1oz/2 tbsp unsalted (sweet) butter
90ml/6 tbsp water
25g/1oz/¼ cup unsweetened cocoa powder
90g/3½oz/½ cup caster (superfine) sugar
5ml/1 tsp vanilla extract
1.5ml/¼ tsp salt
2 eggs
icing (confectioners') sugar, for dusting

1 Preheat the oven to 180°C/350°F/Gas 4. Grease the base and sides of a 20cm/8in square baking tin (pan).

2 Grind the walnuts with a few tablespoons of the caster sugar in a food processor or blender. In a bowl, combine the ground walnuts, remaining sugar and the flour.

3 Rub in the butter using your fingertips or a biscuit (cookie) cutter until the mixture resembles coarse breadcrumbs. Alternatively, use a food processor.

4 Pat the walnut mixture evenly into the base of the baking tin. Bake for 25 minutes.

5 To make the topping, gently melt the butter with the water in a pan. Whisk in the cocoa powder and sugar. Remove from the heat, stir in the vanilla extract and salt until well combined, then cool for 5 minutes.

6 Whisk in the eggs until blended. Pour the topping over the baked crust.

7 Return to the oven and bake until set, about 20 minutes. Set the tin on a wire rack to cool, then cut into bars and dust with icing sugar before serving.

Chunky Chocolate Bars

Chocolate is combined here with dried fruit and nuts to create these heavenly bars.

Makes 12

350g/12oz plain (semisweet) chocolate, chopped into small pieces
115g/4oz/½ cup unsalted (sweet) butter
400g/14oz can condensed milk
225g/8oz digestive biscuits (graham crackers), broken
50g/2oz/⅓ cup raisins
115g/4oz ready-to-eat dried peaches, roughly chopped
50g/2oz/½ cup hazelnuts or pecan nuts, roughly chopped

1 Line a 28 × 18cm/11 × 7in cake tin (pan) with clear film (plastic wrap).

2 Melt the chocolate and butter together in a large heatproof bowl or double boiler set over a pan of simmering water. Stir until well melted and smooth.

3 Pour the condensed milk into the chocolate and butter mixture. Beat with a wooden spoon until creamy.

4 Add the broken biscuits, raisins, chopped peaches and hazelnuts or pecans. Mix well until all the ingredients are coated in the rich chocolate sauce.

5 Tip the mixture into the prepared tin, making sure it is pressed well into the corners. Leave the top craggy. Cool, then chill until set.

6 Lift the cake out of the tin using the clear film and then peel off the film. Cut into 12 bars and serve immediately.

Variations

You can make these chunky bars with a variety of fruits. Try making with dried apricots instead of the peaches, or use glacé (candied) cherries, prunes or dates if you prefer. Preserved stem ginger, in place of the fruit, would make a tasty gingery bar.

Walnut Bars Energy 97kcal/407kJ; Protein 1.5g; Carbohydrate 9.8g, of which sugars 6.5g; Fat 6.1g, of which saturates 2.9g; Cholesterol 26mg; Calcium 16mg; Fibre 0.3g; Sodium 45mg.
Chunky Bars Energy 462kcal/1935kJ; Protein 6.3g; Carbohydrate 53.7g, of which sugars 43g; Fat 26.2g, of which saturates 13.9g; Cholesterol 42mg; Calcium 135mg; Fibre 1.9g; Sodium 220mg.

Chocolate Butterscotch Bars

The blend of chocolate and butterscotch makes these bars exquisitely chewy.

Makes 24
225g/8oz/2 cups plain (all-purpose) flour
2.5ml/½ tsp baking powder
150g/5oz plain (semisweet) chocolate, chopped
115g/4oz/½ cup unsalted (sweet) butter, diced
50g/2oz/⅓ cup light muscovado (brown) sugar
30ml/2 tbsp ground almonds

For the topping
175g/6oz/¾ cup unsalted (sweet) butter, diced
115g/4oz/½ cup caster (superfine) sugar
30ml/2 tbsp golden (light corn) syrup
175ml/6fl oz/¾ cup condensed milk
150g/5oz/1¼ cups whole toasted hazelnuts
225g/8oz plain (semisweet) chocolate, chopped into small pieces

1 Preheat the oven to 160°C/325°F/Gas 3. Grease a shallow 30 × 20 cm/12 × 8 in tin (pan). Sift the flour and baking powder into a large bowl. Melt the chocolate in a bowl over a pan of simmering water.

2 Rub the butter into the flour until the mixture resembles coarse breadcrumbs, then stir in the sugar. Work in the melted chocolate and ground almonds to make a light biscuit dough.

3 Spread the dough roughly in the tin, then use a rubber spatula to press it down evenly into the sides and the corners. Prick the surface with a fork and bake for 25–30 minutes until firm. Leave to cool in the tin.

4 Make the topping. Heat the butter, sugar, golden syrup and condensed milk in a pan, stirring until the butter and sugar have melted. Simmer until golden, then stir in the hazelnuts.

5 Pour over the cooked base. Leave to set.

6 Melt the chocolate for the topping in a heatproof bowl over barely simmering water. Spread evenly over the butterscotch layer, then leave to set again before cutting into bars to serve.

Rocky Road Chocolate Bars

If you have eaten versions of rocky road in various coffee bars and, although delicious, have always thought "I could improve on that" – well, you can, and this recipe is a dream to make with children. They will love smashing up the biscuits, and can do most of the rest, apart from melting the chocolate and lining the pan. Adults will also enjoy the contrast of melting chocolate chips, crunchy biscuits and soft marshmallows all blended together – it's not just kid's stuff.

Makes 16
225g/8oz/1 cup salted butter
115g/4oz dark (bittersweet) chocolate, roughly broken up
30ml/2 tbsp caster (superfine) sugar
30ml/2 tbsp golden (light corn) syrup
30ml/2 tbsp good-quality unsweetened cocoa powder
350g/12oz mixed digestive biscuits (graham crackers) and ginger nut biscuits (gingersnaps)
50g/2oz mini marshmallows
75g/3oz mixed white and milk chocolate chips
icing (confectioners') sugar, for dusting (optional)

1 Line a 20cm/8in square cake pan, measuring about 2.5cm/1in deep, with baking parchment.

2 Put the butter in a pan with the chocolate, sugar, syrup and cocoa powder. Place over a gentle heat until completely melted.

3 Put the biscuits into a large plastic bag and smash with a rolling pin until broken up into rough chunks.

4 Stir the biscuits into the chocolate mixture, followed by the marshmallows and chocolate chips. Mix together well until everything is well coated in chocolate.

5 Spoon the mixture into the pan, but don't press down too much – it should look like a rocky road. Chill for at least 1 hour, or until firm.

6 Remove the cake from the pan and cut into 16 bars. If you like, dust the bars with icing sugar before serving.

Butterscotch Bars Energy 305kcal/1273kJ; Protein 3.5g; Carbohydrate 30g, of which sugars 22.5g; Fat 19.8g, of which saturates 9.7g; Cholesterol 29mg; Calcium 57mg; Fibre 1.2g; Sodium 89mg.
Rocky Road Energy 296kcal/1237kJ; Protein 2.7g; Carbohydrate 28.6g, of which sugars 15.7g; Fat 19.9g, of which saturates 11.6g; Cholesterol 40mg; Calcium 39mg; Fibre 0.9g; Sodium 245mg.

Greek Chocolate Mousse Tartlets

Irresistible Greek-style tartlets with a lightweight chocolate and yogurt filling.

Makes 6 tarts

175g/6oz/1½ cups plain (all-purpose) flour
30ml/2 tbsp unsweetened cocoa powder
30ml/2 tbsp icing (confectioners') sugar
115g/4oz/½ cup butter
60ml/4 tbsp water
melted dark (bittersweet) chocolate, to decorate

For the filling

200g/7oz white chocolate
120ml/4fl oz/½ cup milk
10ml/2 tsp powdered gelatine
25g/1oz/2 tbsp caster (superfine) sugar
5ml/1 tsp vanilla extract
2 eggs, separated
250g/9oz/generous 1 cup Greek (US strained plain) yogurt

1 Preheat the oven to 190°C/375°F/Gas 5. Sift the flour, cocoa and icing sugar into a large bowl.

2 Place the butter in a pan with the water and heat gently until just melted. Cool, then stir into the flour to make a smooth dough. Chill until firm.

3 Roll out the pastry and line six deep 10cm/4in loose-based flan tins (pans). Prick the base of the pastry cases (pie shells), cover with baking parchment, weigh down with baking beans and bake blind for 10 minutes. Remove the beans and paper, return to the oven and bake for 15 minutes until firm. Leave to cool.

4 Make the filling. Melt the broken-up chocolate in a heatproof bowl over hot water. Pour the milk into a pan, sprinkle over the gelatine and heat gently, stirring, until the gelatine has dissolved. Remove from the heat and stir in the chocolate.

5 Whisk the sugar, vanilla and egg yolks in a large bowl, then beat in the chocolate mixture. Beat in the yogurt until mixed.

6 Whisk the egg whites in a clean, grease-free bowl until stiff, then carefully fold into the chocolate mixture. Spoon into the pastry cases and leave to set. Drizzle with melted chocolate to serve.

Chocolate Lemon Tartlets

These delicious individual chocolate desserts have a tasty lemony curd filling.

Makes 12 tartlets

350g/12oz chocolate shortcrust pastry
lemon twists and melted chocolate, to decorate

For the lemon custard sauce

grated rind and juice of 1 lemon
350ml/12fl oz/1½ cups milk
6 egg yolks
50g/2oz/¼ cup caster (superfine) sugar

For the lemon curd filling

grated rind and juice of 2 lemons
175g/6oz/¾ cup unsalted (sweet) butter, diced
450g/1lb/2¼ cups granulated (white) sugar
3 eggs, lightly beaten

For the chocolate layer

175ml/6fl oz/¾ cup double (heavy) cream
175g/6oz dark (bittersweet) or plain (semisweet) chocolate, chopped into small pieces
25g/1oz/2 tbsp unsalted (sweet) butter, cut into pieces

1 Prepare the custard sauce. Boil the rind in a pan with the milk. Remove from the heat and leave for 5 minutes to infuse (steep). Strain the milk into a clean pan and reheat it gently. In a bowl beat the yolks and sugar with a hand-held electric mixer for 2–3 minutes, until pale and thick. Pour over about 250ml/8fl oz/1 cup of the flavoured hot milk, beating vigorously.

2 Return the yolk mixture to the milk in the pan and cook gently, stirring, until the mixture thickens. (Do not allow the sauce to boil or it will curdle.) Strain into a chilled bowl. Stir 30ml/2 tbsp lemon juice into the sauce. Cool, stirring occasionally, then chill until ready to use.

3 Prepare the lemon curd filling. Combine the lemon rind, juice, butter and sugar in the top of a double boiler. Set over simmering water and heat until the butter has melted and the sugar has completely dissolved. Reduce the heat to low. Stir the lightly beaten eggs into the mixture. Gently cook for 15 minutes, stirring constantly, until the mixture thickens. Strain into a bowl and cover with clear film (plastic wrap). Allow to cool, stirring occasionally, then chill to thicken, stirring occasionally.

4 Lightly butter twelve 7.5cm/3in tartlet tins (muffin pans). On a lightly floured surface, roll out the pastry to a thickness of 3mm/⅛in. Using a 10cm/4in fluted cutter, cut out 12 rounds and press each one into a tin. Prick the bases with a fork. Place the tins on a baking sheet and chill for 30 minutes.

5 Preheat the oven to 190°C/375°F/Gas 5. Cut out rounds of foil and line each pastry case (pie shell); fill with baking beans or rice. Bake blind for 5–8 minutes. Remove the foil and beans and bake for 5 minutes, until the cases are golden. Remove to a rack to cool.

6 Prepare the chocolate layer. Boil the cream in a pan. Remove from the heat and add the chocolate; stir until melted. Beat in the butter and cool slightly. Pour the filling into each tartlet to make a layer 5mm/¼in thick. Chill for 10 minutes until set.

7 Fill the tartlets with lemon curd. Set aside. Spoon lemon custard sauce on to a plate and place a tartlet in the centre. Decorate with a lemon twist. Dot with melted chocolate.

Greek Tartlets Energy 555kcal/2320kJ; Protein 11.9g; Carbohydrate 55g, of which sugars 32.2g; Fat 34g, of which saturates 19.7g; Cholesterol 105mg; Calcium 242mg; Fibre 1.5g; Sodium 263mg.
Lemon Tartlets Energy 379kcal/1585kJ; Protein 6.1g; Carbohydrate 40.5g, of which sugars 27g; Fat 22.6g, of which saturates 12.9g; Cholesterol 163mg; Calcium 68mg; Fibre 0.7g; Sodium 127mg.

Fruit Tartlets with Chocolate Pastry

The cream and fresh fruit topping of these delightful tartlets contrast beautifully with the chocolate pastry.

Makes 8 tartlets

150g/5oz/10 tbsp cold butter, cut into pieces
65g/2½oz/5 tbsp dark brown sugar
45ml/3 tbsp unsweetened cocoa powder
175g/6oz/1½ cups plain (all-purpose) flour
1 egg white

For the filling

215g/7½oz/¾ cup redcurrant or grape jelly
15ml/1 tbsp fresh lemon juice
175ml/6fl oz/¾ cup whipping cream
675g/1½lb fresh fruit, such as strawberries, raspberries, kiwi fruit, peaches, grapes or blueberries, peeled and sliced as necessary

1 Make the pastry. Place the butter, brown sugar and cocoa in a medium pan over a low heat. When the butter has melted, remove from the heat and sift over the flour. Stir with a wooden spoon to combine, then add just enough egg white to bind the mixture. Gather into a ball, wrap in baking parchment and chill for at least 30 minutes.

2 Preheat the oven to 180°C/350°F/Gas 4. Grease eight 7.5cm/3in tartlet tins (muffin pans). Roll out the dough between two sheets of baking parchment and stamp out eight 10cm/4in rounds with a fluted cutter.

3 Line the tartlet tins with dough rounds. Prick the pastry bases with a fork. Chill for 15 minutes.

4 Bake for 20–25 minutes until firm. Leave to cool, then remove the tartlets from the tins.

5 Melt the jelly with the lemon juice in a pan over a low heat. Brush a thin layer over the base of the tartlets. Whip the cream in a bowl and spread a thin layer in the tartlet cases (shells). Arrange the fruit on top. Brush evenly with the fruit glaze and serve immediately.

Truffle Filo Tarts

These dainty filo pastry cups, decorated with twists of lemon, can be prepared a day ahead and then stored in an airtight container until they are needed.

Makes 24 tarts

3–6 sheets filo pastry (depending on size), thawed if frozen
45g/1½oz/3 tbsp unsalted (sweet) butter, melted
sugar, for sprinkling
lemon rind, to decorate

For the truffle mixture

250ml/8fl oz/1 cup double (heavy) cream
225g/8oz plain (semisweet) or dark (bittersweet) chocolate, chopped
50g/2oz/¼ cup unsalted (sweet) butter, diced
30ml/2 tbsp brandy

1 To make the truffle mixture, bring the double cream to the boil in a pan over medium heat. Remove from the heat and add the chocolate, stirring until melted. Beat in the butter and add the brandy. Strain into a bowl and chill for 1 hour.

2 Preheat the oven to 200°C/400°F/Gas 6. Grease a bun tray with 24 cups, each 4cm/1½in. Cut each filo sheet into 6cm/2½in squares. Cover with a damp dish towel. Keeping the other filo sheets covered, place one square on a work surface. Brush lightly with melted butter, turn over and brush the other side. Sprinkle with a pinch of sugar.

3 Butter another square and place it over the first at an angle. Sprinkle with sugar. Butter a third square and place over the first two, unevenly, so that the corners form an uneven edge. Press the layered square into the tray. Continue to fill the tray.

4 Bake the filo cups for 4–6 minutes, or until golden. Cool for 10 minutes on a wire rack in the tray. Remove from the tray and cool completely.

5 Stir the chocolate mixture, which should be just thick enough to pipe. Spoon the mixture into a piping (pastry) bag fitted with a medium star nozzle and pipe a swirl into each cup. Decorate with lemon rind.

Fruit Tartlets Energy 440kcal/1841kJ; Protein 5.4g; Carbohydrate 49.3g, of which sugars 32g; Fat 26g, of which saturates 16.1g; Cholesterol 63mg; Calcium 83mg; Fibre 3.5g; Sodium 192mg.
Filo Tarts Energy 149kcal/621kJ; Protein 1.2g; Carbohydrate 10.2g, of which sugars 6.1g; Fat 11.5g, of which saturates 7.1g; Cholesterol 23mg; Calcium 16mg; Fibre 0.4g; Sodium 27mg.

Tia Maria Truffle Tarts

The ideal dessert for a tea or coffee break, these mini coffee pastry cases are filled with a truffle centre and topped with fresh berries.

Serves 6

300ml/½ pint/1¼ cups double (heavy) cream
225g/8oz/generous ¾ cup seedless bramble or raspberry jam
150g/5oz plain (semisweet) chocolate, broken into squares
45ml/3 tbsp Tia Maria liqueur
450g/1lb mixed berries, such as raspberries, small strawberries or blackberries

For the pastry

225g/8oz/2 cups plain (all-purpose) flour
15ml/1 tbsp caster (superfine) sugar
150g/5oz/10 tbsp butter, cubed
1 egg yolk
30ml/2 tbsp very strong brewed coffee, chilled

1 Preheat the oven to 200°C/400°F/Gas 6. Put a baking sheet in the oven to heat. To make the pastry, sift the flour and sugar into a large bowl. Rub in the butter. Stir the egg yolk and coffee together, add to the bowl and mix to a stiff dough. Knead lightly on a floured surface for a few seconds until smooth. Wrap in clear film (plastic wrap) and chill for about 20 minutes.

2 Use the pastry to line six 10cm/4in fluted tartlet tins (pans). Prick the bases with a fork and line with baking parchment and baking beans. Put the tins on the hot baking sheet and bake for 10 minutes. Remove the paper and beans and bake for another 8–10 minutes longer, until cooked. Transfer to a wire rack and leave to cool completely.

3 Make the filling. Bring the cream and 175g/6oz/generous ½ cup of the jam to the boil, stirring continuously until dissolved.

4 Remove from the heat, add the chocolate and 30ml/2 tbsp of the liqueur. Stir until melted. Cool, then spoon into the pastry cases (pie shells) and smooth the tops. Chill for 40 minutes.

5 Heat the remaining jam and liqueur until smooth. Arrange the fruit on top of the tarts, then brush the jam glaze over it. Chill until ready to serve.

Dark Chocolate and Hazelnut Tart

The crisp pastry tastes wonderful combined with a luxurious chocolate filling.

Serves 10

300ml/½ pint/1¼ cups double (heavy) cream
150ml/¼ pint/⅔ cup full-fat (whole) milk
150g/5oz dark (bittersweet) chocolate, chopped
4 eggs
50g/2oz/¼ cup caster (superfine) sugar
5ml/1 tsp vanilla extract
15ml/1 tbsp plain (all-purpose) flour
115g/4oz/1 cup toasted hazelnuts
10ml/2 tsp icing (confectioners') sugar, for dusting

For the pastry

150g/5oz/1¼ cups plain (all-purpose) flour
pinch of salt
40g/1½oz/3 tbsp caster (superfine) sugar
50g/2oz/½ cup ground hazelnuts, toasted
90g/3½oz/scant ½ cup butter, diced
1 egg, lightly beaten

1 Make the pastry. Sift the flour, salt and sugar into a mixing bowl, then mix in the toasted hazelnuts. Rub or cut in the butter until the mixture resembles fine breadcrumbs.

2 Make a well in the centre, add the beaten egg and mix to a firm dough. Knead the dough on a lightly floured surface for a few seconds until smooth. Wrap in clear film (plastic wrap) and chill for 30 minutes.

3 Roll out the pastry on a floured surface and use to line a 23cm/9in loose-based heart-shaped flan tin (pan). Trim the edges. Cover and chill for a further 30 minutes.

4 Re-roll the pastry trimmings into a long strip, about 30cm/12in long. Cut this into six strips, each 5mm/¼in wide, and make two plaits (braids) with three pastry strips in each. Curve into a heart shape and press gently to join together at both ends. Carefully place the heart on a baking sheet lined with baking parchment, and chill.

5 Put a baking sheet in the oven and preheat to 200°C/400°F/Gas 6. Prick the base of the pastry case (pie shell) with a fork. Line with foil and baking beans and bake blind on the sheet for 10 minutes. Remove the foil and beans and bake for a further 5 minutes. Bake the pastry plait on the shelf below for 10 minutes, or until lightly browned.

6 Meanwhile, pour the cream and milk into a pan and bring to the boil. Add the chocolate and stir until melted. Whisk the eggs, caster sugar, vanilla and flour together in a bowl. Pour the hot chocolate cream over the egg mixture, whisking all the time. Stir the chopped hazelnuts into the mixture, stirring until well combined.

7 Pour the chocolate and hazelnut mixture into the pastry case and bake in the oven for 25 minutes, or until just set.

8 Allow the tart to cool completely, then remove from the tin and transfer on to a serving plate. Place the pastry rope on top of the tart, then lightly dust the surface with icing sugar.

Tia Maria Tarts Energy 844kcal/3519kJ; Protein 7.1g; Carbohydrate 79g, of which sugars 50.2g; Fat 55.9g, of which saturates 34.3g; Cholesterol 157mg; Calcium 112mg; Fibre 2.6g; Sodium 182mg.
Dark Tart Energy 544kcal/2261kJ; Protein 8.8g; Carbohydrate 35.6g, of which sugars 22.5g; Fat 41.8g, of which saturates 19.2g; Cholesterol 158mg; Calcium 105mg; Fibre 2g; Sodium 106mg.

Velvety Mocha Tart

A creamy smooth filling tops a dark light-textured base in this wondrous dessert decorated with cream and chocolate-coated coffee beans.

Serves 8

10ml/2 tsp instant espresso coffee
30ml/2 tbsp hot water
175g/6oz plain (semisweet) chocolate
25g/1oz bitter cooking chocolate
350ml/12fl oz/1½ cups whipping cream, slightly warmed
120ml/4fl oz/½ cup whipped cream, to decorate
chocolate-coated coffee beans, to decorate

For the base

150g/5oz/2½ cups crushed chocolate wafers
30ml/2 tbsp caster (superfine) sugar
65g/2½oz/5 tbsp butter, melted

1 To make the base, combine the crushed chocolate wafers with the sugar and butter in a bowl.

2 Press the mixture over the base and sides of a 23cm/9in pie dish. Chill.

3 Dissolve the coffee in the water. Set aside to cool.

4 Melt the plain and bitter chocolates in the top of a double boiler or in a heatproof bowl over a pan of simmering water.

5 Once the chocolate has melted, remove from the double boiler and set the base of the pan in cold water to cool.

6 Whip the cream until light and fluffy. Add the coffee and whip until the cream just holds its shape.

7 When the chocolate is at room temperature, fold it gently into the cream.

8 Pour into the wafer base and chill until firm. Decorate with piped whipped cream and chocolate-coated coffee beans just before serving.

Chocolate and Pine Nut Tart

Orange-flavoured pastry makes this a real winner.

Serves 8

200g/7oz/1¾ cups plain (all-purpose) flour
50g/2oz/¼ cup caster (superfine) sugar
pinch of salt
grated rind of ½ orange
115g/4oz/½ cup unsalted (sweet) butter, cut into small pieces
3 egg yolks, lightly beaten
15–30ml/1–2 tbsp chilled water

For the filling

2 eggs
45ml/3 tbsp caster (superfine) sugar
grated rind of 1 orange
15ml/1 tbsp orange liqueur
250ml/8fl oz/1 cup whipping cream
115g/4oz plain (semisweet) chocolate, cut into small pieces
75g/3oz/¾ cup pine nuts, toasted
thinly pared rind of 1 orange and 50g/2oz/¼ cup granulated (white) sugar, to decorate

1 Process the flour, sugar, salt and orange rind in a food processor, add the butter and process again for 30 seconds. Add the yolks and pulse until the dough begins to stick together. If it seems dry, gradually add the water. Knead, then wrap and chill for 2–3 hours.

2 Grease a 23cm/9in loose-based flan tin (pan). Roll out the dough on a floured surface into a 28cm/11in round. Ease it into the tin and roll a rolling pin over the edge to trim. Prick the base. Chill for 1 hour. Preheat the oven to 200°C/400°F/Gas 6.

3 Line the pastry with foil, fill with baking beans and bake blind for 5 minutes. Remove the foil and beans and bake for 5 minutes more, then cool. Lower the temperature to 180°C/350°F/Gas 4.

4 Beat the eggs, sugar, orange rind and liqueur in a bowl. Stir in the cream. Sprinkle the chocolate and pine nuts over the base of the tart. Pour in the filling. Bake for 20–30 minutes, until golden.

5 Make the decoration. Cut the orange rind into strips. Dissolve the sugar in 120ml/4fl oz/½ cup water over a medium heat, add the rind and boil for 5 minutes. Remove from the heat and stir in 15ml/1 tbsp cold water. Brush the orange syrup over the tart and decorate with the caramelized strips. Serve warm.

Mocha Tart Energy 507kcal/2103kJ; Protein 3.6g; Carbohydrate 30.3g, of which sugars 27g; Fat 42.1g, of which saturates 26.2g; Cholesterol 83mg; Calcium 71mg; Fibre 0.8g; Sodium 83mg.
Pine Nut Tart Energy 543kcal/2261kJ; Protein 7.8g; Carbohydrate 42.7g, of which sugars 23.5g; Fat 38.6g, of which saturates 19.2g; Cholesterol 187mg; Calcium 84mg; Fibre 1.3g; Sodium 118mg.

Chocolate Lemon Tart

In this easy-to-make recipe, the chocolate-flavoured pastry is pressed into the tin rather than rolled out, helping to speed up the preparation. With a simple lemon filling, this is a great dessert for the busy cook.

Serves 8–10

175g/6oz/1½ cups plain (all-purpose) flour
10ml/2 tsp unsweetened cocoa powder
25g/1oz/¼ cup icing (confectioners') sugar
2.5ml/½ tsp salt
115g/4oz/½ cup unsalted (sweet) butter or margarine, plus extra for greasing
15ml/1 tbsp water

For the filling

225g/8oz/1 cup caster (superfine) sugar
6 eggs
grated rind of 2 lemons
175ml/6fl oz/¾ cup freshly squeezed lemon juice
175ml/6fl oz/¾ cup double (heavy) or whipping cream
chocolate curls, to decorate

1 Grease a 25cm/10in loose-based flan tin (pan). Sift the flour, cocoa, icing sugar and salt into a bowl. Set aside.

2 Melt the butter or margarine and water in a pan over a low heat. Add the flour mixture and stir until the flour has absorbed all the liquid and the dough is smooth.

3 Press the dough evenly over the base and side of the prepared tin. Chill the pastry case (pie shell).

4 Preheat the oven to 190°C/375°F/Gas 5, and place a baking sheet inside to heat up. Make the filling. Whisk the caster sugar and eggs in a bowl until the sugar has dissolved. Add the lemon rind and juice and mix well. Stir in the cream. Taste and add more lemon juice or sugar if needed, for a sweet taste with a touch of tartness.

5 Pour the filling into the pastry case and place the tin on the hot baking sheet. Bake for 20–25 minutes or until the filling is set. Cool the tart on a rack, then remove from the tin. Decorate with the chocolate curls and serve.

Chocolate Truffle Tart

A dreamy chilled tart with a chocolate flavoured pastry case and a luscious filling, laced with brandy.

Serves 12

115g/4oz/1 cup plain (all-purpose) flour
40g/1¼oz/⅓ cup unsweetened cocoa powder
50g/2oz/¼ cup caster (superfine) sugar
2.5ml/½ tsp salt
115g/4oz/½ cup unsalted (sweet) butter, cut into pieces
1 egg yolk
15–30ml/1–2 tbsp iced water
25g/1oz good-quality white or milk chocolate, melted
whipped cream for serving (optional)

For the truffle filling

350ml/12fl oz/1½ cups double (heavy) cream
350g/12oz fine plain (semisweet) chocolate, chopped
50g/2oz/4 tbsp unsalted (sweet) butter, cut into small pieces
30ml/2 tbsp brandy or liqueur

1 Make the pastry. Sift the flour and cocoa into a bowl. In a food processor fitted with a metal blade, process the flour mixture with the sugar and salt. Add the butter and process for a further 15–20 seconds, or until the mixture resembles coarse breadcrumbs.

2 Lightly beat the yolk with the iced water in a bowl. Add to the flour mixture and pulse until the dough begins to stick together. Turn out the dough on to a sheet of clear film (plastic wrap). Use the film to help shape the dough into a flat disc. Wrap tightly. Chill for 1–2 hours, until firm.

3 Lightly grease a 23cm/9in flan tin (pan) with a removable base. Let the dough soften briefly, then roll it out between sheets of baking parchment or clear film to a 28cm/11in round, about 5mm/¼in thick. Peel off the top sheet and invert the dough into the flan tin. Remove the bottom sheet. Ease the dough into the tin. Prick all over with a fork. Chill in the refrigerator for 1 hour.

4 Preheat the oven to 180°C/350°F/Gas 4. Line the tart with foil or baking parchment; fill with baking beans. Bake blind for 5–7 minutes. Lift out the foil with the beans, return the pastry case (pie shell) to the oven and bake for a further 5–7 minutes, until the pastry is just set. Leave to cool completely in the tin on a rack.

5 Make the filling. In a medium pan, bring the cream to the boil over a medium heat. Remove the pan from the heat and stir in the chocolate until melted and smooth. Stir in the butter and brandy or liqueur. Strain into the prepared pastry case, tilting the tin slightly to level the surface. Do not touch the surface of the filling or it will spoil the glossy finish.

6 Spoon the melted chocolate into a paper piping (pastry) bag and cut off the tip. Drop rounds of chocolate over the surface of the tart and use a skewer or cocktail stick (toothpick) to draw a point gently through the chocolate to produce a marbled effect. Chill for 2–3 hours, until set.

7 Just before serving, allow the tart to soften slightly at room temperature, then serve with whipped cream, if you like.

Lemon Tart Energy 379kcal/1585kJ; Protein 6.1g; Carbohydrate 40.5g, of which sugars 27g; Fat 22.6g, of which saturates 12.9g; Cholesterol 163mg; Calcium 68mg; Fibre 0.7g; Sodium 127mg.
Truffle Tart Energy 474kcal/1969kJ; Protein 3.7g; Carbohydrate 32.5g, of which sugars 24.6g; Fat 36.8g, of which saturates 22.6g; Cholesterol 88mg; Calcium 48mg; Fibre 1.4g; Sodium 117mg.

Chocolate Apricot Linzer Tart

This makes an excellent dinner party dessert.

Serves 10–12
50g/2oz/⅓ cup blanched almonds
115g/4oz/generous ½ cup caster (superfine) sugar
175g/6oz/1½ cups plain (all-purpose) flour
30ml/2 tbsp unsweetened cocoa powder
5ml/1 tsp ground cinnamon
2.5ml/½ tsp salt
5ml/1 tsp grated orange rind
225g/8oz/1 cup unsalted (sweet) butter, cut into small pieces
75g/3oz/½ cup chocolate chips
icing (confectioners') sugar, for dusting

For the apricot filling
350g/12oz/1½ cups dried apricots
120ml/4fl oz/½ cup orange juice
40g/1½oz/3 tbsp granulated (white) sugar
50g/2oz/2 tbsp apricot jam
2.5ml/½ tsp almond extract

1 For the filling, simmer the apricots, orange juice and 175ml/6fl oz/¾ cup water, stirring, until the liquid is absorbed. Stir in the remaining ingredients. Strain into a bowl, cool, cover and chill.

2 Grease a 28cm/11in loose-based flan tin (pan). Grind the almonds and half the sugar in a food processor. Sift in the flour, cocoa, cinnamon and salt, add the remaining sugar and process. Add the rind and butter. Process for 15–20 seconds until the mixture resembles breadcrumbs. Add 30ml/2 tbsp iced water and pulse, adding more water until the dough holds together.

3 Turn out and knead the dough on a lightly floured surface. Halve and press one piece on to the base and sides of the tin. Prick the base with a fork. Chill for 20 minutes. Roll out the rest of the dough between sheets of clear film (plastic wrap) to a 28cm/11in round, then slide on to a baking sheet and chill for 30 minutes.

4 Preheat the oven to 180°C/350°F/Gas 4. Spread the filling in the pastry case (pie shell) and sprinkle with chocolate chips. Cut the dough round into 1cm/½in strips. Leave to soften, then place the strips over the filling, 1cm/½in apart, to form a lattice. Press the ends on to the side of the tart and trim. Bake for 35–40 minutes, until golden. Cool on a rack and dust with icing sugar.

Chocolate Tiramisu Tart

This tart, based on the Italian dessert, has an utterly delicious creamy filling.

Serves 12–16
115g/4oz/½ cup butter
15ml/1 tbsp coffee liqueur
175g/6oz/1½ cups plain (all-purpose) flour
25g/1oz/¼ cup unsweetened cocoa powder, plus extra for dusting
25g/1oz/¼ cup icing (confectioners') sugar
pinch of salt
2.5ml/½ tsp vanilla extract

For the chocolate layer
350ml/12fl oz/1½ cups double (heavy) cream
15ml/1 tbsp golden (light corn) syrup
115g/4oz plain (semisweet) chocolate, chopped into pieces
25g/1oz/2 tbsp unsalted (sweet) butter, cut into small pieces
30ml/2 tbsp coffee liqueur

For the filling
250ml/8fl oz/1 cup whipping cream
350g/12oz/1½ cups mascarpone, at room temperature
45ml/3 tbsp icing (confectioners') sugar
45ml/3 tbsp cold espresso or strong black coffee
45ml/3 tbsp coffee liqueur
90g/3½oz plain (semisweet) chocolate, grated

1 Make the pastry. Grease a 23cm/9in springform tin (pan). Heat the butter and liqueur until melted. Sift the flour, cocoa, sugar and salt into a bowl. Remove the butter mixture from the heat, stir in the vanilla and stir into the flour mixture until soft dough forms. Knead until smooth. Press on to the base and up the sides of the tin. Prick the dough. Chill for 40 minutes. Preheat the oven to 190°C/375°F/Gas 5. Bake for 8–10 minutes. Cool in the tin on a rack.

2 Mix the cream and syrup in a pan. Bring to a boil. Off the heat, stir in the chocolate until melted. Beat in the butter and liqueur and pour into the pastry case (pie shell). Cool and chill.

3 Make the filling. In one bowl, whip the cream until soft peaks form; in another, beat the cheese until soft, then beat in the sugar until smooth. Add the coffee, liqueur, cream and chocolate. Spoon into the pastry case, on top of the chocolate layer. Level the surface. Chill until ready to serve, dusted with cocoa powder.

Linzer Tart Energy 368kcal/1539kJ; Protein 4.4g; Carbohydrate 44.3g, of which sugars 32.8g; Fat 20.4g, of which saturates 11.4g; Cholesterol 40mg; Calcium 69mg; Fibre 3.1g; Sodium 147mg.
Tiramisu Tart Energy 399kcal/1657kJ; Protein 4.8g; Carbohydrate 24.4g, of which sugars 15.8g; Fat 30.9g, of which saturates 20.4g; Cholesterol 60mg; Calcium 49mg; Fibre 0.9g; Sodium 86mg.

White Chocolate and Mango Cream Tart

A rich, exotic tart designed to tantalize the taste buds.

Serves 8

175g/6oz/1½ cups plain (all-purpose) flour
75g/3oz/1 cup desiccated (dry unsweetened shredded) coconut
115g/4oz/½ cup butter, softened
30ml/2 tbsp caster (superfine) sugar
2 egg yolks
2.5ml/½ tsp almond extract
120ml/4fl oz/½ cup whipping cream, whipped to soft peaks
1 large mango, peeled and sliced
whipped cream and toasted almonds, to decorate

For the filling

150g/5oz good-quality white chocolate, chopped finely
120ml/4fl oz/½ cup whipping cream or double (heavy) cream
75ml/5 tbsp cornflour (cornstarch)
15ml/1 tbsp plain (all-purpose) flour
50g/2oz/¼ cup granulated (white) sugar
350ml/12fl oz/1½ cups milk
5 egg yolks

1 Beat the flour, coconut, butter, sugar, egg yolks and almond extract in a bowl to form a soft dough. Grease a 23cm/9in flan tin (pan) with a removable base and press the pastry into the tin to line. Prick the base with a fork. Chill for 30 minutes.

2 Preheat the oven to 180°C/350°F/Gas 4. Line the pastry case (pie shell) with baking parchment; fill with baking beans and bake blind for 10 minutes. Remove the paper and beans and bake for a further 5–7 minutes, until golden. Cool in the tin on a wire rack.

3 Make the filling. In a pan, melt the chocolate with the cream, stirring until smooth. Combine the cornflour, plain flour and sugar in another pan. Stir in the milk and cook, stirring until thick.

4 Beat the egg yolks in a bowl. Stir in some of the milk mixture. Return the yolk mixture to the rest of the sauce in the pan. Bring to a boil, stirring, until thick. Stir in the melted chocolate. Cool, then fold in the cream. Spoon half the custard into the case and arrange the mango on top. Cover with the rest of the custard. Remove from the tin and decorate with piped cream and nuts.

Rich Chocolate Tart with Blackberry Sauce

This magnificent chocolate tart is a gorgeous way to serve fresh summer berries.

Serves 10

115g/4oz/½ cup unsalted (sweet) butter, softened
90g/3½oz/½ cup caster (superfine) sugar
2.5ml/½ tsp salt
15ml/1 tbsp vanilla extract
50g/2oz/½ cup unsweetened cocoa powder
215g/7½oz/scant 2 cups plain (all-purpose) flour
450g/1lb fresh berries for topping

For the chocolate filling

475ml/16fl oz/2 cups double (heavy) cream
150g/5oz/½ cup seedless blackberry preserve
225g/8oz plain (semisweet) chocolate, chopped
25g/1oz/2 tbsp unsalted (sweet) butter

For the blackberry sauce

225g/8oz blackberries
15ml/1 tbsp lemon juice
25g/1oz/2 tbsp caster (superfine) sugar
30ml/2 tbsp blackberry liqueur

1 Make the pastry. Place the butter, sugar, salt and vanilla in a food processor and process until creamy. Add the cocoa and process for 1 minute. Add the flour all at once and process for 10–15 seconds, until just blended. Place a piece of clear film (plastic wrap) on a work surface. Turn out the dough on to the clear film. Use the clear film to help shape the dough into a flat disc and wrap tightly. Chill for 1 hour.

2 Lightly grease a 23cm/9in loose-based flan tin (pan). Roll out the dough between two sheets of clear film to a 28cm/11in round, about 5mm/¼in thick. Peel off the top sheet of clear film and invert the dough into the prepared tin. Ease the dough into the tin. Remove the clear film.

3 With floured fingers, press the dough on to the base and side of the tin, then roll a rolling pin over the edge of the tin to cut off any excess dough. Prick the base of the dough with a fork. Chill for 1 hour. Preheat the oven to 180°C/350°F/Gas 4. Line the pastry case (pie shell) with foil or baking paper and fill with baking beans. Bake for 10 minutes, then lift out the foil and beans and bake for 5 minutes more, until just set (the pastry may look underdone on the base, but will dry out). Place on a wire rack to cool completely.

4 Make the filling. Place the cream and blackberry preserve in a medium pan over medium heat and bring to the boil. Remove from the heat and add the chocolate, stirring until smooth. Stir in the butter and strain into the cooled tart, then level the surface. Leave the tart to cool completely.

5 Make the sauce. In a food processor, combine the blackberries, lemon juice and sugar and process until smooth. Strain into a small bowl and add the blackberry liqueur. If the sauce is too thick, thin with a little water.

6 To serve, remove the tart from the tin. Place on a serving plate and arrange the berries on top of the tart. With a pastry brush, coat the berries with a little of the blackberry sauce to glaze lightly. Serve the remaining sauce separately.

Mango Tart Energy 802kcal/3336kJ; Protein 12.3g; Carbohydrate 57.3g, of which sugars 30.3g; Fat 59.8g, of which saturates 41.9g; Cholesterol 217mg; Calcium 256mg; Fibre 3.1g; Sodium 195mg.
Rich Tart Energy 653kcal/2722kJ; Protein 6g; Carbohydrate 58.9g, of which sugars 41.8g; Fat 44.9g, of which saturates 27.7g; Cholesterol 96mg; Calcium 95mg; Fibre 3.5g; Sodium 152mg.

Chocolate Pear Tart

Serve slices of this tart drizzled with cream for a special treat.

Serves 8
115g/4oz plain (semisweet) chocolate, grated
3 large firm, ripe pears
1 egg
1 egg yolk
120ml/4fl oz/½ cup single (light) cream
2.5ml/½ tsp vanilla extract
40g/1½oz/3 tbsp caster (superfine) sugar

For the pastry
115g/4oz/1 cup plain (all-purpose) flour
pinch of salt
25g/1oz/2 tbsp caster (superfine) sugar
115g/4oz/½ cup cold unsalted (sweet) butter, cut into pieces
1 egg yolk
15ml/1 tbsp fresh lemon juice

1 Make the pastry. Sift the flour and salt into a bowl. Add the sugar and butter. Cut in with a pastry blender until the mixture resembles coarse crumbs. With a fork, stir in the egg yolk and lemon juice until the mixture forms a dough. Gather into a ball, wrap in baking parchment, and chill for at least 20 minutes.

2 Place a baking sheet in the oven and preheat to 200°C/400°F/Gas 6. On a lightly floured surface, roll out the dough to 3mm/⅛in thick and trim the edge. Use to line a 25cm/10in loose-based flan tin (pan).

3 Sprinkle the base of the pastry all over with the grated plain chocolate.

4 Peel, halve and core the pears. Cut in thin slices crossways, then fan them out slightly. Transfer the pear halves to the tart with a metal spatula and arrange on top of the chocolate in a pattern resembling the spokes of a wheel.

5 Whisk together the egg and egg yolk, cream and vanilla extract. Spoon over the pears, then sprinkle with sugar.

6 Bake for 10 minutes. Reduce the heat to 180°C/350°F/Gas 4 and continue to cook for about 20 minutes until the custard is set and the pears begin to caramelize. Serve warm.

Chocolate Nut Tart

This is a sophisticated tart – strictly for grown-ups.

Serves 6–8
225g/8oz chocolate shortcrust pastry, thawed if frozen
200g/7oz/1¾ cups dry amaretti
90g/3½oz/generous ½ cup blanched almonds
50g/2oz/⅓ cup blanched hazelnuts
45ml/3 tbsp caster (superfine) sugar
200g/7oz plain (semisweet) cooking chocolate
45ml/3 tbsp milk
50g/2oz/¼ cup butter
45ml/3 tbsp amaretto liqueur or brandy
30ml/2 tbsp single (light) cream

1 Grease a shallow loose-based 25cm/10in flan tin (pan). Roll out the pastry on a lightly floured surface, and use it to line the tin. Trim the edge, prick the base with a fork and chill for 30 minutes.

2 Grind the amaretti in a blender or food processor. Tip into a mixing bowl.

3 Set eight whole almonds aside and place the rest in the food processor or blender with the hazelnuts and sugar. Grind to a medium texture. Add the nuts to the amaretti, and mix well to combine thoroughly.

4 Preheat the oven to 190°C/375°F/Gas 5. Slowly melt the chocolate with the milk and butter in the top of a double boiler or in a heatproof bowl over a pan of simmering water. Once the chocolate has melted, stir until smooth.

5 Pour the chocolate mixture into the dry ingredients and mix well. Add the liqueur or brandy and the cream.

6 Spread the filling evenly in the pastry case (pie shell). Bake for 35 minutes, or until the crust is golden brown and the filling has puffed up and is beginning to darken.

7 Allow to cool to room temperature. Split the reserved almonds in half and use to decorate the tart.

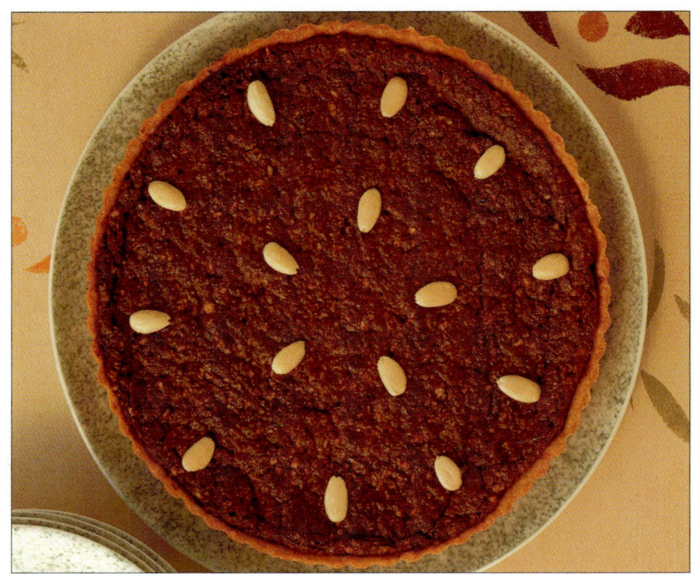

Pear Tart Energy 357kcal/1492kJ; Protein 4.5g; Carbohydrate 39.9g, of which sugars 28.8g; Fat 21.1g, of which saturates 12.3g; Cholesterol 114mg; Calcium 66mg; Fibre 2.9g; Sodium 107mg.
Nut Tart Energy 644kcal/2685kJ; Protein 9.6g; Carbohydrate 56.4g, of which sugars 32g; Fat 42.4g, of which saturates 13.4g; Cholesterol 21mg; Calcium 122mg; Fibre 3g; Sodium 241mg.

Chilled Chocolate and Date Tart

A delicious tart with a crisp gingery base.

Serves 6–8
115g/4oz/½ cup unsalted (sweet) butter, melted
225g/8oz ginger nut biscuits (gingersnaps), finely crushed

For the filling
50g/2oz/⅔ cup stale sponge cake crumbs
75ml/5 tbsp orange juice
115g/4oz/⅔ cup stoned (pitted) dates
25g/1oz/¼ cup finely chopped nuts
175g/6oz dark (bittersweet) chocolate
300ml/½ pint/1¼ cups whipping cream
grated chocolate and icing (confectioners') sugar, to decorate

1 Make the base. Mix the butter and biscuit crumbs in a bowl, then press the mixture on to the sides and base of an 18cm/7in loose-based flan tin (pan). Chill the crust while making the filling.

2 Make the filling. Put the sponge cake crumbs into a bowl. Pour over 60ml/4 tbsp of the orange juice, stir well with a wooden spoon and leave to soak. Put the dates in a pan and add the remaining orange juice. Warm the mixture over a low heat. Mash the warm dates thoroughly and stir in the cake crumbs, with the finely chopped nuts.

3 Mix the chocolate with 60ml/4 tbsp of the cream in a heatproof bowl. Place the bowl over a pan of barely simmering water and stir occasionally until melted. In a separate bowl, whip the rest of the cream to soft peaks, then fold in the melted chocolate.

4 Add the cooled date, crumb and nut mixture to the cream and chocolate and mix lightly but thoroughly. Pour into the crumb crust. Using a metal spatula, level the mixture. Chill until just set, then mark the tart into portions, using a sharp knife dipped in hot water. Chill until firm.

5 To decorate the tart, sprinkle the grated chocolate over the surface and dust with icing sugar. Serve in wedges, with single (light) cream, if desired. Fresh orange segments make an excellent accompaniment.

Black Rum and Chocolate Pie

A totally wicked rum and chocolate creation.

Serves 6–8
250g/9oz/2¼ cups plain (all-purpose) flour
150g/5oz/10 tbsp unsalted (sweet) butter
2 egg yolks
15–30ml/1–2 tbsp chilled water

For the filling
3 eggs, separated
20ml/4 tsp cornflour (cornstarch)
75g/3oz/6 tbsp golden caster (superfine) sugar
400ml/14fl oz/1⅔ cups milk
150g/5oz plain (semisweet) chocolate, chopped into small pieces
5ml/1 tsp vanilla extract
1 sachet powdered gelatine
45ml/3 tbsp water
30ml/2 tbsp dark rum
175ml/6fl oz/¾ cup whipping cream
chocolate curls, to decorate

1 Sift the flour into a bowl and rub in the butter until the mixture resembles coarse breadcrumbs. Stir in the egg yolks with just enough chilled water to bind the mixture to a soft dough. Roll out on a lightly floured surface and line a deep 23cm/9in flan tin (pan). Chill for about 30 minutes.

2 Preheat the oven to 190°C/375°F/Gas 5. Prick the pastry case (pie shell) all over with a fork, cover with baking parchment weighed down with baking beans and bake blind for 10 minutes. Remove the baking beans and the paper, return the pastry case to the oven and bake for 10 minutes, until golden. Cool in the tin.

3 Make the filling. Mix the egg yolks, cornflour and 25g/1oz/2 tbsp of the sugar in a bowl. Heat the milk in a pan until almost boiling, then beat into the egg mixture. Return to the clean pan and stir over a low heat until the custard has thickened and is smooth. Pour half the custard into a bowl.

4 Put the chocolate in a heatproof bowl. Place over a pan of barely simmering water until the chocolate has melted, stirring occasionally until smooth. Stir the melted chocolate into the custard in the bowl, with the vanilla extract.

5 Spread the chocolate filling in the pastry case and cover closely with dampened clear film (plastic wrap) to prevent a skin forming. Allow to cool, then chill until set.

6 Sprinkle the gelatine over the water in a bowl, leave until spongy, then place the bowl over a pan of simmering water until all the gelatine has dissolved. Stir into the remaining custard, then add the rum.

7 Whisk the egg whites in a clean, grease-free bowl until peaks form. Whisk in the remaining sugar, a little at a time, until stiff, then fold the egg whites quickly but evenly into the rum-flavoured custard.

8 Spoon the custard over the chocolate layer in the pastry shell. Level the mixture, making sure that none of the chocolate custard is visible. Chill the pie until the top layer has set, then remove the pie from the tin. Whip the cream, spread it over the top and sprinkle with chocolate curls, to decorate.

Date Tart Energy 575kcal/2394kJ; Protein 5.1g; Carbohydrate 51.3g, of which sugars 37.5g; Fat 40.2g, of which saturates 22.8g; Cholesterol 78mg; Calcium 87mg; Fibre 1.8g; Sodium 214mg.
Black Rum Pie Energy 545kcal/2276kJ; Protein 9.3g; Carbohydrate 51.3g, of which sugars 25.1g; Fat 34.2g, of which saturates 20g; Cholesterol 189mg; Calcium 148mg; Fibre 1.4g; Sodium 173mg.

Rich Chocolate Pie

A delicious rich and creamy pie generously decorated with chocolate curls.

Serves 8

75g/3oz plain (semisweet) chocolate
50g/2oz/¼ cup butter or margarine
45ml/3 tbsp golden (light corn) syrup
3 eggs, beaten
150g/5oz/¾ cup caster (superfine) sugar
5ml/1 tsp vanilla extract
115g/4oz milk chocolate
475ml/16fl oz/2 cups whipping cream

For the pastry

165g/5½oz/1⅓ cups plain (all-purpose) flour
2.5ml/½ tsp salt
115g/4oz/⅔ cup lard or white cooking fat (shortening), diced
30–45ml/2–3 tbsp iced water

1 Preheat the oven to 220°C/425°F/Gas 7. To make the pastry, sift the flour and salt into a bowl. Rub in the fat until the mixture resembles coarse breadcrumbs. Add water until the pastry forms a ball.

2 Roll out the pastry and use to line a 20–23cm/8–9in flan tin (pan). Flute the edge. Prick the base and sides of the pastry case (pie shell) with a fork. Bake for 10–15 minutes until lightly browned. Cool in the tin on a wire rack.

3 Reduce the oven temperature to 180°C/350°F/Gas 4. In the top of a double boiler or in a heatproof bowl over a pan of simmering water, melt the plain chocolate, the butter or margarine, and the golden syrup. Remove from the heat and stir in the eggs, sugar and vanilla extract. Pour the chocolate mixture into the pastry case. Bake until the filling is set, about 35–40 minutes. Cool in the tin on a wire rack.

4 For the decoration, use the heat of your hands to soften the milk chocolate slightly. Use a swivel-headed vegetable peeler to shave off short, wide curls. Chill until needed.

5 Before serving, lightly whip the cream until soft peaks form. Spread the cream over the surface of the chocolate filling. Decorate with the milk chocolate curls.

Black Bottom Pie

Chocolate and rum make a winning combination over a crunchy ginger base.

Serves 8

10ml/2 tsp powdered gelatine
45ml/3 tbsp cold water
2 eggs, separated
150g/5oz/¾ cup caster (superfine) sugar
15g/½oz/2 tbsp cornflour (cornstarch)
2.5ml/½ tsp salt
475ml/16fl oz/2 cups milk
50g/2oz plain (semisweet) chocolate, finely chopped
30ml/2 tbsp rum
1.5ml/¼ tsp cream of tartar
chocolate curls, to decorate

For the crust

175g/6oz/2 cups ginger nut biscuits (gingersnaps), crushed
65g/2½oz/5 tbsp butter, melted

1 Preheat the oven to 180°C/350°F/Gas 4. Mix together the crushed ginger nut biscuits and the melted butter. Press evenly over the base and side of a 23cm/9in pie plate. Bake in the oven for 6 minutes. Sprinkle the gelatine over the water and leave to soften.

2 Beat the egg yolks in a large bowl and set aside. In a pan, combine half the sugar, the cornflour and salt. Gradually stir in the milk. Boil for 1 minute, stirring constantly.

3 Whisk the hot milk mixture into the yolks, pour back into the pan and return to the boil, whisking. Cook for 1 minute, still whisking. Remove from the heat.

4 Pour 225g/8oz of the custard mixture into a bowl. Add the chopped chocolate and stir until melted. Stir in half the rum and pour into the pie crust. Whisk the softened gelatine into the plain custard until dissolved, then stir in the remaining rum. Set the pan in cold water to reach room temperature.

5 Beat the egg whites and cream of tartar until they form stiff peaks. Add the remaining sugar gradually, beating thoroughly after each addition. Fold the cooled custard into the egg whites, then spoon over the chocolate mixture in the pie crust. Chill the pie until it is set, about 2 hours. Decorate with chocolate curls and serve immediately.

Chocolate Pie Energy 712kcal/2962kJ; Protein 7.2g; Carbohydrate 55.8g, of which sugars 40g; Fat 52.7g, of which saturates 28.9g; Cholesterol 164mg; Calcium 121mg; Fibre 1g; Sodium 109mg.
Black Pie Energy 248kcal/1040kJ; Protein 5.2g; Carbohydrate 25.8g, of which sugars 14.6g; Fat 13.7g, of which saturates 7.6g; Cholesterol 69mg; Calcium 111mg; Fibre 0.5g; Sodium 166mg.

Italian Chocolate Ricotta Pie

Savour the full richness of Italy with this de luxe tart.

Serves 6

225g/8oz/2 cups plain (all-purpose) flour
30ml/2 tbsp unsweetened cocoa powder
50g/2oz/¼ cup caster (superfine) sugar
115g/4oz/½ cup unsalted (sweet) butter
60ml/4 tbsp dry sherry

For the filling

2 egg yolks
115g/4oz/generous ½ cup caster (superfine) sugar
500g/1¼lb/2½ cups ricotta cheese
finely grated rind of 1 lemon
90ml/6 tbsp dark (bittersweet) chocolate chips
75ml/5 tbsp mixed (candied) chopped peel
45ml/3 tbsp chopped angelica

1 Sift the flour and cocoa powder into a bowl. Stir in the sugar. Rub in the butter with your fingers. Work in the sherry to form a firm dough.

2 Preheat the oven to 200°C/400°F/Gas 6. Roll out three-quarters of the pastry on a lightly floured surface and line a 24cm/9½in loose-based flan tin (pan).

3 Make the filling. Beat the egg yolks and sugar in a bowl, then beat in the ricotta to mix thoroughly. Stir in the lemon rind, chocolate chips, mixed peel and angelica.

4 Scrape the ricotta mixture into the pastry case (pie shell) and level the surface. Roll out the remaining pastry and cut into strips. Arrange these in a lattice over the pie.

5 Bake for 15 minutes. Lower the oven temperature to 180°C/350°F/Gas 4 and cook for a further 30–35 minutes, until golden brown and firm. Cool the pie in the tin, then serve.

Cook's Tip
This dish is best served at room temperature, so if made in advance, chill it, then bring to room temperature before serving.

Crunchy-topped Coffee Meringue Pie

For a special treat, try this sweet pastry case filled with coffee custard and topped with meringue – crisp on the outside and soft and chewy underneath.

Serves 6

30ml/2 tbsp ground coffee
350ml/12fl oz/1½ cups milk
25g/1oz/¼ cup cornflour (cornstarch)
130g/4½oz/⅔ cup caster (superfine) sugar
4 egg yolks
15g/½oz/1 tbsp butter
chocolate curls, to decorate

For the pastry

175g/6oz/1½ cups plain (all-purpose) flour
15ml/1 tbsp icing (confectioners') sugar
75g/3oz/6 tbsp butter, diced
1 egg yolk
finely grated rind of ½ orange
15ml/1 tbsp orange juice

For the meringue

3 egg whites
1.5ml/¼ tsp cream of tartar
150g/5oz/¾ cup caster (superfine) sugar
15ml/1 tbsp demerara (raw) sugar
25g/1oz/¼ cup skinned hazelnuts

1 Preheat the oven to 200°C/400°F/Gas 6. Make the pastry. Sift the flour and icing sugar into a bowl. Rub or cut in the butter until the mixture resembles fine breadcrumbs. Add the egg yolk, orange rind and juice and mix to form a firm dough. Wrap in clear film (plastic wrap) and chill for 20 minutes.

2 Roll out the pastry and use to line a 23cm/9in loose-based flan tin (pan). Cover again with clear film and chill for 30 minutes more.

3 Prick the pastry all over with a fork, line with foil, fill with baking beans and bake for about 10 minutes. Remove the foil and beans and bake for a further 5 minutes. Lower the oven temperature to 160°C/325°F/Gas 3.

4 Put the coffee in a small bowl. Heat 250ml/8fl oz/1 cup of the milk until near-boiling and pour over the coffee. Leave to infuse (steep) for 4–5 minutes, then strain. Blend the cornflour and sugar with the remaining milk in a pan and whisk in the coffee-flavoured milk. Bring the mixture to the boil, stirring until thickened. Remove from the heat.

5 In a bowl, beat the egg yolks. Stir a little of the coffee mixture into the egg yolks, then add to the remaining coffee mixture in the pan with the butter. Cook the filling over a low heat for 4 minutes, until thick. Pour the coffee filling into the pastry case (pie shell).

6 Make the meringue. Whisk the egg whites and cream of tartar in a small bowl until stiff peaks form. Whisk in the caster sugar, a spoonful at a time.

7 Spoon the meringue over the filling and spread right up to the edge of the pastry, swirling into peaks. Sprinkle with demerara sugar and hazelnuts, leaving some whole and chopping others into pieces.

8 Bake for 30–35 minutes, or until the topping is golden brown and crisp. Cover the top with chocolate curls and serve either warm or cold.

Ricotta Pie Energy 701kcal/2938kJ; Protein 14.2g; Carbohydrate 83.4g, of which sugars 54.1g; Fat 35.6g, of which saturates 21.3g; Cholesterol 144mg; Calcium 115mg; Fibre 3g; Sodium 223mg.
Meringue Pie Energy 540kcal/2274kJ; Protein 9.5g; Carbohydrate 83.6g, of which sugars 57.4g; Fat 21g, of which saturates 10g; Cholesterol 203mg; Calcium 168mg; Fibre 1.2g; Sodium 160mg.

Boston Banoffee Pie

A great American creation, you simply press the biscuity pastry into the tin, rather than rolling it out. Add the toffee filling and sliced banana and chocolate topping and it'll prove irresistible.

Serves 6
115g/4oz/½ cup butter, diced
200g/7oz can skimmed, sweetened condensed milk
115g/4oz/½ cup soft light brown sugar
30ml/2 tbsp golden (light corn) syrup
2 small bananas, sliced
a little lemon juice
whipped cream, to decorate
5ml/1 tsp grated plain (semisweet) chocolate

For the pastry
150g/5oz/1¼ cups plain (all-purpose) flour
115g/4oz/½ cup butter, diced
50g/2oz/¼ cup caster (superfine) sugar

1 Make the pastry. Preheat the oven to 160°C/325°F/Gas 3. In a food processor, process the flour and diced butter until it forms crumbs. Stir in the caster sugar and mix to form a soft, pliable dough.

2 Press into the base and sides of a 20cm/8in loose-based flan tin (pan). Bake for 30 minutes.

3 Make the filling. Place the butter in a medium pan with the condensed milk, brown sugar and syrup. Heat gently, stirring constantly, until the butter has melted and the sugar has completely dissolved.

4 Bring the mixture to a gentle boil, then cook for 7–10 minutes, stirring constantly, until the mixture thickens and turns a light caramel colour.

5 Pour the hot caramel filling into the pastry case (pie shell) and leave until completely cold.

6 Sprinkle the banana slices with lemon juice and arrange in overlapping circles on top of the filling, leaving a gap in the centre. Pipe a generous swirl of whipped cream in the centre and sprinkle with the grated chocolate.

Double Chocolate Banoffee Pie

An extra chocolatey version of the classic American pie.

Serves 12–14
2 x 400ml/14fl oz cans sweetened condensed milk
150g/5oz dark (bittersweet) chocolate, broken in pieces
175ml/6fl oz/¾ cup whipping or double (heavy) cream
10ml/2 tsp corn or glucose syrup
40g/1½oz/3 tbsp unsalted (sweet) butter, cut into pieces
5ml/1 tsp vanilla extract

For the ginger crumb crust
250g/9oz/about 24–26 ginger nut biscuits (gingersnaps), crushed
75g/3oz/6 tbsp butter, melted

For the topping
150g/5oz fine-quality white chocolate
450ml/16fl oz/2 cups double (heavy) cream
3 ripe bananas
white chocolate curls
unsweetened cocoa powder, for dusting

1 Puncture a small hole in each can. Place in a pan large enough to cover with water. Bring to a boil, then reduce the heat and simmer for 2 hours, partially covered. Remove cans and cool.

2 Prepare the crust. Preheat the oven to 180°C/350°F/Gas 4. Grease a 23cm/9in loose-bottomed flan tin (pan), 4cm/1½in deep. Mix the ginger crumbs with the butter and put on to the bottom and side of the tin. Bake for 5–7 minutes until set. Cool on rack.

3 In a pan, simmer the dark chocolate, cream and syrup until melted and smooth. Remove from the heat and beat in the butter and vanilla. Pour over the crust and chill until set, about 1 hour.

4 Empty the cans of milk into a bowl. Whisk until smooth. Spoon over the chocolate layer. In a food processor, process the white chocolate into crumbs. In a pan, heat 125ml/4fl oz/½ cup of the cream. With the machine running, pour in the cream and process until the chocolate has melted. Chill for 25–30 minutes. Whip the remaining cream until stiff. Beat in a spoonful of cream to the chocolate mixture, then fold in the remaining cream.

5 Slice the bananas and arrange over the toffee layer. Spread over the chocolate whipped cream. Decorate with white chocolate curls and a light dusting of cocoa powder.

Boston Banoffee Pie Energy 608kcal/2547kJ; Protein 6.4g; Carbohydrate 78.5g, of which sugars 58.9g; Fat 32g, of which saturates 20.1g; Cholesterol 82mg; Calcium 169mg; Fibre 1.1g; Sodium 299mg.
Double Pie Energy 682kcal/2845kJ; Protein 8.3g; Carbohydrate 64.7g, of which sugars 56.4g; Fat 45.1g, of which saturates 27.6g; Cholesterol 100mg; Calcium 246mg; Fibre 0.8g; Sodium 211mg.

Chocolate, Banana and Toffee Pie

As an alternative to the coffee topping, just decorate the pie with whipped cream and extra banana slices.

Serves 6

65g/2½oz/5 tbsp unsalted (sweet) butter, melted
250g/9oz milk chocolate digestive biscuits (graham crackers), crushed

For the filling

400g/14oz can sweetened condensed milk, unopened
150g/5oz plain (semisweet) chocolate, chopped
120ml/4fl oz/½ cup crème fraîche
15ml/1 tbsp golden (light corn) syrup

For the topping

2 bananas
250ml/8fl oz/1 cup crème fraîche
10ml/2 tsp strong black coffee
chocolate curls, to decorate

1 Mix the butter with the biscuit crumbs. Press on to the base and sides of a 23cm/9in loose-based flan tin (pan). Chill.

2 Make the filling. Place the unopened can of condensed milk in a deep pan of boiling water, making sure that it is completely covered. Lower the heat and simmer, covered, for 2 hours, topping up the water as necessary. The can must remain covered at all times.

3 Remove the pan from the heat and set aside, covered, until the can has cooled down completely in the water. Do not attempt to open the can until it is completely cold.

4 Gently melt the chocolate with the crème fraîche and golden syrup in a heatproof bowl over a pan of simmering water. Stir in the caramelized condensed milk and beat together until thoroughly combined. Pour the chocolate filling into the biscuit crust and spread it evenly.

5 Slice the bananas evenly and arrange them over the chocolate filling in an attractive pattern.

6 Stir the crème fraîche and coffee together in a bowl, then spoon the mixture over the bananas. Sprinkle the chocolate curls on top.

Mississippi Pie

This American biscuit-based pie has a layer of chocolate mousse, topped with a coffee toffee layer and lots of freshly whipped cream.

Serves 8

For the base

275g/10oz digestive biscuits (graham crackers), crushed
150g/5oz/10 tbsp butter, melted

For the chocolate layer

10ml/2 tsp powdered gelatine
30ml/2 tbsp cold water
175g/6oz plain (semisweet) chocolate, broken into squares
2 eggs, separated
150ml/¼ pint/⅔ cup double (heavy) cream

For the coffee toffee layer

30ml/2 tbsp ground coffee
300ml/½ pint/1¼ cups double (heavy) cream
200g/7oz/1 cup caster (superfine) sugar
25g/1oz/4 tbsp cornflour (cornstarch)
2 eggs, beaten
15g/½oz/1 tbsp butter
150ml/¼ pint/⅔ cup whipping cream and chocolate curls, to decorate

1 Grease a 21cm/8½in loose-based tin (pan). Mix the biscuit crumbs and butter and press over the base and sides of the tin. Chill for 30 minutes.

2 Make the chocolate layer. Sprinkle the gelatine over the water. Leave for 5 minutes. Stir in a bowl over a pan of hot water until dissolved. Melt the chocolate in a bowl over hot water. Stir in the gelatine. Blend the egg yolks and cream and stir into the chocolate. Whisk the egg whites and fold into the mixture. Pour into the case and chill for 2 hours.

3 Make the coffee layer. Reserve 60ml/4 tbsp of cream. Heat the remaining cream to near-boiling and pour over the coffee. Leave for 4 minutes. Strain back into the pan. Add the sugar and dissolve. Mix the cornflour with the reserved cream and the eggs. Add to the coffee and cream mixture and simmer for 2–3 minutes. Stir in the butter. Cool for 30 minutes. Spoon over the chocolate layer. Chill for 2 hours.

4 Whip the cream until soft peaks form, and spread thickly over the pie. Decorate with chocolate curls and chill until serving.

Toffee Pie Energy 900kcal/3758kJ; Protein 11.5g; Carbohydrate 90g, of which sugars 73.2g; Fat 57.4g, of which saturates 35.8g; Cholesterol 139mg; Calcium 275mg; Fibre 1.8g; Sodium 368mg.
Mississippi Energy 519kcal/2165kJ; Protein 8.5g; Carbohydrate 48.6g, of which sugars 20.6g; Fat 32.8g, of which saturates 19.3g; Cholesterol 178mg; Calcium 146mg; Fibre 1.2g; Sodium 164mg.

Mississippi Mud Pie

This is a pastry-based version of the Mississippi classic.

Serves 6–8

3 eggs, separated
20ml/4 tsp cornflour (cornstarch)
75g/3oz/6 tbsp sugar
400ml/14fl oz/1⅔ cups milk
150g/5oz plain (semisweet) chocolate, broken up
5ml/1 tsp vanilla extract
15ml/1 tbsp powdered gelatine
45ml/3 tbsp water
30ml/2 tbsp dark rum
175ml/6fl oz/¾ cup double (heavy) cream, whipped
a few chocolate curls, to decorate

For the pastry

250g/9oz/2¼ cups plain (all-purpose) flour
150g/5oz/10 tbsp butter, diced
2 egg yolks
15–30ml/1–2 tbsp chilled water

1 Make the pastry. Sift the flour into a bowl. Rub in the butter until the mixture resembles breadcrumbs. Stir in the yolks with enough chilled water to make a soft dough. Roll out and use to line a deep 23cm/9in flan tin (pan). Chill for 30 minutes. Preheat the oven to 190°C/375°F/Gas 5. Prick the pastry, line with foil and baking beans, and bake blind for 10 minutes. Remove the foil and beans, and return to the oven for 10 minutes until the pastry is crisp and golden. Cool.

2 Mix the yolks, cornflour and 30ml/2 tbsp of the sugar in a bowl. In a pan, bring the milk almost to a boil, then beat into the egg mixture. Return to the pan and stir over a low heat until thickened. Pour half into a bowl. Melt the chocolate in a heatproof bowl over a pan of hot water, then add to the custard in the bowl. Mix in the vanilla extract. Spread in the pastry case (pie shell), cover with baking parchment to prevent a skin forming, cool, then chill until set. Sprinkle the gelatine over the water in a small bowl, leave until spongy, then place over a pan of simmering water until the gelatine dissolves. Stir into the remaining custard, with the rum.

3 Whisk the egg whites until stiff peaks form, whisk in the rest of the sugar, then fold into the gelatine and custard mix before it sets. Spoon over the chocolate custard to cover. Chill until set, then remove from the tin. Spread whipped cream over the top, decorate with chocolate curls and serve immediately.

Chocolate-topped Candied Fruit Pie

Use good-quality candied fruits for the best flavour. Try half digestive biscuits and half ginger nut biscuits for the crust, if you prefer.

Serves 10

15ml/1 tbsp rum
50g/2oz/¼ cup mixed glacé (candied) fruit, chopped
475ml/16fl oz/2 cups milk
20ml/4 tsp powdered gelatine
90g/3½oz/½ cup caster (superfine) sugar
2.5ml/½ tsp salt
3 eggs, separated
250ml/8fl oz/1 cup whipping cream, whipped
chocolate curls, to decorate

For the crust

175g/6oz/2 cups crushed digestive biscuits (graham crackers)
75g/3oz/6 tbsp butter, melted
15ml/1 tbsp caster (superfine) sugar

1 To make the crust mix the digestive biscuits, butter and sugar. Press evenly over the base and sides of a 23cm/9in pie plate. Chill.

2 Stir together the rum and glacé fruit. Set aside. Pour 120ml/4fl oz/½ cup of the milk into a small bowl. Sprinkle over the gelatine and leave for 5 minutes to soften.

3 In the top of a double boiler or in a heatproof bowl over a pan of simmering water, combine 50g/2oz/¼ cup of the sugar, the remaining milk and the salt. Stir in the gelatine mixture. Cook, stirring, until the gelatine dissolves. Whisk in the egg yolks and cook, stirring, until thick enough to coat the back of the spoon. Pour the custard over the glacé fruit mixture, set in a bowl of iced water.

4 Beat the egg whites until they form soft peaks. Add the remaining sugar and beat until just blended. Fold a large dollop of the egg whites into the cooled gelatine mixture. Pour into the remaining egg whites and fold together. Fold in the cream.

5 Pour into the pie crust and chill until firm. Decorate with chocolate curls.

Mississippi Mud Pie Energy 571kcal/2385kJ; Protein 9.4g; Carbohydrate 53.5g, of which sugars 22.7g; Fat 36.2g, of which saturates 21.2g; Cholesterol 196mg; Calcium 160mg; Fibre 1.3g; Sodium 180mg.
Fruit Pie Energy 333kcal/1388kJ; Protein 5.2g; Carbohydrate 28.9g, of which sugars 19.3g; Fat 22.3g, of which saturates 12.8g; Cholesterol 109mg; Calcium 110mg; Fibre 0.6g; Sodium 213mg.

Chocolate Chiffon Pie

Decorate with chocolate curls for a pretty finish.

Serves 8

175g/6oz plain (semisweet) chocolate squares, chopped
25g/1oz dark (bittersweet) chocolate, chopped
250ml/8fl oz/1 cup milk
15ml/1 tbsp powdered gelatine
130g/4½oz/⅔ cup sugar
2 eggs, separated
5ml/1 tsp vanilla extract
350ml/12fl oz/1½ cups whipping cream
pinch of salt
whipped cream, to decorate

For the base

75g/3oz/1½ cups digestive biscuit (graham cracker) crumbs
75g/3oz/6 tbsp butter, melted

1 Place a baking sheet in the oven and preheat to 180°C/350°F/Gas 4. Make the crust. Mix the biscuit crumbs and butter in a bowl. Press the crumbs evenly over the base and sides of a 23cm/9in pie tin (pan). Bake for 8 minutes. Allow to cool.

2 Grind both chocolates in a food processor or blender. Set aside. Place the milk in the top of a double boiler or in a heatproof bowl. Sprinkle over the gelatine. Let stand for 5 minutes to soften.

3 Set the top of the double boiler or heatproof bowl over hot water. Add 50g/2oz/¼ cup of the sugar, the chocolate and egg yolks. Stir until dissolved. Add the vanilla extract.

4 Place the top of the double boiler or the heatproof bowl in a bowl of ice and stir until the mixture reaches room temperature. Remove from the ice and set aside.

5 Whip the cream lightly. Set aside. With an electric whisk, beat the egg whites and salt until they hold soft peaks. Add the remaining sugar and beat only enough to blend. Fold a dollop of egg whites into the chocolate mixture, then pour back into the whites and gently fold in.

6 Fold in the cream and pour into the tin. Freeze for about 5 minutes until just set. If the centre sinks, fill with any remaining mixture. Chill for 3–4 hours. Decorate with whipped cream.

Chocolate, Pear and Pecan Pie

A classic pie gets a tempting new twist.

Serves 8–10

3 small pears, peeled
150ml/¼ pint/⅔ cup water
165g/5½oz/generous ¾ cup caster (superfine) sugar
pared rind of 1 lemon
50g/2oz plain (semisweet) chocolate, broken into pieces
50g/2oz/¼ cup butter, diced
225g/8oz/scant ¾ cup golden (light corn) syrup
3 eggs, beaten
5ml/1 tsp vanilla extract
150g/5oz/1¼ cups pecan nuts, chopped

For the pastry

175g/6oz/1½ cups plain (all-purpose) flour
115g/4oz/½ cup butter, diced
25g/1oz/2 tbsp caster (superfine) sugar
1 egg yolk, lightly beaten with 10ml/2 tsp chilled water

1 Sift the flour into a bowl, rub in the butter and stir in the sugar. Add the egg yolk and mix to a dough, adding more water if necessary. Knead lightly, wrap and chill for 30 minutes.

2 Roll out the pastry and use to line a 23cm/9in flan tin (pan). Chill for 20 minutes. Preheat the oven to 200°F/400°C/Gas 6. Line the pastry case (pie shell) with foil, fill with baking beans and bake for 10 minutes. Lift out the foil and beans and bake for 5 minutes more. Set aside to cool.

3 Halve and core the pears. Bring the water, 50g/2oz/¼ cup of the sugar and the lemon rind to the boil. Add the pears, cover and simmer gently for 10 minutes. Remove the pears from the pan.

4 Melt the chocolate over simmering water, beat in the butter and set aside. Heat the remaining sugar and syrup until the sugar has dissolved. Bring to the boil and simmer for 2 minutes. Whisk the eggs into the chocolate mixture until combined, then whisk in the syrup mixture. Stir in the vanilla and nuts.

5 Slice the pear halves lengthways without cutting all the way through. Arrange them in the pastry case and pour in the nut mixture. Bake for 25–30 minutes. Cool and serve sliced.

Chiffon Pie Energy 509kcal/2120kJ; Protein 5.5g; Carbohydrate 43.2g, of which sugars 37.8g; Fat 36.2g, of which saturates 21.7g; Cholesterol 121mg; Calcium 98mg; Fibre 0.8g; Sodium 158mg.
Pear and Pecan Pie Energy 499kcal/2090kJ; Protein 5.8g; Carbohydrate 59.9g, of which sugars 46.3g; Fat 28g, of which saturates 11g; Cholesterol 113mg; Calcium 68mg; Fibre 2.4g; Sodium 186mg.

Chocolate Cheesecake Tart

You can use all digestive biscuits for the base of this tart, if you prefer.

Serves 8

350g/12oz/1½ cups cream cheese
60ml/4 tbsp whipping cream
225g/8oz/generous 1 cup caster (superfine) sugar
50g/2oz/½ cup unsweetened cocoa powder
2.5ml/½ tsp ground cinnamon
3 eggs
whipped cream and chocolate curls, to decorate

For the base

75g/3oz/1 cup crushed digestive biscuits (graham crackers)
40g/1½oz/scant 1 cup crushed amaretti
75g/3oz/6 tbsp butter, melted

1 Preheat a baking sheet in the oven at 180°C/350°F/Gas 4.

2 To make the base, mix the crushed biscuits and melted butter in a bowl.

3 Press the mixture over the base and sides of a 23cm/9in pie dish. Bake for 8 minutes. Leave to cool, but keep the oven on.

4 Beat the cream cheese and cream together until smooth. Beat in the sugar, cocoa and cinnamon until blended.

5 Add the eggs, one at a time, beating just enough to blend.

6 Pour into the biscuit base and bake on the baking sheet for 25–30 minutes. The filling will sink down as it cools.

7 Decorate the top of the tart with whipped cream and chocolate curls.

Cook's Tip

To make chocolate curls, run a vegetable peeler against the long side of a bar of chocolate.

American Chocolate Cheesecake

This popular variation of the American classic is made with a crunchy cinnamon and chocolate base.

Serves 10–12

175g/6oz plain (semisweet) chocolate, chopped
115g/4oz dark (bittersweet) chocolate, chopped
1.2kg/2½lb/5 cups cream cheese, at room temperature
200g/7oz/1 cup caster (superfine) sugar
10ml/2 tsp vanilla extract
4 eggs, at room temperature
175ml/6fl oz/¾ cup sour cream

For the base

75g/3oz/1½ cups chocolate biscuit (cookie) crumbs
75g/3oz/6 tbsp butter, melted
2.5ml/½ tsp ground cinnamon

1 Preheat the oven to 180°C/350°F/Gas 4. Grease a 23cm/9in springform cake tin (pan).

2 Make the base. Mix the chocolate biscuit crumbs with the butter and cinnamon. Press evenly over the bottom of the tin.

3 Melt the plain and dark chocolate in the top of a double boiler, or in a heatproof bowl set over a pan of simmering water. Set aside.

4 With an electric whisk, beat the cream cheese until smooth, then beat in the sugar and vanilla extract. Add the eggs, one at a time, scraping the bowl with a spatula when necessary.

5 Add the sour cream to the cheese mixture, then stir in the melted chocolate, mixing well.

6 Pour into the tin. Bake for 1 hour. Allow to cool, then remove from the tin. Chill before serving.

Variation

For a chocolate-orange cheesecake, replace the vanilla extract with finely grated orange rind. Serve with sliced oranges coated in a light sugar syrup, flavoured with shredded orange rind.

Tart Energy 514kcal/2139kJ; Protein 6.1g; Carbohydrate 40.8g, of which sugars 32.7g; Fat 37.5g, of which saturates 22.3g; Cholesterol 145mg; Calcium 98mg; Fibre 1g; Sodium 350mg.
Cheesecake Energy 717kcal/2972kJ; Protein 5.2g; Carbohydrate 37.5g, of which sugars 34.9g; Fat 61.8g, of which saturates 38.4g; Cholesterol 118mg; Calcium 131mg; Fibre 0.7g; Sodium 362mg.

Marbled Chocolate Cheesecake

This attractive-looking dessert will be a big hit.

Serves 6

butter or margarine, for greasing
50g/2oz/½ cup unsweetened cocoa powder
75ml/5 tbsp hot water
900g/2lb/4 cups cream cheese, at room temperature
200g/7oz/1 cup caster (superfine) sugar
4 eggs
5ml/1 tsp vanilla extract
75g/3oz digestive biscuits (graham crackers), crushed

1 Preheat the oven to 180°C/350°F/Gas 4. Line a deep 20cm/8in cake tin (pan) with baking parchment. Grease the paper.

2 Sift the cocoa powder into a bowl. Pour over the hot water and stir to dissolve.

3 In another bowl, beat the cheese until smooth, then beat in the sugar, followed by the eggs, one at a time. Do not overmix.

4 Divide the mixture evenly between two bowls. Stir the chocolate mixture into one bowl, then add the vanilla extract to the remaining mixture.

5 Pour a cup or ladleful of the plain mixture into the centre of the tin; it will spread out into an even layer. Slowly pour over a cupful of chocolate mixture in the centre. Continue to alternate the cake mixtures in this way until both are used up. Draw a metal skewer through the cake mixture for a marbled effect.

6 Place the tin in a roasting pan and pour in hot water to come 4cm/1½in up the sides of the cake tin. Bake the cheesecake for about 1½ hours, until the top is golden. (The cake will rise during baking but will sink later.) Cool in the tin on a wire rack.

7 Run a knife around the inside edge of the cheesecake. Invert a flat plate over the tin and turn out the cake. Sprinkle the crushed biscuits evenly over the cake, gently invert another plate on top, and turn over again. Cover and chill for 3 hours, preferably overnight, before serving.

Luxury White Chocolate Cheesecake

A luscious dessert for a special occasion.

Serves 16–20

150g/5oz (about 16–18) digestive biscuits (graham crackers)
50g/2oz/½ cup blanched hazelnuts, toasted
50g/2oz/¼ cup unsalted (sweet) butter, melted, plus extra for greasing
2.5ml/½ tsp ground cinnamon
white chocolate curls, to decorate
unsweetened cocoa powder, for dusting (optional)

For the filling

350g/12oz fine white chocolate, chopped into small pieces
120ml/4fl oz/½ cup whipping cream or double (heavy) cream
675g/1½lb/3 cups cream cheese, softened
50g/2oz/¼ cup granulated (white) sugar
4 eggs
30ml/2 tbsp hazelnut-flavoured liqueur or 15ml/1 tbsp vanilla extract

For the topping

450ml/¾ pint/scant 2 cups sour cream
50g/2oz/¼ cup granulated (white) sugar
15ml/1 tbsp hazelnut-flavoured liqueur or 5ml/1 tsp vanilla extract

1 Preheat the oven to 180°C/350°F/Gas 4. Grease a deep 23cm/9in springform tin (pan).

2 Put the digestive biscuits and hazelnuts in a food processor and process to form fine crumbs. Pour in the butter and cinnamon. Process until the mixture is just blended. Using the back of a spoon, press on to the base and to within 1cm/½in of the top of the sides of the cake tin.

3 Bake the crumb crust for 5–7 minutes, or until it is just set. Cool the crust in the tin on a wire rack. Lower the oven temperature to 150°C/300°F/Gas 2 and place a baking sheet inside to heat up.

4 Make the filling. Melt the white chocolate and cream in a small pan over a low heat, until smooth, stirring frequently. Set aside to cool slightly.

5 Using an electric whisk, beat the cream cheese and sugar in a large bowl until smooth. Add the eggs one at a time, beating well. Slowly beat in the white chocolate mixture and liqueur or vanilla extract.

6 Pour the filling into the baked crust. Place the tin on the heated baking sheet. Bake for 45–55 minutes; be careful to ensure the top does not brown. Transfer to a wire rack while preparing the topping. Increase the oven temperature to 200°C/400°F/Gas 6.

7 Make the topping. In a small bowl whisk the sour cream, sugar and liqueur or vanilla extract until well combined. Pour over the cheesecake, spreading it evenly to the edges, and return to the oven. Bake for a further 5–7 minutes. Turn off the oven, but do not open the door for 1 hour.

8 Serve the cheesecake at room temperature, decorated with the white chocolate curls. Dust lightly with the cocoa powder, if you like.

Marbled Cheesecake Energy 923kcal/3828kJ; Protein 11.3g; Carbohydrate 44.4g, of which sugars 36.5g; Fat 79.3g, of which saturates 47.8g; Cholesterol 274mg; Calcium 206mg; Fibre 1.3g; Sodium 653mg.
Luxury Cheesecake Energy 421kcal/1746kJ; Protein 5.3g; Carbohydrate 22.3g, of which sugars 18.1g; Fat 34.6g, of which saturates 20g; Cholesterol 98mg; Calcium 124mg; Fibre 0.3g; Sodium 206mg.

Raspberry and White Chocolate Cheesecake

An unbeatable combination: raspberries teamed with mascarpone and white chocolate on a crunchy ginger and pecan nut base.

Serves 8

50g/2oz/4 tbsp unsalted (sweet) butter
225g/8oz/2⅓ cups ginger nut biscuits (gingersnaps), crushed
50g/2oz/½ cup chopped pecan nuts or walnuts

For the filling

275g/10oz/1¼ cups mascarpone
175g/6oz/¾ cup fromage frais or soft white (farmer's) cheese
2 eggs, beaten
40g/1½oz/3 tbsp caster (superfine) sugar
250g/9oz white chocolate, broken into squares
225g/8oz/1⅓ cups fresh or frozen raspberries

For the topping

115g/4oz/½ cup mascarpone
75g/3oz/⅓ cup fromage frais or soft white (farmer's) cheese
white chocolate curls and raspberries, to decorate

1 Preheat the oven to 150°C/300°F/Gas 2. Melt the butter in a pan, then stir in the crushed biscuits (cookies) and nuts. Press into the base of a 23cm/9in springform cake tin (pan).

2 Make the filling. Beat the mascarpone and fromage frais or white cheese in a bowl, then beat in the eggs and caster sugar until evenly mixed.

3 Melt the white chocolate gently in a heatproof bowl over a pan of simmering water. Stir the chocolate into the cheese mixture with the raspberries.

4 Turn into the prepared tin and spread evenly, then bake for about 1 hour or until just set. Switch off the oven, but do not remove the cheesecake. Leave it until cold and completely set.

5 Remove the cheesecake from the tin. Make the topping. Mix the mascarpone with the fromage frais and spread over the cheesecake. Decorate with chocolate curls and raspberries.

Baked Chocolate and Raisin Cheesecake

This classic cheesecake will disappear in a flash.

Serves 8–10

75g/3oz/⅔ cup plain (all-purpose) flour
45ml/3 tbsp unsweetened cocoa powder
75g/3oz/½ cup semolina
50g/2oz/¼ cup caster (superfine) sugar
115g/4oz/½ cup unsalted (sweet) butter, softened

For the filling

225g/8oz/1 cup cream cheese
120ml/4fl oz/½ cup natural (plain) yogurt
2 eggs, beaten
75g/3oz/6 tbsp caster (superfine) sugar
finely grated rind of 1 lemon
75g/3oz/½ cup raisins
45ml/3 tbsp plain (semisweet) chocolate chips

For the topping

75g/3oz plain (semisweet) chocolate, chopped into pieces
30ml/2 tbsp golden (light corn) syrup
40g/1½oz/3 tbsp butter

1 Preheat the oven to 150°C/300°F/Gas 2. Sift the flour and cocoa into a mixing bowl and stir in the semolina and sugar. Using your fingertips, work the butter into the flour mixture until it makes a firm dough.

2 Press the dough into the base of a 22cm/8½in springform tin (pan). Prick all over with a fork and bake in the oven for 15 minutes. Remove the tin but leave the oven on.

3 Make the filling. In a large bowl, beat the cream cheese with the yogurt, eggs and sugar until evenly mixed. Stir in the lemon rind, raisins and chocolate chips.

4 Smooth the cream cheese mixture over the chocolate base and bake for a further 35–45 minutes or until the filling is pale gold and just set. Cool in the tin on a wire rack.

5 Make the topping. Melt the chocolate, syrup and butter in a bowl over simmering water, then pour over the cheesecake. Leave until set. Remove the cheesecake from the tin and serve.

Raspberry Cheesecake Energy 551kcal/2305kJ; Protein 12.8g; Carbohydrate 53.9g, of which sugars 41.4g; Fat 33.1g, of which saturates 17g; Cholesterol 88mg; Calcium 170mg; Fibre 1.4g; Sodium 195mg.
Raisin Cheesecake Energy 441kcal/1841kJ; Protein 5.8g; Carbohydrate 41.4g, of which sugars 29.3g; Fat 29.3g, of which saturates 17.7g; Cholesterol 93mg; Calcium 86mg; Fibre 1.4g; Sodium 243mg.

Hot Chocolate Cake

This warm chocolate cake is wonderfully wicked served as a dessert with a white chocolate sauce. The basic cake freezes well – thaw, then warm in the microwave before serving.

Makes 10–12 slices

200g/7oz/1¾ cups self-raising wholemeal (self-rising whole-wheat) flour
25g/1oz/¼ cup unsweetened cocoa powder
pinch of salt
175g/6oz/¾ cup soft margarine
175g/6oz/¾ cup soft light brown sugar
few drops vanilla extract
4 eggs
75g/3oz white chocolate, roughly chopped
chocolate leaves and curls, to decorate

For the chocolate sauce
75g/3oz white chocolate
150ml/¼ pint/⅔ cup single (light) cream
30–45ml/2–3 tbsp milk

1 Preheat the oven to 160°C/325°F/Gas 3. Sift the flour, cocoa and salt into a bowl, adding in the wholemeal flakes from the sieve (strainer).

2 Cream the margarine, sugar and vanilla extract together until light and fluffy, then gently beat in one egg.

3 Gradually stir in the remaining eggs, one at a time, alternately folding in some of the flour mixture, until the eggs and flour have been used up and the mixture is blended in.

4 Stir in the white chocolate and spoon into a 675–900g/1½–2lb loaf tin (pan) or an 18cm/7in greased cake tin (pan). Bake for 30–40 minutes, or until just firm to the touch and shrinking away from the sides of the tin.

5 Meanwhile, make the sauce. Heat the white chocolate and cream very gently in a pan until the chocolate is melted. Add the milk and stir until cool.

6 Serve the cake sliced, in a pool of sauce and decorated with chocolate leaves and curls.

Chocolate Cinnamon Cake with Banana Sauce

This mouthwatering cake, bursting with lovely flavours, is brilliantly complemented by the tasty banana sauce.

Serves 6

25g/1oz plain (semisweet) chocolate, chopped into small pieces
115g/4oz/½ cup unsalted (sweet) butter, at room temperature
15ml/1 tbsp instant coffee powder
5 eggs, separated
225g/8oz/1 cup granulated (white) sugar
115g/4oz/1 cup plain (all-purpose) flour
10ml/2 tsp ground cinnamon

For the banana sauce
4 ripe bananas
45ml/3 tbsp soft light brown sugar
15ml/1 tbsp fresh lemon juice
175ml/6fl oz/¾ cup whipping cream
15ml/1 tbsp rum (optional)

1 Preheat the oven to 180°C/350°F/Gas 4. Grease a 20cm/8in round cake tin (pan).

2 Place the chocolate and butter in the top of a double boiler or in a heatproof bowl set over a pan of simmering water. Stir until the chocolate and butter have melted. Remove from the heat and stir in the coffee. Set aside.

3 Beat the egg yolks with the granulated sugar until thick and lemon-coloured. Add the chocolate mixture and mix until just blended.

4 Stir the flour and cinnamon together in a bowl. In another bowl, beat the egg whites until they hold stiff peaks.

5 Fold a spoonful of whites into the chocolate mixture to lighten it. Fold in the remaining whites in three batches, alternating with the sifted flour mixture.

6 Pour the mixture into the prepared tin. Bake for 40–50 minutes, or until a skewer inserted in the centre comes out clean. Remove from the oven and turn the cake out on to a wire rack. Preheat the grill (broiler).

7 Make the sauce. Slice the bananas into a shallow, flameproof dish. Stir in the brown sugar and lemon juice. Place under the grill for 8 minutes, stirring occasionally, until caramelized.

8 Mash the banana mixture until almost smooth. Tip into a bowl and stir in the cream and rum, if using. Slice the cake and serve with the sauce.

Cook's Tip

Take care when folding the egg white and flour into the chocolate mixture – do not be tempted to stir, otherwise you will break down the air bubbles in the mixture and the cake will not rise well.

Chocolate Cake Energy 343kcal/1432kJ; Protein 5.4g; Carbohydrate 35.7g, of which sugars 23.1g; Fat 20.8g, of which saturates 7.1g; Cholesterol 71mg; Calcium 124mg; Fibre 0.8g; Sodium 221mg.
Cinnamon Cake Energy 642kcal/2691kJ; Protein 8.9g; Carbohydrate 80.9g, of which sugars 64.8g; Fat 33.8g, of which saturates 19.4g; Cholesterol 230mg; Calcium 100mg; Fibre 1.4g; Sodium 186mg.

Rich Chocolate Brioche Bake

This dessert is amazingly easy to make and doesn't require many ingredients. Richly flavoured and quite delicious, it's the perfect dish for entertaining, when you are pushed for time. Serve with a platter of sliced tropical fruit as a foil to the richness of the dish.

Serves 4

40g/1½oz/3 tbsp unsalted (sweet) butter, plus extra for greasing
200g/7oz plain (semisweet) chocolate, chopped into small pieces
60ml/4 tbsp bitter marmalade
4 individual brioches, cut into halves, or 1 large brioche loaf, cut into thick slices
3 eggs
300ml/½ pint/1¼ cups milk
300ml/½ pint/1¼ cups single (light) cream
30ml/2 tbsp demerara (raw) sugar
crème fraîche, to serve

1 Preheat the oven to 180°C/350°F/Gas 4. Using the extra butter, lightly grease a shallow ovenproof dish.

2 Place the plain chocolate with the marmalade and butter in a double boiler or in a heatproof bowl set over a pan of just simmering water, stirring the mixture occasionally, until melted and smooth.

3 Spread the melted chocolate mixture over the brioche slices, then carefully arrange them in the dish so that the slices overlap in neat rows.

4 Beat the eggs in a large bowl, then add the milk and cream and mix well. Transfer to a jug (pitcher) and pour evenly over the slices.

5 Sprinkle the mixture with the demerara sugar and place the dish in the oven. Bake for 40–50 minutes, or until the custard has set lightly and the brioche slices have turned a golden brown colour.

6 Serve immediately, topped with dollops of crème fraîche and a fruit platter, if you like.

Chocolate Orange Marquise

Here is a cake for people who are passionate about the combination of chocolate and orange. The rich, dense chocolate flavour is accentuated by fresh orange to make it a truly delectable treat.

Serves 6–8

200g/7oz/1 cup caster (superfine) sugar
60ml/4 tbsp freshly squeezed orange juice
350g/12oz dark (bittersweet) chocolate, broken into squares
225g/8oz/1 cup unsalted (sweet) butter, diced, plus extra for greasing
5 eggs
finely grated rind of 1 orange
45g/1¾oz/3 tbsp plain (all-purpose) flour
icing (confectioners') sugar and finely pared strips of orange rind, to decorate

1 Preheat the oven to 180°C/350°F/Gas 4. Grease a 23cm/9in shallow cake tin (pan) with a depth of 6cm/2½in. Line the base of the tin with baking parchment.

2 Place 90g/3½oz/½ cup of the sugar in a pan. Add the orange juice and stir over a low heat until dissolved.

3 Remove from the heat and stir in the chocolate until melted, then add the butter, piece by piece, until melted.

4 Whisk the eggs with the remaining sugar in a large bowl, until the mixture is pale and very thick. Add the orange rind, then lightly fold the chocolate mixture into the egg mixture. Sift the flour over the top and fold in.

5 Pour the mixture into the prepared tin. Place in a roasting pan, then pour hot water into the roasting pan to reach about halfway up the sides of the cake tin.

6 Bake for 1 hour, or until the cake is firm to the touch. Remove the tin from the roasting pan and cool for 20 minutes. Turn out the cake on to a baking sheet, place a serving plate upside down on top, then carefully turn the plate and baking sheet over together. Dust with a little icing sugar, decorate with strips of orange rind and serve slightly warm or chilled.

Brioche Bake Energy 987kcal/4143kJ; Protein 25.9g; Carbohydrate 127.8g, of which sugars 59.1g; Fat 45g, of which saturates 25.4g; Cholesterol 213mg; Calcium 460mg; Fibre 4.4g; Sodium 1060mg.
Marquise Energy 553kcal/2309kJ; Protein 3.1g; Carbohydrate 59.1g, of which sugars 54.4g; Fat 35.5g, of which saturates 22g; Cholesterol 63mg; Calcium 41mg; Fibre 1.3g; Sodium 176mg.

Hot Mocha Rum Soufflé

These delicious individual soufflés, flavoured with cocoa and coffee, are light enough to be the ideal dessert for serving after a substantial main course.

Serves 6

25g/1oz/2 tbsp unsalted (sweet) butter, melted
65g/2½oz/9 tbsp unsweetened cocoa powder
75g/3oz/scant ½ cup caster (superfine) sugar
60ml/4 tbsp made-up strong black coffee
30ml/2 tbsp dark rum
6 egg whites
icing (confectioners') sugar, for dusting

1 Preheat the oven to 190°C/375°F/Gas 5. Grease six 250ml/8fl oz/1 cup soufflé dishes with melted butter.

2 Mix 15ml/1 tbsp of the cocoa with 15ml/1 tbsp of the caster sugar in a bowl. Sprinkle the mixture into each of the dishes in turn, rotating them so that they are evenly coated.

3 Mix the remaining cocoa with the coffee and rum in a medium bowl.

4 Whisk the egg whites in a clean, grease-free bowl until they form firm peaks. Whisk in the remaining sugar. Stir a generous spoonful of the egg whites into the cocoa mixture to lighten it, then fold in the remaining whites.

5 Spoon the mixture into the prepared dishes, smoothing the tops. Place on a hot baking sheet, and bake in the oven for 12–15 minutes, or until well risen. Serve immediately, dusted with icing sugar.

Cook's Tip

You can use either a hand whisk or an electric version to beat the egg whites, but take care not to overbeat them if you are using electric beaters. The beaten whites should stand in soft peaks, with the tips gently flopping over. If they are overbeaten they will look dry.

Chocolate and Orange Soufflé

The base in this hot soufflé is an easy-to-make semolina mixture, rather than the thick white sauce that many soufflés call for.

Serves 4

butter, for greasing
600ml/1 pint/2½ cups milk
50g/2oz/generous ⅓ cup semolina
50g/2oz/scant ¼ cup soft light brown sugar
grated rind of 1 orange
90ml/6 tbsp fresh orange juice
3 eggs, separated
75g/3oz plain (semisweet) chocolate, grated
icing (confectioners') sugar, for sprinkling
single (light) cream, to serve

1 Preheat the oven to 200°C/400°F/Gas 6. Butter a shallow 1.75 litre/3 pint/7½ cup ovenproof dish.

2 Pour the milk into a heavy pan, sprinkle over the semolina and sugar, then heat, stirring the mixture constantly, until boiling and thickened.

3 Remove the pan from the heat, beat in the orange rind and juice, egg yolks and all but 15ml/1 tbsp of the grated plain chocolate.

4 Whisk the egg whites until stiff peaks form, then lightly fold one-third into the semolina mixture. Fold in another third, followed by the remaining egg whites. Spoon the mixture into the buttered dish and bake for about 30 minutes, until just set in the centre.

5 Sprinkle the soufflé with the reserved grated chocolate and the icing sugar, then serve immediately, with the cream handed around separately.

Variation

For a sophisticated touch, replace 30ml/2 tbsp of the orange juice with the same amount of orange-flavoured liqueur, such as Cointreau or Grand Marnier.

Hot Mocha Rum Soufflé Energy 148kcal/619kJ; Protein 5g; Carbohydrate 14.3g, of which sugars 13.1g; Fat 5.8g, of which saturates 3.6g; Cholesterol 9mg; Calcium 23mg; Fibre 1.3g; Sodium 190mg.
Orange Soufflé Energy 321kcal/1353kJ; Protein 12.2g; Carbohydrate 43.7g, of which sugars 33.8g; Fat 12.2g, of which saturates 5.9g; Cholesterol 153mg; Calcium 219mg; Fibre 0.8g; Sodium 123mg.

French Chocolate Soufflé

These stylish French soufflés are actually extremely easy to make.

Serves 6

175g/6oz plain (semisweet) chocolate, chopped
150g/5oz/10 tbsp unsalted (sweet) butter, cut into small pieces
4 large (US extra large) eggs, separated
30ml/2 tbsp orange liqueur (optional)
1.5ml/¼ tsp cream of tartar
40g/1½oz/3 tbsp caster (superfine) sugar
icing (confectioners') sugar, for dusting
sprigs of redcurrants and white chocolate roses, to decorate

For the sauce

75g/3oz white chocolate, chopped
90ml/6 tbsp whipping cream
15–30ml/1–2 tbsp orange liqueur
grated rind of ½ orange

1 Generously butter six 150ml/¼ pint/⅔ cup ramekins, custard cups or small ovenproof dishes. Sprinkle each with a little sugar and tap out any excess. Place the dishes on a baking sheet.

2 Melt the chocolate and butter in a heavy pan over a very low heat, stirring until smooth. Remove from the heat and cool slightly, then beat in the egg yolks and orange liqueur, if using. Set aside, stirring occasionally.

3 Preheat the oven to 220°C/425°F/Gas 7. In a grease-free bowl, whisk the egg whites slowly until frothy. Add the cream of tartar, increase the speed and whisk to form soft peaks. Gradually whisk in the sugar until the whites are stiff and glossy. Stir a third of the whites into the cooled chocolate mixture, then fold this into the remaining whites. Spoon into the dishes.

4 Make the sauce. Put the white chocolate and cream in a small pan. Place over a low heat and cook, stirring constantly until smooth. Remove from the heat and stir in the liqueur and orange rind, then pour into a serving jug (pitcher); keep warm.

5 Bake the soufflés for 10–12 minutes until risen and set, but still slightly wobbly in the centre. Dust with icing sugar and decorate with redcurrants and chocolate roses. Serve with the sauce.

Twice-baked Mocha Soufflé

The perfect way to end a meal, these mini mocha soufflés can be made up to 3 hours ahead, then reheated just before you serve them.

Serves 6

75g/3oz/6 tbsp unsalted (sweet) butter, softened
90g/3½oz bittersweet or plain (semisweet) chocolate, grated
30ml/2 tbsp ground coffee
400ml/14fl oz/1⅔ cup milk
40g/1½oz/⅓ cup plain (all-purpose) flour, sifted
15g/½oz/2 tbsp unsweetened cocoa powder, sifted
3 eggs, separated
50g/2oz/¼ cup caster (superfine) sugar
175ml/6fl oz/¾ cup creamy chocolate or coffee liqueur, such as Crème de Caçao or Tia Maria

1 Preheat the oven to 200°C/400°F/Gas 6. Lightly brush six 150ml/¼ pint/⅔ cup dariole moulds or mini pudding bowls with 25g/1oz/2 tbsp of the butter. Coat evenly with 50g/2oz of the grated chocolate.

2 Put the coffee in a bowl. Heat the milk until almost boiling and pour over the coffee. Leave for 5 minutes, then strain.

3 Melt the remaining butter in a pan. Stir in the flour and cocoa to make a roux. Cook for 1 minute, then add the coffee milk, stirring all the time to make a very thick sauce. Simmer for 2 minutes. Remove from the heat and stir in the egg yolks.

4 Cool for 5 minutes, then stir in the remaining chocolate. Whisk the egg whites until stiff, then whisk in the sugar. Fold half into the sauce to loosen, then fold in the remainder.

5 Spoon the mixture into the dariole moulds or bowls and place in a roasting pan. Pour in enough hot water to come two-thirds of the way up the sides of the tins.

6 Bake the soufflés for 15 minutes. Turn them out on to a baking tray and leave to cool completely. Before serving, spoon 15ml/1 tbsp of liqueur over each soufflé and reheat in the oven for 6–7 minutes. Serve with the remaining liqueur poured over.

French Soufflé Energy 543kcal/2256kJ; Protein 7.1g; Carbohydrate 35g, of which sugars 34.7g; Fat 42.3g, of which saturates 25g; Cholesterol 198mg; Calcium 80mg; Fibre 0.7g; Sodium 218mg.
Mocha Soufflé Energy 395kcal/1650kJ; Protein 7.4g; Carbohydrate 33.6g, of which sugars 28.1g; Fat 23.5g, of which saturates 10.9g; Cholesterol 127mg; Calcium 124mg; Fibre 0.9g; Sodium 191mg.

Rich Chocolate and Coffee Pudding

This heavenly dessert boasts a rich sponge topping with a luscious sauce underneath.

Serves 6

90g/3½oz/¾ cup plain (all-purpose) flour
10ml/2 tsp baking powder
pinch of salt
50g/2oz/¼ cup butter or margarine
25g/1oz plain (semisweet) chocolate, chopped into small pieces
115g/4oz/generous ½ cup caster (superfine) sugar
75ml/2½fl oz/⅓ cup milk
1.5ml/¼ tsp vanilla extract
whipped cream, to serve

For the topping

30ml/2 tbsp instant coffee powder or granules
325ml/11fl oz/1⅓ cups hot water
90g/3½oz/½ cup soft dark brown sugar
65g/2½oz/5 tbsp caster (superfine) sugar
30ml/2 tbsp unsweetened cocoa powder

1 Preheat the oven to 180°C/350°F/Gas 4. Grease a 23cm/9in square non-stick baking tin (pan).

2 Sift the flour, baking powder and salt into a small mixing bowl. Set aside.

3 Melt the butter or margarine, chocolate and caster sugar in a heatproof bowl set over a pan of simmering water, stirring occasionally. Remove the bowl from the heat.

4 Add the flour mixture and stir well. Stir in the milk and vanilla extract. Mix well, then pour into the prepared tin.

5 Make the topping. Dissolve the coffee in the water in a bowl. Allow to cool. Mix the brown sugar, caster sugar and cocoa powder in a bowl. Sprinkle the mixture over the pudding mixture in the tin.

6 Pour the coffee evenly over the surface. Bake for 40 minutes, or until the pudding is risen and set on top. The coffee mixture will have formed a delicious creamy sauce underneath. Serve immediately with whipped cream.

Steamed Chocolate and Fruit Pudding with Chocolate Syrup

Some things always turn out well, just like these wonderful little puddings. Dark, fluffy chocolate sponge with tangy cranberries and apple is served with a honeyed chocolate syrup.

Serves 4

butter or oil, for greasing
115g/4oz/½ cup muscovado (molasses) sugar
1 eating apple, peeled and cored
75g/3oz/¾ cup cranberries, thawed if frozen
115g/4oz/½ cup soft margarine
2 eggs
75g/3oz/⅔ cup plain (all-purpose) flour
2.5ml/½ tsp baking powder
45ml/3 tbsp unsweetened cocoa powder

For the chocolate syrup

115g/4oz plain (semisweet) chocolate, broken into squares
30ml/2 tbsp clear honey
15ml/1 tbsp unsalted (sweet) butter
2.5ml/½ tsp vanilla extract

1 Prepare a steamer or half fill a pan with water and bring to the boil. Grease four individual heatproof bowls and sprinkle each one with a little of the muscovado sugar to coat all over.

2 Dice the apple into a bowl. Add the cranberries and mix well. Divide the mixture equally among the prepared bowls.

3 Put the remaining sugar in a mixing bowl. Add the margarine, eggs, flour, baking powder and cocoa. Beat well until smooth.

4 Spoon the mixture on to the fruit, and cover each bowl with a double thickness of foil. Steam for 45 minutes, topping up the water if necessary, until the puddings are well risen and firm.

5 Make the syrup. Mix together the chocolate, honey, butter and vanilla in a small pan. Heat gently, stirring, until smooth.

6 Run a knife around the edge of each pudding to loosen it, then turn out on to individual plates. Serve immediately, with the chocolate syrup poured over the top.

Rich Pudding Energy 325kcal/1371kJ; Protein 3g; Carbohydrate 60.6g, of which sugars 50.5g; Fat 9.5g, of which saturates 5.8g; Cholesterol 19mg; Calcium 66mg; Fibre 1.1g; Sodium 107mg.
Fruit Pudding Energy 672kcal/2811kJ; Protein 8.7g; Carbohydrate 73.1g, of which sugars 57.3g; Fat 40.4g, of which saturates 13.9g; Cholesterol 105mg; Calcium 84mg; Fibre 3.2g; Sodium 366mg.

Chocolate, Date and Walnut Pudding

This tempting pudding is not steamed in the traditional way, but baked in the oven. The finished result is still completely irresistible.

Serves 4

25g/1oz/¼ cup chopped walnuts
25g/1oz/2 tbsp chopped dates
2 eggs, separated
5ml/1 tsp vanilla extract
30ml/2 tbsp golden caster (superfine) sugar
45ml/3 tbsp plain wholemeal (all-purpose whole-wheat) flour
15ml/1 tbsp unsweetened cocoa powder
30ml/2 tbsp skimmed milk

1 Preheat the oven to 180°C/350°F/Gas 4. Grease a 1.2 litre/2 pint/5 cup ovenproof bowl and line with baking parchment. Spoon in the walnuts and dates.

2 Mix the egg yolks, vanilla extract and sugar in a heatproof bowl. Place over a pan of hot water and whisk the mixture until thick and pale, then remove the bowl from the heat.

3 Sift the flour and cocoa over the mixture and fold in with a metal spoon. Stir in the milk, to soften the mixture. Whisk the egg whites to soft peaks, then gradually fold them into the pudding mixture.

4 Spoon the mixture over the walnuts and dates in the bowl and bake for 40–45 minutes, or until well risen and firm to the touch. Run a knife around the pudding to loosen it from the bowl, and then turn it out on to a plate and serve immediately.

Cook's Tips

• *Pudding fans will probably not be satisfied without custard to accompany this dessert. Why not serve a real custard, Crème Anglaise, made using cream, egg yolks, caster (superfine) sugar and a few drops of vanilla extract?*

• *If you wish, the cocoa can be omitted and the sponge mix flavoured with grated orange rind instead.*

Magic Chocolate Mud Cake

Guaranteed to be a big hit, this scrumptious dessert can be put together in no time at all.

Serves 4

50g/2oz/¼ cup butter, plus extra for greasing
90g/3½oz/¾ cup self-raising (self-rising) flour
5ml/1 tsp ground cinnamon
75ml/5 tbsp unsweetened cocoa powder
200g/7oz/1 cup light muscovado (brown) or demerara (raw) sugar
475ml/16fl oz/2 cups milk
crème fraîche, Greek (US strained plain) yogurt or vanilla ice cream, to serve

1 Preheat the oven to 180°C/350°F/Gas 4. Grease a 1.5 litre/2½ pint/6¼ cup ovenproof dish with butter. Place the dish on a baking sheet and set aside.

2 Sift the flour and ground cinnamon into a bowl. Sift in 15ml/1 tbsp of the cocoa and mix well.

3 Place the butter in a pan. Add 115g/4oz/½ cup of the sugar and 150ml/¼ pint/⅔ cup of the milk. Heat gently without boiling, stirring from time to time, until the butter has melted and all the sugar has completely dissolved. Remove the pan from the heat.

4 Stir in the flour mixture, mixing evenly. Pour the mixture into the prepared dish and level the surface.

5 Mix the remaining sugar and cocoa in a bowl, then sprinkle over the pudding mixture. Pour the remaining milk evenly over the pudding.

6 Bake for 45–50 minutes or until the sponge has risen to the top and is firm to the touch. Serve hot, with the crème fraîche, yogurt or ice cream.

Cook's Tip

A delicious sauce 'magically' appears beneath the sponge.

Date Pudding Energy 171kcal/716kJ; Protein 6.2g; Carbohydrate 19.5g, of which sugars 10.5g; Fat 8.2g, of which saturates 1.7g; Cholesterol 96mg; Calcium 55mg; Fibre 1.1g; Sodium 76mg.
Mud Cake Energy 480kcal/2025kJ; Protein 10g; Carbohydrate 77.6g, of which sugars 58.3g; Fat 16.7g, of which saturates 10.2g; Cholesterol 34mg; Calcium 227mg; Fibre 3g; Sodium 309mg.

Chocolate Chip and Banana Pudding

Hot and steamy, this superb light pudding tastes extra special when served with ready-made fresh chocolate sauce or custard.

Serves 4

200g/7oz/1¾ cups self-raising (self-rising) flour
75g/3oz/6 tbsp unsalted (sweet) butter or margarine
2 ripe bananas
75g/3oz/6 tbsp caster (superfine) sugar
60ml/4 tbsp milk
1 egg, beaten
60ml/4 tbsp plain (semisweet) chocolate chips or chopped chocolate
whipped cream and fresh chocolate sauce, to serve

1 Prepare a steamer or half fill a pan with water and bring to the boil. Grease a 1 litre/1¾ pint/4 cup ovenproof bowl.

2 Sift the flour into a bowl and rub in the butter or margarine until the mixture resembles breadcrumbs. Mash the bananas in a bowl. Stir them into the creamed mixture, with the sugar.

3 Whisk the milk with the egg in a bowl, then beat into the pudding mixture. Stir in the chocolate chips.

4 Spoon the mixture into the prepared bowl, cover closely with a double thickness of foil, and steam for 2 hours, topping up the water as required during cooking.

5 Run a knife around the top edge of the pudding to loosen it, then turn it out on to a warm serving dish. Serve hot, with chocolate sauce and a spoonful of whipped cream.

Cook's Tip

If you have a food processor, make a quick-mix version by processing all the ingredients, except the chocolate, until smooth. Then stir in the chocolate, spoon into the prepared bowl and finish as described in the recipe.

Chocolate Pudding with Rum Custard

With melting moments of chocolate in every mouthful, these little treats won't last long. The rum custard turns them into a more adult dessert; you could flavour the custard with vanilla or orange rind instead.

Serves 6

115g/4oz/½ cup butter, plus extra for greasing
115g/4oz/½ cup soft light brown sugar
2 eggs, beaten
drops of vanilla extract
45ml/3 tbsp unsweetened cocoa powder, sifted
115g/4oz/1 cup self-raising (self-rising) flour
75g/3oz plain (semisweet) chocolate, chopped
a little milk, warmed

For the rum custard

250ml/8fl oz/1 cup milk
15ml/1 tbsp caster (superfine) sugar
2 egg yolks
10ml/2 tsp cornflour (cornstarch)
30–45ml/2–3 tbsp rum (optional)

1 Lightly grease a 1.2 litre/2 pint/5 cup heatproof bowl or six individual dariole moulds. Cream the butter and sugar until pale and creamy. Gently blend in the eggs and the vanilla extract.

2 Sift together the cocoa powder and flour, and fold gently into the egg mixture with the chopped chocolate and sufficient milk to give a soft dropping consistency.

3 Spoon the mixture into the bowl or moulds, cover with buttered baking parchment and tie down.

4 Fill a pan with 2.5–5cm/1–2in water, place the puddings in the pan, cover with a lid and bring to the boil. Steam the large pudding for 1½–2 hours and the individual ones for 45–50 minutes, topping up with water if necessary. When firm, turn out on to warm plates.

5 Make the custard. Bring the milk and sugar to the boil. Whisk together the egg yolks and cornflour, then pour on the hot milk, whisking constantly. Return the mixture to the pan and stir while it comes back to the boil. Simmer gently as it thickens, stirring all the time. Remove from the heat and stir in the rum.

Banana Pudding Energy 528kcal/2220kJ; Protein 8.1g; Carbohydrate 79.3g, of which sugars 40.9g; Fat 22g, of which saturates 13g; Cholesterol 89mg; Calcium 222mg; Fibre 2.5g; Sodium 320mg.
Chocolate Pudding Energy 458kcal/1915kJ; Protein 8.3g; Carbohydrate 49g, of which sugars 31.5g; Fat 25.6g, of which saturates 14.5g; Cholesterol 186mg; Calcium 145mg; Fibre 1.8g; Sodium 302mg.

Chocolate Baked Alaska

Children will love the surprise of this classic dessert – hot meringue with chocolate sponge and ice-cold ice cream inside. Here's a variation on the classic version to try out.

Serves 3 to 4

3 large egg whites
150g/5oz/¾ cup caster (superfine) sugar
25g/1oz desiccated (dry unsweetened shredded) coconut
175–225g/6–8oz piece of ready-made chocolate cake
6 slices ripe, peeled pineapple
500ml/17fl oz/generous 2 cups vanilla ice cream, in a brick
a few cherries or figs, to decorate

1 Preheat the oven to 230°C/450°F/Gas 8. Whisk the egg whites in a grease-free bowl until stiff, then whisk in the sugar until the mixture is stiff and glossy. Fold in the coconut.

2 Slice the ready-made cake into two thick layers the same rectangular shape as the ice cream. Cut the pineapple into triangles or quarters, cutting it over the cake to catch any drips.

3 On a baking sheet, arrange the pineapple on top of one layer of cake. Place the ice cream on top of the fruit and then top with the second layer of cake.

4 Spread the meringue over the cake and ice cream, and bake in the oven for 5–7 minutes, or until turning golden. Serve immediately, topped with fruit.

Cook's Tip
Do not use soft-scoop ice cream for this dessert as it will soften too quickly.

Variation
For chocoholics, use chocolate ice cream in place of the vanilla.

Chocolate, Date and Almond Filo Coil

Experience the allure of the Middle East with this delectable dessert. Crisp filo pastry conceals a chocolate and rose water filling studded with dates and almonds.

Serves 6

275g/10oz filo pastry, thawed if frozen
50g/2oz/¼ cup butter, melted
icing (confectioners') sugar, unsweetened cocoa powder and ground cinnamon, for dusting

For the filling
75g/3oz/6 tbsp butter
115g/4oz dark (bittersweet) chocolate, broken up into pieces
115g/4oz/1⅓ cup ground almonds
115g/4oz/⅔ cup chopped dates
75g/3oz/⅔ cup icing (confectioners') sugar
10ml/2 tsp rose water
2.5ml/½ tsp ground cinnamon

1 Preheat the oven to 180°C/350°F/Gas 4. Grease a 22cm/8½in round cake tin (pan). To make the filling, melt the butter with the chocolate in a heatproof bowl set over a pan of simmering water, then remove from the heat and stir in the remaining ingredients to make a thick paste. Leave to cool.

2 Lay one sheet of filo on a flat surface and brush with melted butter. Lay a second sheet on top and brush with more butter.

3 Roll a handful of the chocolate and almond mixture into a long sausage shape and place along one long edge of the layered filo. Roll up the pastry tightly around the filling to make a roll.

4 Fit the filo roll in the cake tin, in such a way that it sits snugly against the outer edge. Make more filo rolls in the same way, adding them to the tin from the outside toward the centre, until the coil fills the tin.

5 Brush the coil with the remaining melted butter. Bake for 30–35 minutes or until the pastry is golden. Transfer to a serving plate. Serve the cake warm, dusted with icing sugar, cocoa and cinnamon.

Alaska Energy 667kcal/2808kJ; Protein 10.8g; Carbohydrate 104.6g, of which sugars 93.9g; Fat 25.7g, of which saturates 9.8g; Cholesterol 33mg; Calcium 215mg; Fibre 2.3g; Sodium 317mg.
Filo Coil Energy 543kcal/2267kJ; Protein 8.2g; Carbohydrate 55.4g, of which sugars 32.4g; Fat 33.6g, of which saturates 15g; Cholesterol 46mg; Calcium 108mg; Fibre 3.2g; Sodium 133mg.

Chocolate Almond Meringue Pie

This dreamy dessert offers a velvety chocolate filling on a light orange pastry case, topped with fluffy meringue.

Serves 6

175g/6oz/1 ½ cups plain (all-purpose) flour
50g/2oz/⅓ cup ground rice
150g/5oz/10 tbsp unsalted (sweet) butter
finely grated rind of 1 orange
1 egg yolk
flaked almonds and melted chocolate, to decorate

For the filling

150g/5oz plain (semisweet) chocolate, broken into squares
50g/2oz/¼ cup unsalted (sweet) butter, softened
75g/3oz/6 tbsp caster (superfine) sugar
10ml/2 tsp cornflour (cornstarch)
4 egg yolks
75g/3oz/¾ cup ground almonds

For the meringue

3 egg whites
150g/5oz/¾ cup caster (superfine) sugar

1 Sift the flour and ground rice into a bowl. Rub in the butter to resemble breadcrumbs. Stir in the orange rind. Add the egg yolk; bring the dough together. Roll out and use to line a 23cm/9in round flan tin (pan). Chill for 30 minutes.

2 Preheat the oven to 190°C/375°F/Gas 5. Prick the pastry base all over with a fork, cover with baking parchment, weighed down with baking beans, and bake blind for 10 minutes. Remove the pastry case from the oven; take out the baking beans and paper.

3 Make the filling. Melt the chocolate in a heatproof bowl over hot water. Cream the butter with the sugar in a bowl, then beat in the cornflour and egg yolks. Fold in the almonds, then the chocolate. Spread in the pastry case. Bake for 10 minutes more.

4 Make the meringue. Whisk the egg whites until stiff, then gradually add half the sugar. Fold in the remaining sugar. Spoon the meringue over the chocolate filling, lifting it up with the back of the spoon to form peaks. Reduce the oven temperature to 180°C/350°F/Gas 4 and bake the pie for 15–20 minutes or until the topping is pale gold. Serve, sprinkled with almonds and drizzled with melted chocolate.

Chocolate Pecan Pie

A delicious version of an American favourite, this pie is great for any occasion.

Serves 6

200g/7oz/1 ¾ cups plain (all-purpose) flour
75ml/5 tbsp caster (superfine) sugar
90g/3½oz/7 tbsp unsalted (sweet) butter, softened
1 egg, beaten
finely grated rind of 1 orange

For the filling

200g/7oz/¾ cup golden (light corn) syrup
45ml/3 tbsp light muscovado (brown) sugar
150g/5oz plain (semisweet) chocolate, chopped into small pieces
50g/2oz/¼ cup butter
3 eggs, beaten
5ml/1 tsp vanilla extract
175g/6oz/1 ½ cups shelled pecan nuts

1 Sift the flour into a bowl and stir in the sugar. Work in the butter evenly with your fingertips until combined.

2 Beat the egg and orange rind in a bowl, then stir into the mixture to make a firm dough. Add a little water if the mixture is too dry, and knead briefly.

3 Roll out the pastry on a lightly floured surface and use to line a deep, 20cm/8in loose-based flan tin (pan). Chill for about 30 minutes.

4 Preheat the oven to 180°C/350°F/Gas 4. Make the filling. Melt the syrup, sugar, chocolate and butter together in a small pan over a low heat.

5 Remove the pan from the heat and beat in the eggs and vanilla extract. Sprinkle the pecan nuts into the pastry case and carefully pour over the chocolate mixture.

6 Place the tin on a baking sheet and bake the pie for 50–60 minutes or until the filling is set.

7 Leave the pie in the tin for 10 minutes, then remove the tin's sides and transfer to a plate. Serve the pie on its own, or with a little single (light) cream.

Meringue Pie Energy 792kcal/3312kJ; Protein 11.4g; Carbohydrate 87g, of which sugars 56g; Fat 46.4g, of which saturates 23.5g; Cholesterol 241mg; Calcium 128mg; Fibre 2.6g; Sodium 248mg.
Pecan Pie Energy 843kcal/3524kJ; Protein 11.6g; Carbohydrate 90.8g, of which sugars 64.8g; Fat 50.8g, of which saturates 19.1g; Cholesterol 178mg; Calcium 112mg; Fibre 3g; Sodium 282mg.

Chocolate Soufflé Crêpes

These tasty pancakes hide a light soufflé filling inside.

Makes 12 crêpes

75g/3oz/¾ cup plain (all-purpose) flour
15ml/1 tbsp unsweetened cocoa powder
5ml/1 tsp caster (superfine) sugar
5ml/1 tsp ground cinnamon
pinch of salt
2 eggs
175ml/6fl oz/¾ cup milk
5ml/1 tsp vanilla extract
50g/2oz/4 tbsp unsalted (sweet) butter, melted
raspberries, pineapple and mint sprigs, to decorate

For the pineapple syrup

½ medium pineapple, peeled, cored and finely chopped
120ml/4fl oz/½ cup water
30ml/2 tbsp natural maple syrup
5ml/1 tsp cornflour (cornstarch)
½ cinnamon stick
30ml/2 tbsp rum

For the soufflé filling

250g/9oz dark (bittersweet) chocolate, chopped into small pieces
75ml/3fl oz/⅓ cup double (heavy) cream
3 eggs, separated
25g/1oz/2 tbsp caster (superfine) sugar

1 Place the ingredients for the syrup in a pan and simmer until thick. Discard the cinnamon. Cool, then chill.

2 Make the crêpes. Sift the flour, cocoa, sugar, cinnamon and salt together. Beat the eggs, milk and vanilla and stir into the mixture. Stir in half the butter and set aside for 1 hour. Butter a 20cm/8in crêpe pan and, when hot, pour in 45ml/3 tbsp of batter and cook over a medium heat for 1–2 minutes, then flip.

3 Make the filling. In a pan, stir the chocolate and cream until melted. In a bowl, beat the yolks with half the sugar until light. Add to the chocolate mixture. In another bowl, whisk the egg whites until soft peaks form. Whisk in the remaining sugar until stiff. Fold a little into the chocolate mixture, then fold in the rest.

4 Preheat the oven to 200°C/400°F/Gas 6. Spread a little filling on a crêpe. Fold in half over the mixture, then halve again. Place on a buttered baking sheet. When all crêpes are made, brush with butter and bake for 15–20 minutes, or until the filling has souffléd. Decorate with the fruits and mint and serve with the syrup.

Chocolate Chip Banana Pancakes

These tasty little pancake morsels will go down well with both children and adults alike.

Makes 16

2 ripe bananas
2 eggs
200ml/7fl oz/scant 1 cup milk
150g/5oz/1¼ cups self-raising (self-rising) flour, sifted
25g/1oz/⅓ cup ground almonds
15g/½oz/1 tbsp caster (superfine) sugar
pinch of salt
15ml/1 tbsp plain (semisweet) chocolate chips
butter, for frying
50g/2oz/½ cup toasted flaked (sliced) almonds

For the topping

150ml/¼ pint/⅔ cup double (heavy) cream
15g/½oz/1 tbsp icing (confectioners') sugar

1 Mash the bananas in a bowl. Beat in the eggs and half the milk. Mix in the flour, ground almonds, sugar and salt. Add the remaining milk and the chocolate chips.

2 Stir the mixture well until it makes a thick batter. Heat a knob (pat) of butter in a non-stick frying pan. Spoon the pancake mixture into the pan in heaps, allowing room for them to spread. When the pancakes are lightly browned underneath and bubbling on top, flip them over to cook the other side. Slide on to a plate and keep hot. Make more pancakes in the same way.

3 Make the topping. Pour the cream into a bowl. Add the icing sugar to sweeten it slightly, and whip to soft peaks. Spoon the cream on to the pancakes and decorate with flaked almonds. Serve immediately.

Variations

- *You could add sliced banana, tossed in lemon juice, to the topping to enhance the banana flavour of the pancakes.*
- *Use yogurt as a low-fat alternative to cream, if you prefer.*

Soufflé Crêpes Energy 273kcal/1143kJ; Protein 5.2g; Carbohydrate 27.7g, of which sugars 22.7g; Fat 16g, of which saturates 9g; Cholesterol 100mg; Calcium 60mg; Fibre 1.3g; Sodium 79mg.
Banana Pancakes Energy 192kcal/798kJ; Protein 3.4g; Carbohydrate 13.7g, of which sugars 6.3g; Fat 14.1g, of which saturates 7.1g; Cholesterol 51mg; Calcium 70mg; Fibre 0.8g; Sodium 89mg.

Chocolate and Orange Scotch Pancakes

Fabulous mini pancakes in a rich orange liqueur sauce.

Serves 4

115g/4oz/1 cup self-raising (self-rising) flour
30ml/2 tbsp unsweetened cocoa powder
2 eggs
50g/2oz plain (semisweet) chocolate, broken into squares
200ml/7fl oz/scant 1 cup milk
finely grated rind of 1 orange
30ml/2 tbsp orange juice
butter or oil, for frying
60ml/4 tbsp chocolate curls, to decorate

For the sauce

2 large oranges
25g/1oz/2 tbsp unsalted (sweet) butter
40g/1½oz/3 tbsp light muscovado (brown) sugar
250ml/8fl oz/1 cup crème fraîche
30ml/2 tbsp orange liqueur

1 Sift the flour and cocoa into a bowl and make a well in the centre. Add the eggs and beat well, gradually incorporating the surrounding dry ingredients to make a smooth batter.

2 Mix the chocolate and milk in a heavy pan. Heat gently until the chocolate has melted, then beat into the batter until smooth and bubbly. Stir in the grated orange rind and juice.

3 Heat a large frying pan. Grease with butter or oil. Drop large spoonfuls of batter on to the hot surface. Cook over a medium heat. When the pancakes are lightly browned underneath and bubbling on top, flip them over to cook the other side. Slide on to a plate and keep hot, then make more in the same way.

4 Make the sauce. Grate the rind of one of the oranges into a bowl and set aside. Peel both oranges, taking care to remove all the pith, then slice the flesh fairly thinly. Heat the butter and sugar in a wide, shallow pan over a low heat, stirring until the sugar dissolves. Stir in the crème fraîche and heat gently.

5 Add the pancakes and orange slices to the sauce, heat gently for 1–2 minutes, then spoon on the liqueur. Sprinkle with the reserved orange rind and chocolate curls.

Chocolate Crêpes with Plums and Port

The crêpes, filling and sauce for this recipe can be made in advance and assembled at the last minute.

Serves 6

50g/2oz plain (semisweet) chocolate, broken into squares
200ml/7fl oz/scant 1 cup milk
120ml/4fl oz/½ cup single (light) cream
30ml/2 tbsp unsweetened cocoa powder
115g/4oz/1 cup plain (all-purpose) flour
2 eggs

For the filling

500g/1¼lb red or golden plums
50g/2oz/¼ cup caster (superfine) sugar
30ml/2 tbsp water
30ml/2 tbsp port
oil, for frying
175g/6oz/¾ cup crème fraîche

For the sauce

150g/5oz plain (semisweet) chocolate, broken into squares
175ml/6fl oz/¾ cup double (heavy) cream
30ml/2 tbsp port

1 Place the chocolate and milk in a heavy pan. Heat gently until the chocolate dissolves. Pour into a blender or food processor and add the cream, cocoa, flour and eggs. Process until smooth. Turn into a jug (pitcher) and chill for 30 minutes.

2 Meanwhile, make the filling. Halve and stone (pit) the plums. Place in a pan with the sugar and water. Bring to the boil, then lower the heat, cover and simmer for about 10 minutes, or until the plums are tender. Stir in the port and simmer for a further 30 seconds. Remove from the heat and keep warm.

3 Heat a crêpe pan, grease with oil, then pour in enough batter to cover the base, swirling to coat it evenly. Cook until the crêpe is set, then flip to cook the other side. Slide on to baking parchment, then cook about ten more crêpes in the same way.

4 Make the sauce. Put the chocolate and cream in a pan. Heat gently, stirring until smooth. Add the port and stir for 1 minute. Divide the plums between the crêpes, add a spoonful of crème fraîche to each and roll up. Serve with the sauce spooned over.

Scotch Pancakes Energy 752kcal/3131kJ; Protein 12.1g; Carbohydrate 58.1g, of which sugars 35.5g; Fat 53.2g, of which saturates 27g; Cholesterol 185mg; Calcium 282mg; Fibre 3.9g; Sodium 304mg.
Chocolate Crêpes Energy 867kcal/3604kJ; Protein 10.6g; Carbohydrate 57.4g, of which sugars 41.7g; Fat 67g, of which saturates 36.7g; Cholesterol 184mg; Calcium 175mg; Fibre 3.4g; Sodium 115mg.

Baked Ravioli with Chocolate and Ricotta Filling

These sweet ravioli have a wonderful chocolate and ricotta cheese filling.

Serves 4

175g/6oz/¾ cup ricotta cheese
50g/2oz/¼ cup caster (superfine) sugar
4ml/¾ tsp vanilla extract
small egg, beaten, plus 1 egg yolk
15ml/1 tbsp mixed glacé (candied) fruits
25g/1oz dark (bittersweet) chocolate, finely chopped

For the pastry

225g/8oz/2 cups plain (all-purpose) flour
65g/2½oz/5 tbsp caster (superfine) sugar
90g/3½oz/7 tbsp butter, diced
1 egg
5ml/1 tsp finely grated chocolate

1 Make the pastry. Place the flour and sugar in a food processor and gradually process in the butter. Keep the motor running while you add the egg and lemon rind to make a dough. Transfer the dough to a sheet of clear film (plastic wrap), cover with another sheet of film and flatten into a round. Chill.

2 Press the ricotta through a strainer into a bowl. Stir in the sugar, vanilla, egg yolk, glacé fruits and dark chocolate.

3 Bring the pastry back to room temperature. Divide in half and roll each between clear film to make rectangles measuring 15 × 56cm/6 × 22in. Preheat the oven to 180°C/350°F/Gas 4.

4 Arrange heaped tablespoonfuls of the filling in two rows along one of the pastry strips, leaving a 2.5cm/1in margin around each strip. Brush the pastry between the mounds of filling with beaten egg. Place the second strip of pastry on top and press down between each mound of filling to seal.

5 Use a 6cm/2½in plain pastry (cookie) cutter to cut around each mound of filling to make small ravioli. Gently pinch each ravioli with your fingertips to seal the edges. Place on a greased baking sheet and bake for 15 minutes, or until they turn golden brown. Serve warm, sprinkled with chocolate.

Luxury Dark Chocolate Ravioli

Serve this special treat with cream and grated chocolate.

Serves 4

175g/6oz/1½ cups plain (all-purpose) flour
25g/1oz/¼ cup unsweetened cocoa powder
salt
30ml/2 tbsp icing (confectioners') sugar
2 large eggs, beaten
15ml/1 tbsp olive oil

For the filling

175g/6oz white chocolate, chopped
350g/12oz/1½ cups cream cheese
1 egg, plus 1 beaten egg to seal

1 Make the pasta. Sift the flour with the cocoa, salt and icing sugar on to a work surface. Make a well in the centre and pour in the eggs and oil. Mix together with your fingers. Knead until smooth. Cover and rest for at least 30 minutes.

2 For the filling, melt the white chocolate in a heatproof bowl placed over a pan of simmering water. Cool slightly. Beat the cream cheese in a bowl, then beat in the chocolate and egg. Spoon into a piping (pastry) bag fitted with a plain nozzle.

3 Cut the dough in half and wrap one portion in clear film (plastic wrap). Roll the pasta out thinly to a rectangle on a lightly floured surface, or use a pasta machine. Cover with a clean damp dish towel and repeat with the remaining pasta.

4 Pipe small mounds (about 5ml/1 tsp) of filling in rows, spacing them at 4cm/1½in intervals across one piece of the dough. Brush the dough between the mounds with beaten egg.

5 Using a rolling pin, lift the remaining sheet of pasta over the dough with the filling. Press down firmly between the pockets of filling, pushing out any trapped air. Cut the filled chocolate pasta into rounds with a ravioli cutter or sharp knife. Transfer to a floured dish towel. Leave for 1 hour to dry out.

6 Bring a frying pan of water to the boil and add the ravioli a few at a time, stirring to prevent sticking. Simmer gently for 3–5 minutes, remove with a perforated spoon and serve.

Baked Ravioli Energy 628kcal/2636kJ; Protein 13.1g; Carbohydrate 81.4g, of which sugars 38.5g; Fat 30.1g, of which saturates 17.7g; Cholesterol 162mg; Calcium 119mg; Fibre 2.1g; Sodium 186mg.
Luxury Ravioli Energy 894kcal/3722kJ; Protein 16.2g; Carbohydrate 68.1g, of which sugars 34g; Fat 63.9g, of which saturates 36.5g; Cholesterol 226mg; Calcium 299mg; Fibre 2.1g; Sodium 424mg.

Fruit Kebabs with Chocolate and Marshmallow Fondue

Children love these barbecued kebab and fondue treats – and with supervision they will happily help you to make them too.

Serves 4

2 bananas
2 kiwi fruit
12 strawberries
15ml/1 tbsp melted butter
15ml/1 tbsp lemon juice
5ml/1 tsp ground cinnamon

For the fondue
225g/8oz plain (semisweet) chocolate
100ml/4fl oz/½ cup single (light) cream
8 marshmallows
2.5ml/½ tsp vanilla extract

1 Peel the bananas and cut each into six thick chunks. Peel the kiwi fruit thinly and quarter them. Thread the bananas, kiwi fruit and strawberries on to four wooden or bamboo skewers.

2 Mix together the butter, lemon juice and cinnamon and brush the mixture over the fruits.

3 Prepare the fondue. Place the plain chocolate, cream and marshmallows in a small pan and heat gently on the barbecue, without boiling, stirring constantly until the mixture has melted and is smooth.

4 Cook the kebabs on the barbecue for 2–3 minutes, turning once, or until golden. Stir the vanilla extract into the fondue and serve it with the kebabs.

Cook's Tips
- *These kebabs taste great straight from the barbecue but if the weather is bad they can easily be cooked under a hot grill (broiler) indoors.*
- *Soak wooden or bamboo skewers in water for 10 minutes before threading with the fruit to avoid them being burned while on the barbecue.*

Chocolate Fruit Fondue

This particular version of a sweet fondue makes a fun dessert that also looks extremely attractive and is appealing to all ages. Guests will enjoy skewering their favourite tropical fruits on to long forks, then dipping them into swirls of decadent hot chocolate fondue.

Serves 6–8

16 fresh strawberries
4 rings fresh pineapple, cut into wedges
2 small nectarines, stoned (pitted) and cut into wedges
1 kiwi fruit, halved and thickly sliced
small bunch of black seedless grapes
2 bananas, chopped
1 small eating apple, cored and cut into wedges
lemon juice, for brushing

For the fondue
225g/8oz plain (semisweet) chocolate
15g/½oz/1 tbsp butter
150ml/¼ pint/⅔ cup single (light) cream
45ml/3 tbsp Irish cream liqueur
15ml/1 tbsp chopped pistachio nuts

1 Arrange the fruit on a serving platter and brush the banana and apple pieces with a little lemon juice. Cover and chill.

2 Place the chocolate, butter, cream and liqueur in a bowl over a pan of simmering water. Stir until smooth.

3 Pour into a warmed serving bowl and sprinkle with the pistachio nuts.

4 To eat, guests skewer the fruits on to forks, then dip them into the hot sauce.

Variation
Other delicious dippers for this fondue include: cubes of sponge cake; sweet biscuits (cookies) such as amaretti; miniature marshmallows; ready-to-eat dried fruit such as apricots; crêpes torn into pieces; and popcorn.

Fruit Kebabs Energy 442kcal/1853kJ; Protein 5.1g; Carbohydrate 57.5g, of which sugars 53.7g; Fat 22.9g, of which saturates 13.9g; Cholesterol 27mg; Calcium 59mg; Fibre 2.7g; Sodium 42mg.
Fruit Fondue Energy 305kcal/1282kJ; Protein 3.6g; Carbohydrate 39.7g, of which sugars 38.9g; Fat 15.2g, of which saturates 8.1g; Cholesterol 16mg; Calcium 51mg; Fibre 2.7g; Sodium 37mg.

Prune Beignets in Chocolate Sauce

Combining soft-textured prunes with a crisp batter coating works brilliantly. The rich chocolate sauce is the perfect finishing touch.

Serves 4

75g/3oz/⅔ cup plain (all-purpose) flour
45ml/3 tbsp ground almonds
45ml/3 tbsp oil or melted butter
1 egg white
60ml/4 tbsp water
oil, for deep frying
175g/6oz/1 cup ready-to-eat pitted prunes
45ml/3 tbsp vanilla sugar
15ml/1 tbsp unsweetened cocoa powder

For the sauce

200g/7oz milk chocolate, chopped into small pieces
120ml/4fl oz/½ cup crème fraîche
30ml/2 tbsp Armagnac or brandy

1 Make the sauce. Melt the chocolate in a bowl over a pan of hot water. Remove from the heat, stir in the crème fraîche until smooth, then add the Armagnac or brandy. Replace the bowl over the water, off the heat, so that the sauce stays warm.

2 Beat the flour, almonds, oil or butter and egg white in a bowl, then beat in enough of the water to make a thick batter.

3 Heat the oil for deep frying to 180°C/350°F or until a cube of dried bread browns in 30–45 seconds. Dip the prunes into the batter and fry a few at a time until the beignets rise to the surface and are golden brown. Remove each batch of beignets with a slotted spoon, drain on kitchen paper and keep hot.

4 Mix the vanilla sugar and cocoa in a bowl or stout paper bag, add the drained beignets and toss well to coat. Serve in individual bowls, with the chocolate sauce poured over the top.

Cook's Tip
Vanilla sugar is available from good food stores, but it's easy to make your own: simply store a vanilla pod in a jar of sugar for a few weeks until the sugar has taken on the vanilla flavour.

Pears in Chocolate Fudge Blankets

This dessert consists of warm poached pears coated in a rich chocolate fudge sauce – who could resist such a treat?

Serves 6

6 ripe eating pears
30ml/2 tbsp fresh lemon juice
75g/3oz/scant ½ cup caster (superfine) sugar
300ml/½ pint/1¼ cups water
1 cinnamon stick

For the sauce

200ml/7fl oz/scant 1 cup double (heavy) cream
150g/5oz/scant 1 cup light muscovado (brown) sugar
25g/1oz/2 tbsp unsalted (sweet) butter
60ml/4 tbsp golden (light corn) syrup
120ml/4fl oz/½ cup milk
200g/7oz plain (semisweet) chocolate, broken into squares

1 Peel the pears thinly, leaving the stalks on. Scoop out the cores from the base. Brush the cut surfaces with lemon juice to prevent browning.

2 Place the sugar and water in a large pan. Heat gently until the sugar dissolves. Add the pears and cinnamon stick with any remaining lemon juice, and, if necessary, a little more water, so that the pears are almost covered.

3 Bring to the boil, then lower the heat, cover the pan and simmer the pears gently for 15–20 minutes.

4 Meanwhile, make the sauce. Place the cream, sugar, butter, golden syrup and milk in a heavy pan. Heat gently until the sugar has dissolved and the butter and syrup have melted, then bring to the boil. Boil, stirring constantly, for about 5 minutes or until thick and smooth.

5 Remove the pan from the heat and stir in the chocolate, a few squares at a time, stirring until it has all melted.

6 Using a slotted spoon, transfer the poached pears to a dish. Keep hot. Boil the syrup rapidly to reduce to 45–60ml/3–4 tbsp. Remove the cinnamon stick and gently stir the syrup into the chocolate sauce. Serve the pears with the sauce spooned over.

Prune Beignets Energy 727kcal/3039kJ; Protein 11.3g; Carbohydrate 71.7g, of which sugars 56.5g; Fat 44.1g, of which saturates 24.2g; Cholesterol 69mg; Calcium 209mg; Fibre 4.8g; Sodium 176mg.
Pears in Blankets Energy 613kcal/2570kJ; Protein 3.6g; Carbohydrate 84.8g, of which sugars 84.5g; Fat 31.2g, of which saturates 19.1g; Cholesterol 58mg; Calcium 90mg; Fibre 4.1g; Sodium 77mg.

Poached Pear Sundae with Chocolate

This is a classic combination of poached dessert pears served with ice cream and a hot chocolate sauce. As a variation, try poaching the pears with white or red wine or a flavoured liqueur.

Serves 4

4 firm dessert pears, peeled
250g/9oz/1¼ cups caster (superfine) sugar
600ml/1 pint/2½ cups water
500ml/17fl oz/2¼ cups vanilla ice cream

For the chocolate sauce
250g/9oz good-quality dark (bittersweet) chocolate (minimum 70 per cent cocoa solids)
40g/1½oz unsalted (sweet) butter
5ml/1 tsp vanilla extract
75ml/5 tbsp double (heavy) cream

1 Cut the pears in half lengthways and remove the core. Place the sugar and water in a large pan and gently heat until the sugar has dissolved completely.

2 Add the pear halves to the pan, then simmer for 20 minutes, or until the pears are tender but not falling apart. Lift out of the sugar syrup with a slotted spoon and leave to cool.

3 To make the chocolate sauce, break the chocolate into small pieces and put into a pan. Add the butter and 30ml/2 tbsp water. Heat gently over a low heat, without stirring, until the chocolate has melted.

4 Add the vanilla extract and cream, and mix gently to combine. Place a scoop of ice cream into each of four glasses.

5 Add two cooled pear halves to each and pour over the hot chocolate sauce. Serve immediately.

Variation
Like apples, there are two types of pear: dessert varieties and those that need cooking. Ensure that you use firm ones, as they will hold their shape when poached, rather than turning to mush.

Bitter Chocolate Fondue with Rosemary and Vanilla Poached Pears

Vanilla-scented poached pears and scoops of ice cream are dipped into a rich chocolate fondue for this splendid dessert. The sprigs of rosemary add a herby flavour.

Serves 4–6

200g/7oz dark (bittersweet) chocolate, broken into pieces
75ml/2½fl oz/⅓ cup strong black coffee
75g/3oz/scant ⅓ cup soft light brown sugar
120ml/4fl oz/½ cup double (heavy) cream
small, firm scoops of vanilla ice cream, to serve

For the poached pears
juice of 1 lemon
90g/3½oz/½ cup vanilla caster (superfine) sugar
1–2 fresh rosemary sprigs
12–18 small pears, or 4–6 large pears

1 To poach the pears, put the lemon juice, sugar, rosemary sprigs and 300ml/½ pint/1¼ cups water in a pan large enough to accommodate the pears all in one layer. Bring to the boil, stirring until the sugar dissolves in the water.

2 Peel the pears, and halve the large ones, if using, but leave the stalks intact. Add to the hot syrup and spoon over to cover.

3 Cook for 5–10 minutes, depending on size and ripeness, spooning the syrup over them and turning frequently, until they are just tender. Transfer to a serving plate, then remove the rosemary sprigs from the syrup. Stir about 15–30ml/1–2 tbsp of the rosemary leaves into the syrup and then leave to cool.

4 Put the chocolate in a heatproof bowl over a pan of barely simmering water. Add the coffee and sugar and heat, without stirring, until the chocolate is melted. Stir in the cream and heat gently. Transfer the fondue to a fondue pot and place on a burner set at a low heat at the table.

5 Serve the pears and syrup together with the vanilla ice cream to dip into the hot chocolate fondue.

Poached Pear Energy 1014kcal/4255kJ; Protein 8.8g; Carbohydrate 145.1g, of which sugars 143.2g; Fat 46.7g, of which saturates 29.6g; Cholesterol 81mg; Calcium 206mg; Fibre 4.9g; Sodium 152mg.
Bitter Fondue Energy 464kcal/1949kJ; Protein 2.8g; Carbohydrate 71.9g, of which sugars 71.6g; Fat 20.3g, of which saturates 12.3g; Cholesterol 29mg; Calcium 59mg; Fibre 5.6g; Sodium 15mg.

Vanilla Poached Pears with Choc-dusted Cappuccino Sauce

Served with a bubbly espresso sauce and finished with a dusting of chocolate, these vanilla-scented pears make a light, elegant dessert.

Serves 6

1 vanilla pod
150g/5oz/¾ cup sugar
400ml/14fl oz/1⅔ cups water
6 slightly underripe pears
juice of ½ lemon

For the cappuccino sauce
3 egg yolks
25g/1oz/2 tbsp caster (superfine) sugar
50ml/2fl oz/¼ cup brewed espresso coffee
50ml/2fl oz/¼ cup single (light) cream
10ml/2 tsp drinking chocolate
2.5ml/½ tsp ground cinnamon

1 Split the vanilla pod lengthways and scrape out the black seeds into a large pan. Add the split pod, sugar and water. Heat gently until the sugar has completely dissolved.

2 Meanwhile, peel and halve the pears, then rub with lemon juice. Scoop out the cores with a melon baller or teaspoon. Add the pears to the syrup and pour in extra water to cover.

3 Cut out a circle of baking parchment and cover the top of the pears. Bring to a light boil, cover the pan with a lid and simmer for 15 minutes, or until tender. Transfer the pears to a serving bowl. Bring the syrup to a rapid boil and cook for 15 minutes, or until reduced by half.

4 Strain the syrup over the pears and leave to cool. Cover with clear film (plastic wrap) and chill for several hours. Allow to come back to room temperature before serving.

5 Make the sauce. Whisk the egg yolks, sugar, coffee and cream in a heatproof bowl over a pan of simmering water until thick and frothy. Remove from the heat and whisk for 2–3 minutes.

6 Arrange the pears on plates and pour sauce over each. Mix the drinking chocolate and cinnamon and dust over the sauce.

Pear Tartlets with Chocolate Sauce

Pears go perfectly with puffy golden pastry, complemented by a rich, warm chocolate sauce.

Serves 6

3 firm pears, peeled
450ml/¾ pint/scant 2 cups water
strip of thinly pared orange rind
1 vanilla pod (bean)
1 bay leaf
50g/2oz/¼ cup sugar
350g/12oz puff pastry
40g/1½oz/⅓ cup unsweetened cocoa powder
75ml/5 tbsp double (heavy) cream
15g/½oz/1 tbsp butter, softened
15ml/1 tbsp soft light brown sugar
25g/1oz/¼ cup walnuts, chopped
1 egg, beaten
15g/½oz/1 tbsp caster (superfine) sugar

1 Cut the pears in half and scoop out just the cores. Put the water in a pan with the orange rind, vanilla pod, bay leaf and sugar. Bring to the boil, stirring well. Add the pears and water to cover. Cover and cook gently for 15 minutes, or until just tender. Remove the pears and set aside to cool. Reserve the syrup.

2 Meanwhile, roll out the pastry and cut out six pear shapes, slightly larger than the pear halves. Place the pastry shapes on greased baking sheets and chill for 30 minutes.

3 Remove the rind, vanilla pod and bay leaf from the syrup, then return the syrup to the heat and boil for 10 minutes. Blend the cocoa powder with 60ml/4 tbsp cold water in a separate pan.

4 Stir a large spoonful of the syrup into the cocoa paste, then whisk the paste into the syrup. Boil until reduced to about 150ml/¼ pint/⅔ cup. Remove the pan from the heat and add the cream to the syrup. Stir well.

5 Preheat the oven to 200°C/400°F/Gas 6. Mix together the butter, sugar and walnuts. and spoon a little of the mixture into each cavity. Brush the pastries with beaten egg. Put a pear half, filled side down, in the centre of each pastry and sprinkle with sugar. Bake for 12 minutes, or until the pastry has puffed up and is golden brown. Drizzle with the warm chocolate sauce.

Poached Pears Energy 228kcal/963kJ; Protein 2.4g; Carbohydrate 47g, of which sugars 47g; Fat 4.6g, of which saturates 1.9g; Cholesterol 105mg; Calcium 52mg; Fibre 3.3g; Sodium 17mg.
Pear Tartlets Energy 443kcal/1847kJ; Protein 6.7g; Carbohydrate 44.2g, of which sugars 22.5g; Fat 28.4g, of which saturates 6.8g; Cholesterol 54mg; Calcium 73mg; Fibre 2.6g; Sodium 277mg.

Chocolate Orange Fondue

This liqueur fondue goes with any fresh fruits.

Serves 4–6

225g/8oz plain (semisweet) chocolate, chopped into pieces
300ml/½ pint/1¼ cups double (heavy) cream
30ml/2 tbsp Grand Marnier
25g/1oz/2 tbsp butter, diced
cherries, strawberries, sliced bananas, mandarin segments and cubes of sponge cake, for dipping

1 Combine the chocolate, cream and Grand Marnier in a fondue pan or small pan. Heat until melted, stirring frequently. Stir the butter into the fondue until melted. Place the fondue pot or pan over a lighted spirit burner.

2 Arrange the fruit and cake on a plate. Guests spear the items of their choice on fondue forks and swirl them in the dip until coated. Anyone who loses his or her dipper pays a forfeit.

Hot Chocolate Zabaglione

This is a delicious twist on the classic Italian dessert.

Serves 6

6 egg yolks
150g/5oz/⅔ cup caster (superfine) sugar
45ml/3 tbsp unsweetened cocoa powder
200ml/7fl oz/scant 1 cup Marsala
unsweetened cocoa powder or icing (confectioners') sugar, for dusting

1 Whisk the egg yolks and sugar in a heatproof bowl over a pan of simmering until pale and all the sugar has dissolved.

2 Add the cocoa and Marsala, then place the bowl back over the simmering water. Whisk until the mixture is thick and foamy.

3 Pour the mixture into tall heatproof glasses, dust with cocoa powder or sugar and serve with chocolate cinnamon tuiles or amaretti biscuits.

Peachy Chocolate Bake

A sublime combination of peaches and chocolate, this lightweight baked dessert is guaranteed to be popular with everyone – and it has the added bonus of being easy to make. For smart presentation, drizzle cream or yogurt over each serving and sprinkle lightly with chocolate powder.

Serves 6

200g/7oz dark (bittersweet) chocolate, chopped into pieces
115g/4oz/½ cup unsalted (sweet) butter, plus extra for greasing
4 eggs, separated
115g/4oz/generous ½ cup caster (superfine) sugar
425g/15oz can peach slices, drained
whipped cream or Greek (US strained plain) yogurt, to serve

1 Preheat the oven to 160°C/325°F/Gas 3. Butter a wide ovenproof dish. Melt the chocolate with the butter in a heatproof bowl over barely simmering water, then remove from the heat.

2 Whisk the egg yolks with the sugar until thick and pale. In a clean, grease-free bowl, whisk the whites until stiff.

3 Beat the melted chocolate into the egg yolk mixture. Stir in a large spoonful of the egg whites, then gently fold in the remaining whites.

4 Fold the peach slices into the mixture, then turn into the prepared dish. Bake for 35–40 minutes or until risen and just firm. Serve hot with cream or yogurt.

Variations

- *Pears also taste delicious with chocolate, and canned pears can be used very successfully in this recipe, instead of the canned peaches.*
- *During the summer months, try using very ripe fresh peaches or a mix of soft berries instead of the canned fruit.*

Fondue Energy 470kcal/1949kJ; Protein 2.7g; Carbohydrate 24.7g, of which sugars 24.4g; Fat 40.8g, of which saturates 25.2g; Cholesterol 80mg; Calcium 38mg; Fibre 0.9g; Sodium 39mg.
Zabaglione Energy 235kcal/989kJ; Protein 4.5g; Carbohydrate 31g, of which sugars 30.1g; Fat 7.1g, of which saturates 2.5g; Cholesterol 202mg; Calcium 48mg; Fibre 0.9g; Sodium 83mg.
Peachy Bake Energy 465kcal/1942kJ; Protein 6.5g; Carbohydrate 48.2g, of which sugars 47.9g; Fat 28.8g, of which saturates 16.6g; Cholesterol 170mg; Calcium 47mg; Fibre 1.4g; Sodium 175mg.

Chocolate Amaretti Peaches

A delicious dish of peaches stuffed with chocolate. This is a simple dessert but nonetheless one that is simply bursting with Italian style and flavour.

Serves 4

115g/4oz amaretti, crushed
50g/2oz plain (semisweet) chocolate, chopped
finely grated rind of ½ orange
15ml/1 tbsp clear honey
1.5ml/¼ tsp ground cinnamon
1 egg white, lightly beaten
4 firm ripe peaches
150ml/¼ pint/⅔ cup white wine
15g/½oz/1 tbsp caster (superfine) sugar
whipped cream, to serve

1 Preheat the oven to 190°C/375°F/Gas 5. Mix together the crushed amaretti, chopped chocolate, orange rind, honey and cinnamon in a bowl. Add the beaten egg white and stir to bind the mixture.

2 Halve the peaches, remove the stones (pits) and fill the cavities with the chocolate mixture, mounding it up slightly.

3 Arrange the stuffed peaches in a lightly buttered, shallow ovenproof dish that will just hold the peaches comfortably in a single layer.

4 Mix the wine and sugar in a jug (pitcher). Pour the wine mixture around the peaches.

5 Bake the peaches for 30–40 minutes, or until they are tender when tested with a metal skewer and the filling has turned a golden colour.

6 Serve immediately with a little cooking juice spooned over. Accompany with cream.

Cook's Tip
To stone (pit) peaches, halve them and twist the two halves apart, then lever out the stone (pit) with the point of a knife.

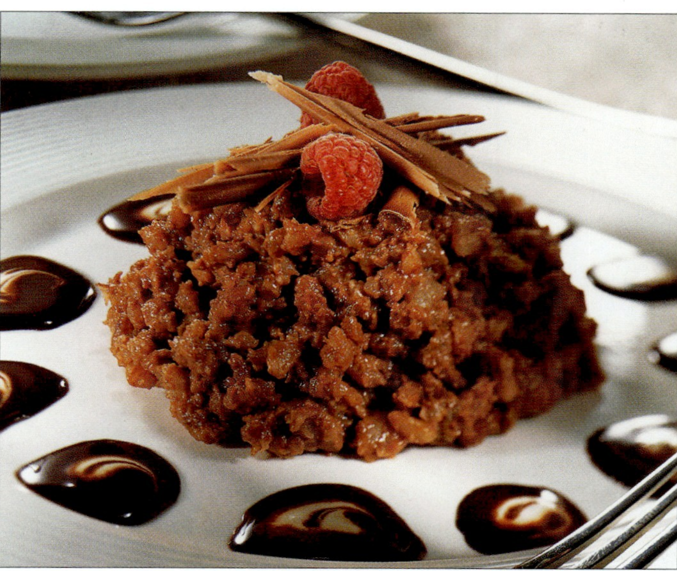

Chocolate Risotto

If you've never tasted a sweet risotto, there's a treat in store. Chocolate risotto is delectable, and children of all ages love it.

Serves 4–6

175g/6oz/scant 1 cup risotto rice
600ml/1 pint/2½ cups milk
75g/3oz plain (semisweet) chocolate, broken into pieces
25g/1oz/2 tbsp butter
about 50g/2oz/¼ cup caster (superfine) sugar
pinch of ground cinnamon
60ml/4 tbsp double (heavy) cream
fresh raspberries and chocolate curls, to decorate
chocolate sauce, to serve

1 Put the rice in a heavy non-stick pan. Pour in the milk and bring to the boil over a low to medium heat. Reduce the heat to the lowest setting and simmer the rice very gently for about 20 minutes, stirring occasionally, until the rice is very soft.

2 Add the chocolate pieces, butter and sugar to the pan. Cook, stirring all the time over a very gentle heat for 1–2 minutes, until the chocolate has melted.

3 Remove the pan from the heat and add the ground cinnamon and the double cream to the pan. Mix thoroughly until well combined. Cover the pan and leave to stand for a few minutes.

4 Spoon the risotto into individual dishes or dessert plates, and decorate with fresh raspberries and chocolate curls. Serve with chocolate sauce.

Cook's Tips
• Ensure that you use the plump Italian risotto rice for this recipe, otherwise it will not work as well. Look out for varieties called arborio or carnaroli.
• Stirring the rice frequently helps it to release the starch contained inside the grains, which gives this dish its delicious creamy texture.

Amaretti Peaches Energy 282kcal/1190kJ; Protein 4.1g; Carbohydrate 47g, of which sugars 34.4g; Fat 7.4g, of which saturates 3.8g; Cholesterol 1mg; Calcium 56mg; Fibre 2.4g; Sodium 117mg.
Risotto Energy 348kcal/1451kJ; Protein 6.3g; Carbohydrate 44.6g, of which sugars 21.2g; Fat 16.3g, of which saturates 10.1g; Cholesterol 37mg; Calcium 138mg; Fibre 0.3g; Sodium 72mg.

Double Chocolate Snowball

This is an ideal dish to make as a party dessert because it can be prepared ahead and decorated on the day.

Serves 12–14

350g/12oz plain (semisweet) chocolate, chopped
285g/10½oz/1½ cups caster (superfine) sugar
275g/10oz/1¼ cups unsalted (sweet) butter, diced
8 eggs
50ml/2fl oz/¼ cup orange-flavoured liqueur (optional)

For the chocolate cream

200g/7oz good-quality white chocolate, broken into pieces
475ml/16fl oz/2 cups double (heavy) or whipping cream
30ml/2 tbsp orange-flavoured liqueur (optional)

1 Preheat the oven to 180°C/350°F/Gas 4. Line a 1.75 litre/3 pint/7½ cup round ovenproof bowl with foil, smoothing the sides. In a bowl over a pan of simmering water, melt the plain chocolate. Add the sugar and stir until it dissolves. Strain into a medium bowl. Using an electric mixer at low speed, beat in the butter, then the eggs, one at a time. Stir in the liqueur, if using, and pour into the lined bowl. Tap to release large air bubbles.

2 Bake for 1¼–1½ hours until the surface is firm and slightly risen, but cracked. The centre will set on cooling. Transfer to a rack to cool. Cover with a plate, then cover completely with clear film (plastic wrap) and chill overnight. To unmould, remove the plate and film and invert the mould on to a plate; shake firmly to release. Peel off foil. Cover until ready to decorate.

3 Work the white chocolate in a food processor to form fine crumbs. In a small pan, heat 120ml/4fl oz/½ cup of the cream until just beginning to simmer. With the processor running, pour in the cream until the chocolate has melted. Strain into a bowl and cool to room temperature, stirring occasionally.

4 Beat the remaining cream until soft peaks form, add the liqueur, if using, and beat for 30 seconds or until the cream just holds its shape. Fold a spoonful of cream into the chocolate then fold in the remaining cream. Spoon into a piping (pastry) bag fitted with a star tip and pipe rosettes over the surface.

Chocolate Amaretto Marquise

This wickedly rich chocolate dessert is truly extravagant.

Serves 10–12

15ml/1 tbsp flavourless vegetable oil, such as groundnut (peanut) or sunflower
75g/3oz/7–8 amaretti, finely crushed
25g/1oz/¼ cup unblanched almonds, toasted and finely chopped
450g/1lb fine-quality plain or dark (bittersweet) chocolate, chopped into small pieces
75ml/5 tbsp Amaretto Disaronno liqueur
75ml/5 tbsp golden (light corn) syrup
475ml/16fl oz/2 cups double (heavy) cream
unsweetened cocoa powder, for dusting

For the Amaretto cream

350ml/12fl oz/1½ cups whipping cream or double (heavy) cream
30–45ml/2–3 tbsp Amaretto Disaronno liqueur

1 Lightly oil a 23cm/9in heart-shaped or springform cake tin (pan). Line the bottom with baking parchment, then oil the paper. In a small bowl, combine the crushed amaretti and the chopped almonds. Sprinkle evenly on to the base of the tin.

2 Place the chocolate, Amaretto liqueur and golden syrup in a medium pan over a very low heat. Stir frequently until the chocolate has melted and the mixture is smooth. Remove from the heat and allow it to cool for about 6–8 minutes, until the mixture feels just warm to the touch.

3 Whip the cream until it just begins to hold its shape. Stir a large spoonful into the chocolate mixture, to lighten it, then quickly add the remaining cream and gently fold in. Pour into the prepared tin, on top of the amaretti mixture. Level the surface. Cover the tin with clear film (plastic wrap) and chill overnight.

4 To unmould, run a slightly warmed, thin-bladed sharp knife around the edge of the dessert, then unmould. Carefully peel off the paper, replacing any crust that sticks to it, and dust with cocoa. In a bowl, whip the cream and Amaretto liqueur to soft peaks. Serve separately.

Snowball Energy 640kcal/2661kJ; Protein 6.7g; Carbohydrate 46.2g, of which sugars 46g; Fat 49g, of which saturates 29.3g; Cholesterol 199mg; Calcium 94mg; Fibre 0.6g; Sodium 185mg.
Marquise Energy 589kcal/2444kJ; Protein 3.9g; Carbohydrate 38.2g, of which sugars 35.1g; Fat 46.4g, of which saturates 27.5g; Cholesterol 87mg; Calcium 63mg; Fibre 1.2g; Sodium 57mg.

Chilled Chocolate Zucotto Sponge

An Italian-style dessert with a rich ricotta, fruit, chocolate and nut filling, zucotto is encased in a moist, chocolate and liqueur-flavoured sponge.

Serves 8

3 eggs
75g/3oz/6 tbsp caster (superfine) sugar
75g/3oz/⅔ cup plain (all-purpose) flour
25g/1oz/¼ cup unsweetened cocoa powder
90ml/6 tbsp Kirsch
250g/9oz/generous 1 cup ricotta cheese
50g/2oz/½ cup icing (confectioners') sugar
50g/2oz plain (semisweet) chocolate, finely chopped
50g/2oz/½ cup blanched almonds, chopped and toasted
75g/3oz/scant ½ cup natural glacé (candied) cherries, quartered
2 pieces preserved stem ginger, finely chopped
150ml/¼ pint/⅔ cup double (heavy) cream
unsweetened cocoa powder, for dusting

1 Preheat the oven to 180°C/350°F/Gas 4. Grease and line a 23cm/9in cake tin (pan). Whisk the eggs and sugar in a heatproof bowl over a pan of simmering water until the whisk leaves a trail. Remove the bowl from the heat and continue to whisk the mixture for 2 minutes.

2 Sift the flour and cocoa into the bowl and fold it in with a large metal spoon. Spoon the mixture into the prepared tin and bake for about 20 minutes until just firm. Leave to cool.

3 Cut the cake horizontally into three layers. Set aside 30ml/2 tbsp of the Kirsch. Drizzle the remaining Kirsch over the layers.

4 Beat the ricotta cheese in a bowl until softened, then beat in the icing sugar, chopped chocolate, toasted almonds, cherries, stem ginger and reserved Kirsch.

5 Pour the cream into a separate bowl and whip it lightly. Using a large metal spoon, fold the cream into the ricotta mixture. Chill. Cut a 20cm/8in circle from one sponge layer, using a plate as a guide, and set it aside.

6 Use the remaining sponge to make the case for the zucotto. Cut the cake to fit the bottom of a 2.8–3.4 litre/5–6 pint/12½–15 cup freezerproof mixing bowl lined with clear film (plastic wrap). Cut more sponge for the sides of the bowl, fitting the pieces together and taking them about one-third of the way up.

7 Spoon the ricotta filling into the bowl up to the height of the sponge, and level the surface.

8 Fit the reserved circle of sponge on top of the filling. Trim off the excess sponge around the edges. Cover the bowl and freeze overnight.

9 Transfer the zucotto to the refrigerator 45 minutes before serving, so that the filling softens slightly. Invert it on to a serving plate and peel away the clear film. Dust with cocoa powder and serve immediately in slices.

Fruity Chocolate Ricotta Creams

Ricotta is an Italian soft cheese with a smooth texture and a mild, slightly sweet flavour. Served here with candied fruit peel and delicious chocolate, it is quite irresistible.

Serves 4

350g/12oz/1½ cups ricotta cheese
30–45ml/2–3 tbsp Cointreau or other orange liqueur
10ml/2 tsp grated lemon rind
30ml/2 tbsp icing (confectioners') sugar
150ml/¼ pint/⅔ cup double (heavy) cream
150g/5oz/scant 1 cup candied peel, such as orange, lemon and grapefruit, finely chopped
50g/2oz plain (semisweet) chocolate, finely chopped
chocolate curls, to decorate
amaretti, to serve (optional)

1 Using the back of a wooden spoon, push the ricotta through a fine sieve (strainer) into a large bowl.

2 Add the liqueur, lemon rind and icing sugar to the ricotta and beat well until the mixture is light and smooth.

3 Whip the cream in a large bowl until it forms soft peaks.

4 Gently fold the cream into the ricotta mixture with the candied peel and chopped chocolate.

5 Spoon the mixture into four individual glass dishes and chill for about 1 hour. Decorate the ricotta creams with chocolate curls and serve with amaretti, if you like.

Cook's Tips

• *For this uncooked, Italian-style dessert, you need to buy candied fruits in large pieces from a good delicatessen – tubs of chopped candied peel are too tough to eat raw, and should only be used in baking.*

• *The desserts can also be topped with a sprinkling of raspberries to add an extra fruitiness.*

Zucotto Sponge Energy 391kcal/1631kJ; Protein 8.7g; Carbohydrate 33.8g, of which sugars 26.1g; Fat 22.7g, of which saturates 11.4g; Cholesterol 111mg; Calcium 66mg; Fibre 1.4g; Sodium 64mg.
Ricotta Creams Energy 546kcal/2276kJ; Protein 9.4g; Carbohydrate 43.1g, of which sugars 43g; Fat 36.7g, of which saturates 22.6g; Cholesterol 89mg; Calcium 75mg; Fibre 2.1g; Sodium 115mg.

Tiramisu in Chocolate Cups

Here is an Italian favourite served in an elegant new way, in chocolate cups.

Serves 6
1 egg yolk
30ml/2 tbsp caster (superfine) sugar
2.5ml/½ tsp vanilla extract
250g/9oz/generous 1 cup mascarpone
120ml/4fl oz/½ cup strong black coffee
15ml/1 tbsp unsweetened cocoa powder, plus extra for dusting
30ml/2 tbsp coffee liqueur
16 amaretti

For the chocolate cups
175g/6oz plain (semisweet) chocolate, chopped
25g/1oz/2 tbsp unsalted (sweet) butter

1 Make the chocolate cups. Cut out six 15cm/6in rounds of baking parchment. Melt the chocolate with the butter in a heatproof bowl over a pan of simmering water. Stir until smooth, then spread a spoonful of the chocolate mixture over each circle, to within 2cm/¾in of the edge.

2 Carefully lift each paper round and drape it over an upturned teacup or ramekin so that the edges curve into frills. Leave until completely set, then carefully peel away the paper.

3 Make the filling. Using a hand-held electric mixer, beat the egg yolk and sugar in a bowl until smooth, then stir in the vanilla extract. Soften the mascarpone if necessary, then stir it into the egg yolk mixture. Beat until smooth.

4 In a separate bowl, mix the coffee, cocoa and liqueur. Break up the amaretti roughly, then stir them into the mixture.

5 Place the chocolate cups on individual plates. Divide half the amaretti mixture among them, then spoon over half the mascarpone mixture.

6 Spoon over the remaining amaretti mixture (including any free liquid), top with the rest of the mascarpone mixture and dust lightly with cocoa. Chill for 30 minutes before serving.

Rice Pudding with Chocolate Sauce

Cook a rice pudding on top of the stove for a light creamy texture, which is particularly good served cold and topped with chocolate sauce and fruit.

Serves 4
50g/2oz/⅓ cup pudding rice
600ml/1 pint/2½ cups milk
5ml/1 tsp vanilla extract
2.5ml/½ tsp ground cinnamon
40g/1½oz sugar

To serve
strawberries, raspberries or blueberries
chocolate sauce
flaked toasted almonds

1 Put the rice, milk, vanilla extract, cinnamon and sugar into a medium-sized pan. Bring to the boil, stirring constantly, and then turn down the heat to a gentle simmer.

2 Cook the rice for about 30–40 minutes, stirring occasionally. You may need to add extra milk if the liquid in the pan reduces down too quickly.

3 Test the grains to make sure they are soft, then remove the pan from the heat and set aside to allow the rice to cool, stirring it occasionally. When the rice has gone cold, chill it in the refrigerator.

4 Just before serving, stir the rice and spoon into four sundae dishes. Top with fruits, chocolate sauce and almonds.

Variations

- *Milk puddings are at last enjoying something of a comeback in popularity. Instead of simple pudding rice try using a Thai fragrant or jasmine rice for a delicious natural flavour. For a firmer texture, an Italian risotto rice, such as arborio, with its high starch content makes a good pudding, too.*
- *There's no need to use a lot of full-fat (whole) milk or cream either. A pudding made with semi-skimmed (low-fat) milk or even fat-free milk can be just as nice and is much more healthy for you.*

Tiramisu Energy 351kcal/1469kJ; Protein 6.9g; Carbohydrate 34.5g, of which sugars 29.6g; Fat 20.4g, of which saturates 12.1g; Cholesterol 62mg; Calcium 33mg; Fibre 1.2g; Sodium 86mg.
Rice Pudding Energy 185kcal/782kJ; Protein 6.9g; Carbohydrate 34.8g, of which sugars 24.8g; Fat 2.7g, of which saturates 1.6g; Cholesterol 9mg; Calcium 204mg; Fibre 1.1g; Sodium 71mg.

Chocolate Vanilla Timbales

These elegantly turned-out timbales look particularly impressive if they are set in fluted moulds. It's worth investing in some.

Serves 6

350ml/12fl oz/1½ cups semi-skimmed (low-fat) milk
30ml/2 tbsp unsweetened cocoa powder, plus extra for dusting
2 eggs
10ml/2 tsp vanilla extract
45ml/3 tbsp caster (superfine) sugar
15ml/1 tbsp/1 sachet powdered gelatine
45ml/3 tbsp hot water
fresh mint sprigs, to decorate (optional)

For the sauce

115g/4oz/½ cup light Greek (US strained plain) yogurt
25ml/1½ tbsp vanilla extract

1 Place the milk and cocoa in a pan and stir until the milk is boiling. Separate the eggs and beat the egg yolks with the vanilla extract and sugar in a bowl, until the mixture is pale and smooth. Gradually pour in the chocolate milk, beating well.

2 Return the mixture to the pan and stir constantly over a gentle heat, without boiling, until it is slightly thickened and smooth in consistency.

3 Remove the pan from the heat. Pour the gelatine into the hot water and stir until it is completely dissolved, then quickly stir it into the milk mixture. Put this mixture aside and allow it to cool until almost setting.

4 Whisk the egg whites until they hold soft peaks. Fold the egg whites quickly into the milk mixture. Spoon the timbale mixture into six individual moulds. Chill them until set.

5 To serve, run a knife around the edge, dip the moulds quickly into hot water and turn out on to serving plates. For the sauce, stir together the yogurt and vanilla extract and spoon on to the plates next to the timbales. Lightly dust with cocoa and decorate with mint sprigs, if using.

Chocolate and Chestnut Pots

The chestnut purée adds substance and texture to these mousses. Crisp, delicate cookies, such as langues-de-chat, provide a good foil to the richness.

Serves 6

250g/9oz plain (semisweet) chocolate
60ml/4 tbsp Madeira
25g/1oz/2 tbsp butter, diced
2 eggs, separated
225g/8oz/scant 1 cup unsweetened chestnut purée
crème fraîche or whipped double (heavy) cream, to decorate

1 Make a few chocolate curls for decoration by rubbing a grater along the length of the bar of chocolate. Break the rest of the chocolate into squares and melt it in a pan with the Madeira over a gentle heat. Remove from the heat and add the butter, a few pieces at a time, stirring until melted and smooth.

2 Beat the egg yolks quickly into the mixture, then beat in the chestnut purée, mixing until smooth.

3 Whisk the egg whites in a clean, grease-free bowl until stiff. Stir about 15ml/1 tbsp of the whites into the chestnut mixture to lighten it, then fold in the rest smoothly and evenly.

4 Spoon the mixture into six small ramekin dishes and chill in the refrigerator until set.

5 Remove the pots from the refrigerator about 30 minutes before serving to allow the flavours to 'ripen'. Serve the pots topped with a generous spoonful of crème fraîche or whipped cream and decorated with chocolate curls.

Cook's Tips

- *If Madeira is not available, use brandy or rum instead.*
- *These chocolate pots can be frozen successfully for up to 2 months, making them ideal for a prepare-ahead dessert.*

Vanilla Timbales Energy 89kcal/372kJ; Protein 6.2g; Carbohydrate 3.7g, of which sugars 3.1g; Fat 5.9g, of which saturates 2.8g; Cholesterol 67mg; Calcium 115mg; Fibre 0.6g; Sodium 110mg.
Chocolate Pots Energy 348kcal/1455kJ; Protein 5g; Carbohydrate 41.4g, of which sugars 29.9g; Fat 18g, of which saturates 9.9g; Cholesterol 75mg; Calcium 42mg; Fibre 2.6g; Sodium 56mg.

Mocha Velvet Cream Pots

These dainty pots of chocolate heaven are a fabulous way to round off a special meal.

Serves 8

15ml/1 tbsp instant coffee powder
475ml/16fl oz/2 cups milk
75g/3oz/6 tbsp caster (superfine) sugar
225g/8oz plain (semisweet) chocolate, chopped into small pieces
10ml/2 tsp vanilla extract
30ml/2 tbsp coffee-flavoured liqueur (optional)
7 egg yolks
whipped cream and crystallized mimosa balls, to decorate

1 Preheat the oven to 160°C/325°F/Gas 3. Place eight 120ml/4fl oz/½ cup custard cups or ramekins in a roasting pan. Set the pan aside.

2 Put the instant coffee in a saucepan. Stir in the milk, then add the sugar and place the pan over medium heat. Bring to the boil, stirring constantly, until both the coffee and the sugar have dissolved completely.

3 Remove the pan from the heat and add the chocolate. Stir until it has melted and the sauce is smooth. Stir in the vanilla extract and coffee liqueur, if using.

4 In a bowl, whisk the egg yolks to blend them lightly. Slowly whisk in the chocolate mixture until well mixed, then strain the mixture into a large jug (pitcher) and divide equally among the cups or ramekins. Pour enough boiling water into the roasting pan to come halfway up the sides of the cups or ramekins. Carefully place the roasting pan in the oven.

5 Bake for 30–35 minutes, until the custard is just set and a knife inserted into the custard comes out clean. Remove the cups or ramekins from the roasting pan and allow to cool. Place on a baking sheet, cover and chill completely.

6 Decorate the pots with whipped cream and crystallized mimosa balls, if you wish.

Petits Pots de Cappuccino

These very rich coffee custards, with a cream topping and a light dusting of drinking chocolate, look wonderful presented in fine china coffee cups.

Serves 6–8

75g/3oz/1 cup roasted coffee beans
300ml/½ pint/1¼ cups milk
300ml/½ pint/1¼ cups single (light) cream
1 whole egg
4 egg yolks
50g/2oz/4 tbsp caster (superfine) sugar
2.5ml/½ tsp vanilla extract

For the topping

120ml/4fl oz/½ cup whipping cream
45ml/3 tbsp iced water
10ml/2 tsp drinking chocolate

1 Preheat oven to 160°C/325°F/Gas 3. Put the coffee beans in a pan over a low heat for about 3 minutes, shaking the pan frequently. Pour the milk and cream over the beans. Heat until almost boiling; cover and leave to infuse (steep) for 30 minutes.

2 Whisk the egg, the egg yolks, sugar and vanilla together. Return the milk to boiling and pour through a sieve (strainer) on to the egg mixture. Discard the beans.

3 Pour the mixture into eight 75ml/5 tbsp coffee cups or six 120ml/4fl oz/½ cup ramekins. Cover each with a small piece of foil. Put in a roasting pan with hot water reaching about two-thirds of the way up the sides of the dishes. Bake for 30–35 minutes, or until lightly set. Let cool. Chill in the refrigerator for at least 2 hours.

4 Whisk the whipping cream and iced water until thick and frothy, and spoon on top of the custards. Dust with drinking chocolate before serving.

Cook's Tip

These petits pots may also be served warm, topped with a spoonful of clotted cream. Serve straight away, with the clotted cream just starting to melt.

Mocha Cream Pots Energy 261kcal/1095kJ; Protein 6g; Carbohydrate 30.5g, of which sugars 30.2g; Fat 13.7g, of which saturates 6.7g; Cholesterol 182mg; Calcium 106mg; Fibre 0.7g; Sodium 36mg.
Petits Pots Energy 226kcal/939kJ; Protein 5.6g; Carbohydrate 10.5g, of which sugars 10.5g; Fat 18.3g, of which saturates 10g; Cholesterol 197mg; Calcium 110mg; Fibre 0g; Sodium 49mg.

Belgian Chocolate Mousse

Every Belgian family has its favourite recipe for this culinary classic, usually involving some combination of melted chocolate with fresh eggs and cream, butter, coffee and liqueur. Whatever the recipe calls for, the essential ingredient is the chocolate, which must be of excellent quality. For professional results you can use callets (drop-like pieces of chocolate) made by the Belgian company Callebaut, or substitute other good-quality Belgian chocolate. The finished dish is magnificent.

Serves 4

150g/5oz Callebaut callets (semisweet bits) or other good-quality Belgian chocolate, cut into small pieces
200ml/7fl oz/scant 1 cup whipping or double (heavy) cream
75g/3oz/6 tbsp caster (superfine) sugar
2 eggs, separated, at room temperature
chocolate curls or sprinkles, roasted almond slivers, strips of candied orange peel, unsweetened cocoa powder or extra whipped cream, to decorate (optional)

1 Put the chocolate in a heatproof bowl over a small pan of simmering water. Melt the chocolate, stirring occasionally. When it is smooth, scrape it into a large bowl and leave to cool to room temperature.

2 In a clean bowl, whip the cream with 15ml/1 tbsp of the sugar until it stands in soft peaks. Set aside.

3 In a separate, grease-free, bowl, whisk the egg whites, gradually adding 50g/2oz/4 tbsp of the remaining sugar, until they are stiff and silky.

4 Whisk the egg yolks in a third bowl, gradually adding the last of the sugar, until foamy. Fold the yolks into the chocolate.

5 Using a spatula, fold in the whipped cream and then the egg whites, taking care not to deflate the mixture. Spoon or pipe into ramekins, dessert glasses or chocolate cups and leave to set for at least 4 hours. Serve plain or with any of the suggested decorations.

Heavenly Mud

This divine chocolate mousse, appropriately christened 'heavenly mud', is a dreamy combination of dark chocolate, eggs and cream. It is rich and full of flavour – the height of self-indulgence, and a classic sweet dessert dish in the Netherlands.

Serves 4

100g/3¾oz dark (bittersweet) chocolate, chopped
30ml/2 tbsp milk
4 eggs, separated
25ml/1½ tbsp soft light brown sugar
whipped double (heavy) cream and grated chocolate, to decorate

1 Put the chocolate and milk in a heatproof bowl and melt over a pan of barely simmering water, stirring constantly until smooth.

2 Beat the egg yolks with the sugar in another bowl. Stir the mixture into the melted chocolate mixture and warm briefly, stirring constantly, until slightly thickened.

3 Whisk the egg whites in a grease-free bowl until they are very stiff. Remove the chocolate mixture from the heat and fold it into the egg whites.

4 Divide the mixture among four individual dishes and chill in the refrigerator for at least 1 hour, until set. Decorate with whipped cream and grated chocolate.

Variation
To make another chocolate dessert called Mud from Gerritje, substitute icing (confectioners') sugar for the brown sugar and add some vanilla and ground cinnamon to the chopped chocolate. Stir 30ml/2 tbsp brandy into the chocolate mixture just before folding it into the egg whites.

Belgian Mousse Energy 550kcal/2290kJ; Protein 5.9g; Carbohydrate 44.3g, of which sugars 43.9g; Fat 40.1g, of which saturates 23.8g; Cholesterol 166mg; Calcium 61mg; Fibre 1g; Sodium 50mg.
Heavenly Mud Energy 226kcal/947kJ; Protein 7.8g; Carbohydrate 22g, of which sugars 21.8g; Fat 12.7g, of which saturates 5.8g; Cholesterol 192mg; Calcium 49mg; Fibre 0.6g; Sodium 75mg.

Bitter Chocolate Mousse

A classic and ever-popular dessert, these dishes of liqueur-flavoured chocolate mousse make a stylish and memorable finish to any dinner party.

Serves 8

225g/8oz plain (semisweet) chocolate, chopped into small pieces
60ml/4 tbsp water
30ml/2 tbsp orange-flavoured liqueur or brandy
25g/1oz/2 tbsp unsalted (sweet) butter, cut into small pieces
4 eggs, separated
90ml/6 tbsp whipping cream
1.5ml/¼ tsp cream of tartar
45ml/3 tbsp caster (superfine) sugar
crème fraîche and chocolate curls, to decorate

1 Melt the chocolate with the water in a heatproof bowl set over a pan of barely simmering water, stirring until completely smooth. Remove from the heat and whisk in the liqueur or brandy and butter.

2 With a hand-held electric mixer, beat the egg yolks for 2–3 minutes until thick and creamy, then slowly beat into the melted chocolate until well blended. Set aside.

3 Whip the cream until soft peaks form and stir a spoonful into the chocolate mixture to lighten it. Fold in the remaining cream.

4 In a grease-free bowl, beat the egg whites slowly until frothy. Add the cream of tartar, increase the speed and continue beating until they form soft peaks. Gradually sprinkle over the sugar and continue beating until the whites are stiff and glossy.

5 Using a rubber spatula or large metal spoon, stir a quarter of the egg whites into the chocolate mixture, then gently fold in the remaining whites, cutting down to the bottom, along the sides and up to the top in a semicircular motion until they are just combined. Gently spoon into eight individual dishes. Chill for at least 2 hours or until set.

6 Spoon a little crème fraîche over each mousse and decorate with the chocolate curls.

White Chocolate Mousse with Dark Sauce

In this delicious dessert, creamy, white chocolate mousse is set off by a dark rum and chocolate sauce.

Serves 6–8

200g/7oz white chocolate, broken into squares
2 eggs, separated
60ml/4 tbsp caster (superfine) sugar
300ml/½ pint/1¼ cups double (heavy) cream
15ml/1 tbsp/1 sachet powdered gelatine
150ml/¼ pint/⅔ cup Greek (US strained plain) yogurt
10ml/2 tsp vanilla extract

For the sauce

50g/2oz plain (semisweet) chocolate, broken into squares
30ml/2 tbsp dark rum
60ml/4 tbsp single (light) cream

1 Line a 1 litre/1¾ pint/4 cup loaf tin (pan) with baking parchment or clear film (plastic wrap). Melt the chocolate in a heatproof bowl over hot water, then remove from the heat.

2 Whisk the egg yolks and sugar in a bowl until pale and thick, then beat in the melted chocolate.

3 Heat the cream in a small pan until almost boiling, then remove from the heat. Sprinkle the powdered gelatine over, stirring gently until it is completely dissolved. Then pour on to the chocolate mixture, whisking vigorously to combine the gelatine until smooth.

4 Whisk the yogurt and vanilla extract into the mixture. In a clean, grease-free bowl, whisk the egg whites until stiff, then fold them into the mixture. Turn into the prepared loaf tin, level the surface and chill until set.

5 Make the sauce. Melt the chocolate with the rum and cream in a heatproof bowl over barely simmering water. Cool.

6 Remove the mousse from the tin with the aid of the lining. Serve sliced with the chocolate sauce poured around.

Bitter Mousse Energy 276kcal/1152kJ; Protein 4.8g; Carbohydrate 24.1g, of which sugars 23.9g; Fat 17.6g, of which saturates 9.9g; Cholesterol 115mg; Calcium 34mg; Fibre 0.7g; Sodium 61mg.
White Mousse Energy 433kcal/1796kJ; Protein 6g; Carbohydrate 25g, of which sugars 24.9g; Fat 34.4g, of which saturates 20.5g; Cholesterol 103mg; Calcium 133mg; Fibre 0.2g; Sodium 69mg.

Black and White Chocolate Mousse

Dark and dreamy or white and creamy – if you can't decide which mousse you prefer, have both.

Serves 8

For the white mousse

200g/7oz white chocolate, broken into squares
60ml/4 tbsp white rum
30ml/2 tbsp coconut cream
1 egg yolk
60ml/4 tbsp caster (superfine) sugar
250ml/8fl oz/1 cup double (heavy) cream
2 egg whites

For the black mousse

200g/7oz plain (semisweet) chocolate, broken into squares
30ml/2 tbsp unsalted (sweet) butter
60ml/4 tbsp dark rum
3 eggs, separated
chocolate curls, to decorate

1 Make the white chocolate mousse. Melt the chocolate with the rum and coconut cream in a heatproof bowl over barely simmering water. Remove from the heat.

2 Beat the egg yolk and sugar in a separate bowl, then whisk into the chocolate mixture. Whip the cream until it just begins to hold its shape, then carefully fold it into the chocolate mixture.

3 Whisk the egg whites in a clean, grease-free bowl until they form soft peaks, then fold quickly and evenly into the chocolate mixture. Chill until cold and set.

4 Make the dark chocolate mousse. Melt the chocolate with the butter and rum in a heatproof bowl over barely simmering water, stirring until smooth. Remove from the heat and beat in the egg yolks.

5 Whisk the egg whites to soft peaks, then fold them quickly and evenly into the chocolate mixture. Chill until cold and set.

6 Spoon the white and dark chocolate mixtures alternately into tall glasses or into one large glass serving bowl. Decorate with chocolate curls and serve.

Rich Chocolate Mousse with Glazed Kumquats

Perfumed kumquats, glazed in orange-flavoured liqueur, turn this mousse into a very special treat.

Serves 6

225g/8oz plain (semisweet) chocolate, broken into squares
4 eggs, separated
30ml/2 tbsp orange-flavoured liqueur
90ml/6 tbsp double (heavy) cream

For the glazed kumquats

275g/10oz/2¾ cups kumquats
115g/4oz/generous ½ cup sugar
150ml/¼ pint/⅔ cup water
15ml/1 tbsp orange-flavoured liqueur

1 To make the glazed kumquats, halve the fruit lengthways and place cut side up in a shallow serving dish.

2 Place the sugar in a small pan with the water. Heat gently, stirring constantly, until the sugar has dissolved, then bring to the boil and boil rapidly, without stirring, until a golden-brown caramel forms.

3 Remove the pan from the heat and very carefully stir in 60ml/4 tbsp boiling water. Stir in the orange-flavoured liqueur, then pour the caramel sauce over the kumquat slices and leave to cool. Once completely cold, cover and chill.

4 Line a shallow 20cm/8in round cake tin (pan) with clear film (plastic wrap). Melt the chocolate in a bowl over a pan of barely simmering water, then remove the bowl from the heat.

5 Beat the egg yolks and liqueur into the chocolate, then gently fold in the cream. In a separate mixing bowl, whisk the egg whites until stiff, then gently fold them into the chocolate mixture. Pour the mixture into the prepared tin and level the surface. Chill for several hours until set.

6 Turn the mousse out on to a plate and cut into slices. Serve with the glazed kumquats alongside.

Black and White Energy 569kcal/2366kJ; Protein 7.5g; Carbohydrate 39.1g, of which sugars 38.9g; Fat 39.9g, of which saturates 24.2g; Cholesterol 149mg; Calcium 111mg; Fibre 0.6g; Sodium 103mg.
Rich Mousse Energy 431kcal/1805kJ; Protein 6.9g; Carbohydrate 49.8g, of which sugars 49.5g; Fat 22.3g, of which saturates 12.4g; Cholesterol 150mg; Calcium 71mg; Fibre 1.7g; Sodium 56mg.

Chocolate and Orange Soya Mousse

There's no hint of deprivation in this dairy-free dessert, made with dark chocolate flavoured with brandy. It makes a great treat when entertaining.

Serves 8

175g/6oz good-quality dark (bittersweet) chocolate, broken into squares
grated rind and juice of 1½ large oranges, plus extra pared rind for decoration
5ml/1 tsp powdered gelatine
4 size 2 eggs, separated
90ml/6 tbsp unsweetened soya cream
60ml/4 tbsp brandy
chopped pistachio nuts, to decorate

1 Melt the chocolate in a heatproof bowl over a pan of barely simmering water, stirring until smooth. Put 30ml/2 tbsp of the orange juice in a heatproof bowl and sprinkle the gelatine on top. When the gelatine is spongy, stand the bowl over a pan of hot water and stir until it has dissolved.

2 Let the chocolate cool slightly, then beat in the orange rind, egg yolks, soya cream and brandy, followed by the gelatine mixture and the remaining orange juice. Set aside.

3 Whisk the egg whites in a grease-free bowl until they form soft peaks. Gently fold the whites into the chocolate and orange mixture.

4 Spoon or pour the mixture into six sundae dishes or glasses, or into a single glass bowl. Cover and chill until the mousse sets. Decorate with the chopped pistachio nuts and extra pared orange rind before serving.

Cook's Tip
The percentage of cocoa solids in the chocolate influences not only the taste but also the texture of the mousse. The higher the percentage of the cocoa the firmer the mousse will become. Try to use a chocolate with a minimum of 70 per cent cocoa solids if you can.

Liqueur-spiked Dark Chocolate Orange Mousse

Everything about this mousse is seductive and sophisticated. The smooth, creamy chocolate lingers on the tongue after being slowly sucked off the spoon. Only the best chocolates can create this divine effect, so save your most expensive, cocoa-solids-packed variety for this ultimate indulgence.

Serves 4

200g/7oz orange-flavoured dark (bittersweet) chocolate with more than 60 per cent cocoa solids
45ml/3 tbsp Grand Marnier or other orange-flavoured liqueur
25g/1oz/2 tbsp unsalted (sweet) butter
3 large (US extra large) eggs
salt
candied orange peel, to serve

1 Break the chocolate into pieces and put in a small bowl over a pan of barely simmering water. Pour in the liqueur and add the butter. Leave undisturbed for about 10 minutes until melted.

2 Separate the eggs and put the whites into a large mixing bowl with a tiny pinch of salt. Stir the chocolate mixture and remove from the heat. Quickly mix in the egg yolks.

3 Whisk the egg whites until stiff but not dry. Fold one large spoonful into the chocolate sauce to loosen the mixture, then carefully, but thoroughly, fold in the remaining egg whites.

4 Spoon the mixture into little pots or ramekins, cover and chill for at least 6 hours, or until set. Serve with thin strips of candied orange peel.

Cook's Tip
Grand Marnier is a liqueur made with cognac and orange extract. A common name for an orange liqueur is 'triple sec', and there are many brands, with Grand Marnier being one of the most famous. Also look out for Cointreau, which, along with Grand Marnier, has a high alcohol content of 40 per cent.

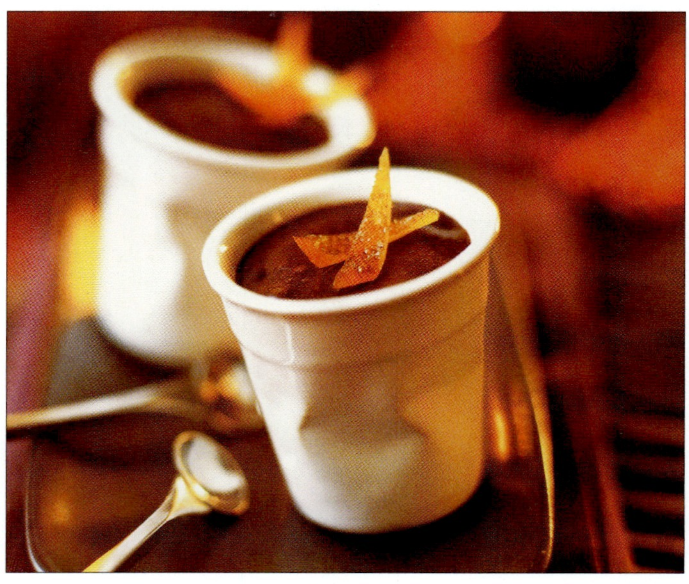

Orange Energy 230kcals/966kJ; Fat, total 12.4g; saturated fat 4.6g;polyunsaturated fat 0.6g; monounsaturated fat 3.4g; Carbohydrate 17.3g; sugar, total 17g; Starch 0.2g; Fibre 0.55g; Sodium 113mg.
Liqueur Energy 382kcal/1593kJ; Protein 7.2g; Carbohydrate 31.8g, of which sugars 31.4g; Fat 23.3g, of which saturates 12.8g; Cholesterol 159mg; Calcium 39mg; Fibre 1.3g; Sodium 94mg.

White Amaretto Mousse with Chocolate Sauce

These little desserts are extremely rich, and derive their flavour from amaretto, an almond-flavoured liqueur, and amaretti, little almond-flavoured cookies.

Serves 8

115g/4oz amaretti, ratafia or macaroon biscuits (cookies)
60ml/4 tbsp amaretto liqueur
350g/12oz white chocolate, broken into squares
15g/½oz powdered gelatine, soaked in 45ml/3 tbsp cold water
450ml/¾ pint/scant 2 cups double (heavy) cream

For the chocolate sauce

225g/8oz dark (bittersweet) chocolate, broken into squares
300ml/½ pint/1¼ cups single (light) cream
50g/2oz/4 tbsp caster (superfine) sugar

1 Lightly oil eight individual 120ml/4floz moulds and line the base of each with oiled baking parchment. Put the biscuits into a large bowl and crush finely with a rolling pin.

2 Melt the liqueur and white chocolate in a bowl over a pan of simmering water. Remove from the pan and leave to cool.

3 Melt the gelatine over hot water and stir into the chocolate mixture. Whisk the cream until it holds soft peaks. Fold in the chocolate mixture, with 60ml/4 tbsp of the crushed biscuits.

4 Put a teaspoonful of the crushed biscuits into the bottom of each mould and spoon in the chocolate mixture. Tap each mould to disperse any air bubbles. Level the tops and sprinkle the remaining biscuits on top. Press down and chill for 4 hours.

5 To make the chocolate sauce, put all the ingredients in a small pan and heat gently to melt the chocolate and dissolve the sugar. Simmer for 2–3 minutes. Leave to cool completely.

6 Slip a knife around the sides of each mould, and turn out on to individual plates. Remove the baking parchment and pour round a little dark chocolate sauce.

Chocolate and Coffee Mousse

A light chocolate mousse is always a popular way to end a meal. This Polish version is made with a good strong chocolate flavoured with coffee and rum, Polish spirit or vodka. You can omit all or any of these, depending on your preference.

Serves 4–6

250g/9oz good-quality dark (bittersweet) chocolate (minimum 70 per cent cocoa solids)
60ml/4 tbsp cooled strong black coffee
8 eggs, separated
200g/7oz/1 cup caster (superfine) sugar
60ml/4 tbsp rum, or 95 per cent proof Polish spirit or vodka

1 Break the chocolate into small pieces and melt in a heatproof bowl over a pan of gently simmering water. Ensure the water in the pan does not touch the base of the bowl, or the chocolate may go hard.

2 Once the chocolate has completely melted, stir in the cold coffee. Leave to cool slightly.

3 Beat the egg yolks with half the sugar until it is pale, thick and creamy. Add the rum, Polish spirit or vodka and stir in the melted chocolate mixture.

4 Whisk the egg whites in a separate clean bowl until stiff peaks form.

5 Stir in the remaining sugar, then fold into the chocolate cream mixture. Spoon into chilled glasses or ramekins and chill for at least an hour before serving.

Variation
For a slightly less intense mousse, whip 300ml/½ pint/1¼ cups double (heavy) cream until soft peaks form, then fold into the mixture at the end of step 3.

Amaretto Mousse Energy 837kcal/3484kJ; Protein 7.9g; Carbohydrate 64.9g, of which sugars 58.4g; Fat 60.6g, of which saturates 37g; Cholesterol 99mg; Calcium 210mg; Fibre 0.9g; Sodium 121mg.
Coffee Mousse Energy 464kcal/1951kJ; Protein 10.6g; Carbohydrate 61.3g, of which sugars 60.9g; Fat 19.1g, of which saturates 9.1g; Cholesterol 256mg; Calcium 70mg; Fibre 1.1g; Sodium 98mg.

Chilled Chocolate and Espresso Mousse in Chocolate Cups

Heady, aromatic espresso coffee adds a distinctive flavour to this rich mousse.

Serves 4

225g/8oz plain (semisweet) chocolate
45ml/3 tbsp brewed espresso
25g/1oz/2 tbsp unsalted (sweet) butter
4 eggs, separated
sprigs of fresh mint, to decorate (optional)
mascarpone or clotted cream, to serve (optional)

For the chocolate cups
225g/8oz plain (semisweet) chocolate

1 For each chocolate cup, cut a double thickness, 15cm/6in square of foil. Mould it around a small orange, leaving the edges and corners loose to make a cup shape. Remove the orange and press the bottom of the foil case gently on a surface to make a flat base. Repeat to make four foil cups.

2 Break the plain chocolate into a heatproof bowl set over a pan of simmering water. Stir until the chocolate has melted and is smooth. Spoon the chocolate into the foil cups, spreading it up the sides with the back of a spoon to give a ragged edge. Chill for 30 minutes or until set hard. Gently peel away the foil, starting at the top edge.

3 To make the chocolate mousse, put the plain chocolate and brewed espresso into a bowl set over a pan of hot water and melt as before. When it is smooth and liquid, add the unsalted butter, a little at a time. Remove the pan from the heat, then stir in the egg yolks.

4 Whisk the egg whites in a bowl until stiff, but not dry, then fold them into the chocolate mixture. Pour into a bowl and refrigerate for at least 3 hours.

5 To serve, scoop the chilled mousse into the chocolate cups. Add a scoop of mascarpone or clotted cream and decorate with a sprig of fresh mint, if you wish.

Iced Coffee Mousse in a Chocolate Case

A dark chocolate bowl is filled with a light, iced coffee mousse.

Serves 8

1 sachet powdered gelatine
60ml/4 tbsp very strong brewed coffee
30ml/2 tbsp coffee liqueur, such as Tia Maria, Kahlúa or Toussaint
3 eggs, separated
75g/3oz/scant ½ cup caster (superfine) sugar
150ml/¼ pint/⅔ cup whipping cream, lightly whipped

For the chocolate case
225g/8oz plain (semisweet) chocolate squares, plus extra for decoration

1 Grease and line a deep 18cm/7in loose-based cake tin (pan) with baking parchment. Melt the chocolate in a bowl over a pan of simmering water. Using a pastry brush, brush a layer of chocolate over the base of the tin and about 7.5cm/3in up the sides, finishing with a ragged edge. Allow the chocolate to set before repeating. Put in the freezer to harden.

2 Sprinkle the gelatine over the coffee in a bowl and leave to soften for 5 minutes. Put the bowl over a pan of simmering water, stirring until dissolved. Remove from the heat and stir in the liqueur. Whisk the egg yolks and sugar in a bowl over the simmering water until thick enough to leave a trail. Remove from the pan and whisk until cool. Whisk the egg whites until stiff.

3 Pour the dissolved gelatine into the egg yolk mixture in a thin stream, stirring gently. Chill in the refrigerator for 20 minutes, or until just beginning to set, then fold in the cream, followed by the whisked egg whites.

4 Remove the chocolate case from the freezer and peel away the lining. Put it back in the tin, then pour in the mousse. Return to the freezer for at least 3 hours. Remove from the tin, place on a plate and allow to soften in the refrigerator for 40 minutes before serving. Decorate with grated chocolate. Use a knife dipped in hot water and wiped dry to cut into slices to serve.

Espresso Mousse Energy 694kcal/2901kJ; Protein 11.9g; Carbohydrate 71.5g, of which sugars 70.5g; Fat 42.2g, of which saturates 23.7g; Cholesterol 210mg; Calcium 67mg; Fibre 2.8g; Sodium 115mg.
Iced Coffee Mousse Energy 464kcal/1950kJ; Protein 10.6g; Carbohydrate 61.3g, of which sugars 60.9g; Fat 19.1g, of which saturates 9.1g; Cholesterol 256mg; Calcium 69mg; Fibre 1g; Sodium 98mg.

Luxury Mocha Mousse

As a variation, use an orange-flavoured liqueur, brandy or even water in place of the coffee.

Serves 6

225g/8oz fine-quality bittersweet chocolate, chopped
50ml/2fl oz/¼ cup espresso or strong coffee
25g/1oz/2 tbsp butter, diced
30ml/2 tbsp brandy or rum
3 eggs, separated
pinch of salt
40g/1½oz/3 tbsp caster (superfine) sugar
120ml/4fl oz/½ cup whipping cream
30ml/2 tbsp coffee liqueur, such as Tia Maria or Kahlúa
chocolate coffee beans to decorate (optional)

1 In a medium pan over medium heat, melt the chocolate and coffee, stirring frequently until smooth. Remove from the heat and beat in the butter and brandy or rum.

2 In a bowl, beat the yolks lightly, then beat into the melted chocolate; the mixture will thicken. Set aside to cool. In a large bowl, beat the whites to 'break' them. Add a pinch of salt and beat until soft peaks form. Beat in the sugar, 15ml/1 tbsp at a time, beating well after each addition until the egg whites become glossy and stiff, but do not overbeat or they will become dry.

3 Beat 1 large spoonful of whites into the chocolate mixture to lighten it, then fold the chocolate into the remaining whites. Pour into a large glass serving bowl or six individual dishes and refrigerate for at least 3–4 hours before serving.

4 In a medium bowl, beat the cream and coffee-flavour liqueur until soft peaks form. Spoon into an icing (pastry) bag fitted with a medium star tip and pipe rosettes or shells on to the surface of the mousse. Garnish with a chocolate coffee bean.

Cook's Tip
It is essential to whip the egg whites while slowly adding the sugar; otherwise the whites will separate and become watery.

Coffee, Vanilla and Chocolate Stripe

This looks really special layered in wine glasses and decorated with cream.

Serves 6

285g/10½oz/1½ cups caster (superfine) sugar
90ml/6 tbsp cornflour (cornstarch)
900ml/1½ pints/3¾ cups milk
3 egg yolks
75g/3oz/6 tbsp unsalted (sweet) butter, at room temperature
20ml/generous 1 tbsp instant coffee powder
10ml/2 tsp vanilla extract
30ml/2 tbsp unsweetened cocoa powder

1 To make the coffee layer, place 90g/3½oz/½ cup of the sugar and 30ml/2 tbsp of the cornflour in a heavy pan. Gradually add one-third of the milk, whisking until well blended. Over a medium heat, whisk in one of the egg yolks and bring to the boil, whisking. Boil for 1 minute.

2 Remove the pan from the heat. Stir in 25g/1oz/2 tbsp of the butter and the instant coffee. Set aside the pan to cool slightly.

3 Divide the coffee mixture among six wine glasses. Smooth the tops before the mixture sets. Wipe any dribbles on the insides and outsides of the glasses with damp kitchen paper.

4 To make the vanilla layer, place half of the remaining sugar and cornflour in a heavy pan. Whisk in half the milk. Over a medium heat, whisk in another egg yolk and bring to the boil, whisking. Boil for 1 minute.

5 Remove the pan from the heat and stir in 25g/1oz/2 tbsp of the butter and the vanilla. Leave to cool slightly, then spoon into the glasses on top of the coffee layer. Smooth the tops.

6 To make the chocolate layer, place the remaining sugar and cornflour in a heavy pan. Gradually whisk in the remaining milk until blended. Over a medium heat, whisk in the last egg yolk and bring to the boil, whisking. Boil for 1 minute. Remove from the heat, stir in the remaining butter and the cocoa. Leave to cool slightly, then spoon on top of the vanilla layer. Chill to set.

Luxury Mousse Energy 389kcal/1621kJ; Protein 5.5g; Carbohydrate 32.5g, of which sugars 32.2g; Fat 25.5g, of which saturates 14.3g; Cholesterol 127mg; Calcium 43mg; Fibre 0.9g; Sodium 72mg.
Coffee Stripe Energy 448kcal/1891kJ; Protein 7.9g; Carbohydrate 71.1g, of which sugars 56.8g; Fat 16.8g, of which saturates 9.6g; Cholesterol 136mg; Calcium 228mg; Fibre 0.6g; Sodium 203mg.

Fruits of the Forest with White Chocolate Creams

Colourful fruits macerated in a mixture of white coconut rum and sugar make a fantastic accompaniment to a delightfully creamy white chocolate mousse.

Serves 4

75g/3oz white cooking chocolate, in squares
150ml/¼ pint/⅔ cup double (heavy) cream
30ml/2 tbsp crème fraîche
1 egg, separated
5ml/1 tsp powdered gelatine
30ml/2 tbsp cold water
a few drops of pure vanilla extract
115g/4oz/¾ cup small strawberries, sliced
75g/3oz/½ cup raspberries
75g/3oz/¾ cup blueberries
45ml/3 tbsp caster (superfine) sugar
75ml/5 tbsp white coconut rum
strawberry leaves, to decorate

1 Melt the chocolate in a heatproof bowl set over a pan of hot water. Heat the cream in a separate pan until almost boiling, then stir into the chocolate with the crème fraîche. Cool slightly, then beat in the egg yolk.

2 Sprinkle the gelatine over the water in another heatproof bowl and set aside for a few minutes to swell. Set the bowl in a pan of hot water until the gelatine has dissolved, then stir into the chocolate mixture and add the vanilla extract. Set aside.

3 Brush four dariole moulds or individual soufflé dishes with oil; line the base of each with baking parchment.

4 In a grease-free bowl, whisk the egg white to soft peaks, then fold into the chocolate mixture. Spoon the mixture into the moulds or dishes. Level the surface and chill for 2 hours until firm.

5 Meanwhile, place the fruits in a bowl. Add the sugar and coconut rum and stir to mix. Cover and chill until required.

6 Ease the chocolate cream away from the moulds or dishes and turn out on to plates. Spoon the fruits around the outside. Decorate with the strawberry leaves.

Chocolate and Lemon Fromage Frais

What better excuse to add iron to your diet than by eating some good dark chocolate? Contrast the richness with the tanginess of fromage frais.

Serves 4

150g/5oz dark (bittersweet) chocolate
45ml/3 tbsp water
15ml/1 tbsp rum, brandy or whisky (optional)
grated rind of 1 lemon
200g/7oz low-fat fromage frais or low-fat cream cheese
sliced kumquats and sprigs of mint, to decorate

1 Break up the chocolate into a heatproof bowl. Add the water and melt very slowly over a pan of gently simmering water, stirring constantly until smooth. Alternatively, melt it in a microwave on full power for 2 minutes.

2 Stir well until smooth and allow the chocolate to cool for 10 minutes. Stir in the rum, brandy or whisky, if using, and the lemon rind and fromage frais or cream cheese.

3 Spoon into four elegant wine glasses and chill until set. Decorate with kumquats and sprigs of mint.

Cook's Tips

- *Fromage frais (French for 'fresh cheese') can be hard to find in the US. Look for specialist stores and markets that stock European food or try to order some from on-line or mail-order retailers. If none is available, then low-fat cream cheese will also work in this recipe.*
- *Chocolate can be melted very successfully in the microwave. Place the pieces of chocolate in a plastic measuring jug (cup) or bowl. The chocolate may scorch if placed in a glass bowl. Microwave on high power for 1 minute, stir, and then heat again for up to 1 minute, checking halfway through to see if it is melted.*

Fruits Energy 397kcal/1643kJ; Protein 4.5g; Carbohydrate 17g, of which sugars 16.2g; Fat 30.4g, of which saturates 18.4g; Cholesterol 107mg; Calcium 90mg; Fibre 1.2g; Sodium 50mg.
Fromage Frais Energy 220kcal/925kJ; Protein 5.7g; Carbohydrate 27.2g, of which sugars 26.9g; Fat 10.6g, of which saturates 6.4g; Cholesterol 3mg; Calcium 56mg; Fibre 1g; Sodium 19mg.

Chocolate Blancmange

An old-fashioned dessert that is worthy of a revival. Serve with pouring cream for a touch of luxury.

Serves 4
60ml/4 tbsp cornflour (cornstarch)
600ml/1 pint/2½ cups milk
45ml/3 tbsp sugar
50–115g/2–4oz plain (semisweet) chocolate, chopped
few drops of vanilla extract
white and plain (semisweet) chocolate curls, to decorate

1 Rinse a 750ml/1¼ pint/3 cup fluted mould with cold water and leave it upside down to drain. Blend the cornflour to a smooth paste with a little of the milk in a medium bowl.

2 Bring the remaining milk to the boil, preferably in a non-stick pan, then pour on to the blended paste, stirring constantly, until smooth in consistency.

3 Pour all the milk back into the pan and bring slowly back to the boil over a low heat, stirring constantly until the mixture boils and thickens.

4 Remove the pan from the heat, then add the sugar, chopped chocolate and vanilla extract and stir constantly until the sauce is smooth, all the sugar has dissolved and the chocolate pieces have melted completely.

5 Carefully pour the chocolate mixture into the mould, cover the top closely with dampened baking parchment (to prevent the formation of a skin) and leave in a cool place for several hours to set.

6 To unmould the blancmange, place a large serving plate upside down on top of the mould. Holding the plate and mould firmly together, turn them both over in one quick motion. Give both plate and mould a gentle but firm shake to loosen the blancmange, then carefully lift off the mould.

7 To serve, sprinkle the chocolate curls over the top.

Chocolate Mandarin Trifle

Rich chocolate custard is combined with mandarin oranges to make this delicious trifle that is too tempting to resist.

Serves 6–8
4 trifle sponges
14 amaretti
60ml/4 tbsp Amaretto Disaronno or sweet sherry
8 mandarin oranges

For the custard
200g/7oz plain (semisweet) chocolate, broken into squares
25g/1oz/2 tbsp cornflour (cornstarch) or custard powder
25g/1oz/2 tbsp caster (superfine) sugar
2 egg yolks
200ml/7fl oz/scant 1 cup milk
250g/9oz/generous 1 cup mascarpone

For the topping
250g/9oz/generous 1 cup mascarpone or fromage frais
chocolate shapes
mandarin slices

1 Break up the trifle sponges and place them in a large glass serving dish. Crumble the amaretti over and then sprinkle with Amaretto or sweet sherry.

2 Squeeze the juice from two of the mandarins and sprinkle into the dish. Segment the rest and put in the dish.

3 Make the custard. Melt the chocolate in a heatproof bowl over hot water. In a separate bowl, mix the cornflour or custard powder, sugar and egg yolks to a smooth paste.

4 Heat the milk in a small pan until almost boiling, then pour in a steady stream on to the egg yolk mixture, stirring constantly. Return to the pan and stir over a low heat until the custard has thickened slightly and is smooth.

5 Stir in the mascarpone until melted, then add the melted chocolate; mix well. Spread over the trifle, cool, then chill to set.

6 To finish, spread the mascarpone or fromage frais over the custard, then decorate with chocolate shapes and the remaining mandarin slices just before serving.

Blancmange Energy 230kcal/975kJ; Protein 5.9g; Carbohydrate 40.6g, of which sugars 26.6g; Fat 6.2g, of which saturates 3.7g; Cholesterol 10mg; Calcium 192mg; Fibre 0.3g; Sodium 74mg.
Mandarin Trifle Energy 569kcal/2394kJ; Protein 12.5g; Carbohydrate 80.3g, of which sugars 61.3g; Fat 23.1g, of which saturates 12.8g; Cholesterol 135mg; Calcium 162mg; Fibre 2.9g; Sodium 115mg.

Chocolate and Mandarin Truffle Slice

Chocoholics will love this rich dessert. The mandarins impart a delicious tang.

Serves 8

400g/14oz plain (semisweet) chocolate
4 egg yolks
3 mandarin oranges
200ml/7fl oz/scant 1 cup crème fraîche
30ml/2 tbsp raisins
chocolate curls, to decorate

For the sauce

30ml/2 tbsp Cointreau
120ml/4fl oz/½ cup crème fraîche

1 Grease a 450g/1lb loaf tin (pan) and line it with clear film (plastic wrap). Break the chocolate in to a large heatproof bowl. Place over a pan of hot water until melted. Remove the bowl of chocolate from the heat and whisk in the egg yolks.

2 Pare the rind from the mandarins, taking care to leave the pith behind. Cut the rind into slivers.

3 Stir the slivers of mandarin rind into the chocolate with the crème fraîche and raisins. Beat until smooth, then spoon the mixture into the prepared loaf tin and chill for 4 hours.

4 Cut the pith and any remaining rind from the mandarins, then slice thinly.

5 For the sauce, stir the Cointreau into the crème fraîche. Remove the truffle loaf from the tin, peel off the clear film and slice. Serve each slice on a dessert plate with some sauce and mandarin slices, and decorate.

Cook's Tip

Chocolate-tipped mandarin slices would also make a superb decoration. Use small segments; pat dry on kitchen paper, then half-dip them in melted chocolate. Leave on baking parchment until the chocolate has set.

Mango and Chocolate Crème Brûlée

Fresh mangoes, topped with a wickedly rich chocolate cream and a layer of crunchy caramel, make a fantastic dessert.

Serves 6

2 ripe mangoes, peeled, stoned (pitted) and chopped
300ml/½ pint/1¼ cups double (heavy) cream
300ml/½ pint/1¼ cups crème fraîche
1 vanilla pod (bean)
115g/4oz plain (semisweet) chocolate, chopped into small pieces
4 egg yolks
15ml/1 tbsp clear honey
90ml/6 tbsp demerara (raw) sugar, for the topping

1 Divide the mangoes among six flameproof dishes set on a baking sheet.

2 Mix the cream, crème fraîche and vanilla pod in a large heatproof bowl. Place the bowl over a pan of barely simmering water.

3 Heat the cream mixture for 10 minutes. Do not let the bowl touch the water or the cream may overheat. Remove the vanilla pod and stir in the chocolate, a few pieces at a time, until melted. When smooth, remove the bowl, but leave the pan of water over the heat.

4 Whisk the egg yolks and clear honey in a second heatproof bowl, then gradually pour in the chocolate cream, whisking constantly. Place over the pan of simmering water and stir constantly until the chocolate custard thickens enough to coat the back of a wooden spoon.

5 Remove from the heat and spoon the custard over the mangoes. Cool, then chill in the refrigerator until set.

6 Preheat the grill (broiler) to high. Sprinkle 15ml/1 tbsp demerara sugar evenly over each dessert and spray lightly with a little water. Grill (broil) briefly, as close to the heat as possible, until the sugar melts and caramelizes. Chill again before serving.

Chocolate Truffle Slice Energy 456kcal/1899kJ; Protein 5g; Carbohydrate 35.3g, of which sugars 34.7g; Fat 32.8g, of which saturates 20.1g; Cholesterol 152mg; Calcium 54mg; Fibre 1.3g; Sodium 19mg.
Mango Crème Brûlée Energy 670kcal/2782kJ; Protein 5.2g; Carbohydrate 38.9g, of which sugars 38.4g; Fat 56g, of which saturates 34.6g; Cholesterol 261mg; Calcium 90mg; Fibre 1.8g; Sodium 31mg.

White Chocolate Parfait

The ultimate cold dessert – white and dark chocolate in one mouthwatering slice.

Serves 10

225g/8oz white chocolate, chopped
600ml/1 pint/2½ cups whipping cream
120ml/4fl oz/½ cup milk
10 egg yolks
15ml/1 tbsp caster (superfine) sugar
25g/1oz/scant ½ cup desiccated (dry unsweetened shredded) coconut
120ml/4fl oz/½ cup canned sweetened coconut milk
150g/5oz/1¼ cups unsalted macadamia nuts

For the chocolate icing

225g/8oz plain (semisweet) chocolate
75g/3oz/6 tbsp butter
20ml/generous 1 tbsp golden (light corn) syrup
175ml/6fl oz/¾ cup whipping cream
curls of fresh coconut, to decorate

1 Line the base and sides of a 1.4 litre/2⅓ pint/6 cup terrine mould (25 × 10cm/10 × 4in) with clear film (plastic wrap).

2 Place the white chocolate and 120ml/4fl oz/½ cup of the cream in the top of a double boiler or in a heatproof bowl set over hot water. Stir until melted and smooth. Set aside.

3 Put 250ml/8fl oz/1 cup of the cream and the milk in a pan and bring to boiling point.

4 Meanwhile, whisk the egg yolks and caster sugar together in a large bowl, until thick and pale.

5 Add the hot cream mixture to the yolks, beating constantly. Pour back into the pan and cook over a low heat for 2–3 minutes, until thickened. Stir constantly and do not boil. Remove the pan from the heat. Add the melted chocolate, desiccated coconut and coconut milk, then stir well and leave to cool.

6 Whip the remaining cream until thick, then fold into the chocolate and coconut mixture.

7 Put 475ml/16fl oz/2 cups of the parfait mixture in the prepared mould and spread evenly. Cover and freeze for about 2 hours, until just firm. Cover the remaining mixture and chill.

8 Sprinkle the macadamia nuts evenly over the frozen parfait. Pour in the remaining parfait mixture. Cover the terrine and freeze for 6–8 hours or overnight, until the parfait is firm.

9 To make the icing, melt the chocolate with the butter and syrup in the top of a double boiler set over hot water. Stir occasionally. Heat the cream in a pan, until just simmering, then stir into the chocolate mixture. Remove from the heat; cool.

10 To turn out the parfait, wrap the terrine in a hot towel and invert on to a plate. Lift off the mould and clear film and place the parfait on a rack over a baking sheet. Pour the chocolate icing over the top and quickly smooth it down the sides with a palette knife. Leave to set slightly, then freeze for 3–4 hours. To serve, slice with a knife dipped in hot water and decorate with coconut curls.

Chocolate and Brandy Parfait

This parfait is traditionally made with a mixture of chocolate and coffee, but here it is blended with cocoa powder. Melted Belgian chocolate and a kick of brandy are the secret of its superb flavour.

Serves 6

45ml/3 tbsp unsweetened cocoa powder
60ml/4 tbsp boiling water
150g/5oz dark (bittersweet) chocolate, broken into squares
4 egg yolks
115g/4oz/generous ½ cup caster (superfine) sugar
120ml/4fl oz/½ cup water
300ml/½ pint/1¼ cups double (heavy) cream
60–75ml/4–5 tbsp brandy
drizzled white chocolate rings, to decorate

1 Mix the cocoa to a paste with the boiling water. Put the chocolate into a heatproof bowl. Bring a pan of water to the boil, remove from the heat and place the bowl on top until the chocolate melts, stirring constantly. In a separate bowl, whisk the yolks until frothy.

2 Heat the sugar and measured water gently in a small pan, stirring occasionally, until completely dissolved, then boil for 4–5 minutes, without stirring, until it registers 115°C/239°F on a sugar thermometer. You can also test the temperature by dropping a little syrup into cold water. The syrup should make a soft ball.

3 Quickly whisk the syrup into the yolks. Lift the bowl of melted chocolate off the pan and bring the water to a simmer. Place the bowl with the yolk mixture on top and whisk until very thick. Lift it off the pan and continue whisking until the mixture cools slightly.

4 Whisk in the cocoa mixture, then fold in the melted chocolate. Whip the cream lightly and fold it in, along with the brandy. Pour the mixture into six or eight freezerproof serving dishes, then freeze for 4 hours or until they are firm. Decorate with white chocolate rings, made by drizzling melted white chocolate on to baking parchment and leaving it to set before carefully peeling from the paper.

White Parfait Energy 792kcal/3280kJ; Protein 9.2g; Carbohydrate 34.8g, of which sugars 34.5g; Fat 69.4g, of which saturates 36g; Cholesterol 301mg; Calcium 165mg; Fibre 1.7g; Sodium 169mg.
Brandy Parfait Energy 537kcal/2235kJ; Protein 5.5g; Carbohydrate 37.6g, of which sugars 36.5g; Fat 39.1g, of which saturates 22.9g; Cholesterol 204mg; Calcium 68mg; Fibre 1.5g; Sodium 91mg.

Chocolate Loaf with Coffee Sauce

This rich chocolate dessert is popular in many French restaurants, where it is called *Marquise au Chocolat*.

Serves 6–8

175g/6oz plain (semisweet) chocolate, chopped
50g/2oz/¼ cup butter, softened
4 large (US extra large) eggs, separated
30ml/2 tbsp rum or brandy (optional)
pinch of cream of tartar
chocolate curls and chocolate coffee beans, to decorate

For the coffee sauce

600ml/1 pint/2½ cups milk
9 egg yolks
50g/2oz/¼ cup caster (superfine) sugar
5ml/1 tsp vanilla extract
15ml/1 tbsp instant coffee powder, dissolved in 30ml/2 tbsp hot water

1 Line a 1.2 litre/2 pint/5 cup terrine or loaf tin (pan) with clear film (plastic wrap), smoothing it evenly.

2 Put the chocolate in a bowl over a pan of hot water and stir until melted. Remove the bowl from the pan and quickly beat in the butter, egg yolks, one at a time, and rum or brandy, if using.

3 In a clean grease-free bowl, using an electric mixer, beat the egg whites until frothy. Add the cream of tartar, increase the speed and mix until they form soft peaks, then stiffer peaks. Stir a third of the whites into the chocolate mixture, then fold in the remaining whites. Pour into the terrine or tin and smooth the top. Cover and freeze.

4 To make the coffee sauce, bring the milk to a simmer over a medium heat. Whisk the egg yolks and sugar until thick and creamy, then add the hot milk and return the mixture to the pan. Stir over a low heat until the sauce thickens and coats the back a spoon. Strain into a chilled bowl, stir in the vanilla extract and coffee and set aside to cool, stirring occasionally. Chill.

5 To serve, uncover the terrine or tin and dip the base into hot water for 10 seconds. Invert the dessert on to a board and peel off the clear film. Slice the loaf and serve with the coffee sauce. Decorate with the chocolate curls and coffee beans.

Pear and Hazelnut Meringue Torte

This stunning dessert with chocolate cream will raise gasps of admiration.

Serves 8–10

175g/6oz/generous ¾ cup granulated (white) sugar
1 vanilla pod (bean), split
475ml/16fl oz/2 cups water
4 ripe pears, peeled, halved and cored
30ml/2 tbsp hazelnut- or pear-flavoured liqueur
150g/5oz/1¼ cups hazelnuts, toasted
6 egg whites
pinch of salt
350g/12oz/3 cups icing (confectioners') sugar
5ml/1 tsp vanilla extract
50g/2oz plain (semisweet) chocolate, melted

For the chocolate cream

275g/10oz plain (semisweet) chocolate, chopped into small pieces
475ml/16fl oz/2 cups whipping cream
60ml/4 tbsp hazelnut- or pear-flavoured liqueur

1 In a pan large enough to hold the pears in a single layer, combine the sugar, vanilla pod and water. Over a high heat, bring to the boil, stirring, until the sugar dissolves. Lower the heat, add the pears to the syrup, cover and simmer gently for 12–15 minutes until tender. Remove the pan from the heat and allow the pears to cool in their poaching liquid. Carefully lift the pears out of the liquid and drain on kitchen paper. Transfer them to a plate, sprinkle with liqueur, cover and chill overnight.

2 Preheat the oven to 180°C/350°F/Gas 4. With a pencil, draw a 23cm/9in circle on each of two sheets of baking parchment. Turn the paper over on to two baking sheets (so that the pencil marks are underneath). Grind the toasted hazelnuts.

3 In a large bowl, beat the whites with a hand-held electric mixer until frothy. Add the salt and beat on high speed until soft peaks form. Reduce the mixer speed and gradually add the icing sugar, beating well after each addition until all the sugar has been added and the whites are stiff. Gently fold in the nuts and vanilla extract to the mixture and spoon the meringue on to the circles on the baking sheets, smoothing the tops and sides.

4 Bake for 1 hour until the tops are dry and firm. Turn off the oven and cool in the oven for 2–3 hours or overnight, until dry.

5 Make the chocolate cream. Melt the chocolate in a heatproof bowl set over a pan of simmering water and stir until melted and smooth. Cool to room temperature. Whip the cream in a bowl to soft peaks. Quickly fold the cream into the chocolate; fold in the liqueur. Spoon about one-third of the chocolate cream into a piping (pastry) bag fitted with a star tip. Set aside.

6 Thinly slice each pear in half lengthways. Place one meringue layer on a serving plate, spread with half the chocolate cream, and arrange half the pears on top. Pipe rosettes around the edge.

7 Top with the second meringue layer, spread with the remaining chocolate cream and arrange the remaining pear slices on top. Pipe a border of rosettes around the edge. Spoon the melted chocolate into a small paper cone and drizzle the chocolate over the pears. Chill for at least 1 hour before serving.

Loaf Energy 323kcal/1347kJ; Protein 10.1g; Carbohydrate 24g, of which sugars 23.8g; Fat 21.5g, of which saturates 10.3g; Cholesterol 341mg; Calcium 142mg; Fibre 0.6g; Sodium 117mg.
Meringue Torte Energy 706kcal/2960kJ; Protein 6.9g; Carbohydrate 86.1g, of which sugars 85.5g; Fat 37.4g, of which saturates 17.9g; Cholesterol 52mg; Calcium 97mg; Fibre 3.1g; Sodium 64mg.

Chocolate Pavlova with Passion Fruit Cream

This meringue dessert has a scrumptious chewy centre that is hard to resist.

Serves 6
4 egg whites
200g/7oz/1 cup caster (superfine) sugar
20ml/4 tsp cornflour (cornstarch)
45g/1¾oz/3 tbsp unsweetened cocoa powder
5ml/1 tsp vinegar
chocolate leaves, to decorate

For the filling
150g/5oz plain (semisweet) chocolate, chopped into small pieces
250ml/8fl oz/1 cup double (heavy) cream
150g/5oz/⅔ cup Greek (US strained plain) yogurt
2.5ml/½ tsp vanilla extract
4 passion fruit

1 Preheat the oven to 140°C/275°F/Gas 1. Cut a piece of baking parchment to fit a baking sheet. Draw on a 23cm/9in circle.

2 Whisk the egg whites in a clean, grease-free bowl until stiff. Gradually whisk in the sugar and continue to whisk until the mixture is stiff again. Whisk in the cornflour, cocoa and vinegar.

3 Place the baking parchment upside down on the baking sheet. Spread the mixture over the circle, making a slight dip in the centre. Bake for 1½–2 hours.

4 Make the filling. Melt the chocolate in a heatproof bowl over barely simmering water, then remove from the heat and cool slightly. In a separate bowl, whip the cream with the yogurt and vanilla extract until thick. Fold 60ml/4 tbsp into the chocolate, then set both mixtures aside.

5 Halve all the passion fruit and scoop out the pulp. Stir half into the plain cream mixture. Carefully transfer the meringue shell to a serving plate. Fill with the passion fruit cream, then spoon over the chocolate mixture and the remaining passion fruit pulp. Decorate with chocolate leaves. Serve immediately.

Meringue Gateau with Chocolate Mascarpone

A chocolatey meringue treat, ideal for a special occasion.

Serves about 10
4 egg whites
pinch of salt
175g/6oz/generous ¾ cup caster (superfine) sugar
5ml/1 tsp ground cinnamon
75g/3oz plain (semisweet) chocolate, grated
icing (confectioners') sugar and rose petals, to decorate

For the filling
115g/4oz plain (semisweet) chocolate, chopped into small pieces
5ml/1 tsp vanilla extract or rose water
115g/4oz/½ cup mascarpone

1 Preheat the oven to 150°C/300°F/Gas 2. Line two large baking sheets with baking parchment. Whisk the egg whites with the salt in a clean, grease-free bowl until they form stiff peaks.

2 Gradually whisk in half the sugar, then add the rest and whisk until stiff and glossy. Add the cinnamon and chocolate and mix.

3 Draw a 20cm/8in circle on the parchment on one of the sheets, replace it upside down and spread the circle evenly with about half the meringue. Spoon the remaining meringue in 28–30 small heaps on the sheets. Bake for 1½ hours, until crisp.

4 Make the filling. Melt the chocolate in a heatproof bowl over hot water. Cool slightly, then add the vanilla extract (or rose water) and cheese. Cool the mixture until it holds its shape.

5 Spoon the chocolate mixture into a large piping (pastry) bag and sandwich the meringues together in pairs, reserving a small amount of filling for assembling the gateau.

6 Peel off the parchment from the large round of meringue, then pile the filled meringues on top, piling them in a pyramid. Keep them in position with a few dabs of the reserved filling. Dust the pyramid with icing sugar, sprinkle with the rose petals and serve immediately.

Pavlova Energy 541kcal/2260kJ; Protein 7.3g; Carbohydrate 56.4g, of which sugars 52.3g; Fat 33.6g, of which saturates 20.4g; Cholesterol 59mg; Calcium 96mg; Fibre 1.9g; Sodium 146mg.
Meringue Gateau Energy 701kcal/2941kJ; Protein 8.2g; Carbohydrate 94.2g, of which sugars 93.1g; Fat 35g, of which saturates 21g; Cholesterol 12mg; Calcium 49mg; Fibre 3g; Sodium 31mg.

Mini Praline Pavlovas

Melt-in-the-mouth meringue topped with rich, velvety chocolate and nutty praline.

Makes 14

2 large (US extra large) egg whites
large pinch of ground cinnamon
90g/3½oz/½ cup caster (superfine) sugar
50g/2oz/½ cup pecan nuts, finely chopped

For the filling

50g/2oz/¼ cup unsalted (sweet) butter, diced
100g/3¾oz/scant 1 cup icing (confectioners') sugar, sifted
50g/2oz plain (semisweet) chocolate, broken into pieces

For the praline

50g/2oz/¼ cup caster (superfine) sugar
15g/½oz/1 tbsp finely chopped toasted almonds

1 Preheat the oven to 140°C/275°F/Gas 1. Line two baking sheets with baking parchment. Whisk the egg whites until stiff. Stir the cinnamon into the sugar. Add a spoonful of sugar to the egg whites and whisk well. Continue whisking in the sugar, a spoonful at a time, until thick and glossy. Stir in the pecan nuts, until well combined.

2 Place 14 spoonfuls of meringue on the prepared baking sheets, well spaced. Using the back of a wet teaspoon, make a small hollow in the top of each meringue. Bake in the oven for 45–60 minutes until dry and just beginning to colour. Cool.

3 Make the filling. Beat together the butter and icing sugar until light and creamy. Place the chocolate in a heatproof bowl. Set over a pan of barely simmering water and stir occasionally until melted. Cool the chocolate slightly, then add to the butter mixture and stir well. Divide the filling among the meringues.

4 Make the praline. Put the sugar in a small non-stick frying pan. Heat gently until the sugar melts to form a clear liquid. When the mixture begins to turn brown, stir in the nuts. When the mixture is a golden brown, remove from the heat and pour immediately on to a lightly oiled or non-stick baking sheet. Leave to cool completely and then break into small pieces. Sprinkle over the meringues and serve.

Mint Chocolate Meringues

These mini meringues are perfect for a child's birthday party and could be tinted pink or green. Any spares are delicious crunched into your next batch of vanilla ice cream.

Makes about 50

2 egg whites
115g/4oz/generous ½ cup caster (superfine) sugar
50g/2oz chocolate mint sticks, chopped
unsweetened cocoa powder, sifted (optional)

For the filling

150ml/¼ pint/⅔ cup double or whipping cream
5–10ml/1–2 tsp crème de menthe, or mint extract

1 Preheat the oven to 110°C/225°F/Gas ¼. Line two or three large baking sheets with baking parchment.

2 Whisk the egg whites until stiff, then gradually whisk in the sugar until the mixture becomes thick and glossy.

3 Carefully fold in the chopped mint sticks to the mixture until well combined.

4 Place heaped teaspoons of the mixture on the prepared baking sheets.

5 Bake for 1 hour, or until crisp. Remove from the oven and allow to cool, then dust with cocoa powder, if using.

6 Lightly whip the cream, stir in the crème de menthe, and sandwich the meringues together just before serving.

Cook's Tips

- *You can store these meringues in airtight tins or jars; they will keep for several days.*
- *Crème de menthe is an alcoholic mint-flavoured liqueur, available in green or clear varieties. Use the mint extract if you plan on making these meringues for children.*

Mini Pavlovas Energy 148kcal/621kJ; Protein 1.3g; Carbohydrate 21.2g, of which sugars 21.1g; Fat 7g, of which saturates 2.7g; Cholesterol 8mg; Calcium 16mg; Fibre 0.3g; Sodium 32mg.
Mint Meringues Energy 30kcal/123kJ; Protein 0.2g; Carbohydrate 3.1g, of which sugars 3.1g; Fat 1.9g, of which saturates 1.2g; Cholesterol 4mg; Calcium 3mg; Fibre 0g; Sodium 3mg.

Meringues with Chestnut Cream

This dessert is a great way to end a dinner party or other special-occasion meal.

Serves 6

2 egg whites
pinch of cream of tartar
90g/3½oz/½ cup caster (superfine) sugar
2.5ml/½ tsp vanilla extract
chocolate shavings, to decorate

For the chestnut cream

65g/2½oz/generous ¼ cup caster (superfine) sugar
120ml/4fl oz/½ cup water
450g/1lb can unsweetened chestnut purée
5ml/1 tsp vanilla extract
350ml/12fl oz/1½ cups double (heavy) cream

For the chocolate sauce

225g/8oz plain (semisweet) chocolate, chopped
175ml/6fl oz/¾ cup whipping cream
30ml/2 tbsp rum or brandy (optional)

1 Preheat the oven to 140°C/275°F/Gas 1. Line a baking sheet with baking parchment. Use a saucer to outline six 9cm/3½in circles and turn the paper over. Whisk the egg whites until frothy. Add the cream of tartar, and beat until soft peaks form. Gradually add the sugar, beating until the whites are stiff. Beat in the vanilla.

2 Spoon the whites into a piping (pastry) bag fitted with a medium plain or star nozzle and pipe six spirals following the outlines on the paper. Bake for about 1 hour, until the meringues feel firm. Transfer to a wire rack to cool completely.

3 Make the chestnut cream. Boil the sugar and water in a pan until dissolved. Boil for 5 minutes. Put the chestnut purée in a food processor and process until smooth. Add the sugar syrup until the purée is soft, but holds its shape. Add the vanilla. Whisk the cream until soft peaks form, then stir a spoonful into the mixture. Spoon the chestnut cream into a piping bag and pipe swirls on to the meringues. Pipe the cream on top.

4 Make the chocolate sauce. Heat the chocolate and cream in a pan. Remove from the heat and stir in the rum or brandy. Set aside to cool. To serve, place each meringue on a plate and sprinkle with chocolate shavings. Serve the sauce separately.

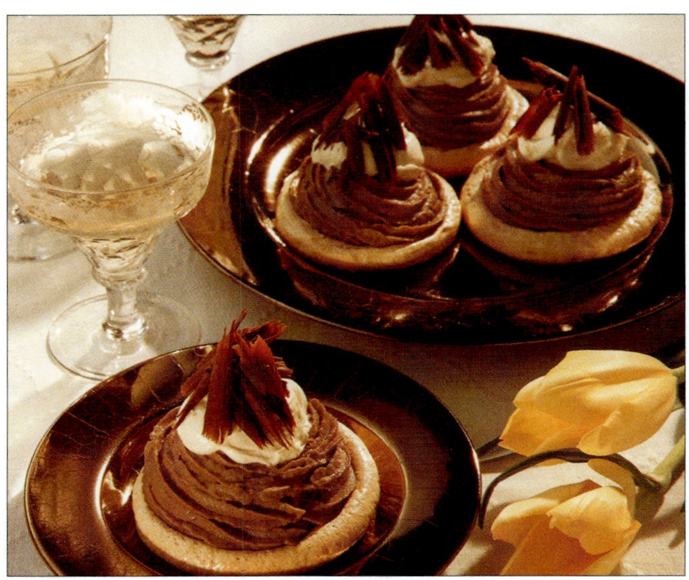

Chocolate Meringues with Mixed Fruit Compote

A glamorous dessert that is very hard to beat.

Serves 6

105ml/7 tbsp unsweetened red grape juice
105ml/7 tbsp unsweetened apple juice
30ml/2 tbsp clear honey
450g/1lb/4 cups mixed fresh summer berries, such as blackcurrants, redcurrants, raspberries and blackberries

For the meringues

3 egg whites
150g/5oz/¾ cup caster (superfine) sugar
75g/3oz good-quality plain (semisweet) chocolate, finely grated
175g/6oz/¾ cup crème fraîche

1 Preheat the oven to 110°C/225°F/Gas ¼. Grease and line two large baking sheets with baking parchment.

2 Make the meringues. Whisk the egg whites in a large mixing bowl until stiff. Gradually whisk in half the sugar, then fold in the remaining sugar, using a metal spoon. Gently fold in the grated plain chocolate. Carefully spoon the meringue mixture into a large piping (pastry) bag fitted with a large star nozzle. Pipe small round whirls of the mixture on to the prepared baking sheets. Bake the meringues for 2½–3 hours until they are firm and crisp. Remove from the oven. Carefully peel the meringues off the paper, then transfer them to a wire rack to cool.

3 Meanwhile, make the compote. Heat the fruit juices and honey in a pan until the mixture is almost boiling. Place the mixed berries in a large bowl and pour over the hot fruit juice and honey mixture. Stir gently to mix, then set aside and leave to cool. Once cool, cover the bowl with clear film (plastic wrap) and chill until required.

4 To serve, sandwich the cold meringues together with crème fraîche. Spoon the mixed fruit compote on to individual plates, top with the meringues and serve immediately.

Meringues with Cream Energy 825kcal/3439kJ; Protein 6g; Carbohydrate 80g, of which sugars 57.5g; Fat 55.6g, of which saturates 33.5g; Cholesterol 113mg; Calcium 107mg; Fibre 4g; Sodium 53mg.
Meringues with Fruit Energy 343kcal/1442kJ; Protein 4g; Carbohydrate 50.2g, of which sugars 50g; Fat 15.4g, of which saturates 10.1g; Cholesterol 34mg; Calcium 61mg; Fibre 2.2g; Sodium 44mg.

Dark Chocolate and Coffee Mousse Cake

This double treat will prove irresistible – rich sponge filled with a delicious creamy coffee mousse.

Serves 8

4 eggs
115g/4oz/generous ½ cup caster (superfine) sugar
75g/3oz/⅔ cup plain (all-purpose) flour, sifted
25g/1oz/¼ cup unsweetened cocoa powder, sifted
60ml/4 tbsp coffee liqueur, such as Tia Maria, Kahlúa or Toussaint
icing (confectioners') sugar, to dust

For the coffee mousse
30ml/2 tbsp dark-roasted ground coffee beans
350ml/12fl oz/1½ cups double (heavy) cream
115g/4oz/generous ½ cup granulated (white) sugar
120ml/4fl oz/½ cup water
4 egg yolks

1 Preheat the oven to 180°C/350°F/Gas 4. Grease and line the bases of a 20cm/8in square and a 23cm/9in round cake tin (pan) with baking parchment. Whisk the eggs and sugar in a bowl over a pan of hot water until thick. Remove from the heat.

2 Fold in the flour and cocoa. Pour a third into the square tin and the remainder into the round tin. Bake the square sponge for 15 minutes and the round for 30 minutes. Cool on a wire rack, then halve the round cake horizontally. Place the bottom half back in the tin. Sprinkle with half the liqueur. Trim the edges of the square sponge and cut into four strips to line the sides of the tin.

3 Make the mousse. Heat 50ml/2fl oz/¼ cup of the cream and pour over the coffee in a bowl, stirring until dissolved. Heat the sugar and water until dissolved. Increase the heat and boil until the syrup reaches 107°C/225°F. Cool for 5 minutes, then pour on to the egg yolks, whisking until the mixture is very thick.

4 Add the coffee cream to the remaining cream and beat until soft peaks form. Fold into the egg mixture. Spoon into the sponge case and freeze for 20 minutes. Sprinkle the remaining liqueur over the second half and place on top of the mousse. Freeze for 4 hours. Remove from the tin and dust with icing sugar.

Cappuccino Chocolate Torte

The famous and much loved beverage of freshly brewed coffee, whipped cream, chocolate and cinnamon is transformed here into a sensational dessert.

Serves 6–8

75g/3oz/6 tbsp butter, melted
275g/10oz shortbread biscuits (cookies), crushed
1.5ml/¼ tsp ground cinnamon
25ml/1½ tbsp powdered gelatine
45ml/3 tbsp cold water
2 eggs, separated
115g/4oz/½ cup soft light brown sugar
115g/4oz plain (semisweet) chocolate, chopped
175ml/6fl oz/¾ cup brewed espresso
400ml/14fl oz/1⅔ cups whipping cream
whole coffee beans and ground cinnamon, to decorate

1 Mix the butter with the biscuits and cinnamon until thoroughly combined. Spoon into the base of a 20cm/8in loose-based tin (pan) and press down well. Chill in the refrigerator while making the filling.

2 Sprinkle the gelatine over the cold water. Leave to soften for 5 minutes, then place the bowl over a pan of hot water and stir to dissolve.

3 Whisk the egg yolks and sugar until thick. Put the chocolate in a bowl with the coffee and stir until melted. Add to the egg mixture, then cook gently in a pan for 1–2 minutes until thickened. Stir in the gelatine. Leave until just beginning to set, stirring occasionally.

4 Whip 150ml/¼ pint/⅔ cup of the cream until soft peaks form. Whisk the egg whites until stiff. Gently fold the cream into the coffee mixture, followed by the egg whites. Pour the mixture over the biscuit base and chill for 2 hours.

5 When ready to serve, remove the torte from the tin and transfer to a serving plate. Whip the remaining cream in a bowl until it has thickened slightly and place a dollop on top. Decorate the top with a little ground cinnamon and place a few whole coffee beans on each plate.

Mousse Cake Energy 465kcal/1940kJ; Protein 7g; Carbohydrate 40.1g, of which sugars 32.6g; Fat 31.1g, of which saturates 16.6g; Cholesterol 262mg; Calcium 82mg; Fibre 0.7g; Sodium 88mg.
Cappuccino Torte Energy 584kcal/2429kJ; Protein 5.5g; Carbohydrate 47.3g, of which sugars 30.8g; Fat 42.7g, of which saturates 26.6g; Cholesterol 146mg; Calcium 81mg; Fibre 1g; Sodium 181mg.

Raspberry Chocolate Mousse Gateau

A lavish quantity of raspberries gives this chocolatey-based gateau its vibrant colour and full flavour. Make it at the height of summer, when raspberries are plentiful.

Serves 8–10

2 eggs
50g/2oz/¼ cup caster (superfine) sugar
50g/2oz/½ cup plain (all-purpose) flour
30ml/2 tbsp unsweetened cocoa powder
600g/1lb 5oz/3½ cups raspberries
115g/4oz/1 cup icing (confectioners') sugar
60ml/4 tbsp whisky (optional)
300ml/½ pint/1¼ cups whipping cream
2 egg whites

1 Preheat the oven to 180°C/350°F/Gas 4. Grease and line a 23cm/9in springform cake tin (pan). Whisk the eggs and sugar in a heatproof bowl set over a pan of simmering water until it leaves a trail. Remove from the heat and whisk for 2 minutes.

2 Sift the flour and cocoa powder over the mixture and fold in. Spoon into the tin and spread to the edges. Bake for 12–15 minutes until just firm. Leave to cool, then remove the cake from the tin and place it on a wire rack. Wash and dry the tin.

3 Line the sides of the clean tin with baking parchment and lower the cake back in. Freeze until the filling is ready. Set aside 200g/7oz/generous 1 cup of the raspberries. Put the remainder in a bowl, stir in the icing sugar and process to a purée in a food processor or blender. Strain into a bowl, then stir in the whisky, if using.

4 Whip the cream to form soft peaks. Whisk the egg whites until stiff. Fold the cream, then the whites into the purée. Spread half the filling over the cake. Sprinkle with the reserved raspberries. Spread the remaining filling on top and level the surface. Cover and freeze the gateau overnight.

5 Transfer the gateau to the refrigerator at least 1 hour before serving. Remove it from the tin, place on a serving plate and serve in slices.

Rich Chocolate Mousse Gateau

Because this gateau is heavily laced with liqueur, you can easily get away with a bought sponge. The mousse is rich, so serve small portions.

Serves 12

400g/14oz chocolate-flavoured sponge cake
75ml/5 tbsp Cointreau or other orange-flavoured liqueur
finely grated rind and juice of 1 orange
300g/11oz plain (semisweet) chocolate, broken into pieces
25g/1oz/¼ cup unsweetened cocoa powder
45ml/3 tbsp golden (light corn) syrup
3 eggs
300ml/½ pint/1¼ cups whipping cream
150ml/¼ pint/⅔ cup double (heavy) cream, lightly whipped
unsweetened cocoa powder, for dusting

1 Cut the cake into 5mm/¼in thick slices. Set a third aside, and use the remainder to make a case for the mousse. Line the bottom of a 23cm/9in springform or loose-based cake tin (pan) with cake, trimming to fit neatly, then use more for the sides, making a case about 4cm/1½ in deep.

2 Mix 30ml/2 tbsp of the liqueur with the orange juice and drizzle over the sponge case. Put the chocolate in a heatproof bowl. Add the cocoa powder, syrup and remaining liqueur and place the bowl over a pan of simmering water. Leave until melted and smooth, then remove from the heat.

3 Whisk the eggs with the orange rind in a mixing bowl until they are thick and pale. Whip the whipping cream until it forms soft peaks. Fold the chocolate mixture into the whisked eggs, using a large metal spoon, then fold in the cream. Scrape the mixture into the sponge case and level the surface.

4 Cover with the reserved chocolate cake, trimming the pieces to fit. Cover and freeze overnight.

5 Transfer the gateau to the refrigerator 30 minutes before serving. Invert on to a plate, spread with the double cream and dust with cocoa powder.

Raspberry Gateau Energy 238kcal/996kJ; Protein 4.4g; Carbohydrate 25g, of which sugars 20.9g; Fat 14.1g, of which saturates 8.3g; Cholesterol 70mg; Calcium 58mg; Fibre 2g; Sodium 65mg.
Rich Mousse Gateau Energy 488kcal/2032kJ; Protein 6g; Carbohydrate 37.4g, of which sugars 29.6g; Fat 34.4g, of which saturates 15.3g; Cholesterol 92mg; Calcium 61mg; Fibre 1.2g; Sodium 175mg.

White Chocolate and Brownie Torte

An exceedingly rich dessert, this quick but impressive-looking dish is guaranteed to appeal to chocolate lovers. The great thing about this recipe is that it uses very few ingredients, making shopping a breeze.

Serves 10
300g/11oz white chocolate, broken into pieces
600ml/1 pint/2½ cups double (heavy) cream
250g/9oz rich chocolate brownies
unsweetened cocoa powder, for dusting

1 Dampen the sides of a 20cm/8in springform tin (pan) and line with a strip of baking parchment. Put the chocolate in a small pan. Add 150ml/¼ pint/⅔ cup of the cream and heat very gently until the chocolate has melted. Stir until smooth, then pour into a bowl and leave to cool.

2 Break the chocolate brownies into chunky pieces and sprinkle these on the bottom of the prepared tin. Pack them down lightly to make a fairly dense base.

3 Whip the remaining cream until it forms soft peaks, then fold in the white chocolate mixture.

4 Spoon into the tin to cover the layer of brownies, then tap the tin gently on the work surface to level the chocolate mixture. Cover the tin and freeze for a few hours or overnight.

5 Transfer the torte to the refrigerator about 45 minutes before serving, then remove the tin to serve. Decorate with a light dusting of cocoa powder before serving.

Cook's Tips
- *If you are unable to find good-quality brownies, use a moist chocolate sponge instead.*
- *Serve with a fresh fruit salad as a foil to the richness. A mix of summer fruit topped with a purée made from lightly cooked raspberries is the perfect partner.*

Chocolate and Brandied Fig Torte

A seriously rich torte for chocolate lovers. If you dislike figs, use dried prunes, dates or apricots instead.

Serves 8
250g/9oz/1½ cups dried figs
60ml/4 tbsp brandy
200g/7oz ginger nut biscuits (gingersnaps)
175g/6oz/¾ cup unsalted (sweet) butter, softened
150ml/¼ pint/⅔ cup milk
250g/9oz plain (semisweet) chocolate, broken into pieces
45ml/3 tbsp caster (superfine) sugar
unsweetened cocoa powder, for dusting
whipped cream, to serve

1 Chop the figs and put them into a bowl, pour over the brandy and leave for 2–3 hours until most of the brandy has been absorbed. Break the ginger nut biscuits into large chunks, put the pieces in a strong plastic bag and crush them with a rolling pin.

2 Melt half the butter and stir in the crumbs until combined. Pack on to the bottom and up the sides of a 20cm/8in loose-based flan tin (pan) that is about 3cm/1¼in deep. Leave in the refrigerator to chill.

3 Pour the milk into a pan, add the chocolate pieces and heat gently until the chocolate has melted and the mixture is smooth, stirring frequently. Pour the chocolate mixture into a bowl and leave to cool.

4 In a separate bowl, beat the remaining butter with the caster sugar until the mixture is pale and creamy.

5 Add the chocolate mixture, whisking until it is well mixed. Fold in the figs, and any remaining brandy, and spoon the mixture into the chilled flan case. Level the surface, cover and freeze overnight.

6 Transfer the frozen torte to the refrigerator about 30 minutes before serving so that the filling softens slightly. Lightly dust the surface with cocoa powder and serve in slices, with dollops of lightly whipped cream.

Brownie Torte Energy 570kcal/2365kJ; Protein 5.2g; Carbohydrate 31.1g, of which sugars 25.7g; Fat 48.1g, of which saturates 25.6g; Cholesterol 82mg; Calcium 129mg; Fibre 0g; Sodium 154mg.
Fig Torte Energy 539kcal/2257kJ; Protein 5g; Carbohydrate 63.9g, of which sugars 54.2g; Fat 29.7g, of which saturates 17.7g; Cholesterol 50mg; Calcium 172mg; Fibre 4.1g; Sodium 241mg.

Iced Praline Chocolate Torte

This lovely torte will serve you well on any occasion.

Serves 8

115g/4oz/1 cup almonds
115g/4oz/generous ½ cup caster (superfine) sugar
115g/4oz/⅔ cup raisins
90ml/6 tbsp rum or brandy
115g/4oz dark (bittersweet) chocolate, broken into squares
30ml/2 tbsp milk
450ml/¾ pint/scant 2 cups double (heavy) cream
30ml/2 tbsp strong black coffee
16 sponge fingers

To finish

150ml/¼ pint/⅔ cup double (heavy) cream
50g/2oz/½ cup flaked (sliced) almonds, toasted
15g/½oz dark (bittersweet) chocolate, melted

1 To make the praline, oil a baking sheet. Put the nuts into a heavy pan with the sugar and heat gently until the sugar melts and coats the nuts. Cook slowly until the nuts brown and the sugar caramelizes. Transfer the nuts quickly to the sheet; leave until cold. Break up and grind to a fine powder in a blender.

2 Soak the raisins in 45ml/3 tbsp of the rum or brandy for at least an hour to soften and absorb the rum. Melt the chocolate with the milk in a bowl over a pan of hot, but not boiling water. Remove and leave until cold. Lightly grease a 1.2 litre/2 pint/5 cup loaf tin (pan) and line it with baking parchment.

3 Whisk the cream in a bowl until it holds soft peaks. Whisk in the chocolate. Fold in the praline and the raisins, with any liquid.

4 Mix the coffee and remaining rum or brandy in a shallow dish. Dip in the sponge fingers and arrange half in a layer over the base of the prepared loaf tin. Cover with the chocolate mixture and add another layer of soaked sponge fingers. Leave in the freezer overnight.

5 To finish, whip the double cream. Dip the tin briefly in warm water and turn the torte out on to a serving plate. Cover with the whipped cream, sprinkle the top with toasted almonds and drizzle with melted chocolate. Freeze until needed.

Iced Paradise Chocolate Cake

Serve this rich and creamy delight chilled.

Makes one 23 x 13cm/9 x 5in cake

3 eggs
75g/3oz/scant ½ cup caster (superfine) sugar
65g/12½oz/9 tbsp plain (all-purpose) flour, sifted
15g/½oz/2 tbsp cornflour (cornstarch), sifted
90ml/6 tbsp dark rum
250g/9oz/1½ cups plain (semisweet) chocolate chips
30ml/2 tbsp golden (light corn) syrup
30ml/2 tbsp water
115g/4oz/generous 1 cup desiccated (dry unsweetened shredded) coconut, toasted
400ml/14fl oz/1⅔ cups double (heavy) cream, whipped
25g/1oz/2 tbsp unsalted (sweet) butter
30ml/2 tbsp single (light) cream
50g/2oz/⅓ cup white chocolate chips, melted
coconut curls, to decorate
unsweetened cocoa powder, to dust

1 Preheat the oven to 200°C/400°F/Gas 6. Grease and flour two baking sheets. Line a 23 × 13cm/9 × 5in loaf tin (pan) with clear film (plastic wrap).

2 Whisk the eggs and sugar together in a heatproof bowl. Place over a pan of simmering water and whisk until pale and thick. Whisk off the heat until cool. Fold in the flour and cornflour. Pipe 30 7.5cm/3in sponge fingers on to the baking sheets. Bake for 8–10 minutes. Cool slightly, then transfer to a wire rack.

3 Line the base and sides of the loaf tin with sponge fingers. Brush with rum. Melt 75g/3oz/½ cup chocolate chips, the syrup, water and 30ml/2 tbsp rum in a bowl over simmering water.

4 Stir the chocolate mixture and coconut into the cream. Pour into the tin and top with the remaining fingers. Brush with the remaining rum. Cover with clear film and freeze until firm.

5 Melt the remaining chocolate with the butter and single cream as before, then cool slightly. Turn the cake out on to a wire rack. Coat with the icing then chill. Drizzle with white chocolate zigzags and chill again. Sprinkle with coconut curls and dust with cocoa powder.

Praline Torte Energy 636kcal/2650kJ; Protein 7.7g; Carbohydrate 49.5g, of which sugars 43.5g; Fat 43.9g, of which saturates 22.3g; Cholesterol 134mg; Calcium 104mg; Fibre 1.9g; Sodium 47mg.
Paradise Energy 5502kcal/22864kJ; Protein 62.6g; Carbohydrate 349.1g, of which sugars 226.4g; Fat 416.4g, of which saturates 267.8g; Cholesterol 1204mg; Calcium 760mg; Fibre 26.4g; Sodium 653mg.

White Chocolate, Frosted Raspberry and Coffee Terrine

A white chocolate and raspberry layer and a contrasting smooth coffee layer make this attractive-looking terrine dessert doubly delicious.

Serves 6–8

30ml/2 tbsp ground coffee, e.g. mocha orange-flavoured
250ml/8fl oz/1 cup milk
4 eggs, separated
50g/2oz/¼ cup caster (superfine) sugar
30ml/2 tbsp cornflour (cornstarch)
150ml/¼ pint/⅔ cup double (heavy) cream
150g/5oz white chocolate, roughly chopped
115g/4oz/⅔ cup raspberries
shavings of white chocolate and cocoa powder, to decorate

1 Line a 1.5 litre/2½ pint/6¼ cup loaf tin (pan) with clear film (plastic wrap) and chill in the freezer. Put the coffee in a jug (pitcher). Heat 100ml/3½fl oz/scant ½ cup of the milk to near-boiling point and pour over the coffee. Leave to infuse (steep).

2 Blend the egg yolks, sugar and cornflour together in a pan and whisk in the remaining milk and the cream. Bring to the boil, stirring all the time, until thickened.

3 Divide the mixture between two bowls and add the white chocolate to one, stirring until melted. Strain the coffee into the other bowl and mix well. Leave until cool, stirring occasionally.

4 Whisk two of the egg whites until stiff. Fold into the coffee custard. Spoon into the tin. Freeze for 30 minutes. Whisk the remaining whites and fold into the chocolate mixture with the raspberries. Spoon into the tin and level. Freeze for 4 hours.

5 Turn the terrine out on to a flat serving plate and peel off the clear film. Cover with shavings and dust with cocoa powder.

Cook's Tip
Soften the terrine in the refrigerator for 20 minutes before slicing.

Classic Triple Chocolate Terrine

This variation on Neapolitan ice cream is made with smooth dark, milk and white chocolate.

Serves 8–10

6 egg yolks
115g/4oz/generous ½ cup caster (superfine) sugar
5ml/1 tsp cornflour (cornstarch)
450ml/¾ pint/scant 2 cups semi-skimmed (low-fat) milk
115g/4oz dark (bittersweet) chocolate, broken into squares
115g/4oz milk chocolate, broken into squares
115g/4oz white chocolate, broken into squares
2.5ml/½ tsp natural vanilla extract
450ml/¾ pint/scant 2 cups whipping cream

1 Whisk the egg yolks, sugar and cornflour until thick. Pour the milk into a pan and bring to the boil. Pour it on to the yolk mixture, whisking constantly, then return the mixture to the pan and simmer, stirring, until the custard thickens and is smooth.

2 Divide the custard among three bowls. Add the chocolates: the dark to one, milk to another, and white and vanilla to the third. Stir with separate spoons until the chocolate has melted. Cool, then chill. Line a 25 × 7.5 × 7.5cm/10 × 3 × 3in terrine or large loaf tin (pan) with clear film (plastic wrap).

3 Stir a third of the cream into each bowl, then churn the milk chocolate custard mixture until thick. Return the remaining bowls of flavoured custard and cream mixture to the refrigerator. Spoon the milk chocolate ice cream into the terrine or tin, level the surface and freeze the ice cream until it is firm.

4 Churn the white chocolate ice cream in an ice cream maker until it is thick and smooth, then spoon it into the tin. Level the surface and freeze the ice cream until it is firm. Finally, churn the dark chocolate ice cream and spread it in the tin to form the top layer, making sure the surface is smooth and level.

5 Cover the terrine with clear film, then freeze it overnight. To serve, remove the clear film cover, then invert on to a plate. Peel off the clear film and serve in slices.

Raspberry Terrine Energy 285kcal/1189kJ; Protein 6.2g; Carbohydrate 23.4g, of which sugars 19.9g; Fat 19.2g, of which saturates 10.8g; Cholesterol 123mg; Calcium 119mg; Fibre 0.4g; Sodium 76mg.
Chocolate Terrine Energy 453kcal/1889kJ; Protein 6.6g; Carbohydrate 35.9g, of which sugars 35.8g; Fat 32.5g, of which saturates 18.9g; Cholesterol 174mg; Calcium 160mg; Fibre 0.4g; Sodium 60mg.

Mocha, Prune and Armagnac Terrine

A sophisticated iced chocolate dessert for entertaining in style.

Serves 6

115g/4oz/½ cup ready-to-eat pitted prunes, chopped
90ml/6 tbsp Armagnac
90g/3½oz/½ cup caster (superfine) sugar
150ml/¼ pint/⅔ cup water
45ml/3 tbsp coffee beans
150g/5oz plain (semisweet) chocolate, broken into pieces
300ml/½ pint/1¼ cups double (heavy) cream
unsweetened cocoa powder, for dusting

1 Put the prunes in a small bowl. Pour over 75ml/5 tbsp of the Armagnac and leave to soak for at least 3 hours or overnight in the refrigerator. Line the bases of six 100ml/3½fl oz/scant ½ cup ramekins with baking parchment.

2 Put the sugar and water in a heavy pan and heat gently until the sugar dissolves, stirring occasionally. Add the soaked prunes and any of the Armagnac that remains in the bowl; simmer the prunes gently in the syrup for 5 minutes.

3 Using a slotted spoon, lift the prunes out of the pan and set them aside. Add the coffee beans to the syrup and simmer gently for 5 minutes.

4 Lift out the coffee beans and put about a third of them in a bowl. Spoon over 120ml/4fl oz/½ cup of the syrup and stir in the remaining Armagnac.

5 Add the chocolate to the pan containing the remaining syrup and leave until melted. Whip the cream until it just holds its shape. Using a large metal spoon, fold the chocolate mixture and prunes into the cream until just combined. Spoon the mixture into the lined ramekins, cover and freeze for at least 3 hours.

6 To serve, loosen the edges of the ramekins with a knife, then dip in very hot water for 2 seconds and invert on to serving plates. Decorate with the syrup and a dusting of cocoa powder.

Iced Pear Terrine with Calvados and Chocolate Sauce

This terrine makes a refreshing and impressive end to a meal. Ensure the pears are ripe and juicy.

Serves 8

1.5kg/3–3½lb ripe Williams pears
juice of 1 lemon
115g/4oz/generous ½ cup caster (superfine) sugar
10 whole cloves
90ml/6 tbsp water
julienne strips of orange rind, to decorate

For the sauce

200g/7oz plain (semisweet) chocolate
60ml/4 tbsp hot strong black coffee
200ml/7fl oz/1 cup double (heavy) cream
30ml/2 tbsp Calvados or brandy

1 Peel, core and slice the pears. Place them in a pan with the lemon juice, sugar, cloves and water. Cover and simmer for 10 minutes. Remove the cloves. Allow the pears to cool.

2 Process the pears with their juice, in a food processor or blender, until smooth. Pour the purée into a freezerproof bowl, cover and freeze until firm.

3 Meanwhile, line a 900g/2lb loaf tin (pan) with clear film (plastic wrap). Allow the film to overhang the sides of the tin. Remove the frozen pear purée from the freezer and spoon it into a food processor or blender. Process until smooth. Pour into the prepared tin, cover and freeze until firm.

4 Make the sauce. Break the chocolate into a large heatproof bowl over a pan of simmering water, stirring until melted and smooth. Stir in the coffee and the cream and then the Calvados or brandy. Set the sauce aside.

5 About 20 minutes before serving, remove the tin from the freezer. Invert on to a plate, lift off the clear film and place the terrine in the refrigerator to soften slightly. Heat the sauce over hot water. Slice the terrine and spoon over some of the sauce. Decorate with julienne strips of orange rind.

Mocha Terrine Energy 495kcal/2060kJ; Protein 2.6g; Carbohydrate 38.9g, of which sugars 38.7g; Fat 33.9g, of which saturates 20.9g; Cholesterol 70mg; Calcium 47mg; Fibre 1.7g; Sodium 16mg.
Pear Terrine Energy 392kcal/1638kJ; Protein 2.3g; Carbohydrate 50.1g, of which sugars 49.9g; Fat 20.6g, of which saturates 12.6g; Cholesterol 36mg; Calcium 49mg; Fibre 4.8g; Sodium 14mg.

Chocolate and Vanilla Ice Cream

To make this popular classic, use good-quality chocolate to give the best flavour.

Serves 6

750ml/1¼ pints/3 cups milk
10cm/4in piece of vanilla pod (bean)
4 egg yolks
150g/5oz/¾ cup granulated (white) sugar
225g/8oz dark (bittersweet) chocolate, melted

1 To make the custard, heat the milk with the vanilla pod in a small pan. Remove from the heat as soon as small bubbles start to form. Do not boil.

2 Beat the egg yolks with a wire whisk or electric beater. Gradually incorporate the sugar, and continue beating for about 5 minutes until the mixture is pale yellow. Strain the milk and slowly add it to the egg mixture, drop by drop.

3 Pour the mixture into a double boiler with the melted chocolate. Stir over moderate heat until the water in the pan is boiling, and the custard thickens enough to lightly coat the back of a spoon. Remove from the heat and allow to cool.

4 Pour the mixture into a freezer container and freeze until set, about 3 hours. Remove from the container and chop roughly into 7.5cm/3in pieces. Place in the bowl of a food processor and process until smooth. Return to the freezer container, and freeze again until firm. Repeat the freezing and chopping process two or three times, until a smooth consistency is reached, then freeze until required. Alternatively, you can use an ice cream maker and freeze the mixture following the manufacturer's instructions.

Cook's Tip
If you do not have a double boiler, cook the custard in a heatproof bowl set over a pan of water. Make sure that the custard does not boil, otherwise it will curdle.

Chocolate Flake Ice Cream

This enticing ice cream, speckled with chocolate, is difficult to resist. Serve with slices of tropical fruit, such as pineapple and mango, for a perfect balance.

Serves 6

300ml/½ pint/1¼ cups whipping cream, chilled
90ml/6 tbsp Greek (US strained plain) yogurt
75–90ml/5–6 tbsp caster (superfine) sugar
few drops of vanilla extract
150g/5oz/10 tbsp flaked or roughly grated chocolate
flaked chocolate pieces, to decorate

1 Have ready a 600–900ml/1–1½ pint/2½–3¾ cup freezer container, preferably with a lid.

2 Gently whip the cream in a large bowl until thickened slightly then fold in the yogurt, sugar, vanilla extract and chocolate. Stir gently to combine thoroughly, and then transfer to the freezer container.

3 Smooth the surface of the ice cream, then cover and freeze. Gently stir with a fork every 30 minutes for up to 4 hours until the ice cream is too hard to stir.

4 Alternatively, use an ice cream maker. Freeze the cream and chocolate mixture following the manufacturer's instructions.

5 Transfer to the refrigerator 15 minutes before serving to soften slightly. Serve in scoops, decorated with chocolate flakes.

Cook's Tips
• *Transferring the ice cream from the freezer to the refrigerator for a short time before serving allows the full flavour of the dessert to develop and makes it easier to scoop it into neat balls for serving.*
• *Use a metal scoop to serve the ice cream. Dipping the scoop briefly in warm water between servings helps to stop the ice cream sticking to the scoop.*

Chocolate Energy 388kcal/1634kJ; Protein 8.2g; Carbohydrate 55.8g, of which sugars 55.5g; Fat 16.3g, of which saturates 8.7g; Cholesterol 144mg; Calcium 191mg; Fibre 0.9g; Sodium 64mg.
Flake Energy 385kcal/1600kJ; Protein 3.3g; Carbohydrate 30.6g, of which sugars 30.4g; Fat 28.7g, of which saturates 17.6g; Cholesterol 54mg; Calcium 66mg; Fibre 0.6g; Sodium 25mg.

White Chocolate Raspberry Ripple

A truly luscious treat that always impresses. Note that an ice cream maker is required for this recipe.

Serves 6

250ml/8fl oz/1 cup milk
475ml/16fl oz/2 cups whipping cream
7 egg yolks
30ml/2 tbsp sugar
225g/8oz good white chocolate, chopped into small pieces
5ml/1 tsp vanilla extract
mint sprigs, to decorate

For the sauce

275g/10oz raspberry preserve or 275g/10oz frozen raspberries in light syrup
10ml/2 tsp golden (light corn) syrup
15ml/1 tbsp lemon juice
15ml/1 tbsp cornflour (cornstarch), if using frozen fruit in syrup, mixed with 15ml/1 tbsp water

1 For the sauce, put the preserve in a pan with the golden syrup, the lemon juice and the water but not the cornflour. If using frozen fruit, press the fruit and its syrup through a sieve (strainer) into a pan and add all the other sauce ingredients. Bring to the boil, stirring. Simmer for 2 minutes. Pour into a bowl, cool, then chill.

2 In a pan, combine the milk and 250ml/8fl oz/1 cup of the cream and bring to the boil. In a bowl, beat the yolks and sugar with a hand-held mixer for 2–3 minutes until thick and creamy. Gradually pour the hot milk mixture over the yolks and return to the pan. Cook over a medium heat, stirring constantly, until the custard coats the back of a wooden spoon.

3 Remove the pan from the heat and stir in the white chocolate until melted and smooth. Pour the remaining cream into a large bowl. Strain in the hot custard, mix well, then stir in the vanilla extract. Cool, then freeze in an ice cream maker.

4 When frozen but soft, transfer a third of the ice cream to a freezerproof bowl. Set aside half the sauce, spooning a third of the rest over the ice cream. Cover with another third of the ice cream and more sauce. Repeat. With a knife, lightly marble the mixture. Cover and freeze. Soften the ice cream for 15 minutes. Serve with the rest of the raspberry sauce, and the mint.

Chocolate Cookie Ice Cream

This wickedly indulgent ice cream is a favourite in the USA. To make the result even more luxurious, use freshly baked home-made cookies with large chunks of chocolate and nuts.

Serves 4–6

4 egg yolks
75g/3oz/scant ½ cup caster (superfine) sugar
5ml/1 tsp cornflour (cornstarch)
300ml/½ pint/1¼ cups semi-skimmed (low-fat) milk
5ml/1 tsp natural vanilla extract
300ml/½ pint/1¼ cups whipping cream
150g/5oz chunky chocolate and hazelnut cookies, crumbled into chunky pieces

1 Whisk the egg yolks, sugar and cornflour in a bowl until the mixture is thick and foamy. Pour the milk into a heavy pan, bring it just to the boil, then pour it on to the yolk mixture in the bowl, whisking constantly.

2 Return to the pan and cook over a gentle heat, stirring until the custard thickens and is smooth. Pour it back into the bowl and cover closely. Leave to cool, then chill.

3 Stir the vanilla into the custard. Stir in the whipping cream and churn in an ice cream maker until thick.

4 Scrape the ice cream into a freezerproof container. Fold in the cookie chunks and freeze for 2–3 hours until firm.

5 Remove the ice cream from the freezer about 15 minutes before serving to allow it to soften slightly.

Cook's Tip

• *Experiment with different types of cookie to find the type that gives the best results.*
• *Softening the ice cream before serving will not only help make the ice cream tastier, but will also ensure the pieces of cookie inside are the perfect texture.*

Raspberry Ripple Energy 735kcal/3066kJ; Protein 10.3g; Carbohydrate 63.3g, of which sugars 61g; Fat 50.8g, of which saturates 29.2g; Cholesterol 321mg; Calcium 242mg; Fibre 1.2g; Sodium 110mg.
Cookie Energy 428kcal/1782kJ; Protein 6.2g; Carbohydrate 36.3g, of which sugars 27.1g; Fat 29.7g, of which saturates 16.4g; Cholesterol 189mg; Calcium 135mg; Fibre 0.5g; Sodium 129mg.

Ice Cream Sundae with Chocolate Sauce

This immensely popular sundae dessert consists of good-quality vanilla ice cream with a decadent warm chocolate sauce.

Serves 4

350ml/12fl oz/1½ cups milk
250ml/8fl oz/1 cup double (heavy) cream
1 vanilla pod (bean)
4 egg yolks
90g/3½oz/½ cup caster (superfine) sugar

For the chocolate sauce

60ml/4 tbsp double (heavy) cream
150ml/¼ pint/⅔ cup milk
250g/9oz Callebaut callets (semisweet bits) or other good-quality chocolate, cut into small pieces
15ml/1 tbsp brandy, rum or liqueur such as Cointreau (optional)
sweetened whipped cream, chopped nuts, chocolate curls and ice cream wafers (optional), to serve

1 Pour 250ml/8fl oz/1 cup of the milk into a heavy pan. Add the cream. Slit the vanilla pod, scrape the seeds into the pan, then heat the mixture until nearly boiling. Remove from the heat and leave to stand for 10 minutes.

2 Beat the egg yolks and sugar in a bowl until thick and creamy. Still beating, add a third of the milk mixture in a steady stream. Add the remaining milk mixture and whisk for 2 minutes more.

3 Return to the pan and cook over medium-high heat, stirring, for 5 minutes, until the custard coats the back of a spoon. Remove the pan from the heat and stir in the remaining milk. When cooled, cover and chill. Scrape the chilled mixture into a freezer container and freeze until firm, whisking occasionally.

4 Make the chocolate sauce. Simmer the cream and milk in a pan. Remove from the heat and stir in the chocolate bits until dissolved. Stir in the brandy or liqueur, if using.

5 Pour about 20ml/4 tsp of the warm chocolate sauce into ice cream coupes or cups. Top with scoops of ice cream and more sauce. Pipe cream on top, add chopped nuts, curls and a wafer.

Chocolate Fudge and Banana Sundae

A banana and ice cream treat, highlighted with coffee.

Serves 4

4 scoops each vanilla and coffee ice cream
2 small ripe bananas
whipped cream
toasted flaked (sliced) almonds

For the sauce

50g/2oz/¼ cup soft light brown sugar
120ml/4fl oz/½ cup golden (light corn) syrup
45ml/3 tbsp strong black coffee
5ml/1 tsp ground cinnamon
150g/5oz plain (semisweet) chocolate, chopped into small pieces
75ml/2½fl oz/⅓ cup whipping cream
45ml/3 tbsp coffee-flavoured liqueur (optional)

1 Make the sauce. Place the sugar, syrup, coffee and cinnamon in a heavy pan. Bring to the boil, then boil for about 5 minutes, stirring the mixture constantly.

2 Turn off the heat and stir in the chocolate pieces. When the chocolate has melted and the mixture is smooth, stir in the cream and the coffee-flavoured liqueur, if using. Set the sauce aside to cool slightly.

3 Fill four glasses with a scoop each of vanilla and coffee ice cream.

4 Peel the bananas and slice them thinly. Sprinkle the sliced bananas over the ice cream. Pour the warm fudge sauce over the bananas, then top each sundae with a generous swirl of whipped cream. Sprinkle the sundaes with toasted almonds and serve immediately.

Cook's Tip

To make life easier you can make the chocolate sauce ahead of time and reheat it gently, until just warm, when you are ready to make the sundaes. Assemble the sundaes just before serving.

Ice Cream Energy 930kcal/3869kJ; Protein 11.2g; Carbohydrate 72.3g, of which sugars 71.7g; Fat 68.2g, of which saturates 40.2g; Cholesterol 324mg; Calcium 229mg; Fibre 1.6g; Sodium 80mg.
Fudge Energy 642kcal/2690kJ; Protein 5.5g; Carbohydrate 85.9g, of which sugars 84g; Fat 33.1g, of which saturates 20.5g; Cholesterol 64mg; Calcium 115mg; Fibre 1.4g; Sodium 132mg.

French-style Coupe Glacée with Chocolate Ice Cream

This dessert can be made with bought ice cream, but this extra rich chocolate ice cream is the main feature.

Serves 6–8

225g/8oz dark (bittersweet) chocolate, chopped
250ml/8fl oz/1 cup milk mixed with 250ml/8fl oz/1 cup single (light) cream
3 egg yolks
50g/1¾oz/¼ cup sugar
350ml/12fl oz/1½ cups double (heavy) cream
15ml/1 tbsp vanilla extract
chocolate triangles, to decorate

For the espresso cream

45g/3 tbsp instant espresso powder, dissolved in 45ml/3 tbsp boiling water, cooled
350ml/12fl oz/1½ cups double (heavy) cream
30ml/2 tbsp coffee-flavoured liqueur

For the sauce

300ml/10fl oz/1¼ cups double (heavy) cream
30g/2 tbsp instant espresso powder, dissolved in 45ml/3 tbsp boiling water
320g/11oz dark (bittersweet) chocolate, chopped
30ml/2 tbsp coffee-flavoured liqueur

1 Melt the chocolate in a pan over a low heat with 120ml/4fl oz/½ cup of the milk mixture. In another pan, boil the remaining milk mixture. Beat the egg yolks and sugar in a bowl until thick and creamy. Pour the milk mixture over the yolks, whisking, and return to the pan. Heat until it thickens, stirring. Pour over the melted chocolate, stirring until blended.

2 Pour the cream into a bowl, and strain in the custard with the vanilla. Blend, then cool. Refrigerate until cold. Transfer to an ice cream maker and freeze according to instructions.

3 Make the espresso cream. Stir the espresso powder into the cream and beat until soft peaks form. Add the liqueur and mix. Spoon into a piping (pastry) bag fitted with a star tip and chill.

4 Prepare the sauce. Boil the cream and espresso powder. Remove from the heat and stir in the chocolate and liqueur. Pipe a layer of espresso cream into six wine goblets. Add the ice cream. Spoon on the sauce and top with rosettes of espresso cream.

Black Forest Sundae

There's more than one way to enjoy the classic Black Forest gateau. Here the traditional ingredients are layered in a sundae glass to make a superb cold sweet.

Serves 4

400g/14oz can stoned (pitted) black cherries in syrup
15ml/1 tbsp cornflour (cornstarch)
45ml/3 tbsp Kirsch
150ml/¼ pint/⅔ cup whipping cream
15ml/1 tbsp icing (confectioners') sugar
600ml/1 pint/2½ cups chocolate ice cream
115g/4oz chocolate-flavoured sponge cake
8 fresh cherries
vanilla ice cream, to serve

1 Strain the cherry syrup from the can into a pan. Spoon the cornflour into a small bowl and stir in 30ml/2 tbsp of the strained cherry syrup.

2 Bring the syrup in the pan to the boil. Stir in the cornflour and syrup mixture. Simmer briefly, stirring constantly, until the syrup thickens.

3 Add the drained canned cherries, stir in the Kirsch and spread on a metal tray to cool.

4 Whip the cream in a large bowl with the icing sugar until the mixture thickens.

5 Place a spoonful of the cherry mixture in the bottom of four sundae glasses. Continue with layers of ice cream, cake, cream and more cherry mixture until the glasses are full.

6 Finish with a piece of chocolate cake, two scoops of ice cream and more cream. Decorate with the fresh cherries.

Cook's Tip

Bottled black cherries often have a better flavour than canned ones, especially if the stones are left in. You needn't remove the stones – just remember to warn your guests.

Coupe Energy 1062kcal/4400kJ; Protein 8.6g; Carbohydrate 50.9g, of which sugars 50.3g; Fat 92.4g, of which saturates 56.4g; Cholesterol 262mg; Calcium 152mg; Fibre 1.8g; Sodium 55mg.
Black Forest Energy 727kcal/3031kJ; Protein 9.4g; Carbohydrate 68g, of which sugars 58.2g; Fat 45.4g, of which saturates 23.1g; Cholesterol 39mg; Calcium 213mg; Fibre 0.7g; Sodium 233mg.

Rocky Road Ice Cream

A gloriously rich chocolate ice cream with lots of texture.

Serves 6
115g/4oz plain (semisweet) chocolate, chopped into small pieces
150ml/¼ pint/⅔ cup milk
300ml/½ pint/1¼ cups double (heavy) cream
115g/4oz/2 cups marshmallows, chopped
115g/4oz/½ cup glacé (candied) cherries, chopped
50g/2oz/½ cup crumbled shortbread
30ml/2 tbsp chopped walnuts
chocolate sauce and wafers, to serve (optional)

1 Melt the chocolate in the milk in a pan over a gentle heat, stirring from time to time. Pour into a bowl and leave to cool.

2 Whip the cream in a separate bowl until it just holds its shape. Beat in the chocolate mixture, a little at a time, until the mixture is smooth and creamy.

3 Pour the chocolate mixture into a freezer container and transfer to the freezer. Freeze until ice crystals form around the edges, then whisk with a strong hand whisk or hand-held electric mixer until smooth. Alternatively, use an ice cream maker and churn the mixture until almost frozen, following the manufacturer's instructions.

4 Stir the marshmallows, glacé cherries, crumbled shortbread and nuts into the iced mixture, then return to the freezer container and freeze until firm.

5 Allow the ice cream to soften at room temperature for 15–20 minutes before serving in scoops. Add a wafer and chocolate sauce to each portion, if you wish.

Cook's Tip
Do not allow the ice cream mixture to freeze too hard before step 4, otherwise it will be difficult to stir in the remaining ingredients.

Chocolate Bombes with Hot Sauce

These individual ice cream bombes, with a surprise vanilla and chocolate-chip centre, are served with a hot toffee cream sauce to make a truly indulgent hot-and-cold dessert.

Serves 6
1 litre/1¾ pints/4 cups soft-scoop chocolate ice cream
475ml/16fl oz/2 cups soft-scoop vanilla ice cream
50g/2oz/⅓ cup plain (semisweet) chocolate chips

For the sauce
115g/4oz toffees
75ml/5 tbsp double (heavy) cream

1 Divide the chocolate ice cream equally among six small cups. Push it roughly to the base and up the sides, leaving a small cup-shaped dip in the middle. Put them in the freezer and leave for 45 minutes. Take the cups out again and smooth the ice cream in each to make cup shapes with hollow centres. Return to the freezer.

2 Put the vanilla ice cream in a small bowl and break it up slightly with a spoon. Stir in the chocolate chips and use this mixture to fill the hollows in the cups of chocolate ice cream. Smooth the tops, then cover the cups with clear film (plastic wrap), return to the freezer and leave overnight.

3 Melt the toffees with the cream in a small pan over a very low heat, stirring constantly until smooth, warm and creamy.

4 Turn out the bombes on to individual plates and pour the toffee sauce over the top. Serve immediately.

Cook's Tips
• *To make it easier to unmould the bombes, dip them briefly in hot water, then turn out immediately on to serving plates. If you wish, you can return the unmoulded bombes to the freezer for about 10 minutes to firm up.*
• *Serve with crisp little biscuits (cookies) for a crunchy contrast.*

Rocky Road Energy 545kcal/2271kJ; Protein 4.7g; Carbohydrate 48.3g, of which sugars 40.6g; Fat 38.4g, of which saturates 22g; Cholesterol 77mg; Calcium 85mg; Fibre 1g; Sodium 57mg.
Bombes Energy 715kcal/2975kJ; Protein 10.6g; Carbohydrate 59.6g, of which sugars 55.1g; Fat 49.7g, of which saturates 29.7g; Cholesterol 21mg; Calcium 269mg; Fibre 0.2g; Sodium 216mg.

Layered Chocolate, Chestnut and Brandy Bombes

Using an ice cream maker takes all the effort out of making these triple-flavoured ice creams, which taste delicious and look stunning.

Serves 6

3 egg yolks
75g/3oz/scant ½ cup caster (superfine) sugar
5ml/1 tsp cornflour (cornstarch)
300ml/½ pint/1 ¼ cups milk
115g/4oz plain (semisweet) chocolate, chopped
150g/5oz/generous 1 cup sweetened chestnut purée
30ml/2 tbsp brandy or Cointreau
130g/4½oz/generous 1 cup mascarpone
5ml/1 tsp vanilla extract
450ml/¾ pint/scant 2 cups double (heavy) cream
50g/2oz plain (semisweet) chocolate, to decorate

1 Whisk the egg yolks in a bowl with the sugar and cornflour. Boil the milk in a pan and pour over the egg mixture, whisking well. Return to the pan and cook over a gentle heat, stirring until thickened. Divide among three bowls. While hot, add the chocolate to one bowl, stirring until melted. Cool, then chill.

2 Beat the chestnut purée until soft, then beat it into the second bowl with the brandy or Cointreau. Beat the mascarpone and vanilla extract into the third bowl. Cool, then chill.

3 Add a third of the cream to each mixture. Turn the chestnut mixture into the ice cream maker and churn until it has a softly set consistency. Divide among six 150ml/¼ pint/⅔ cup metal moulds, level the surface and freeze.

4 Add the chocolate mixture to the ice cream maker and churn to the same consistency. Spoon into the moulds, level the top and freeze. Churn the remaining mixture to the same consistency. Spoon into moulds, level the surface and freeze for several hours or overnight.

5 To serve, melt the chocolate for the decoration in a bowl over a pan of simmering water. Transfer to a piping (pastry) bag and pipe lines on to plates. Soften the ice cream slightly, then serve.

Rainbow Ice Cream with Chocolate Candies

Speckled with roughly chopped sugar-coated chocolate sweets, this will soon be a family favourite with youngsters and adults alike, and it is especially good at children's parties.

Serves 6

4 egg yolks
75g/3oz/6 tbsp caster (superfine) sugar
5ml/1 tsp cornflour (cornstarch)
300ml/½ pint/1 ¼ cups semi-skimmed (low-fat) milk
300ml/½ pint/1 ¼ cups double (heavy) cream
5ml/1 tsp vanilla extract
115g/4oz sugar-coated chocolate sweets (candies)
whole sweets (candies), to decorate

1 Whisk the egg yolks, sugar and cornflour together in a bowl until thick and pale. Pour the milk into a heavy pan, bring it just to the boil, then gradually pour it on to the egg yolk mixture, whisking constantly.

2 Return the mixture to the pan and cook over a gentle heat, stirring constantly until the custard has thickened and is smooth.

3 Pour it back into the bowl, cover, leave to cool, then chill. Mix the cream and vanilla extract into the cooled custard, then pour into an ice cream maker. Churn until thick.

4 Roughly chop the sweets, stir them into the ice cream and churn for a minute or two until firm enough to scoop. Transfer to a plastic container and freeze until it is required.

5 Scoop into bowls or cones and decorate with the sweets.

Cook's Tip
The sugar coating on the sweets will dissolve slightly into the ice cream, but this just adds to the swirly coloured effect.

Bombes Energy 671kcal/2786kJ; Protein 7.9g; Carbohydrate 40.2g, of which sugars 31.1g; Fat 53.1g, of which saturates 31.7g; Cholesterol 217mg; Calcium 133mg; Fibre 1.5g; Sodium 48mg.
Rainbow Energy 438kcal/1823kJ; Protein 5.1g; Carbohydrate 30.4g, of which sugars 29.8g; Fat 33.8g, of which saturates 20g; Cholesterol 176mg; Calcium 132mg; Fibre 0g; Sodium 49mg.

Cranberry and White Chocolate Ice Cream

A traditional American combination – the creamy sweet white chocolate ice cream complements the slight sharpness of the ruby-red fruits for a richly contrasting marbled ice cream.

Serves 6

150g/5oz/1 ¼ cups frozen cranberries
125g/4½oz/scant ¾ cup caster (superfine) sugar
4 egg yolks
5ml/1 tsp cornflour (cornstarch)
300ml/½ pint/1 ¼ cups semi-skimmed (low-fat) milk
150g/5oz white chocolate
5ml/1 tsp vanilla extract
200ml/7fl oz/scant 1 cup double (heavy) cream
extra cranberries, to decorate

1 Put the cranberries into a pan with 60ml/4 tbsp water and cook uncovered for 5 minutes until softened. Drain off any fruit juices, mix in 60ml/4 tbsp of the sugar and leave to cool.

2 Whisk the egg yolks, remaining sugar and cornflour together in a bowl until thick and pale. Pour the milk into a heavy pan, bring it just to the boil, then gradually pour it on to the egg yolk mixture, whisking constantly.

3 Return the mixture to the pan and cook over a gentle heat, stirring constantly until the custard thickens and is smooth. Pour it back into the bowl.

4 Finely chop 50g/2oz of the chocolate and set aside. Break the remainder into pieces and stir into the hot custard until melted. Mix in the vanilla extract then cover, cool and chill.

5 Pour the cooled chocolate custard and cream into an ice cream maker and churn until thick. Gradually mix in the cooled cranberries and diced chocolate and churn for a few more minutes until firm enough to scoop. Transfer to a freezer container and freeze until required.

6 Scoop into tall glasses and decorate with a few cranberries.

Classic Dark Chocolate Ice Cream

Rich, dark and wonderfully luxurious, this ice cream can be served solo, with chocolate shavings or drizzled with warm chocolate sauce. If you are making it in advance, don't forget to soften the ice cream before serving so that the full intense flavour of the dark chocolate comes through.

Serves 4–6

4 egg yolks
75g/3oz/scant ½ cup caster (superfine) sugar
5ml/1 tsp cornflour (cornstarch)
300ml/½ pint/1 ¼ cups semi-skimmed (low-fat) milk
200g/7oz dark (bittersweet) chocolate
300ml/½ pint/1 ¼ cups whipping cream
shaved chocolate, to decorate

1 Whisk the egg yolks, sugar and cornflour in a bowl until thick and foamy. Pour the milk into a pan, bring just to the boil, then gradually whisk it into the yolk mixture.

2 Return the mixture to the pan and cook over a gentle heat, stirring constantly until the custard thickens and is smooth. Remove the pan from the heat.

3 Break the chocolate into small pieces and stir into the hot custard until it has melted. Leave to cool, then chill.

4 Whip the cream until it has thickened but still falls from a spoon. Fold into the custard, then pour into a freezer container. Freeze for 6 hours or until firm enough to scoop, beating once or twice with a fork or in a food processor as it thickens.

5 Alternatively, use an ice cream maker. Mix the chocolate custard with the whipped cream. Churn until the mixture is firm enough to scoop. Serve in scoops, decorated with chocolate shavings.

Cook's Tip
For the best flavour use a good-quality chocolate with at least 70 per cent cocoa solids, such as fine Belgian chocolate.

Cranberry Energy 296kcal/1245kJ; Protein 5.4g; Carbohydrate 41.8g, of which sugars 41g; Fat 13.1g, of which saturates 7g; Cholesterol 108mg; Calcium 153mg; Fibre 0.4g; Sodium 57mg.
Dark Chocolate Energy 349kcal/1461kJ; Protein 4.8g; Carbohydrate 36.8g, of which sugars 35.8g; Fat 21.4g, of which saturates 11.9g; Cholesterol 162mg; Calcium 78mg; Fibre 0.7g; Sodium 29mg.

Chocolate Double Mint Ice Cream

Full of body and flavour, this creamy, smooth ice cream combines the sophistication of dark chocolate with the satisfying coolness of fresh chopped mint.

Serves 4

4 egg yolks
75g/3oz/scant ½ cup caster (superfine) sugar
5ml/1 tsp cornflour (cornstarch)
300ml/½ pint/1¼ cups semi-skimmed (low-fat) milk
200g/7oz dark (bittersweet) chocolate, broken into squares
40g/1½oz/¼ cup peppermints
60ml/4 tbsp chopped fresh mint
300ml/½ pint/1¼ cups whipping cream
sprigs of fresh mint dusted with icing (confectioners') sugar, to decorate

1 Put the egg yolks, sugar and cornflour in a bowl and whisk until thick and foamy. Pour the milk into a heavy pan, bring slowly to the boil, then gradually whisk the hot milk into the yolk mixture.

2 Scrape the mixture back into the pan and cook over a gentle heat, stirring constantly, until the custard thickens and is smooth. Scrape it back into the bowl, add the chocolate, a little at a time, and stir until melted and smooth. Cool, then chill.

3 Put the peppermints in a strong plastic bag and crush them with a rolling pin. Stir them into the custard with the chopped fresh mint.

4 Mix the custard and cream together and churn the mixture in an ice cream maker until firm enough to scoop.

5 Serve the ice cream in scoops and then decorate with mint sprigs dusted with sifted icing sugar.

Cook's Tip

If you freeze the ice cream in a tub, don't beat it in a food processor when breaking up the ice crystals, or the crunchy texture of the crushed peppermints will be lost.

Double White Chocolate Ice Cream

Crunchy chunks of white chocolate are a bonus in this delicious ice cream. Serve it scooped in waffle cones dipped in dark chocolate for a truly sensational treat.

Serves 8

4 egg yolks
75g/3oz/scant ½ cup caster (superfine) sugar
5ml/1 tsp cornflour (cornstarch)
300ml/½ pint/1¼ cups semi-skimmed (low-fat) milk
250g/9oz white chocolate, chopped into pieces
10ml/2 tsp natural vanilla extract
300ml/½ pint/1¼ cups whipping cream
8 chocolate-dipped cones, to serve

1 Whisk the egg yolks, sugar and cornflour in a bowl until the mixture is thick and foamy. Pour the milk into a heavy pan, bring it to the boil, then gradually pour the hot milk on to the yolk mixture, whisking constantly.

2 Return the custard mixture to the pan and cook over a gentle heat, stirring constantly, until the custard begins to thicken and is smooth. Pour the hot custard back into the same bowl.

3 Add 150g/5oz of the chopped white chocolate to the hot custard, along with the vanilla extract. Gently stir until the chocolate has completely melted, leave to cool to room temperature, then chill.

4 Stir the cream into the custard, then churn the mixture in an ice cream maker until thick. Add the remaining white chocolate and churn for 5–10 minutes until firm. Serve in cones dipped in dark chocolate.

Variation

If you prefer, scoop the ice cream into glass dishes and decorate with white chocolate curls or extra diced chocolate. Ice cream served this way won't go quite as far, so will only serve 4–6.

Double Mint Energy 757kcal/3159kJ; Protein 9.8g; Carbohydrate 68.3g, of which sugars 66.7g; Fat 51.4g, of which saturates 29.8g; Cholesterol 299mg; Calcium 186mg; Fibre 1.3g; Sodium 66mg.
White Chocolate Energy 395kcal/1646kJ; Protein 6g; Carbohydrate 31.4g, of which sugars 30.8g; Fat 28.2g, of which saturates 16.4g; Cholesterol 142mg; Calcium 168mg; Fibre 0g; Sodium 65mg.

Chocolate and Hazelnut Brittle Ice Cream

For nut lovers and chocoholics everywhere, this luxurious ice cream is the ultimate indulgence. Rich, smooth dark chocolate is combined with crisp little chunks of sweet hazelnut brittle that provide a satisfying contrast. For a change, use other types of nuts, such as almonds, walnuts or pecan nuts.

Serves 4–6

4 egg yolks
175g/6oz/scant 1 cup sugar
5ml/1 tsp cornflour (cornstarch)
300ml/½ pint/1¼ cups semi-skimmed (low-fat) milk
150g/5oz dark (bittersweet) chocolate, broken into squares
115g/4oz/1 cup hazelnuts
60ml/4 tbsp water
300ml/½ pint/1¼ cups whipping cream

1 Whisk the egg yolks, sugar and cornflour in a bowl until thick and foamy. Pour the milk into a pan, bring it just to the boil, then gradually whisk it into the yolk mixture. Scrape back into the pan and cook over a gentle heat, stirring constantly, until the custard has thickened and is smooth.

2 Take the pan off the heat and stir in the chocolate, a few squares at a time. Cool, then chill. Lightly oil a baking sheet.

3 Meanwhile, put the hazelnuts, remaining sugar and water in a large frying pan. Gently heat without stirring until the sugar has dissolved. Increase the heat slightly and cook until the syrup has turned pale golden. Pour the mixture on to the oiled baking sheet and leave to stand until the hazelnut brittle hardens.

4 Pour the chocolate custard into the ice cream maker and add the cream. Churn for 25 minutes or until it is thick and firm enough to scoop.

5 Break the nut brittle into pieces. Reserve a few pieces for decoration and finely chop the rest. Scrape the ice cream into a tub and stir in the nut brittle. Freeze for 2–3 hours or until firm enough to scoop. Scoop on to plates and decorate with the reserved hazelnut brittle.

Chunky Chocolate Ice Cream

This creamy milk chocolate ice cream, topped with delicious chunks of milk, dark and white chocolate will satisfy even the sweetest tooth and will be a hit with adults as well as children.

Serves 4–6

4 egg yolks
75g/3oz/scant ½ cup caster (superfine) sugar
5ml/1 tsp cornflour (cornstarch)
300ml/½ pint/1¼ cups semi-skimmed (low-fat) milk
200g/7oz milk chocolate
50g/2oz dark (bittersweet) chocolate, plus extra, to decorate
50g/2oz white chocolate
300ml/½ pint/1¼ cups whipping cream

1 Whisk the egg yolks, caster sugar and cornflour in a bowl until thick and foamy. Heat the milk in a pan and bring it to the boil, then pour it on to the egg mixture, whisking constantly.

2 Return the custard mixture to the pan and cook over a gentle heat, stirring constantly with a wooden spoon until the custard thickens and is smooth.

3 Pour the custard back into the bowl. Break 150g/5oz of the milk chocolate into squares, stir these into the hot custard, then cover closely. Leave to cool, then chill.

4 Chop the remaining milk, dark and white chocolate finely and set aside. Mix the chocolate custard and the whipping cream and churn in an ice cream maker for 25–30 minutes until thick.

5 Scoop the ice cream out of the machine and into a plastic tub. Fold in the pieces of chocolate and freeze for 2–3 hours until firm enough to scoop. To serve, scoop into glasses or bowls and decorate with more pieces of chopped chocolate.

Cook's Tip
For maximum flavour, use good-quality chocolate or your favourite chocolate bar. Avoid dark, milk or white cake covering.

Hazelnut Brittle Energy 614kcal/2559kJ; Protein 8.3g; Carbohydrate 52g, of which sugars 50.6g; Fat 42.9g, of which saturates 19g; Cholesterol 158mg; Calcium 151mg; Fibre 1.9g; Sodium 43mg.
Chunky Energy 564kcal/2352kJ; Protein 7.9g; Carbohydrate 47.7g, of which sugars 47.5g; Fat 39.3g, of which saturates 23g; Cholesterol 197mg; Calcium 175mg; Fibre 0.8g; Sodium 64mg.

Chocolate Ripple Ice Cream

This creamy, dark chocolate ice cream, unevenly rippled with swirls of rich chocolate sauce, will stay deliciously soft even after freezing.

Serves 4–6

4 egg yolks
75g/3oz/scant ½ cup caster (superfine) sugar
5ml/1 tsp cornflour (cornstarch)
300ml/½ pint/1¼ cups semi-skimmed (low-fat) milk
250g/9oz dark (bittersweet) chocolate, broken into squares
25g/1oz/2 tbsp butter, diced
30ml/2 tbsp golden (light corn) syrup
90ml/6 tbsp single (light) cream or cream and milk mixed
300ml/½ pint/1¼ cups whipping cream

1 Put the egg yolks, sugar and cornflour in a bowl and whisk until thick and foamy. Pour the milk into a heavy pan, bring just to the boil, then gradually pour the milk on to the yolk mixture, whisking constantly.

2 Return the mixture to the pan and cook over a gentle heat, stirring constantly until the custard thickens and is smooth. Pour back into the bowl and stir in 150g/5oz of the chocolate until melted. Cover the custard closely, leave to cool, then chill.

3 Whip the cream in a bowl until it has thickened, but is still soft enough to fall from a spoon. Fold it into the custard. Pour the mixture into a freezer container and freeze for 5 hours until thick, beating twice with a fork or in a food processor during this time.

4 Alternatively, use an ice cream maker. Stir the whipped cream into the cooled custard and churn the mixture for 20–25 minutes until thick.

5 Put the remaining chocolate in a pan with the butter and golden syrup. Heat gently, stirring, until melted. Stir in the single cream or cream and milk mixture. Heat gently, stirring, until smooth, then leave to cool.

6 Add alternate spoonfuls of ice cream and sauce to a large freezer container. Freeze for 5–6 hours until firm.

Gingered Semi-freddo in Dark Chocolate Cases

This ice cream is made with a boiled sugar syrup rather than an egg custard.

Serves 6

4 egg yolks
115g/4oz/generous ½ cup caster (superfine) sugar
120ml/4fl oz/½ cup cold water
300ml/½ pints/1¼ cups double (heavy) cream
115g/4oz/⅔ cup drained stem ginger, finely chopped, plus extra slices, to decorate
45ml/3 tbsp whisky (optional)

For the chocolate cases
175g/6oz dark (bittersweet) chocolate, melted

1 Put the egg yolks in a large heatproof bowl and whisk until frothy. Bring a pan of water to the boil and simmer gently.

2 Mix the sugar and cold water in a pan and heat gently, stirring, until the sugar has dissolved. Increase the heat and boil for 4–5 minutes without stirring, until the syrup registers 115°C/239°F on a sugar thermometer. Pour the water away. You should be able to mould the syrup into a ball.

3 Put the bowl of egg yolks over the pan of simmering water and whisk in the sugar syrup. Continue whisking until the mixture is very thick. Remove from the heat and whisk until cool.

4 Whip the cream and lightly fold it into the yolk mixture, with the chopped ginger and whisky, if using. Pour into a plastic tub or similar freezerproof container and freeze for 1 hour.

5 To make cases, spread the melted chocolate over six squares of baking parchment in circles about 13cm/5in in diameter. Drape over upturned tumblers. Leave to cool and harden. Ease off the tumblers, then gently peel away the paper.

6 Stir the semi-freddo to bring any ginger that has sunk to the bottom of the tub to the top, then return to the freezer for 5–6 hours until firm. Scoop into the chocolate cases. Decorate with slices of ginger.

Chocolate Ripple Energy 594kcal/2474kJ; Protein 7.3g; Carbohydrate 48.3g, of which sugars 47.2g; Fat 42.6g, of which saturates 25.2g; Cholesterol 209mg; Calcium 140mg; Fibre 1.1g; Sodium 87mg.
Semi-freddo Energy 371kcal/1539kJ; Protein 3g; Carbohydrate 22.4g, of which sugars 22.3g; Fat 30.6g, of which saturates 17.8g; Cholesterol 203mg; Calcium 55mg; Fibre 0.5g; Sodium 23mg.

Minty Choc Madness Ice Cream

This creamy smooth peppermint ice cream is speckled with crushed peppermints and shards of chocolate-covered peppermint crisps, and looks particularly good served scooped in delicate glasses.

Serves 6

4 egg yolks
75g/3oz/scant ½ cup caster (superfine) sugar
5ml/1 tsp cornflour (cornstarch)
300ml/½ pint/1¼ cups semi-skimmed (low-fat) milk
250ml/8fl oz/1 cup crème fraîche
5ml/1 tsp peppermint extract
50g/2oz mint imperials or other hard mints
75g/3oz chocolate-covered peppermint crisps and chocolate curls, to decorate

1 Whisk the egg yolks, sugar and cornflour together in a bowl until thick and pale. Pour the milk into a pan, bring it just to the boil, then pour it on to the yolk mixture, whisking constantly. Return to the pan and cook over a gentle heat, stirring, until the custard thickens. Pour it back into the bowl, cover, cool, then chill.

2 Whisk the crème fraîche and peppermint extract into the chilled custard. Pour into an ice cream maker and churn until thick.

3 Put the mints into a plastic bag and roughly crush them with a rolling pin. Roughly chop the peppermint crisps with a knife. Stir both into the ice cream and churn until firm enough to scoop. Transfer to a freezer container and freeze.

4 Scoop the ice cream into glasses and sprinkle with extra pieces of peppermint crisps and chocolate curls.

Cook's Tip

To make delicate chocolate curls, hold a bar of dark, white or milk chocolate over a plate and pare curls away from the edge of the bar, using a swivel-blade vegetable peeler. Lift the pared curls carefully with a flat blade or a palette knife and arrange as desired.

Black Forest and Kirsch Ice Cream

All the flavours of boozy soaked dark cherries, cream and chocolate sponge combined in a light ice cream dessert.

Serves 6

425g/15oz can black cherries
90ml/6 tbsp Kirsch
4 egg yolks
75g/3oz/scant ½ cup caster (superfine) sugar
5ml/1 tsp cornflour (cornstarch)
300ml/½ pint/1¼ cups semi-skimmed (low-fat) milk
300ml/½ pint/1¼ cups double (heavy) cream
6 double chocolate muffins, each one weighing about 75g/3oz

To decorate

fresh cherries, on stalks
a little sifted unsweetened cocoa powder

1 Drain the cherries, discarding the juice, then put into a bowl and spoon over 30ml/2 tbsp of the Kirsch. Leave to soak for 2 hours or overnight.

2 Whisk the egg yolks, sugar and cornflour together in a bowl until thick and pale. Pour the milk into a heavy pan, bring it just to the boil, then gradually pour it on to the egg yolk mixture, whisking constantly.

3 Return the mixture to the pan and cook over a gentle heat, stirring constantly until the custard thickens and is smooth. Pour it back into the bowl, cover, leave to cool, then chill well.

4 Stir the cream into the custard, then pour into an ice cream maker. Churn until thick.

5 Gradually mix in the soaked cherries and any Kirsch juices and gently churn together.

6 Meanwhile, cut each muffin into two horizontal slices and drizzle with the remaining Kirsch.

7 To serve, sandwich the muffin slices back together with ice cream, arrange on serving plates and decorate with the fresh cherries and a light dusting of cocoa powder.

Minty Choc Madness Energy 338kcal/1414kJ; Protein 4.2g; Carbohydrate 36.7g, of which sugars 35.8g; Fat 20.4g, of which saturates 12.6g; Cholesterol 151mg; Calcium 104mg; Fibre 0g; Sodium 38mg.
Black Forest Energy 726kcal/3034kJ; Protein 9.1g; Carbohydrate 69.4g, of which sugars 50.7g; Fat 44.1g, of which saturates 26.1g; Cholesterol 224mg; Calcium 234mg; Fibre 1.6g; Sodium 234mg.

Chocolate Ice Cream in Florentine Baskets

A similar mixture to that used when making florentines is perfect for shaping fluted baskets for holding scoops of ice cream. For convenience, make the baskets a couple of days in advance, but dip the edges in chocolate on the day you serve them.

Serves 8

115g/4oz/½ cup butter, plus extra for greasing
50g/2oz/¼ cup caster (superfine) sugar
90ml/6 tbsp golden (light corn) syrup
90g/3½oz/scant 1 cup plain (all-purpose) flour
50g/2oz/½ cup flaked (sliced) almonds
50g/2oz/¼ cup glacé (candied) cherries, finely chopped
25g/1oz/3 tbsp raisins, chopped
15ml/1 tbsp finely chopped preserved stem ginger
90g/3½oz plain (semisweet) chocolate, broken into pieces
about 750ml/1¼ pints/3 cups chocolate ice cream

1 Preheat oven to 190°C/375°F/Gas 5. Line two baking sheets with greased baking parchment. Melt the butter, sugar and syrup in a pan. Stir in the flour, almonds, cherries, raisins and ginger.

2 Place a shallow tablespoonful of the mixture at either end of a baking sheet and spread to a 13cm/5in round. Bake for 5 minutes until they look lacy and golden. Spread more circles on the second baking sheet ready to put in the oven. Have ready several metal dariole moulds for shaping the baskets.

3 Leave the biscuits (cookies) on the sheet for 2 minutes to firm up. Lay a biscuit over an upturned dariole mould. Shape the biscuit into flutes around the sides of the mould. Leave for 2 minutes until cool, then lift away. Process the remaining mixture until you have eight baskets.

4 Melt the chocolate in a heatproof bowl over a pan of gently simmering water. Carefully dip the edges of the baskets in the melted chocolate and place on individual dessert plates. Scoop the chocolate ice cream into the baskets to serve.

Ice Cream with Mexican Chocolate

This rich ice cream has a wonderfully complex flavour, thanks to the cinnamon and almonds in the chocolate.

Serves 4

2 large eggs
115g/4oz/generous ½ cup caster (superfine) sugar
2 bars Mexican chocolate, total weight about 115g/4oz
400ml/14fl oz/1⅔ cups double (heavy) cream
200ml/7fl oz/scant 1 cup full-fat (whole) milk
chocolate curls, to decorate

1 Put the eggs in a bowl and whisk them with an electric whisk until they are thick, pale and fluffy. Gradually whisk in the sugar.

2 Gently heat the chocolate in a heatproof bowl over a pan of simmering water, stirring until melted and smooth. Add it to the egg mixture and mix thoroughly.

3 Whisk in the cream to the chocolate mixture. Stir in the milk, a little at a time.

4 Cool the mixture, then chill. Pour the mixture into an ice cream maker and churn until thick.

5 Alternatively, freeze the mixture in a shallow plastic box in the fast-freeze section of the freezer for several hours, until ice crystals have begun to form around the edges. Process to break up the ice crystals, then freeze again. To serve, decorate with chocolate curls.

Cook's Tip

Mexican chocolate is richly flavoured with cinnamon, almonds and vanilla, and has a much grainier texture than other chocolates. It is available in Mexican food stores and some supermarkets. If you can't find it, then 25g/1oz plain (semisweet) chocolate, 2.5ml/½ tsp ground cinnamon and 1 drop of almond extract can be substituted for every 25g/1oz Mexican chocolate.

Baskets Energy 525kcal/2191kJ; Protein 6.8g; Carbohydrate 53.9g, of which sugars 45g; Fat 32.8g, of which saturates 18.2g; Cholesterol 31mg; Calcium 141mg; Fibre 1.2g; Sodium 180mg.
Mexican Chocolate Energy 966kcal/4016kJ; Protein 9.3g; Carbohydrate 69.7g, of which sugars 69.2g; Fat 74.2g, of which saturates 44.9g; Cholesterol 243mg; Calcium 156mg; Fibre 1.4g; Sodium 84mg.

Crumbled Chocolate Brownie Ice Cream

A double-chocolate dessert that combines chocolate ice cream with soft brownies.

Serves 6
1.2 litres/2 pints/5 cups good-quality chocolate or chocolate chip ice cream

For the chocolate brownies
75g/3oz dark (bittersweet) chocolate, broken into pieces
115g/4oz/½ cup butter
4 eggs, beaten
10ml/2 tsp vanilla extract
400g/14oz/2 cups caster (superfine) sugar
115g/4oz/1 cup plain (all-purpose) flour
25g/1oz/¼ cup unsweetened cocoa powder
115g/4oz packet dark (bittersweet) chocolate chips
115g/4oz/1 cup chopped walnuts

1 Make the brownies. Preheat the oven to 190°C/375°F/Gas 5. Grease an 18 × 28cm/7 × 11in shallow baking tin (pan) and line the base with baking parchment. Melt the chocolate with the butter in a heatproof bowl over a pan of simmering water, stirring until smooth. Remove the bowl from the heat and stir in the beaten eggs, vanilla and sugar. Mix together well.

2 Sift the flour with the cocoa powder and beat into the chocolate mixture. Gently stir in the chocolate chips and walnuts. Pour the mixture into the pan and level the surface.

3 Bake for about 35 minutes. To test if the brownies are fully cooked, insert a metal skewer in the centre. The cake should be set but still moist. (Overcooking will make the brownies dry.) If you prefer a drier texture – which is better for the ice cream – cook for 10–15 minutes more. Leave the brownies to cool in the pan. When completely cold, cut into squares or bars.

4 To make the chocolate brownie ice cream, cut about 175g/6oz of the brownies into small cubes. Soften the ice cream and lightly stir in the chopped brownies. Spoon the mixture into a large freezerproof container, cover and freeze for at least 2 hours before serving.

White Chocolate and Brownie Ice Cream

This scrumptious recipe combines an irresistible contrast between the white chocolate ice cream and luscious chunks of chocolate brownie. Use good-quality bought chocolate brownies, or even better still, make your own.

Serves 6
4 egg yolks
2.5ml/½tsp cornflour (cornstarch)
300ml/½ pint/1¼ cups full cream (whole) milk
200g/7oz white chocolate, chopped
200g/7oz chocolate brownies
300ml/½ pint/1¼ cups whipping cream

1 Put the egg yolks and cornflour in a bowl and whisk lightly to combine. Bring the milk to the boil in a heavy pan. Pour the milk over the whisked mixture, whisking constantly until the mixture is well combined.

2 Pour the custard back into the pan and cook over a very gentle heat, stirring continually until it slightly thickens and becomes smooth.

3 Pour into a bowl and add the chopped chocolate. Leave until the chocolate has melted, stirring frequently. Leave to cool.

4 Crumble the brownies into small pieces. Stir the cream into the chocolate custard and pour into the ice cream maker. Churn the mixture until it is thick.

5 Sprinkle the crumbled brownies over the ice cream mixture and churn until just mixed. Scoop into glasses or transfer to a freezerproof container and freeze the ice cream until ready to serve.

Variation
As an alternative, you could use chopped dark (bittersweet) chocolate in place of the white chocolate, and white chocolate brownies or 'blondies' in place of the dark chocolate brownies.

Brownie Energy 1255kcal/5248kJ; Protein 19.4g; Carbohydrate 139.4g, of which sugars 123.7g; Fat 72.8g, of which saturates 36.1g; Cholesterol 170mg; Calcium 319mg; Fibre 2.6g; Sodium 330mg.
White Chocolate Energy 570kcal/2365kJ; Protein 5.2g; Carbohydrate 31.1g, of which sugars 25.7g; Fat 48.1g, of which saturates 25.6g; Cholesterol 82mg; Calcium 129mg; Fibre 0g; Sodium 154mg.

Chocolate and Coffee Bombe with Marsala

For the best results, use a good-quality ice cream for this delicious Italian dessert. The assembled bombe is very impressive.

Serves 6–8

15–18 sponge fingers
about 175ml/6fl oz/¾ cup sweet Marsala
75g/3oz amaretti
about 475ml/16fl oz/2 cups coffee ice cream, softened
about 475ml/16fl oz/2 cups vanilla ice cream, softened
50g/2oz dark (bittersweet) or plain (semisweet) chocolate, grated
chocolate curls and sifted cocoa powder or icing (confectioners') sugar, to decorate

1 Line a 1 litre/1¾ pint/4 cup freezerproof bowl with a large piece of damp muslin (cheesecloth), letting it hang over the top edge. Trim the sponge fingers to fit the bowl, if necessary. Pour the Marsala into a shallow dish. Dip a sponge finger in the Marsala, turning it quickly so that it becomes saturated but does not disintegrate. Stand it against the side of the bowl, sugared side out. Repeat with the remaining sponge fingers to line the bowl fully. Fill in the base and any gaps around the side with any trimmings and sponge fingers cut to fit. Chill for 30 minutes.

2 Put the amaretti in a large bowl and crush them with a rolling pin. Add the coffee ice cream and any remaining Marsala, and beat until mixed. Spoon into the sponge-finger-lined bowl. Press the ice cream against the sponge to form an even layer with a hollow. Freeze for 2 hours.

3 Put the vanilla ice cream and grated chocolate in a bowl and beat together until evenly mixed. Spoon into the hollow in the centre of the mould. Smooth the top, then cover with the overhanging muslin. Place in the freezer overnight.

4 To serve, run a spatula between the muslin and the bowl, then unfold the top of the muslin. Place a chilled serving plate on top of the bombe, then invert so that the bombe is upside down on the plate. Carefully peel off the muslin. Decorate with the chocolate curls, then sift cocoa powder or icing sugar over.

Chocolate Ice Cream with Hot Cherry Sauce

Hot cherry sauce transforms chocolate ice cream into a delicious dessert for any occasion. Serve immediately to ensure that the sauce is still warm to the taste.

Serves 4

425g/15oz can stone (pitted) black cherries in juice
10ml/2 tsp cornflour (cornstarch)
finely grated rind of 1 lemon, plus 10ml/2 tsp juice
15ml/1 tbsp caster (superfine) sugar
2.5ml/½ tsp ground cinnamon
30ml/2 tbsp brandy or Kirsch (optional)
400ml/14fl oz/1⅔ cups dark (bittersweet) chocolate ice cream
400ml/14fl oz/1⅔ cups classic vanilla ice cream
drinking chocolate powder, for dusting

1 Drain the cherries, reserving the canned juice. Spoon the cornflour into a small pan and blend to a paste with a little of the reserved juice.

2 Stir in the remaining canned juice with the lemon rind and juice, sugar and cinnamon. Bring to the boil, stirring, until smooth and glossy. Add the cherries, with the brandy or kirsch, if using. Stir gently, then cook for 1 minute.

3 Scoop the chocolate and vanilla ice cream into shallow dishes. Spoon the sauce around, dust with drinking chocolate powder and serve.

Variation
The hot cherry sauce also makes a delicious filling for pancakes. For a speedy dessert, you can use heated, ready-made sweet pancakes – just spread a little sauce in the centre of each pancake and fold into a triangle shape or roll up. Then arrange in a serving dish and spoon the rest of the sauce over the top. Finish with spoonfuls of thick yogurt or whipped cream.

Bombe Energy 391kcal/1631kJ; Protein 8.7g; Carbohydrate 33.8g, of which sugars 26.1g; Fat 22.7g, of which saturates 11.4g; Cholesterol 111mg; Calcium 66mg; Fibre 1.3g; Sodium 64mg.
Ice Cream with Cherry Energy 529kcal/2213kJ; Protein 8.4g; Carbohydrate 59.5g, of which sugars 57g; Fat 30.2g, of which saturates 18.1g; Cholesterol 0mg; Calcium 218mg; Fibre 0.7g; Sodium 130mg.

Chunky Chocolate-coffee Bean and Kahlúa Ice Cream

A wonderful combination of creamy dark coffee with a hint of coffee liqueur, peppered with crunchy chocolate-covered coffee beans. The beans used here have been coated with white, dark and milk chocolate, but all dark chocolate-covered beans would work just as well.

Serves 6
4 egg yolks
75g/3oz/scant ½ cup caster (superfine) sugar
5ml/1 tsp cornflour (cornstarch)
300ml/½ pint/1¼ cups semi-skimmed (low-fat) milk
30ml/2 tbsp instant coffee granules or powder
300ml/½ pint/1¼ cups double (heavy) cream
120ml/4fl oz/½ cup Kahlúa or other coffee liqueur
115g/4oz assorted chocolate-covered coffee beans
a little sifted unsweetened cocoa powder, to decorate

1 Whisk the egg yolks, sugar and cornflour in a bowl until the mixture is thick and pale. Heat the milk in a pan, then gradually whisk into the yolk mixture. Return the custard to the pan and cook over a gentle heat, stirring constantly so that it does not catch on the bottom and burn.

2 When the custard has thickened and is smooth, pour it back into the bowl and mix in the instant coffee granules or powder, stirring continuously until all of the coffee has completely dissolved. Cover the custard with clear film (plastic wrap) to prevent a skin from forming, leave to cool, then chill well before churning.

3 Stir the cream and Kahlúa into the coffee custard, then pour into an ice cream maker. Churn until thick. Roughly chop 75g/3oz of the chocolate-covered coffee beans, add to the ice cream and churn until firm enough to scoop. Transfer to a freezer container and freeze until required.

4 Scoop the ice cream into coffee cups and decorate with the remaining chocolate-covered coffee beans and a light dusting of cocoa powder.

White Chocolate Brûlées with Blackberry Coulis

This ice cream is topped with caramel shards and fresh blackberries.

Serves 6
4 egg yolks
50g/2oz/¼ cup caster (superfine) sugar
5ml/1 tsp cornflour (cornstarch)
300ml/½ pint/1¼ cups semi-skimmed (low-fat) milk
150g/5oz white chocolate, broken into pieces
5ml/1 tsp vanilla extract
115g/4oz/generous 1 cup granulated (white) sugar
300ml/½ pint/1¼ cups double (heavy) cream
blackberries, for decoration

For the coulis
200g/7oz/scant 2 cups blackberries

1 Whisk the egg yolks, sugar and cornflour together until thick and pale. Pour the milk into a pan, bring it just to the boil, then pour it on to the egg yolk mixture, whisking constantly. Return to the pan and cook gently, stirring, until the custard thickens.

2 Take the pan off the heat and add the chocolate pieces and vanilla extract and stir until the chocolate has completely melted. Cover, leave to cool, then chill.

3 For the coulis, put the blackberries into a pan with 60ml/4 tbsp water, then cover and cook for 5 minutes until softened. Purée the berries in a liquidizer or food processor and strain, discarding the seeds. Stir in 30–45ml/2–3 tbsp extra water to make a sauce.

4 Put the granulated sugar in a small pan with 45ml/3 tbsp water and heat, without stirring, until the sugar has dissolved. Increase the heat and boil for 4–5 minutes until golden. Pour on to an oiled baking sheet. Leave to harden, then break into pieces.

5 Pour the cooled white chocolate custard and cream into an ice cream maker and churn until firm enough to scoop. Transfer to a freezer container and store in the freezer until required.

6 Scoop the ice cream into bowls and top with caramel pieces and whole blackberries. Serve with the coulis.

Bean and Kahlúa Energy 504kcal/2094kJ; Protein 4.9g; Carbohydrate 32.2g, of which sugars 31.3g; Fat 38.2g, of which saturates 20.8g; Cholesterol 173mg; Calcium 112mg; Fibre 0.4g; Sodium 57mg.
White Brûlées Energy 553kcal/2307kJ; Protein 6.4g; Carbohydrate 49g, of which sugars 48.2g; Fat 38.3g, of which saturates 22.6g; Cholesterol 172mg; Calcium 192mg; Fibre 1g; Sodium 67mg.

Chocolate Teardrops with Cherry Brandy Sauce

These stunning chocolate cases look impressive but are easy to make.

Serves 6

90g/3½oz plain (semisweet) chocolate, broken into pieces
115g/4oz amaretti
450ml/¾ pint/scant 2 cups double (heavy) cream
2.5ml/½ tsp almond extract
40g/1½oz/⅓ cup icing (confectioners') sugar
30ml/2 tbsp brandy or almond liqueur
75ml/5 tbsp full-fat (whole) milk
fresh cherries, to decorate

For the sauce
2.5ml/½ tsp cornflour (cornstarch)
75ml/5 tbsp water
225g/8oz pitted cherries, halved
45ml/3 tbsp caster (superfine) sugar
10ml/2 tsp lemon juice
45ml/3 tbsp brandy or almond liqueur

1 Cut out six 25 × 3cm/10 × 1¼in strips of Perspex (Plexiglas). Melt the chocolate in a heatproof bowl over a pan of hot water. Line a baking sheet with baking parchment.

2 Coat the underside of the Perspex strips in chocolate, apart from 1cm/½in at each end. Bring the ends together so the chocolate is on the inside. Secure the ends with paper clips, then set on the baking sheet. Chill until completely hardened.

3 Put the amaretti in a plastic bag and crush with a rolling pin. Put the cream in a bowl and beat in the almond extract, icing sugar and liqueur. Churn in an ice cream maker until thick. Spoon in the milk and crushed amaretti. Churn until mixed. Spoon carefully into the chocolate cases, making sure they're filled to the rim. Freeze for at least 2 hours or overnight.

4 Make the sauce. Put the cornflour in a pan and stir in a little of the water to make a paste. Stir in the remaining water with the cherries, sugar and lemon juice. Bring to the boil and stir until thick. Remove from the heat and cool. Stir in the liqueur.

5 Peel away the Perspex from the cases and put on a plate. Spoon sauce beside the cases and decorate with cherries.

Miniature Choc Ices

For summer entertaining, these little chocolate-coated ice creams make a fun alternative to the more familiar after-dinner chocolates. You can be creative with toppings and adapt them to suit the occasion, from chopped nuts for adults to multicoloured sprinkles for children.

Makes about 25

750ml/1¼ pints/3 cups vanilla, chocolate or coffee ice cream
200g/7oz plain (semisweet) chocolate, broken into small pieces
25g/1oz milk chocolate, broken into small pieces
25g/1oz/¼ cup chopped hazelnuts, lightly toasted

1 Put a baking sheet in the freezer for 15 minutes. Use a melon baller to scoop balls of each of the different ice cream flavours on to the baking sheet. Freeze for 1 hour until firm.

2 Line a second baking sheet with baking parchment and place in the freezer for 15 minutes. Melt the plain and milk chocolates in separate heatproof bowls set over a pan of simmering water.

3 Transfer the ice cream scoops to the paper-lined sheet. Spoon a little plain chocolate over a scoop so that most of it is coated. Sprinkle with chopped nuts, before the chocolate sets.

4 Coat the remaining scoops with the dark chocolate. Sprinkle chopped nuts over half of the chocolate-covered scoops, working quickly so that the chocolate does not set.

5 Once the chocolate has set on the half that are not topped with nuts, drizzle each with milk chocolate, using a teaspoon. Freeze until ready to serve.

Cook's Tip
If the melted milk chocolate is very runny, leave it for a few minutes to thicken up slightly before spooning it over the ice cream scoops. The milk chocolate can be piped on the choc ices, using a bag fitted with a writing nozzle.

Teardrops Energy 441kcal/1839kJ; Protein 3.3g; Carbohydrate 45g, of which sugars 36.1g; Fat 26.9g, of which saturates 16.3g; Cholesterol 53mg; Calcium 72mg; Fibre 1.1g; Sodium 78mg.
Choc Ices Energy 117kcal/488kJ; Protein 1.8g; Carbohydrate 10.7g, of which sugars 10.6g; Fat 7.7g, of which saturates 4.3g; Cholesterol 1mg; Calcium 36mg; Fibre 0.3g; Sodium 19mg.

Cappuccino Choc Cones

White and dark chocolate cones are filled with swirls of cappuccino cream and topped with a dusting of unsweetened cocoa powder.

Serves 6

115g/4oz each good-quality plain (semisweet) and white cooking chocolate

For the cappuccino cream

30ml/2 tbsp ground espresso or other strong-flavoured coffee
30ml/2 tbsp near-boiling water
300ml/½ pint/1¼ cups double (heavy) cream
45ml/3 tbsp icing (confectioners') sugar, sifted
15ml/1 tbsp unsweetened cocoa powder, for dusting

1 Cut nine 13 × 10cm/5 × 4in rectangles from baking parchment, then cut each rectangle in half diagonally to make 18 triangles. Roll up each to make a cone and secure with tape.

2 Heat the plain chocolate in a heatproof bowl over a pan of gently simmering water, stirring, until melted. Using a small pastry brush, thickly brush the insides of half the paper cones with chocolate. Chill until set. Repeat with the white chocolate. Carefully peel away the paper and keep the cones in the refrigerator until needed.

3 To make the cappuccino cream, put the coffee in a small bowl. Pour the hot water over. Leave to infuse (steep) for 4 minutes, then strain into a bowl. Leave to cool. Add the cream and sugar and whisk until soft peaks form. Spoon into a piping (pastry) bag fitted with a medium star nozzle.

4 Pipe the cream into the chocolate cones. Put on a baking sheet and freeze for at least 2 hours or until solid. Arrange on individual plates, allowing three cones per person and dusting with cocoa powder before serving.

Cook's Tip
When melting the chocolate in bowls over pans of water, make sure that the water doesn't boil or touch the bottom of the bowl, otherwise the chocolate will overheat and stiffen.

Iced Chocolate Nut Gateau

A divine dessert of rich chocolate ice cream encased in brandy-soaked sponge.

Serves 6–8

75g/3oz/¾ cup shelled hazelnuts
about 32 sponge fingers
150ml/¼ pint/⅔ cup cold strong black coffee
30ml/2 tbsp brandy
475ml/16fl oz/2 cups double (heavy) cream
75g/3oz/⅔ cup icing (confectioners') sugar, sifted
150g/5oz plain (semisweet) chocolate, chopped into small pieces
icing (confectioners') sugar and unsweetened cocoa powder, for dusting

1 Preheat the oven to 200°C/400°F/Gas 6. Spread out the hazelnuts on a baking sheet and toast them in the oven for 5 minutes until golden. Turn the nuts on to a clean dish towel and rub off the skins while still warm. Cool, then chop finely.

2 Line a 1.2 litre/2 pint/5 cup loaf tin (pan) with clear film (plastic wrap) and cut the sponge fingers to fit the base and sides. Reserve the remaining fingers. Mix the coffee with the brandy in a shallow dish. Dip the sponge fingers briefly into the coffee mixture and return to the tin, sugar side down, to fit.

3 Whip the cream with the icing sugar until it holds soft peaks. Fold half the chopped chocolate into the cream with the hazelnuts. Use a gentle figure-of-eight action to distribute the chocolate and nuts evenly.

4 Melt the remaining chocolate in a bowl set over a pan of barely simmering water. Cool, then fold into the cream mixture. Spoon into the tin.

5 Moisten the remaining fingers in the coffee mixture – take care not to soak the fingers, otherwise they will go soft and collapse. Lay the moistened fingers over the filling. Wrap and freeze until firm.

6 To serve, remove from the freezer 30 minutes before serving to allow the ice cream to soften slightly. Turn out on to a serving plate and dust with icing sugar and cocoa powder.

Cones Energy 485kcal/2013kJ; Protein 3.8g; Carbohydrate 32.3g, of which sugars 31.9g; Fat 38.7g, of which saturates 23.8g; Cholesterol 70mg; Calcium 90mg; Fibre 0.8g; Sodium 58mg.
Nut Gateau Energy 573kcal/2380kJ; Protein 5.8g; Carbohydrate 36.8g, of which sugars 30.8g; Fat 44.9g, of which saturates 23.9g; Cholesterol 140mg; Calcium 73mg; Fibre 1.3g; Sodium 37mg.

Chocolate Mint Ice Cream Pie

This chocolate-flavoured cereal pie case is incredibly easy to make and offers a simple way to turn ready-made ice cream into a smart-looking dessert.

Serves 8

75g/3oz plain (semisweet) chocolate chips
40g/1½oz/3 tbsp butter or margarine
50g/2oz crisped rice cereal
1 litre/1¾ pints/4 cups mint-chocolate-chip ice cream
chocolate curls, to decorate

1 Line a 23cm/9in pie tin (pan) with foil. Place a round of baking parchment over the foil in the bottom of the tin.

2 Put the chocolate chips and butter or margarine in a heatproof bowl that will fit over a pan of simmering water. Place the bowl over the pan and melt the chocolate and butter.

3 Remove the bowl from the heat and gently stir in the cereal, a little at a time.

4 Press the chocolate-cereal mixture evenly over the base and up the sides of the prepared tin, forming a 1cm/½in rim. Chill until completely hard.

5 Carefully remove the cereal case from the tin and peel off the foil and paper. Return the case to the pie tin.

6 Remove the ice cream from the freezer. Let it soften for 10 minutes and spread it evenly in the cereal case. Freeze until firm.

7 Sprinkle the ice cream with chocolate curls just before serving.

Variation
Use any flavour of ice cream that marries well with chocolate – coffee, orange or raspberry ripple would be a good choice. Try plain, milk or white chocolate for the base.

Chocolate Millefeuille Slice

This stunning dessert takes a little time to prepare but can be assembled days in advance, ready to impress dinner guests.

Serves 8

4 egg yolks
10ml/2 tsp cornflour (cornstarch)
300ml/½ pint/1¼ cups milk
175ml/6fl oz/¾ cup maple syrup
250ml/8fl oz/1 cup crème fraîche
115g/4oz/1 cup pecan nuts, chopped

To finish
200g/7oz plain (semisweet) chocolate, broken into pieces
300ml/½ pint/1¼ cups double (heavy) cream
45ml/3 tbsp icing (confectioners') sugar
30ml/2 tbsp brandy
lightly toasted pecan nuts

1 Whisk the egg yolks in a bowl with the cornflour and a little of the milk until smooth. Pour the remaining milk into a pan, bring to the boil, then pour over the yolk mixture, stirring. Return the mixture to the pan and stir in the maple syrup and crème fraîche. Heat gently, stirring until thick. Pour into a bowl, cover and cool.

2 Churn in an ice cream maker until thick, then add the pecan nuts. Scrape into a freezerproof container and freeze overnight.

3 Melt 150g/5oz of the chocolate in a bowl over a pan of hot water. On baking parchment draw four rectangles, each about 19 × 12cm/7½ × 4½in. Spoon the melted chocolate equally on to the rectangles, spreading to the edges. Leave to set. Make thin curls from the remaining chocolate using a potato peeler.

4 Whip the cream with the sugar and brandy until it forms soft peaks. Peel away the paper from a rectangle and place on a plate. Spread a third of the cream over the chocolate. Lay small scoops of ice cream over the cream. Cover with a second rectangle. Repeat the layering, finishing with chocolate.

5 Sprinkle with the toasted pecan nuts and chocolate curls. Freeze overnight until firm. Transfer the frozen dessert to the refrigerator 30 minutes before serving to soften it slightly. Serve in slices.

Mint Ice Cream Pie Energy 378kcal/1573kJ; Protein 6.1g; Carbohydrate 32g, of which sugars 27.2g; Fat 25.9g, of which saturates 15.5g; Cholesterol 11mg; Calcium 183mg; Fibre 0.2g; Sodium 108mg.
Millefeuille Energy 667kcal/2772kJ; Protein 6.7g; Carbohydrate 43.3g, of which sugars 42.6g; Fat 53.1g, of which saturates 27.2g; Cholesterol 191mg; Calcium 117mg; Fibre 1.3g; Sodium 99mg.

Chocolate, Rum and Raisin Roulade

This richly flavoured dessert can be assembled and frozen a week or two in advance.

Serves 6

For the roulade

115g/4oz plain (semisweet) chocolate, broken into pieces
4 eggs, separated
115g/4oz/generous ½ cup caster (superfine) sugar, plus extra for dusting

For the filling

75g/3oz/generous ½ cup raisins
60ml/4 tbsp dark rum
425g/15oz can custard
50g/2oz/¼ cup light muscovado (brown) sugar
200ml/7fl oz/scant 1 cup whipping cream
unsweetened cocoa powder and icing (confectioners') sugar, to decorate

1 Make the roulade. Preheat the oven to 180°C/350°F/Gas 4. Line a 33 × 23cm/13 × 9in Swiss roll tin (jelly roll pan) with baking parchment. Melt the chocolate in a heatproof bowl set over a pan of simmering water.

2 Whisk the egg yolks and sugar together until thick and pale. Fold in the melted chocolate. Whisk the egg whites until stiff and fold one quarter of the egg whites into the chocolate mixture to loosen it, then gently fold in the remainder.

3 Pour the mixture into the tin. Bake for about 20 minutes or until the cake has risen and is just firm. Leave to cool in the tin covered with a piece of baking parchment and a clean dish towel.

4 Meanwhile, warm the raisins in the rum in a small pan for a few minutes, then leave them to cool and soak for 2 hours.

5 Make the ice cream. Mix together the custard, sugar and cream and pour into an ice cream maker. Churn until it is thick, then add the raisins and churn until it is stiff enough to spread.

6 Turn the roulade out on to baking parchment dusted with caster sugar. Spread with the ice cream, then roll up from one of the short sides, using the paper to help. Cover and freeze. Dust with cocoa powder and icing sugar before slicing and serving.

White Chocolate Castles with Fresh Summer Berries

These romantic-looking chocolate cases serve a wide variety of uses. They can be frozen with iced mousses or filled with scoops of your favourite ice cream and succulent fresh blueberries.

Serves 6

225g/8oz white chocolate, broken into pieces
250ml/8fl oz/1 cup white chocolate ice cream
250ml/8fl oz/1 cup dark (bittersweet) chocolate ice cream
115g/4oz/1 cup blueberries
unsweetened cocoa powder, for dusting

1 Put the white chocolate in a heatproof bowl, set it over a pan of gently simmering water and leave until melted. Line a baking sheet with baking parchment. Cut out six 30 × 13cm/12 × 5in strips of baking parchment, then fold each in half lengthways.

2 Stand a 7.5cm/3in pastry (cookie) cutter on the baking sheet. Roll one strip of paper into a circle and fit inside the cutter with the folded edge on the base paper. Stick the edges together with tape.

3 Remove the cutter and make more paper collars in the same way, leaving the cutter in place around the final collar.

4 Spoon a little of the melted chocolate into the base of the collar supported by the cutter. Using a teaspoon, spread the chocolate over the base and up the sides of the collar, making the top edge uneven. Carefully lift away the cutter.

5 Make five more chocolate cases in the same way, using the cutter for extra support each time. Leave the cases in a cool place or in the refrigerator to set.

6 Carefully peel the baking parchment from the sides of the chocolate cases, then lift the cases off the base. Transfer to serving plates. Using a teaspoon, scoop the ice creams into the cases and decorate with the fruit. Dust with cocoa powder.

Roulade Energy 486kcal/2023kJ; Protein 10.2g; Carbohydrate 32.8g, of which sugars 32.4g; Fat 34.5g, of which saturates 19.9g; Cholesterol 190mg; Calcium 41mg; Fibre 1.3g; Sodium 143mg.
Castles Energy 351kcal/1463kJ; Protein 6g; Carbohydrate 34.3g, of which sugars 34.2g; Fat 22g, of which saturates 13.1g; Cholesterol 0mg; Calcium 182mg; Fibre 1.2g; Sodium 84mg.

Chocolate Ice Cream with Lime Sabayon

Sabayon sauce has a light, foamy texture that perfectly complements the rich, smooth flavour of ice cream. This tangy lime version is particularly delicious when spooned generously over chocolate ice cream.

Serves 4

2 egg yolks
65g/2½oz/5 tbsp caster (superfine) sugar
finely grated rind and juice of 2 limes
60ml/4 tbsp white wine or apple juice
45ml/3 tbsp single (light) cream
500ml/17fl oz/generous 2 cups chocolate chip or dark (bittersweet) chocolate ice cream
pared strips of lime rind, to decorate

1 Put the egg yolks and sugar in a heatproof bowl and beat until combined. Beat in the lime rind and juice, then the white wine or apple juice.

2 Whisk the mixture over a pan of gently simmering water until the sabayon is smooth and thick, and the mixture leaves a trail when the whisk is lifted from the bowl.

3 Lightly whisk in the cream. Remove the bowl from the pan and cover with a lid or plate.

4 Working quickly, scoop the ice cream into four glasses. Spoon the sabayon sauce over the ice cream, decorate with the strips of lime rind and serve immediately.

Variation

The tangy lime sauce marries just as well with vanilla ice cream. It is also very good served with individual servings of sliced tropical fruit – pineapple, papaya and kiwi would look pretty. Try the sabayon sauce as a topping for a selection of soft summer fruits, too.

Chocolate Sorbet

This is a delicious cooling treat for chocolate lovers. Serve with crisp little biscuits as a light way to end a meal.

Serves 6

150g/5oz dark (bittersweet) chocolate, chopped
115g/4oz plain (semisweet) chocolate, grated
225g/8oz/1 cup caster (superfine) sugar
475ml/16fl oz/2 cups water
chocolate curls, to decorate

1 Put all of the chocolate in a food processor, fitted with a metal blade, and process for approximately 20–30 seconds, or until finely chopped.

2 Place the sugar and water in a pan over medium heat. Bring to the boil, stirring until all of the sugar has completely dissolved. Boil for about 2 minutes, then remove the pan from the heat.

3 While the machine is running, carefully add the hot sugar-and-water syrup to the chocolate in the food processor. Keep the food processor running for 1–2 minutes until the chocolate is completely melted and the mixture is smooth. Scrape down the bowl once or twice to catch any mixture that is clinging to the sides.

4 Strain the chocolate mixture into a large measuring jug (cup) or bowl. Leave to cool completely, then chill, making sure that you stir the mixture occasionally.

5 Pour the chilled mixture into a freezer container and freeze until it is slushy.

6 Whisk the mixture until smooth, then freeze again until it is almost firm. Whisk it for a second time and return it to the freezer.

7 Allow to soften slightly before serving decorated with the chocolate curls.

Lime Sabayon Energy 395kcal/1648kJ; Protein 6.8g; Carbohydrate 38.3g, of which sugars 38.2g; Fat 23.8g, of which saturates 13.5g; Cholesterol 107mg; Calcium 157mg; Fibre 0g; Sodium 84mg.
Chocolate Sorbet Energy 301kcal/1266kJ; Protein 2.3g; Carbohydrate 48.1g, of which sugars 47.7g; Fat 12.4g, of which saturates 7.4g; Cholesterol 3mg; Calcium 25mg; Fibre 1.1g; Sodium 4mg.

Chocolate Sorbet with Red Fruits

Mouthwatering chocolate-flavoured sorbet tastes and looks stunning when served with a selection of luscious red berries.

Serves 6

475ml/16fl oz/2 cups water
45ml/3 tbsp clear honey
90g/3½oz/½ cup caster (superfine) sugar
75g/3oz/⅔ cup unsweetened cocoa powder
50g/2oz plain (semisweet) or dark (bittersweet) chocolate, chopped into small pieces
400g/14oz soft red fruits, such as raspberries, redcurrants or strawberries

1 Put the water in a pan with the honey, sugar and cocoa powder. Heat the mixture gently, stirring occasionally, until the sugar has completely dissolved.

2 Remove the pan from the heat, add the chocolate pieces and stir until melted. Leave until cool.

3 Pour the chocolate mixture into a freezer container and freeze until slushy. Whisk quickly until smooth, then return the mixture to the freezer again and freeze until almost firm. Whisk the iced mixture for a second time, cover the container and freeze until firm.

4 Alternatively, use an ice cream maker to freeze the mixture, following the manufacturer's instructions.

5 Remove the sorbet from the freezer 10–15 minutes before serving to soften slightly. Serve in scoops, in chilled dessert bowls, with the soft fruits.

Cook's Tip

Chocolate curls make an attractive decoration for a dessert and are very simple to create. Simply chill a bar of chocolate, then use a vegetable peeler to shave off curls along the length of the bar.

Choca Mocha Sherbet

This delicious dark chocolate sherbet is a cross between a water ice and light cream-free ice cream. It is an ideal way to end a meal for chocoholics who are trying to count calories but still feel the need to have an occasional taste of chocolate.

Serves 4–6

600ml/1 pint/2½ cups semi-skimmed (low-fat) milk
40g/1½oz/⅓ cup good-quality unsweetened cocoa powder
115g/4oz/generous ½ cup caster (superfine) sugar
5ml/1 tsp instant coffee granules
chocolate-covered raisins, to decorate

1 Heat the milk in a pan. Meanwhile, put the cocoa powder in a bowl, add a little of the hot milk and mix to a paste.

2 Add the remaining milk to the cocoa mixture, stirring all the time, then pour the chocolate milk back into the pan. Bring to the boil, stirring continuously.

3 Take the pan off the heat and add the sugar and the coffee granules, stirring until the sugar and coffee have dissolved. Pour into a jug (pitcher), leave to cool, then chill well.

4 To make by hand, pour the mixture into a plastic tub or similar freezerproof container and freeze for 6 hours until firm, beating once or twice with a fork, electric mixer or in a food processor to break up the ice crystals. Allow to soften slightly before scooping into dishes. Sprinkle each portion with a few chocolate-covered raisins.

5 To make in an ice cream maker, churn the chilled mixture until very thick. Scoop into dishes. Sprinkle each portion with a few chocolate-covered raisins.

Cook's Tip

Use good-quality cocoa powder and don't overheat the milk mixture or the finished ice may taste bitter. If there are any lumps of cocoa in the milk, beat with a balloon whisk.

Sorbet Energy 179kcal/758kJ; Protein 3.8g; Carbohydrate 31.2g, of which sugars 29.7g; Fat 5.3g, of which saturates 3.1g; Cholesterol 1mg; Calcium 44mg; Fibre 3.4g; Sodium 123mg.
Choca Mocha Energy 142kcal/604kJ; Protein 4.7g; Carbohydrate 25.5g, of which sugars 24.7g; Fat 3.2g, of which saturates 1.9g; Cholesterol 6mg; Calcium 139mg; Fibre 0.8g; Sodium 108mg.

Coffee with Mocha Ice Cream

This coffee and mocha ice cream combination is a speciality of Belgium. You can enjoy it as an afternoon treat or serve it after dinner as the perfect way to finish off a good meal. The chocolatey topping – either a dusting of cocoa, shavings of chocolate or a chocolate-coated coffee bean – make an attractive and delicious decoration.

Serves 1

100ml/3 1fl oz/scant ½ cup double (heavy) cream
15ml/1 tbsp icing (confectioners') sugar
45ml/3 tbsp freshly brewed espresso coffee
10ml/2 tsp granulated (white) sugar
2 scoops mocha ice cream
2.5ml/½ tsp unsweetened cocoa powder, 5ml/1 tsp shaved chocolate curls, or 3 chocolate coffee beans, to decorate

1 Pour the cream into a bowl. Add the icing sugar and whip by hand or with an electric mixer until stiff.

2 Sweeten the espresso coffee by stirring in the granulated sugar.

3 Place the scoops of ice cream in a tall or wide heat-resistant glass.

4 Pour over the hot, sweet espresso and top with the whipped cream.

5 Decorate with a dusting of cocoa, a few shavings of chocolate or the chocolate coffee beans. Serve immediately.

Cook's Tip
Chill the espresso before pouring it over the ice cream, if you prefer.

Turkish Delight Sorbet with White Chocolate Drizzle

Anyone who likes Turkish delight will adore the taste and aroma of this intriguing dessert. Because of its sweetness, it is best served in small portions and is delicious with after-dinner coffee. Decorate with drizzled white chocolate and sugared almonds or slices of Turkish delight.

Serves 8

250g/9oz rose water-flavoured Turkish delight
25g/1oz/2 tbsp caster (superfine) sugar
750ml/1¼ pints/3 cups water
30ml/2 tbsp lemon juice
50g/2oz white chocolate, broken into pieces
roughly chopped sugared almonds, to decorate

1 Cut the cubes of Turkish delight into small pieces. Put half of the pieces in a heavy pan with the sugar. Pour in half of the water. Heat gently until the Turkish delight has dissolved.

2 Cool, then stir in the lemon juice with the remaining water and Turkish delight. Chill well. Churn the mixture in an ice cream maker until it is firm enough to hold its shape.

3 While the sorbet is freezing, dampen eight very small plastic cups or glasses. Line them with clear film (plastic wrap).

4 Spoon the sorbet into the cups and tap them lightly on the surface to compact the mixture. Cover with the overlapping film and freeze for at least 3 hours or overnight.

5 Make a paper piping (pastry) bag. Put the chocolate in a heatproof bowl over a pan of gently simmering water, and stir until melted.

6 Meanwhile, remove the sorbets from the freezer, let them stand at room temperature for 5 minutes, then pull them out of the cups. Transfer to serving plates and peel away the film. Spoon the melted chocolate into the piping bag, snip off the tip and scribble a design on the sorbet and the plate. Sprinkle the sugared almonds over and serve.

Coffee with Mocha Energy 925kcal/3855kJ; Protein 6.2g; Carbohydrate 82.9g, of which sugars 81.6g; Fat 64g, of which saturates 40.7g; Cholesterol 166mg; Calcium 198mg; Fibre 0g; Sodium 97mg.
Turkish Delight Energy 280kcal/1188kJ; Protein 1.4g; Carbohydrate 63.8g, of which sugars 58g; Fat 3.9g, of which saturates 2.3g; Cholesterol 0mg; Calcium 44mg; Fibre 0g; Sodium 34mg.

Creamy Fudge

A good selection of fudge always makes a welcome change from more traditional sweets and chocolate confections.

Makes 900g/2lb

50g/2oz/¼ cup unsalted (sweet) butter, plus extra for greasing
450g/1lb/2 cups sugar
300ml/½ pint/1¼ cups double (heavy) cream
150ml/¼ pint/⅔ cup milk
45ml/3 tbsp water (or use orange, apricot or cherry brandy, or strong coffee)

For the flavourings
225g/8oz/1⅓ cups plain (semisweet) or milk chocolate chips
115g/4oz/1 cup chopped almonds, hazelnuts, walnuts or brazil nuts
115g/4oz/½ cup chopped glacé (candied) cherries, dates or ready-to-eat dried apricots

1 Butter a 20cm/8in shallow square tin (pan). Place the sugar, cream, butter, milk and water or other flavouring into a pan. Heat very gently, stirring occasionally, until all the sugar has dissolved.

2 Bring the mixture to a boil, and boil steadily, stirring only occasionally to prevent the mixture from burning over the base of the pan. Boil until the fudge forms a soft ball if a spoonful is dropped in iced water; 110°C/225°F for a soft fudge.

3 If you are making chocolate-flavoured fudge, add the chocolate at this stage. Remove the pan from the heat and beat thoroughly until the mixture thickens and becomes opaque. Just before this consistency has been reached, add chopped nuts for a nutty fudge, or glacé cherries or dried fruit for a fruity fudge.

4 Pour the fudge into the prepared pan, taking care as the mixture is exceedingly hot. Leave the mixture until cool and almost set. Using a sharp knife, mark the fudge into small squares and leave in the tin until quite firm.

5 Turn the fudge out on to a board and invert. Using a long-bladed knife, cut into neat squares. You can dust some with icing (confectioners') sugar and drizzle others with melted chocolate, if desired.

Easy Chocolate Hazelnut Fudge

An easy way to make a batch of delicious nutty fudge.

Makes 16 squares

150ml/¼ pint/⅔ cup evaporated milk
350g/12oz/1½ cups sugar
large pinch of salt
50g/2oz/½ cup hazelnuts, halved
350g/12oz/2 cups plain (semisweet) chocolate chips

1 Generously grease a 20cm/8in square cake tin (pan).

2 Place the evaporated milk, sugar and salt in a heavy pan. Bring to the boil over a medium heat, stirring constantly until smooth. Lower the heat and simmer gently, stirring, for about 5 minutes.

3 Remove the pan from the heat and add the hazelnuts and chocolate chips. Stir gently with a metal spoon until the chocolate has completely melted.

4 Quickly pour the fudge mixture into the prepared tin and spread evenly, ensuring that it is spread right into the corners. Leave to cool and set.

5 When the chocolate hazelnut fudge has set, cut it into 2.5cm/1in squares. Store in an airtight container, separating the layers of fudge with sheets of baking parchment to stop them sticking together.

Variation

For two-tone fudge, make the Easy Chocolate Hazelnut Fudge and spread it in a 23cm/9in square cake tin (pan), to make a slightly thinner layer than for the main recipe. While it is cooling, make a batch of plain fudge, substituting white chocolate chips for the plain chocolate chips and leaving out the hazelnuts. Leave the plain fudge to cool slightly before pouring it carefully over the darker chocolate layer. Use a metal spatula to evenly spread the plain layer to the corners, then leave to set as detailed in the recipe above. Cut into squares.

Creamy Energy 5886kcal/24635kJ; Protein 40.4g; Carbohydrate 708.8g, of which sugars 704.5g; Fat 340.8g, of which saturates 171g; Cholesterol 540mg; Calcium 874mg; Fibre 14.1g; Sodium 512mg.
Hazelnut Fudge Energy 231kcal/975kJ; Protein 2.4g; Carbohydrate 38.3g, of which sugars 38g; Fat 8.7g, of which saturates 4.2g; Cholesterol 3mg; Calcium 48mg; Fibre 0.8g; Sodium 14mg.

Rich Chocolate Pistachio Fudge

This rich melt-in-the-mouth chocolate fudge is extremely rich – so you should try to eat it sparingly.

Makes 36

250g/9oz/1¼ cup sugar
375g/13oz can sweetened condensed milk
50g/2oz/¼ cup unsalted (sweet) butter
5ml/1 tsp vanilla extract
115g/4oz plain (semisweet) chocolate, grated
75g/3oz/½ cup pistachio nuts, almonds or hazelnuts

1 Lightly grease a 19cm/7½in square cake tin (pan) and line with baking parchment.

2 Mix the sugar, condensed milk and butter in a heavy pan. Heat gently, stirring occasionally, until the sugar has dissolved completely and the mixture is smooth.

3 Bring the mixture to the boil, stirring occasionally, and boil until it registers 116°C/240°F on a sugar thermometer, or until a small amount of the mixture dropped into a cup of iced water forms a soft ball.

4 Remove the pan from the heat and beat in the vanilla extract, chocolate and nuts. Beat vigorously until the mixture is smooth and creamy.

5 Pour the mixture into the prepared cake tin and spread evenly. Leave until just set, then mark into squares.

6 Leave the fudge to set completely before cutting into squares and removing from the tin. Store in an airtight container in a cool place.

Variation
Try making this fudge with different varieties of nut. Almonds, hazelnuts and brazil nuts will all work as well as the pistachios. Simply substitute the same quantity in the recipe.

Chocolate Fudge Triangles

A fun way to prepare fudge, with a plain chocolate layer sandwiched between layers of white chocolate fudge.

Makes about 48 triangles

600g/1lb 6oz fine-quality white chocolate, chopped into small pieces
375g/13oz can sweetened condensed milk
15ml/1 tbsp vanilla extract
7.5ml/1½ tsp lemon juice
pinch of salt
175g/6oz/1½ cups hazelnuts or pecan nuts, chopped (optional)
175g/6oz plain (semisweet) chocolate, chopped into small pieces
40g/1½ oz/3 tbsp unsalted (sweet) butter, cut into pieces
50g/2oz dark (bittersweet) chocolate, for drizzling

1 Line a 20cm/8in square baking tin (pan) with foil. Brush the foil lightly with oil.

2 In a pan over low heat, melt the white chocolate and condensed milk until smooth, stirring frequently. Remove from the heat and stir in the vanilla extract, lemon juice and salt. Stir in the nuts, if using. Spread half the mixture in the tin. Chill for 15 minutes.

3 In a pan over a low heat, melt the plain chocolate and butter until smooth, stirring frequently. Remove from the heat, cool slightly, then pour over the chilled white layer and chill for 15 minutes until set.

4 Gently reheat the remaining white chocolate mixture and pour over the set chocolate layer. Smooth the top, then chill for 2–4 hours, until set.

5 Using the foil as a guide, remove the fudge from the pan and turn it on to a cutting board. Carefully lift off the foil and use a sharp knife to cut the fudge into 24 squares. Cut each square into a triangle.

6 Melt the dark chocolate in a heatproof bowl over a pan of barely simmering water. Leave to cool slightly, then drizzle over the triangles.

Pistachio Fudge Energy 112kcal/472kJ; Protein 1.5g; Carbohydrate 18.2g, of which sugars 18.1g; Fat 4.2g, of which saturates 2.1g; Cholesterol 7mg; Calcium 39mg; Fibre 0.2g; Sodium 35mg.
Fudge Triangles Energy 120kcal/503kJ; Protein 1.5g; Carbohydrate 15.3g, of which sugars 15.1g; Fat 6.3g, of which saturates 3.8g; Cholesterol 6mg; Calcium 28mg; Fibre 0.4g; Sodium 17mg.

Chocolate Almond Torrone

Torrone is a type of Italian nougat believed to be of Roman origin. This delicious version is an ideal way to finish a dinner party.

Makes about 20 slices

115g/4oz plain (semisweet) chocolate, chopped into pieces
50g/2oz/¼ cup unsalted (sweet) butter
1 egg white
115g/4oz/generous ½ cup caster (superfine) sugar
75g/3oz/¾ cup chopped toasted almonds
50g/2oz/½ cup ground almonds
75ml/5 tbsp chopped mixed (candied) peel

For the coating

175g/6oz white chocolate, chopped into small pieces
25g/1oz/2 tbsp unsalted (sweet) butter
115g/4oz/1 cup flaked (sliced) almonds, toasted

1 Melt the chocolate with the butter in a heatproof bowl over a pan of barely simmering water until smooth.

2 In a clean, grease-free bowl, whisk the egg white with the sugar until stiff. Gradually beat in the melted chocolate mixture, then stir in the toasted almonds, ground almonds and peel.

3 Transfer the mixture on to a sheet of baking parchment and shape into a thick roll.

4 As the mixture cools, use the paper to press the roll firmly into a triangular shape. When you are satisfied with the shape, twist the paper over the triangular roll and chill until it is completely set.

5 Make the coating. Melt the white chocolate with the butter in a heatproof bowl over a pan of simmering water. Unwrap the chocolate roll and with a clean knife spread the white chocolate quickly over the surface. Press the flaked almonds in a thin even coating over the chocolate, working quickly before the chocolate sets.

6 Chill the coated chocolate roll again until firm, then cut the torrone into fairly thin slices to serve.

Chocolate Nut Clusters

The classic combination of chocolate and nuts are here made into tasty morsels, perfect for a mouthful of chocolate heaven.

Makes about 30

550ml/18fl oz/2½ cups double (heavy) cream
25g/1oz/2 tbsp unsalted (sweet) butter, cut into small pieces
350ml/12fl oz/1½ cups golden (light corn) syrup
200g/7oz/1 cup sugar
75g/3oz/scant ½ cup soft light brown sugar
pinch of salt
15ml/1 tbsp vanilla extract
350g/12oz/3 cups combination of hazelnuts, pecans, walnuts, brazil nuts and unsalted peanuts
400g/14oz plain (semisweet) chocolate, chopped into pieces
15g/½oz/1 tbsp white vegetable fat (shortening)

1 Lightly brush two baking sheets with vegetable oil. In a pan over a low heat, cook the cream, butter, golden syrup, sugars and salt, stirring until the sugars dissolve and the butter melts.

2 Bring to the boil and continue cooking, stirring, for about 1 hour, until the caramel reaches 119°C/238°F on a sugar thermometer, or until a small amount of caramel dropped into a cup of iced water forms a hard ball. Plunge the bottom of the pan into cold water to stop the cooking process. Cool slightly, then stir in the vanilla extract.

3 Stir the nuts into the caramel until well coated. Using an oiled tablespoon, drop spoonfuls of nut mixture on to the prepared sheets, about 2.5cm/1in apart. If the mixture hardens, return to the heat to soften. Chill the clusters for 30 minutes until firm and cold, or leave in a cool place until hardened.

4 Using a metal spatula, transfer the clusters to a wire rack placed over a baking sheet to catch drips. In a pan, over a low heat, melt the chocolate with the white vegetable fat, stirring until the mixture is smooth. Set aside to cool slightly.

5 Spoon chocolate over each cluster, being sure to cover completely. Place on the wire rack. Allow to set for 2 hours until hardened. Store in an airtight container.

Almond Torrone Energy 186kcal/775kJ; Protein 3.7g; Carbohydrate 11.8g, of which sugars 11.4g; Fat 14.1g, of which saturates 5.1g; Cholesterol 8mg; Calcium 60mg; Fibre 1.2g; Sodium 48mg.
Nut Clusters Energy 311kcal/1298kJ; Protein 2.7g; Carbohydrate 28.3g, of which sugars 27.9g; Fat 21.6g, of which saturates 9.2g; Cholesterol 27mg; Calcium 36mg; Fibre 1.1g; Sodium 46mg.

Chocolate-coated Nut Brittle

This chocolatey version of the classic nut praline will prove to be an instant, and very short-lived, success.

Makes 20–24 pieces

115g/4oz/1 cup mixed pecan nuts and whole almonds
115g/4oz/generous ½ cup caster (superfine) sugar
60ml/4 tbsp water
200g/7oz plain (semisweet) chocolate, chopped into small pieces

1 Lightly grease a baking sheet with butter or oil.

2 Mix the nuts, sugar and water in a heavy pan. Place the pan over a gentle heat, stirring frequently until all the sugar has completely dissolved.

3 Bring the mixture to the boil, then lower the heat to moderate. Cook until the mixture turns a rich golden brown and registers 155°C/310°F on a sugar thermometer. If you do not have a sugar thermometer, test the syrup by adding a few drops to a cup of iced water. The mixture should solidify to a very brittle mass.

4 Quickly remove the pan from the heat and tip the mixture on to the prepared baking sheet, spreading it around evenly with a metal spatula. Leave until completely cold and hard.

5 Break the nut brittle into bitesize pieces. Melt the chocolate in a heatproof bowl set over a pan of barely simmering water. Stir frequently until the chocolate is melted and smooth.

6 While the chocolate is still warm, dip in the nut brittle pieces to half-coat them. Leave on a sheet of baking parchment to set.

Cook's Tip
If the nut brittle proves too hard to break by hand, then cover with a clean dish towel and hit gently with a rolling pin or, if you have one, a toffee hammer.

Chocolate Christmas Cups

These fabulous little confections would be perfect to serve during the Christmas festivities. You will need about 70–80 paper or foil sweet cases in which to make and serve them.

Makes about 35 cups

275g/10oz plain (semisweet) chocolate, broken into pieces
175g/6oz cooked, cold Christmas pudding
75ml/2½fl oz/⅓ cup brandy or whisky
chocolate leaves and a few crystallized cranberries, to decorate

1 Place the chocolate in a double boiler or in a bowl over a pan of hot water. Heat gently until the chocolate is melted, stirring until the chocolate is smooth.

2 Using a pastry brush, brush or coat the base and sides of about 35 paper or foil sweet (candy) cases. Allow to set, then repeat, reheating the melted chocolate if necessary, and apply a second coat. Leave to cool and set completely, for 4–5 hours or overnight. Reserve the remaining chocolate.

3 Crumble the Christmas pudding in a small bowl, sprinkle with the brandy or whisky and allow to stand for 30–40 minutes, until the spirit is absorbed.

4 Spoon a little of the pudding mixture into each cup, smoothing the top. Reheat the remaining chocolate and spoon over the top of each cup to cover the surface of each cup to the edge. Leave to set.

5 When the cups are completely set, peel off the cases and place in clean foil cases. Decorate with chocolate leaves and crystallized cranberries.

Cook's Tip
To crystallize cranberries for decoration, beat an egg white until frothy. Dip each berry in egg white, then in sugar. Leave to dry.

Nut Brittle Energy 94kcal/395kJ; Protein 0.9g; Carbohydrate 10.6g, of which sugars 10.4g; Fat 5.7g, of which saturates 1.7g; Cholesterol 1mg; Calcium 8mg; Fibre 0.4g; Sodium 1mg.
Christmas Cups Energy 59kcal/249kJ; Protein 0.6g; Carbohydrate 7.5g, of which sugars 6.6g; Fat 2.7g, of which saturates 1.3g; Cholesterol 0mg; Calcium 7mg; Fibre 0.3g; Sodium 10mg.

Chocolate Citrus Candies

Home-candied peel makes a superb sweetmeat, especially when dipped in melted chocolate. You can also use bought candied peel for this recipe, but make sure it is the very best quality. If you buy the peel in one piece, it can then be simply sliced and dipped.

Makes about 100g/4oz petits fours
1 orange or 2 lemons
25g/1oz/2 tbsp sugar
about 50g/2oz good-quality plain (semisweet) chocolate

1 Using a vegetable knife or peeler, cut the rind from the orange or lemons. Take care not to cut off too much of the pith. Slice into matchsticks.

2 Blanch the chopped peel in boiling water for 4–5 minutes, until beginning to soften, then refresh under cold water and drain thoroughly.

3 In a small pan, heat the sugar and 30ml/2 tbsp water gently together until the sugar has completely dissolved. Add the strips of fruit peel and simmer gently for about 8–10 minutes, or until the water has evaporated and the matchsticks of peel have turned transparent.

4 Lift out the peel with a slotted spoon and spread out on a sheet of baking parchment to cool. When cold, the peel can be stored in an airtight container in the refrigerator for up to 2 days before using, if required.

5 To coat, melt the chocolate carefully in a double boiler or in a heatproof bowl over a pan of hot water. Spear each piece of peel on to a cocktail stick (toothpick) and dip one end into the melted chocolate.

6 To set the chocolate on the candies, stick the cocktail sticks into a large potato. When the chocolate is completely dry, remove the sticks and then arrange the citrus candies attractively on a dish to serve as petits fours.

Marzipan Chocolate Logs

These rich confections are made from orange-flavoured marzipan rolled into logs then covered in a variety of tasty toppings. They will help to liven up any festive table, or serve at any other special occasion feast.

Makes about 12
225g/8oz marzipan, at room temperature
115g/4oz/⅔ cup candied orange peel, chopped
30ml/2 tbsp orange-flavoured liqueur
15ml/1 tbsp soft light brown sugar
edible gold powder
75g/3oz plain (semisweet) chocolate
gold-coated sweets (candies)

1 Knead the marzipan well on a lightly floured surface, then mix in the chopped peel and liqueur. Set aside for about 1 hour, to dry out.

2 Break off small pieces of the mixture and roll them into log shapes in the palms of your hands.

3 Separate the marzipan logs into two equal batches. Dip half of the logs in the brown sugar and brush them lightly with the edible gold powder using a clean, dry pastry brush or a small paintbrush, if available.

4 Melt the chocolate in a double boiler or heatproof bowl over a pan of barely simmering water. Stir the chocolate until it is completely melted and smooth.

5 Dip the remaining logs in the melted chocolate. Place on baking parchment and press a gold-coated sweet in the centre of each. When set, arrange all the logs on a plate.

Cook's Tip
There are a variety of orange-flavoured liqueurs on the market. Look out for Cointreau or Grand Marnier. The mandarin-flavoured Mandarine Napoleon will also work here.

Citrus Candies Energy 438kcal/1845kJ; Protein 4.4g; Carbohydrate 74g, of which sugars 72.6g; Fat 15.8g, of which saturates 8.9g; Cholesterol 15mg; Calcium 208mg; Fibre 3.6g; Sodium 270mg.
Marzipan Logs Energy 138kcal/584kJ; Protein 1.3g; Carbohydrate 24.4g, of which sugars 24.4g; Fat 4.2g, of which saturates 1.2g; Cholesterol 0mg; Calcium 28mg; Fibre 1g; Sodium 31mg.

Double Chocolate-dipped Fruit

These sweets have a multi-coloured chocolate layer covering various fruits.

Makes 24 coated pieces

fruits – about 24 pieces (strawberries, cherries, orange segments, large seedless grapes, physalis, kumquats, pitted prunes, pitted dates, ready-to-eat dried apricots, dried peaches or dried pears)
115g/4oz white chocolate, chopped into small pieces
115g/4oz dark (bittersweet) or plain (semisweet) chocolate, chopped into small pieces

1 Clean and prepare fruits; wipe strawberries with a soft cloth or brush gently with a pastry brush. Wash firm-skinned fruits such as cherries and grapes and dry well. Peel and leave whole or cut up any other fruits being used.

2 Melt the white chocolate. Remove from the heat and cool to tepid (about 29°C/84°F), stirring frequently. Line a baking sheet with baking parchment.

3 Holding each fruit by the stem or end and at an angle, dip about two-thirds of the fruit into the chocolate. Allow the excess to drip off and place on the baking sheet. Chill the fruits for about 20 minutes until the chocolate has completely set.

4 Melt the dark or plain chocolate, stirring frequently until smooth. Remove the chocolate from the heat and cool to just below body temperature, about 30°C/86°F.

5 Take each white chocolate-coated fruit in turn from the baking sheet and, holding by the stem or end and at the opposite angle, dip the bottom third of each piece into the darker chocolate, creating a chevron effect. Set on the baking sheet. Chill for 15 minutes or until set.

6 Allow the fruit to stand at room temperature for about 15 minutes before serving.

Swedish Rose Chocolates

These rich chocolate balls are simple to make and completely delicious. They are a popular Swedish Christmas treat, where they might be offered as a gift or served on Christmas Eve. Here, they are served with crystallized rose petals.

Makes 12

150g/5oz plain (semisweet) chocolate
30ml/2 tbsp ground almonds
30ml/2 tbsp caster (superfine) sugar
2 egg yolks
10ml/2 tsp strong brewed coffee
15ml/1 tbsp dark rum
15ml/1 tbsp rose water
40g/1½oz/¼ cup chocolate vermicelli (sprinkles)
crystallized rose petals, for decoration

1 Grate the chocolate finely or grind in batches in a coffee or spice mill. Place in a bowl and add the ground almonds, caster sugar, egg yolks, coffee and rum.

2 Roll the mixture into balls by rolling small teaspoonfuls between your fingers. Chill well.

3 Dip each of the chocolate balls into the rose water, then roll in the chocolate vermicelli until completely coated.

4 Wrap the chocolate balls individually in cellophane tied with natural raffia before packing them in decorative boxes, or pile them high on a serving plate, sprinkled with crystallized rose petals.

Cook's Tip

For crystallized rose petals, coat clean and dry petals with a thin and even layer of beaten egg white and, working quickly, sprinkle with sifted icing (confectioners') sugar. Allow the petals to dry for 30 minutes on a wire rack. The petals will keep for up to a week, stored in an airtight container between layers of paper towels.

Chocolate-dipped Fruit Energy 54kcal/227kJ; Protein 0.8g; Carbohydrate 6.8g, of which sugars 6.8g; Fat 2.8g, of which saturates 1.7g; Cholesterol 0mg; Calcium 17mg; Fibre 0.3g; Sodium 7mg.
Rose Chocolates Energy 114kcal/476kJ; Protein 1.9g; Carbohydrate 13.3g, of which sugars 10.5g; Fat 5.8g, of which saturates 2.5g; Cholesterol 34mg; Calcium 16mg; Fibre 0.5g; Sodium 3mg.

Chocolate Apricots

You can use almost any dried fruit for this sophisticated sweetmeat. In this recipe, the sweet but sharp flavour of apricots contrasts beautifully with the velvet-smooth chocolate.

Makes 24–36
50g/2oz plain (semisweet) chocolate
12 large ready-to-eat dried apricots

1 Take a length of foil or baking parchment and use it to line a baking sheet. Set the baking sheet aside.

2 Break the chocolate into a double pan or a heatproof bowl set over a pan of barely simmering water. Heat until melted, stirring occasionally.

3 Cut each dried apricot into 2–3 strips. Dip the long cut side of each strip into the melted chocolate and immediately place it on the prepared baking sheet. Repeat the process until all the apricots are covered.

4 Chill the chocolate apricots in the freezer for about 30 minutes, until set.

5 Use a metal spatula to slide the apricots off the foil or baking paper, or press them from underneath. Store the apricots in a cool place, in an airtight container.

Cook's Tips
- *To melt this quantity of chocolate in the microwave, put it on a plate and cook on high for about 1 minute. If the chocolate in the bowl starts to set before you have finished dipping all of the apricots, put the bowl back over the heat for a minute or two, or microwave again briefly.*
- *These chocolate treats will make an excellent gift for a loved one. Simply pack the apricots into a pretty gift box, protecting them with some coloured tissue paper.*

Stuffed Chocolate Prunes

Chocolate-covered prunes, soaked in liqueur, hide a delicious melt-in-the-mouth coffee filling.

Makes approximately 30
225g/8oz/1 cup unpitted prunes
50ml/2fl oz/¼ cup Armagnac
30ml/2 tbsp ground coffee
150ml/¼ pint/⅔ cup double (heavy) cream
350g/12oz plain (semisweet) chocolate, broken into squares
10g/¼oz/½ tbsp vegetable fat
30ml/2 tbsp unsweetened cocoa powder, sifted, for dusting

1 Put the unpitted prunes in a bowl and pour the Armagnac over. Stir, then cover with clear film (plastic wrap) and set aside for 2 hours, or until the prunes have absorbed the liquid.

2 Make a slit along each prune to remove the pit, making a hollow for the filling, but leaving the fruit intact.

3 Put the coffee and cream in a pan and heat almost to boiling point. Cover, infuse (steep) for 4 minutes, then heat again until almost boiling. Put 115g/4oz of the chocolate into a bowl and pour over the coffee cream through a sieve (strainer).

4 Stir until the chocolate has melted and the mixture is smooth. Leave to cool, until it has the consistency of softened butter.

5 Fill a piping (pastry) bag with a small plain nozzle with the chocolate mixture. Pipe into the cavities of the prunes. Chill in the refrigerator for 20 minutes.

6 Melt the remaining chocolate in a bowl over a pan of hot water. Using a fork, dip the prunes one at a time into the chocolate to give them a generous coating. Place on a sheet of baking parchment until they have hardened. Dust each with a little cocoa powder.

Cook's Tip
Dates can be used instead of prunes, if preferred.

Chocolate Apricots Energy 207kcal/872kJ; Protein 3.3g; Carbohydrate 34.2g, of which sugars 33.9g; Fat 7.3g, of which saturates 4.2g; Cholesterol 2mg; Calcium 45mg; Fibre 3.8g; Sodium 9mg.
Stuffed Prunes Energy 100kcal/419kJ; Protein 0.9g; Carbohydrate 10.1g, of which sugars 9.9g; Fat 6.3g, of which saturates 3.8g; Cholesterol 8mg; Calcium 10mg; Fibre 0.8g; Sodium 7mg.

Cognac and Ginger Creams

Ginger is arguably the perfect partner to rich and creamy plain chocolate. Add in some cognac and these confections become utterly irresistible.

Makes 18–20

300g/11oz plain (semisweet) chocolate, chopped into pieces
45ml/3 tbsp double (heavy) cream
30ml/2 tbsp cognac
4 pieces of stem ginger, finely chopped, plus 15ml/1 tbsp syrup from the jar
crystallized ginger, to decorate

1 Polish the insides of 18–20 chocolate moulds carefully with cotton wool.

2 Melt about two-thirds of the chocolate in a heatproof bowl over a pan of barely simmering water, then spoon a little into each mould. Reserve a little of the melted chocolate for sealing the creams.

3 Using a small brush, sweep the chocolate up the sides of the moulds to coat them evenly, then invert them on to a sheet of baking parchment. Set aside in a cool place until the chocolate has completely set.

4 Melt the remaining chopped chocolate over simmering water, then stir in the cream, cognac, stem ginger and ginger syrup, mixing well.

5 Spoon the mixture into the chocolate-lined moulds. If the reserved chocolate has solidified, melt, then spoon a little into each mould to seal.

6 Leave the chocolates in a cool place (not the refrigerator) until set. To remove them from the moulds, gently press them out on to a cool surface, such as a marble slab.

7 Decorate each cream with small pieces of crystallized ginger. Keep the chocolates cool if you are not planning on serving them immediately.

Peppermint Chocolate Sticks

These minty treats are perfect with an after-dinner cup of coffee.

Makes about 80

115g/4oz/generous ½ cup sugar
150ml/¼ pint/⅔ cup water
2.5ml/½ tsp peppermint extract
200g/7oz plain (semisweet) chocolate, chopped into small pieces
60ml/4 tbsp toasted desiccated (dry unsweetened shredded) coconut

1 Lightly oil a large baking sheet. Place the sugar and water in a pan and heat gently, stirring until the sugar has dissolved.

2 Bring to the boil and boil rapidly without stirring until the syrup registers 138°C/280°F on a sugar thermometer. Remove the pan from the heat and stir in the peppermint extract.

3 Pour the mixture on to the greased baking sheet and leave until set.

4 Break up the peppermint mixture into a small bowl and use the end of a rolling pin to crush it into small pieces.

5 Melt the chocolate. Remove from the heat and stir in the mint pieces and desiccated coconut.

6 Lay a 30 × 25cm/12 × 10in sheet of baking parchment on a flat surface. Spread the chocolate mixture over the paper, leaving a narrow border all around, to make a rectangle measuring about 25 × 20cm/10 × 8in. Leave to set. When firm, use a sharp knife to cut into thin sticks, each about 6cm/2½in long.

Variations

- *Make orange chocolate sticks by replacing the peppermint extract with the same amount of an orange-flavoured liqueur.*
- *You can replace the coconut with the same quantity of ginger nut biscuits (gingersnaps) for crunchy gingery sticks.*

Cognac Creams Energy 92kcal/383kJ; Protein 0.8g; Carbohydrate 10.2g, of which sugars 10g; Fat 5.4g, of which saturates 3.3g; Cholesterol 4mg; Calcium 6mg; Fibre 0.4g; Sodium 3mg.
Peppermint Sticks Energy 23kcal/96kJ; Protein 0.2g; Carbohydrate 3.1g, of which sugars 3.1g; Fat 1.2g, of which saturates 0.8g; Cholesterol 0mg; Calcium 2mg; Fibre 0.2g; Sodium 0mg.

Chocolate and Coffee Mint Thins

These coffee-flavoured chocolate squares contain pieces of crisp minty caramel and are ideal for serving with after-dinner coffee.

Makes 16

75g/3oz/scant ½ cup sugar
75ml/5 tbsp water
3 drops oil of peppermint
15ml/1 tbsp strong-flavoured ground coffee
75ml/5 tbsp near-boiling double (heavy) cream
225g/8oz plain (semisweet) chocolate
10g/¼oz/½ tbsp unsalted (sweet) butter

1 Line an 18cm/7in square tin (pan) with baking parchment. Gently heat the sugar and water in a heavy pan until dissolved. Add the peppermint, and boil until a light caramel colour.

2 Pour the caramel on to an oiled baking sheet and leave to harden, then crush into small pieces.

3 Put the coffee in a small bowl and pour the hot cream over. Leave to infuse (steep) for about 4 minutes, then strain through a fine sieve (strainer).

4 Melt the chocolate and unsalted butter in a bowl over barely simmering water. Remove from the heat and beat in the hot coffee cream. Stir in the mint caramel.

5 Pour the mixture into the prepared tin and smooth the surface level. Leave in a cool place to set for at least 4 hours, preferably overnight.

6 Carefully turn out the chocolate on to a board and peel off the lining paper. Cut the chocolate into squares with a sharp knife and store in an airtight container until needed.

Cook's Tip
Don't put the chocolate in the refrigerator to set, or it may lose its glossy appearance and become too brittle to cut easily into neat squares.

Chocolate and Cherry Colettes

Tasty maraschino cherries are hidden inside these double-chocolate treats. A perfect gift for adults.

Makes 18–20

115g/4oz plain (semisweet) chocolate, chopped into pieces
75g/3oz white or milk chocolate, chopped into small pieces
25g/1oz/2 tbsp unsalted (sweet) butter, melted
15ml/1 tbsp Kirsch or brandy
60ml/4 tbsp double (heavy) cream
18–20 maraschino cherries or liqueur-soaked cherries
milk chocolate curls, to decorate

1 Melt the dark chocolate in a heatproof bowl over a pan of simmering water, then remove it from the heat. Spoon into 18–20 foil sweet cases, spread evenly up the sides with a small brush, then leave the cases in a cool place until the chocolate has completely set.

2 Melt the white or milk chocolate in a pan with the butter over a gentle heat. Remove from the heat and stir in the Kirsch or brandy, then the cream. Cool until the mixture is thick enough to hold its shape.

3 Carefully peel away the paper from the chocolate cases. Place one cherry in each chocolate case.

4 Spoon the white or milk chocolate cream mixture into a piping (pastry) bag fitted with a small star nozzle and pipe over the cherries until the cases are full.

5 Top each colette with a generous swirl of the chocolate, and decorate each one with milk chocolate curls. Leave to set before serving.

Cook's Tip
To make the chocolate curls for the decoration, put a bar of chocolate in the fridge until well chilled and then run a vegetable peeler down the long edge of the bar.

Chocolate Mint Thins Energy 118kcal/494kJ; Protein 0.8g; Carbohydrate 13.9g, of which sugars 13.8g; Fat 7g, of which saturates 4.3g; Cholesterol 9mg; Calcium 10mg; Fibre 0.4g; Sodium 6mg.
Cherry Colettes Energy 163kcal/675kJ; Protein 0.7g; Carbohydrate 6.9g, of which sugars 6.8g; Fat 14.7g, of which saturates 9.2g; Cholesterol 31mg; Calcium 17mg; Fibre 0.2g; Sodium 82mg.

Fruit Fondant Chocolates

These chocolates are simple to make using pre-formed plastic moulds, yet look very professional. Fruit fondant is available from sugarcraft stores and comes in a variety of flavours including coffee and nut. Try a mixture of flavours using a small quantity of each, or use just a single flavour.

Makes 24

225g/8oz plain (semisweet), milk or white chocolate
115g/4oz/1 cup real fruit liquid fondant
15–20ml/3–4tsp cooled boiled water
15ml/1 tbsp melted plain (semisweet), milk or white chocolate, to decorate

1 Melt the chocolate in a bowl over a pan of hot water. Use a piece of cotton wool to polish the insides of plastic chocolate moulds, ensuring that they are clean. Fill up the shapes in one plastic tray to the top with the chocolate, leave for a few seconds, then invert the tray over the bowl of melted chocolate allowing the excess chocolate to fall back into the bowl. Sit the tray on the work surface and draw a metal spatula across the top to remove the excess chocolate and to neaten the edges. Chill until set. Repeat to fill the remaining trays.

2 Sift the fruit fondant mixture into a bowl. Gradually stir in enough water to give it the consistency of thick cream. Place the fondant in a baking parchment piping (pastry) bag, fold down the top and snip off the end. Fill each chocolate case almost to the top by piping in the fondant. Leave for about 30 minutes, or until a skin has formed on the surface of the fondant.

3 Spoon the remaining melted chocolate over the fondant to fill each mould level with the top. Chill until the chocolate has set hard. Invert the tray and press out the chocolates one by one. Place the melted chocolate of a contrasting colour into a baking parchment piping bag, fold down the top, snip off the point and pipe lines across the top of each chocolate. Allow to set, then pack into pretty boxes and tie with ribbon.

Chocolate Fondant Hearts

If you're looking for a gift for your Valentine, look no further.

Makes 50

60ml/4 tbsp liquid glucose
50g/2oz plain (semisweet) chocolate, plus extra for decorating
50g/2oz white chocolate, plus extra for decorating
1 egg white
450g/1lb/4 cups icing (confectioners') sugar, sifted, plus extra for dusting

1 Divide the glucose between two heatproof bowls. Place each bowl over a pan of barely simmering water and heat gently. Break the two types of chocolate into pieces. Add the plain chocolate to one bowl and the white chocolate to the other and continue to heat until melted.

2 Remove both bowls of chocolate from the heat and set them aside to cool. Whisk the egg white until stiff, then add one-third to each bowl, reserving the remaining third.

3 Divide the icing sugar equally between the bowls and stir in thoroughly to mix. Turn the mixtures out of the bowls and knead each piece separately, with your hands, until smooth and pliable.

4 Lightly dust a work surface with icing sugar and roll out each piece of fondant to a 3mm/⅛in thickness.

5 Brush the surface of the dark chocolate fondant with the remaining egg white and place the white chocolate fondant on top. Roll the surface of the fondants with a rolling pin to press the pieces together.

6 Using a heart-shaped cutter, stamp out about 50 hearts from the fondant. Melt the extra plain and white chocolate and pipe or drizzle over the top of each chocolate heart.

7 Leave to set completely before packing in an airtight container, or put them in a decorative gift box.

Fruit Chocolates Energy 88kcal/368kJ; Protein 0.7g; Carbohydrate 13.1g, of which sugars 10.8g; Fat 4g, of which saturates 2.4g; Cholesterol 1mg; Calcium 5mg; Fibre 0.4g; Sodium 8mg.
Fondant Hearts Energy 50kcal/212kJ; Protein 0.2g; Carbohydrate 11.6g, of which sugars 11.1g; Fat 0.6g, of which saturates 0.4g; Cholesterol 0mg; Calcium 8mg; Fibre 0g; Sodium 5mg.

Chocolate Birds' Nests

These delightful crispy chocolate nests make a perfect Easter tea-time treat and are a real favourite with kids. They're so quick and easy to make and young children can have great fun shaping the chocolate mixture inside the paper cases and tucking the pastel-coloured chocolate eggs inside.

Makes 12

200g/7oz milk chocolate
25g/1oz/2 tbsp unsalted (sweet) butter, diced
90g/3½oz shredded wheat cereal
36 small pastel-coloured, sugar-coated chocolate eggs

1 Line the sections of a tartlet tin (muffin pan) with 12 decorative paper cake cases.

2 Break the milk chocolate into pieces and put in a heatproof bowl with the butter. Rest the bowl over a pan of gently simmering water and stir frequently until melted. Remove the bowl from the heat and leave to cool for a few minutes.

3 Using your fingers, crumble the Shredded Wheat into the melted chocolate. Stir well until the cereal is completely coated in chocolate.

4 Divide the mixture among the paper cases, pressing it down gently with the back of a spoon, and make a slight indentation in the centre. Tuck three eggs into each nest and leave to set for about 2 hours.

Cook's Tip

Bags of sugar-coated chocolate eggs are widely available in supermarkets and food stores around Easter time. However, if you have trouble finding them out of season, try visiting an old-fashioned sweet (candy) store. Often these stores have large jars of this type of chocolate sweet, which they sell all year round, and you can choose how many to buy.

Fruit-and-nut White Chocolate Clusters

This is a no-bake recipe that children will like, although if they are making it themselves, supervision for melting the chocolate is recommended.

Makes 24

225g/8oz white chocolate
50g/2oz/⅓ cup sunflower seeds
50g/2oz/½ cup flaked (sliced) almonds
50g/2oz/¼ cup sesame seeds
50g/2oz/⅓ cup seedless raisins
5ml/1 tsp ground cinnamon

1 Break the white chocolate into small pieces. Put the chocolate in a microwave-proof container and cook in a microwave on medium for 2–3 minutes, following the manufacturer's instructions.

2 Alternatively, melt the chocolate by putting it into a heatproof bowl set over a pan of barely simmering water on a low heat. Do not allow the water to touch the base of the bowl, or the chocolate may become too hot and stiffen.

3 Stir the melted chocolate constantly until it takes on a smooth and glossy appearance.

4 Mix the remaining ingredients together until thoroughly combined. Pour on the melted chocolate and stir well until all the ingredients are evenly covered in chocolate.

5 Using a teaspoon, spoon the mixture into paper cases supported in a bun tin (pan) if necessary. When all the cases are full, leave in a cool place to set, but do not put the clusters in the refrigerator.

Cook's Tip

As with any recipe that contains nuts, always check that the people who will be eating the cookies do not have nut allergies. You could always substitute other dried fruit, such as dates or apricots, for the nuts.

Birds' Nests Energy 214kcal/896kJ; Protein 3.4g; Carbohydrate 24.4g, of which sugars 19g; Fat 12.1g, of which saturates 7.2g; Cholesterol 12mg; Calcium 77mg; Fibre 1g; Sodium 42mg.
Fruit-and-nut Clusters Energy 93kcal/386kJ; Protein 2g; Carbohydrate 7.5g, of which sugars 7g; Fat 6.3g, of which saturates 2.1g; Cholesterol 0mg; Calcium 48mg; Fibre 0.5g; Sodium 12mg.

White Chocolate Snowballs

These little spherical cookies are particularly popular during the Christmas season. They're simple to make, yet utterly delicious and bursting with creamy, buttery flavours. If you like, make them in advance of a special tea as they will keep well in the refrigerator for a few days.

Makes 16

200g/7oz white chocolate
25g/1oz/2 tbsp butter, diced
90g/3½oz/generous 1 cup desiccated (dry unsweetened shredded) coconut
90g/3½oz syrup sponge or Madeira cake
icing (confectioners') sugar, for dusting

1 Break the chocolate into pieces and put in a heatproof bowl with the butter. Rest the bowl over a pan of gently simmering water and stir frequently until melted. Remove the bowl from the heat and set aside for a few minutes.

2 Meanwhile, put 50g/2oz/⅔ cup of the coconut on a plate and set aside.

3 Crumble the sponge or Madeira cake and add to the melted chocolate with the remaining coconut. Mix well to form a chunky paste.

4 Take spoonfuls of the mixture and roll into balls, about 2.5cm/1in in diameter, and immediately roll them in the reserved coconut. Place the balls on baking parchment and leave to set.

5 Before serving, dust the snowballs liberally with plenty of icing sugar.

Cook's Tip
Be prepared to shape the mixture into balls as soon as you've mixed in the desiccated coconut and the cake. The mixture will set extremely quickly and you won't be able to shape it once it has hardened.

Florentine Bites

Extremely sweet and rich, these little mouthfuls – based on a classic Italian biscuit – are really delicious when served with after-dinner coffee and liqueurs. Nicely wrapped, they would also make a very special gift for anyone – your dinner party host, for example.

Makes 36

200g/7oz good-quality plain (semisweet) chocolate (minimum 70 per cent cocoa solids)
50g/2oz/2½ cups cornflakes
50g/2oz/scant ½ cup sultanas (golden raisins)
115g/4oz/1 cup toasted flaked (sliced) almonds
115g/4oz/½ cup glacé (candied) cherries, halved
50g/2oz/⅓ cup mixed (candied) peel
200ml/7fl oz/scant 1 cup sweetened condensed milk

1 Preheat the oven to 180°C/350°F/Gas 4. Line the base of a shallow 20cm/8in cake tin (pan) with baking parchment. Lightly grease the sides.

2 Melt the chocolate in a heatproof bowl over a pan of barely simmering water on a low heat. Stir and spread the melted chocolate over the base of the tin. Chill in the refrigerator until set.

3 Meanwhile, put the cornflakes, sultanas, almonds, cherries and mixed peel in a large bowl.

4 Pour the condensed milk over the cornflake mixture and toss the mix gently, using a fork.

5 Spread the mixture evenly over the chocolate base and bake for 12–15 minutes, or until golden brown.

6 Put the cooked florentine mixture aside in the tin until completely cooled, then chill for 20 minutes.

7 Cut into approximately 36 tiny squares and serve.

Snowballs Energy 133kcal/554kJ; Protein 1.6g; Carbohydrate 10.9g, of which sugars 9.7g; Fat 9.5g, of which saturates 6.6g; Cholesterol 3mg; Calcium 38mg; Fibre 0.8g; Sodium 46mg.
Florentine Bites Energy 87kcal/364kJ; Protein 1.6g; Carbohydrate 12g, of which sugars 10.7g; Fat 3.9g, of which saturates 1.4g; Cholesterol 2mg; Calcium 30mg; Fibre 0.5g; Sodium 28mg.

Chocolate Cherry Brandy Truffles

Gloriously rich chocolate truffles are given a really wicked twist in this recipe simply by the addition of a small quantity of cherry brandy – the perfect indulgent way to end a special dinner party. Instead of adding cherry brandy, try experimenting with some other of your favourite alcoholic spirits or liqueurs.

Makes 18

50g/2oz/½ cup plain (all-purpose) flour
25g/1oz/¼ cup unsweetened cocoa powder
2.5ml/½ tsp baking powder
90g/3½oz/½ cup caster (superfine) sugar
25g/1oz/2 tbsp butter, diced
1 egg, beaten
5ml/1 tsp cherry brandy
50g/2oz/½ cup icing (confectioners') sugar

1 Preheat the oven to 200°C/400°F/Gas 6. Line two baking sheets with baking parchment.

2 Sift the flour, cocoa and baking powder into a bowl and stir in the sugar.

3 Rub the butter into the flour mixture with your fingertips until the mixture resembles coarse breadcrumbs.

4 Mix together the beaten egg and cherry brandy and stir thoroughly into the flour mixture. Cover with clear film (plastic wrap) and chill for approximately 30 minutes.

5 Put the icing sugar in a bowl. Shape walnut-size pieces of dough roughly into a ball and drop into the icing sugar. Toss until thickly coated, then place on the baking sheets.

6 Bake for about 10 minutes, or until just set. Transfer to a wire rack to cool completely.

Variation
If you are making these for children try using fresh orange juice instead of cherry brandy.

Mixed Chocolate Truffles

Give these delectable truffles as a gift and you will have a friend for life.

Makes 20 large or 30 medium truffles

250ml/8fl oz/1 cup double (heavy) cream
275g/10oz fine-quality dark (bittersweet) or plain (semisweet) chocolate, chopped into small pieces
40g/1½oz/3 tbsp unsalted (sweet) butter, cut into small pieces
unsweetened cocoa powder, for dusting (optional)
finely chopped pistachio nuts, to decorate (optional)
400g/14oz dark (bittersweet) chocolate, to decorate (optional)

1 Pour the cream into a pan. Bring to the boil over a medium heat. Remove from the heat and add the chocolate. Stir gently until melted. Stir in the butter. Strain into a bowl and cool to room temperature. Cover with clear film (plastic wrap) and chill for 4 hours or overnight.

2 Line a baking sheet with baking parchment. Using a small ice cream scoop, melon baller or tablespoon, form the mixture into 20 large or 30 medium balls and place on the baking sheet.

3 If dusting with cocoa powder, sift a thick layer of cocoa on to a plate. Roll the truffles in the cocoa, rounding them between the palms of your hands. Do not worry if the truffles are not perfectly round as an irregular shape looks more authentic. Alternatively, roll the truffles in very finely chopped pistachios. Chill on the paper-lined baking sheet until firm. Keep in the refrigerator for up to 10 days or freeze for up to 2 months.

4 If coating with chocolate, do not roll the truffles in cocoa, but freeze them for 1 hour. For perfect results, temper the chocolate. Alternatively, simply melt it in a heatproof bowl over a pan of barely simmering water. Using a fork, dip the truffles, one at a time, into the melted chocolate, tapping the fork on the edge of the bowl to shake off excess. Place on a baking sheet, lined with baking parchment. If the chocolate begins to thicken, reheat it gently until smooth. Chill the truffles until set.

Cherry Brandy Truffles Energy 60kcal/251kJ; Protein 0.9g; Carbohydrate 10.5g, of which sugars 8.2g; Fat 1.8g, of which saturates 1g; Cholesterol 14mg; Calcium 12mg; Fibre 0.3g; Sodium 26mg.
Mixed Truffles Energy 169kcal/705kJ; Protein 1.3g; Carbohydrate 14.4g, of which sugars 14.2g; Fat 11.9g, of which saturates 7.3g; Cholesterol 16mg; Calcium 12mg; Fibre 0.6g; Sodium 11mg.

Chocolate Truffle Medley

These are popular with almost everybody; simply use different combinations of chocolate and flavourings to make your favourites.

Makes 60
115g/4oz plain (semisweet) chocolate
115g/4oz milk chocolate
175g/6oz white chocolate
175ml/6fl oz/¾ cup double (heavy) cream

For the flavouring
30ml/2 tbsp dark rum
30ml/2 tbsp Tia Maria
30ml/2 tbsp apricot brandy

For the coating
45g/3 tbsp coarsely grated plain (semisweet) chocolate
45g/3 tbsp coarsely grated milk chocolate
45g/3 tbsp coarsely grated white chocolate

1 Melt each type of chocolate in a separate bowl. Place the cream in a small pan and heat gently until hot but not boiling. Allow to cool. Stir one-third of the cream into each of the bowls and blend evenly.

2 Add the rum to the plain chocolate and whisk until the mixture becomes lighter in colour. Whisk the Tia Maria into the milk chocolate, and lastly whisk the apricot brandy into the white chocolate.

3 Allow the three mixtures to thicken, giving them an occasional stir, until they are thick enough to divide into equal spoonfuls. Line three baking sheets with baking parchment. Place about 20 teaspoons of each flavoured chocolate mixture, well spaced apart, on to the three baking sheets and chill until firm enough to roll into small balls.

4 Place each of the grated chocolates into separate dishes. Shape the plain chocolate truffles into neat balls and roll in grated plain chocolate to coat evenly.

5 Repeat with the milk chocolate truffles and grated milk chocolate, and the white chocolate truffles and grated white chocolate. Chill the truffles until firm, then arrange neatly in boxes, bags or tins and tie with festive ribbon.

Classic Belgian Chocolate Truffles

When made with the best dark Belgian chocolate, these sweet truffles are the ultimate heavenly indulgence.

Makes 30
250g/9oz Belgian dark (bittersweet) chocolate, such as Callebaut, finely chopped
150g/5oz/10 tbsp unsalted (sweet) butter, diced and softened
100ml/3½fl oz/scant ½ cup double (heavy) cream
15–30ml/1-2 tbsp brandy or liqueur of own choice
15ml/1 tbsp vanilla extract (optional)
100g/3¾oz sifted unsweetened cocoa powder, icing (confectioners') or caster (superfine) sugar, chopped nuts or grated coconut, for coating

1 Melt the chocolate in a heatproof bowl over just boiled water, stirring until smooth. Stir in the butter until melted. Pour the cream into a pan and bring it to simmering point. Remove from the heat and leave to stand for 2 minutes.

2 Pour the cream into the chocolate, stirring until blended. Stir in the brandy or liqueur, with the vanilla extract, if using. Cover and refrigerate for at least 4 hours, stirring frequently, until the mixture is stiff but still malleable.

3 Transfer the chocolate mixture to a glass tray or shallow dish and spread it out so that it is about 3cm/1¼in deep. Cover and put in the refrigerator for 5 hours or overnight.

4 Line a baking sheet with baking parchment. Scoop up the teaspoonfuls of chocolate mixture and transfer to the baking sheet. Continue until all the chocolate has been shaped. Put the mixture back in the refrigerator for 30 minutes.

5 Working quickly, roll each piece of chocolate into a ball. Place slightly apart on parchment-lined baking sheets. Cover lightly with clear film (plastic wrap) and chill again for 1 hour.

6 To coat the truffles, roll them in separate bowls of cocoa powder, icing sugar, caster sugar, chopped nuts or grated coconut until coated. Cover and chill for 10 minutes to firm up again. Store in an airtight container for up to a week.

Chocolate Truffle Medley Energy 65kcal/269kJ; Protein 0.7g; Carbohydrate 5.4g, of which sugars 5.4g; Fat 4.3g, of which saturates 2.6g; Cholesterol 5mg; Calcium 18mg; Fibre 0.1g; Sodium 7mg.
Belgian Chocolate Truffles Energy 108kcal/447kJ; Protein 1.1g; Carbohydrate 5.8g, of which sugars 5.3g; Fat 9g, of which saturates 5.5g; Cholesterol 16mg; Calcium 10mg; Fibre 0.6g; Sodium 63mg.

Coffee Chocolate Truffles

Because these classic chocolates contain fresh cream, they should be stored in the refrigerator and eaten within a few days.

Makes 24

350g/12oz plain (semisweet) chocolate
75ml/5 tbsp double (heavy) cream
30ml/2 tbsp coffee liqueur, such as Tia Maria, Kahlúa or Toussaint
115g/4oz good-quality white dessert chocolate
115g/4oz good-quality milk dessert chocolate

1 Melt 225g/8oz of the plain chocolate in a bowl over a pan of barely simmering water. Stir in the cream and liqueur, then chill the mixture in the refrigerator for 4 hours, until firm.

2 Divide the mixture into 24 equal pieces and quickly roll each into a ball. Chill for one more hour, or until they are firm again.

3 Melt the remaining plain, white and milk chocolate in separate small bowls. Using two forks, carefully dip eight of the truffles, one at a time, into the melted milk chocolate.

4 Repeat with the white and plain chocolate. Place the truffles on a board, covered with baking parchment or foil. Leave to set before removing and placing in a serving bowl or individual paper cases.

Variations

Ginger: *Stir in 40g/1½oz/¼ cup finely chopped crystallized ginger.*
Candied fruit: *Stir in 50g/2oz/⅓ cup finely chopped candied fruit, such as pineapple and orange.*
Pistachio: *Stir in 25g/1oz/¼ cup, chopped, skinned pistachio nuts.*
Hazelnut: *Roll each ball of chilled truffle mixture around a whole skinned hazelnut.*
Raisin: *Soak 40g/1½oz/generous ¼ cup raisins overnight in 15ml/1 tbsp coffee liqueur, such as Tia Maria or Kahlúa and stir into the truffle mixture.*

Malt Whisky Truffles

Whisky aficionados will adore these heavenly alcoholic-flavoured chocolate truffles.

Makes 25–30

200g/7oz plain (semisweet) chocolate, chopped into small pieces
150ml/¼ pint/⅔ cup double (heavy) cream
45ml/3 tbsp malt whisky
115g/4oz/1 cup icing (confectioners') sugar
unsweetened cocoa powder, for coating

1 Melt the chocolate in a heatproof bowl or a double boiler set over a pan of simmering water, stir until smooth, then allow to cool slightly.

2 Using a wire whisk, whip the cream with the whisky in a bowl until thick enough to hold its shape.

3 Stir in the melted chocolate and icing sugar, mixing evenly until well combined. Leave the mixture until it is firm enough to handle. Chill it for about 30 minutes in the refrigerator if necessary.

4 Dust your hands with a little cocoa powder to stop the mixture from sticking to them. Shape the mixture into bitesize balls by rolling a small portion of the mixture between your hands.

5 Coat each ball in cocoa powder and pack them into pretty cases or gift boxes. Store in an airtight container in the refrigerator for up to 3–4 days if necessary.

Variation

Try this recipe with your favourite brand of whisky, whether Scottish or Irish, but try to use malt whisky for its superior taste. American bourbon such as Jack Daniel's or Jim Beam will work just as well as Scotch in this recipe. Simply replace the malt whisky with the same quantity of bourbon.

Coffee Truffles Energy 143kcal/599kJ; Protein 1.5g; Carbohydrate 15.2g, of which sugars 15.1g; Fat 8.7g, of which saturates 5.3g; Cholesterol 6mg; Calcium 30mg; Fibre 0.4g; Sodium 11mg.
Malt Whisky Truffles Energy 77kcal/323kJ; Protein 0.4g; Carbohydrate 8.3g, of which sugars 8.3g; Fat 4.6g, of which saturates 2.8g; Cholesterol 7mg; Calcium 7mg; Fibre 0.2g; Sodium 2mg.

Gingered Truffles

Wonderfully creamy, these rich chocolate truffles are flecked with ginger, coated in dark chocolate and piped with melted white chocolate: a truly impressive gift.

Makes about 30

150ml/¼ pint/⅔ cup double (heavy) cream
400g/14oz plain (semisweet) chocolate, broken into squares
25g/1oz butter
25g/1oz/2 tbsp brandy
30ml/2 tbsp glacé (candied) ginger, finely chopped
15ml/1 tbsp unsweetened cocoa powder
50g/2oz white chocolate, broken into squares

1 Place the cream in a heavy pan and bring to the boil. Remove from the heat and add 150g/5oz of the plain chocolate and the butter. Leave to stand for 5 minutes, stirring, until the chocolate and butter have melted. Return the pan to the heat for a few seconds if the chocolate and butter don't melt completely. Stir in the brandy, then, using an electric whisk, beat for 4–5 minutes, until the mixture is thick. Add 15ml/1 tbsp of the glacé ginger and stir well. Cover and chill for 2–3 hours until firm.

2 For the decoration, dip a teaspoon of the mixture in the cocoa powder and roll it into a ball, using your hands. Set aside and continue until all the mixture is used up. Freeze the truffles for 30 minutes until hard.

3 Place the remaining dark chocolate in a bowl set over a pan of simmering water. Heat until melted, stirring occasionally. Holding a truffle on a fork, spoon the melted chocolate over it until completely coated.

4 Carefully transfer to a baking sheet lined with baking parchment. Sprinkle the remaining glacé ginger over the truffles and leave to cool and harden. Melt the white chocolate and spoon into a baking parchment piping (pastry) bag. Pipe squiggly lines over the truffles and leave in the refrigerator to harden. Pack the truffles into petit four cases and arrange in boxes. Cover with a lid or some clear film (plastic wrap) and tie with a decorative ribbon.

Bourbon Balls

This rich American delicacy laces biscuit and pecan nut truffles with an enticing dash of bourbon.

Makes about 25

175g/6oz Nice biscuits (cookies)
115g/4oz/1 cup pecan nuts, chopped
30ml/2 tbsp unsweetened cocoa powder
75g/3oz/⅔ cup icing (confectioners') sugar, sifted
30ml/2 tbsp clear honey
120ml/4fl oz/½ cup bourbon

1 Put the biscuits in a plastic bag, sealing the open end, and crush them finely, using a rolling pin.

2 Transfer the crumbs into a bowl and add the chopped nuts, cocoa powder and half of the icing sugar. Stir until the mixture is well combined.

3 Add the honey and bourbon to the biscuit mixture. Stir until the mixture forms a stiff paste, adding a touch more bourbon if necessary.

4 Coat your hands in a little cocoa powder and shape the mixture into small balls. Place the balls on a plate and chill in the refrigerator until firm.

5 Roll the balls in the remaining icing sugar, then chill in the refrigerator for 15 minutes and roll again in the sugar.

6 Store in an airtight container until ready to serve, or pack in a decorative gift box.

Variations

• *Nice biscuits are a plain coconut-flavoured biscuit, which have been made in the UK for over 100 years. If you can't find them, use any variety of plain coconut-flavoured biscuit or cookie.*
• *Brandy snaps can also be used and cognac or brandy in place of bourbon.*

Gingered Truffles Energy 111kcal/463kJ; Protein 0.97g; Carbohydrate 9.58g, of which sugars 9.41g; Fat 7.7g, of which saturates 4.7g; Cholesterol 9mg; Calcium 12mg; Fibre 0.4g; Sodium 14mg.
Bourbon Balls Energy 93kcal/389kJ; Protein 1.1g; Carbohydrate 8.8g, of which sugars 6g; Fat 5g, of which saturates 1.2g; Cholesterol 2.6mg; Calcium 12mg; Fibre 0.46g; Sodium 37mg.

Mocha Truffles with Café Noir

The combination of coffee liqueur and chocolate is irresistible. These mocha truffles would make a perfect after-dinner treat.

Makes about 25

175g/6oz plain (semisweet) chocolate
50g/2oz/¼ cup unsalted (sweet) butter
10ml/2 tsp instant coffee granules
30ml/2 tbsp double (heavy) cream
225g/8oz/4 cups Madeira cake crumbs
50g/2oz/½ cup ground almonds
30ml/2 tbsp coffee-flavoured liqueur
unsweetened cocoa powder, chocolate vermicelli (sprinkles) or ground almonds, to coat

1 Break the chocolate into a heatproof bowl with the butter and instant coffee. Set the bowl over a pan of barely simmering water and heat gently until the chocolate and butter have melted and the coffee has dissolved.

2 Remove from the heat and stir in the cream, cake crumbs, ground almonds and coffee-flavoured liqueur.

3 Chill the mixture in the refrigerator until it has firmed up and is more easily handled.

4 Shape into small balls, roll in the cocoa powder, chocolate vermicelli or ground almonds, and place in foil petit four cases. Pack the truffles in gift boxes or arrange them on a decorative plate ready for serving.

Cook's Tip

There are a number of coffee-flavoured liqueurs that are widely available. The Jamaican liqueur Tia Maria is a little drier and lighter than Kahlúa, which has been made in Mexico for over 50 years. Kahlúa is more complex, with chocolate and vanilla flavours as well as coffee. Toussaint, from Haiti, is drier still and is the ideal choice for anybody who finds Tia Maria and Kahlúa a little too sweet.

Rose Petal Truffles

These glamorous chocolates are fun to make as a Valentine gift or for an engagement.

Makes about 25

500g/1¼lb plain (semisweet) chocolate
300ml/½ pint/1¼ cups double (heavy) cream
15ml/1 tbsp rose water
2 drops rose essential oil
250g/9oz plain (semisweet) chocolate, for coating
crystallized rose petals, for decoration

1 Break the chocolate into a heatproof bowl or into the top of a double boiler. Add the cream and set over a pan of barely simmering water. Heat gently, stirring constantly, until the chocolate has melted and the mixture is smooth.

2 Mix in the rose water and the essential oil, then pour into a baking tin (pan) lined with baking parchment and set aside to allow the mixture to cool.

3 When almost firm, take teaspoonfuls of the chocolate and shape into balls, using your hands. Coat your hands in a little cocoa powder if you find the mixture is sticking to them. Chill the truffles until they are hard.

4 Melt the chocolate for the coating in a heatproof bowl over a pan of simmering water. Skewer a truffle and dip it into the melted chocolate.

5 Decorate with a crystallized rose petal before the chocolate has set, then leave on a sheet of baking parchment until the truffles have set completely.

6 Sprinkle the truffles with crystallized rose petals before packing in a box.

Cook's Tip

Look out for crystallized rose petals in specialist food stores and large supermarkets.

Mocha Truffles Energy 108kcal/450kJ; Protein 1.36g; Carbohydrate 10.2g, of which sugars 8.2g; Fat 6.9g, of which saturates 3.5g; Cholesterol 6mg; Calcium 13mg; Fibre 0.43g; Sodium 47.5mg.
Rose Petal Truffles Energy 212kcal/886kJ; Protein 1.7g; Carbohydrate 19.2g, of which sugars 19g; Fat 14.8g, of which saturates 9g; Cholesterol 18mg; Calcium 16mg; Fibre 0.75g; Sodium 4.5mg

Truffle Christmas Puddings

Chocolate truffle Christmas puddings are great fun both to make and receive.

Makes 20

15ml/1 tbsp unsweetened cocoa powder
15ml/1 tbsp icing (confectioners') sugar
225g/8oz/1 cup white chocolate, melted
50g/2oz/¼ cup white marzipan
green and red food colouring
yellow food colouring dust

For the truffle mixture

175ml/6fl oz/¾ cup double (heavy) cream
275g/10oz plain (semisweet) chocolate, chopped
25g/1oz/2 tbsp unsalted (sweet) butter, cut into pieces
30–45ml/2–3 tbsp brandy (optional)

1 Prepare the truffle mixture. In a pan over a medium heat, bring the cream to a boil. Remove from the heat and add the chocolate, stirring until melted. Beat in the butter and add the brandy if using. Strain into a bowl, cover and chill overnight.

2 Line a large baking sheet with baking parchment. Using two teaspoons, form the truffle mixture into 20 balls and place in lines on the paper. Chill if the mixture becomes soft.

3 Sift the cocoa and icing sugar together and coat the truffles. Spread ⅔ of the white chocolate over a new sheet of baking parchment. Using a small daisy cutter, stamp out 20 rounds. Put a truffle on the centre of each daisy, securing with a little of the reserved melted chocolate.

4 Colour ⅔ of the marzipan green and the rest red, using the food colourings. Roll out the green marzipan thinly and stamp out 40 leaves with a tiny holly leaf cutter. Mark the veins with a sharp knife. Mould lots of tiny red marzipan beads.

5 Colour the remaining white chocolate with yellow food colouring and place in a baking parchment piping bag. Fold down the top of the bag, cut off the tip and and pipe the chocolate over the top of each truffle to resemble custard. Arrange the holly leaves and berries on the top of the puddings. Leave until completely set.

Chocolate Mint Truffle Filo Parcels

These exquisite little mint truffle parcels are utterly irresistible: there will be no leftovers. The use of fresh mint in the recipe gives a wonderfully fresh flavour.

Makes 18 parcels

15ml/1 tbsp very finely chopped fresh mint
75g/3oz/¾ cup ground almonds
50g/2oz plain (semisweet) chocolate, grated
115g/4oz/½ cup crème fraîche or fromage frais
2 dessert apples, peeled and grated
9 large sheets filo pastry
75g/3oz/6 tbsp butter, melted
15ml/1 tbsp icing (confectioners') sugar, to dust
15ml/1 tbsp unsweetened cocoa powder, to dust

1 Mix the chopped fresh mint, almonds, grated chocolate, crème fraîche or fromage frais and grated apple in a large mixing bowl. Set aside.

2 Cut the filo pastry sheets into 7.5cm/3in squares and cover with a damp cloth to prevent the sheets from drying out while you prepare the parcels.

3 Brush a square of filo with melted butter, lay on a second sheet, brush again and place a spoonful of filling in the middle of the top sheet. Bring in all four corners and twist to form a purse shape. Repeat to make 18 parcels.

4 Place the filo parcels on a griddle or baking sheet, well brushed with melted butter. Cook on a medium-hot barbecue for about 10 minutes, until the filo pastry is crisp.

5 Leave to cool, then dust lightly with sifted icing sugar and then with sifted cocoa powder.

Cook's Tip
If you can't find crème fraîche or fromage frais, then low-fat cream cheese would work equally well in this recipe.

Truffle Puddings Energy 169kcal/705kJ; Protein 1.3g; Carbohydrate 14.4g, of which sugars 14.2g; Fat 11.9g, of which saturates 7.3g; Cholesterol 16mg; Calcium 12mg; Fibre 0.6g; Sodium 11mg.
Filo Parcels Energy 140kcal/584kJ; Protein 2.3g; Carbohydrate 12.7g, of which sugars 4.1g; Fat 9.2g, of which saturates 4.6g; Cholesterol 16mg; Calcium 32mg; Fibre 0.9g; Sodium 28mg.

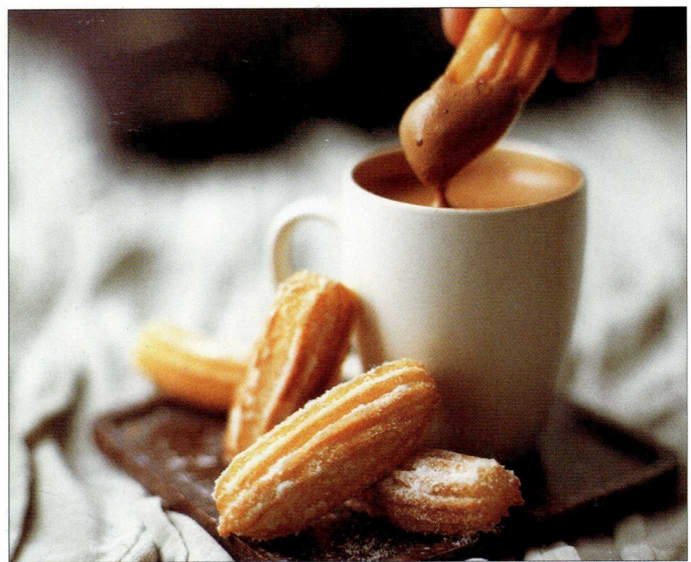

Real Hot Chocolate

There are few better ways to enjoy the heavenly pleasures of chocolate than with a warming mug of proper hot chocolate. If you want a more chocolatey flavour, then simply increase the amount of chocolate. It's all a matter of taste.

Serves 2

115g/4oz plain (semisweet) chocolate with more than 60 per cent cocoa solids
400ml/14fl oz/1⅔ cups milk

1 Break up the chocolate and put it in a heatproof bowl or double boiler set over a pan of barely simmering water.

2 Leave the chocolate in the bowl for 10 minutes until it has completely melted and is smooth.

3 Add the milk to a small pan and, over a medium heat, bring it just to a boil.

4 Stir a little of the hot milk into the melted chocolate.

5 Whisk in the remaining milk – a hand-held blender is good for this – until frothy.

6 Pour the hot chocolate into mugs and drink while hot.

Cook's Tips

- *This is the essence of real hot chocolate. The powdered version that comes in a packet doesn't even compare. Try to make it with the best chocolate you can afford – you'll really notice the difference if you use a cheaper version. This is how the Spanish and Mexicans have been making hot chocolate for centuries, and it's pure heaven.*
- *For an utterly indulgent treat, enjoy your hot chocolate with your favourite chocolate treat, be it a cookie, truffle, cake or other delight. The perfect way to wind down from a busy day and give yourself a treat at supper time.*

Frothy Hot Chocolate

Good hot chocolate should be made with the finest chocolate available. The vanilla pod will impart a delicious flavour to the milk. This is true comfort in a mug, the perfect way to unwind from a busy day after work or after a walk on a cold winter's day.

Serves 4

1 litre/1¾ pints/4 cups milk
1 vanilla pod (bean)
50–115g/2–4oz good-quality dark (bittersweet) chocolate, minimum 60 per cent cocoa solids, grated

1 Pour the milk into a small pan and gently heat.

2 Split the vanilla pod lengthways using a sharp knife to reveal the seeds.

3 Add the pod to the milk and leave for a couple of minutes to let the milk take on the flavour of the vanilla.

4 Add the grated chocolate.

5 Heat the chocolate milk gently, stirring until all the chocolate has melted and the mixture is smooth, then whisk until the mixture boils.

6 Remove the vanilla pod from the pan and divide the drink among four mugs or heatproof glasses.

7 Serve the hot chocolate immediately.

Cook's Tips

- *Large mugs are essential for this drink. They will provide plenty of room to accommodate the lip-smackingly good froth as well as the dark, rich chocolate underneath.*
- *The amount of chocolate to use depends on personal taste – start with a smaller amount if you are unsure of the flavour and taste at the beginning of step 4, adding more if necessary.*

Real Chocolate Energy 386kcal/1619kJ; Protein 9.7g; Carbohydrate 45.9g, of which sugars 45.4g; Fat 19.5g, of which saturates 11.8g; Cholesterol 15mg; Calcium 259mg; Fibre 1.5g; Sodium 90mg.
Frothy Chocolate Energy 179kcal/755kJ; Protein 9.1g; Carbohydrate 19.7g, of which sugars 19.6g; Fat 7.8g, of which saturates 4.8g; Cholesterol 16mg; Calcium 304mg; Fibre 0.3g; Sodium 108mg.

Mexican Hot Chocolate

The Mexicans have been drinking hot chocolate and other chocolate drinks for many hundreds of years. With drinks that taste this good it is easy to see why. Enjoy this drink at any time of day, or night.

Serves 4
1 litre/1 3/4 pints/4 cups milk
1 cinnamon stick
2 whole cloves
115g/4oz plain (semisweet) chocolate, chopped into small pieces
2–3 drops of almond extract

1 Put the milk into a small pan over a gentle heat.

2 Add the cinnamon stick and whole cloves to the pan and heat until the milk is almost boiling.

3 Stir in the plain chocolate over a medium heat until melted and smooth.

4 Strain the mixture into a blender, discarding the whole spices.

5 Add the almond extract and whizz on high speed for about 30 seconds until frothy. Alternatively, whisk the mixture in a bowl with a hand-held electric mixer or wire whisk.

6 Pour into warmed heatproof glasses and serve immediately.

Cook's Tips

• *This drink is a recreation of Mexican chocolate, which is flavored with cinnamon, almonds and vanilla, and has a much grainier texture than other chocolates. It is available in Mexican food stores and some supermarkets. If you can find some, why not try grating a little over the top of your drink for a full Mexican experience.*

• *Few cultures have a longer history of cultivating and consuming chocolate than the Mexicans. The word itself comes from the Aztecs, who lived in Mexico over 500 years ago. They made a drink from cocoa beans called 'xocolatl', meaning 'bitter water'. No wonder this version of hot chocolate is one of the best.*

Champurrada

This popular version of *atole* is made with Mexican chocolate. A special wooden whisk called a *molinollo* is traditionally used when making this frothy drink.

Serves 6
115g/4oz Mexican chocolate, about 2 discs
1.2 litres/2 pints/5 cups water or milk, or a mixture
200g/7oz white masa harina
30ml/2 tbsp soft dark brown sugar

1 Put the chocolate in a mortar and grind with a pestle until it becomes a fine powder. Alternatively, grind the chocolate in a food processor.

2 Put the liquid in a heavy pan and gradually stir in all the masa harina until a smooth paste is formed. Use a traditional wooden *molinollo*, if you have one, or use a wire whisk to create a frothier drink.

3 Place the pan over a moderate heat and bring the mixture to the boil, stirring all the time until the frothy drink thickens.

4 Stir in the ground chocolate, then add the sugar, stirring until the sugar has completely dissolved.

5 Pour into warmed glasses or mugs and serve immediately.

Cook's Tips

• Atole *is a very thick beverage that's popular in Mexico and some parts of the American South-west. It's a combination of masa harina (a heavy type of white flour made from maize), water or milk, crushed fruit and sugar or honey. Latin markets sell instant* atole, *which can be mixed with milk or water.* Atole *can be served hot or at room temperature.*

• *This version of champurrada is also very popular in Mexico. In the morning in Mexican cities you will see people crowd around street-corner tamale carts as non-alcoholic champurrada is served in styrofoam cups or in plastic bags with straws as part of an on-the-go breakfast.*

Mexican Chocolate Energy 220kcal/924kJ; Protein 8.1g; Carbohydrate 25.3g, of which sugars 25.1g; Fat 10.4g, of which saturates 6.4g; Cholesterol 13mg; Calcium 248mg; Fibre 0.6g; Sodium 88mg.
Champurrada Energy 250kcal/1048kJ; Protein 6g; Carbohydrate 41.6g, of which sugars 18.8g; Fat 6.8g, of which saturates 3.5g; Cholesterol 5mg; Calcium 89mg; Fibre 1.1g; Sodium 30mg.

White Hot Chocolate

This rich beverage is a delicious variation on the traditional dark chocolate drink. Flavoured with coffee and orange liqueur, it is the perfect way to round off a dinner party with friends or any other special-occasion meal.

Serves 4
1.75 litres/3 pints/7½ cups milk
175g/6oz white chocolate, chopped into small pieces
10ml/2 tsp coffee powder
10ml/2 tsp orange-flavoured liqueur (optional)
whipped cream and ground cinnamon, to serve

1 Pour the milk into a large heavy pan and heat until it is almost boiling.

2 As soon as bubbles form around the edge of the pan remove the milk from the heat.

3 Add the white chocolate pieces, coffee powder and the orange-flavoured liqueur, if using.

4 Stir the mixture until all the chocolate has melted and the mixture is smooth.

5 Pour the hot chocolate into four mugs.

6 Top each with a swirl or spoonful of whipped cream and a sprinkling of ground cinnamon. Serve immediately.

Variations
A variety of different flavoured liqueurs can be substituted in this recipe for the orange-flavoured liqueur.
Crème de cacao: *Use this chocolate liqueur to make the drink extra chocolatey. Only use the clear version, however, rather than the dark brown variety.*
Crème de banane: *Give your drink a banana flavour with this liqueur.*
Maraschino: *Try this bittersweet cherry-flavoured liqueur to give the drink a hint of maraschino cherries.*

Iced Mint and Chocolate Cooler

This delicious chocolate drink is suprisingly invigorating thanks to the inclusion of peppermint extract and fresh mint leaves. For an even bigger minty kick, replace the chocolate ice cream for some mint chocolate chip ice cream.

Serves 4
60ml/4 tbsp drinking chocolate
400ml/14fl oz/1⅔ cups chilled milk
150ml/¼ pint/⅔ cup natural (plain) yogurt
2.5ml/½ tsp peppermint extract
4 scoops of chocolate ice cream, (or mint chocolate chip ice cream, if you prefer)
mint leaves and chocolate shapes, to decorate

1 Place the drinking chocolate in a small pan and stir in about 120ml/4fl oz/½ cup of the milk. Heat gently, stirring, until almost boiling, then remove the pan from the heat.

2 Pour the hot chocolate milk into a heatproof bowl or large jug (pitcher) and whisk in the remaining milk. Add the natural yogurt and peppermint extract and whisk again.

3 Pour the mixture into four tall glasses, filling them no more than three-quarters full. Top each drink with a scoop of chocolate ice cream. Decorate with mint leaves and chocolate shapes. Serve immediately.

Variations
Use this recipe as a base for other delicious milk drinks.
Chocolate vanilla cooler: *Make the drink as in the main recipe, but use single (light) cream instead of the natural yogurt and 5ml/1 tsp natural vanilla extract instead of the peppermint extract.*
Mocha cooler: *Make the drink as in the main recipe, but dissolve the chocolate in 120ml/4fl oz/½ cup strong black coffee, and reduce the amount of milk to 300ml/½ pint/1¼ cups. Use single (light) cream instead of natural yogurt and omit the peppermint extract and mint leaves.*

White Chocolate Energy 433kcal/1821kJ; Protein 18.4g; Carbohydrate 46.1g, of which sugars 46.1g; Fat 21g, of which saturates 12.7g; Cholesterol 26mg; Calcium 643mg; Fibre 0g; Sodium 236mg.
Mint Cooler Energy 231kcal/968kJ; Protein 8.1g; Carbohydrate 27.9g, of which sugars 27.5g; Fat 10.5g, of which saturates 6.3g; Cholesterol 6mg; Calcium 247mg; Fibre 0g; Sodium 138mg.

Irish Chocolate Velvet

Few things are more deliciously indulgent than this velvety chocolate drink, heavily spiked with Irish whiskey. It is the perfect way to enjoy the end of a splendid feast.

Serves 4

250ml/8fl oz/1 cup double (heavy) cream
400ml/14fl oz/1⅔ cups milk
115g/4oz milk chocolate, chopped into small pieces
30ml/2 tbsp unsweetened cocoa powder
60ml/4 tbsp Irish whiskey
whipped cream, for topping
chocolate curls, to decorate

1 Using a hand-held electric mixer, whip half the cream in a bowl until it is thick enough to hold its shape.

2 Place the milk and chocolate in a pan and heat gently, stirring, until the chocolate has melted and the mxture is smooth and glossy.

3 Whisk in the cocoa, then bring to the boil. Remove from the heat and stir in the remaining cream and the Irish whiskey.

4 Pour quickly into four warmed heatproof mugs or glasses.

5 Top each serving with a generous spoonful of the whipped cream, then the chocolate curls.

6 Serve with peppermint sticks for extra indulgence.

Cook's Tips
• *If you don't have any Irish whiskey, then this recipe will work equally well with your favourite brand of Scotch whisky. Even American bourbon makes a successful substitute.*
• *To make quick chocolate curls, chill a bar of your preferred chocolate in the refrigerator until hard. Run a vegetable peeler down the long side of the bar to peel off curls.*

Warm Chocolate Float

Hot chocolate milkshake, scoops of chocolate ice cream and vanilla ice cream are combined here to make a meltingly delicious drink which will prove a big success with children and adults alike.

Serves 2

115g/4oz plain chocolate, broken into pieces
250ml/8fl oz/1 cup milk
15ml/1 tbsp caster sugar
4 large scoops vanilla ice cream
4 large scoops dark chocolate ice cream
a little lightly whipped cream
grated chocolate or chocolate curls, to decorate

1 Put the chocolate in a saucepan and add the milk and sugar.

2 Heat gently, stirring with a wooden spoon until the chocolate has melted and the mixture is smooth.

3 Place two scoops of each type of ice cream alternately in two heatproof tumblers.

4 Pour the chocolate milk over and around the ice cream. Top with lightly whipped cream and grated chocolate or big chocolate curls.

Variation
For a simpler – and decadently rich – version of a chocolate smoothie, try making the recipe with just two ingredients. Break 150g/5oz good-quality chocolate into pieces and place in a heatproof bowl set over a pan of simmering water, making sure that the bowl does not rest in the water. Add 60ml/4 tbsp full cream (whole) milk and leave until the chocolate melts, stirring occasionally with a wooden spoon. Remove the bowl from the heat, pour another 290ml/10fl oz/1 cup milk over the chocolate and stir to combine. Pour the mixture into a blender or food processor and blend until frothy. Pour into glasses, add ice and chocolate curls or shavings, to serve.

Irish Velvet Energy 390kcal/1623kJ; Protein 7.5g; Carbohydrate 22.4g, of which sugars 21.6g; Fat 28.3g, of which saturates 17.3g; Cholesterol 54mg; Calcium 208mg; Fibre 1.1g; Sodium 145mg.
Warm Float Energy 918kcal/3834kJ; Protein 16.9g; Carbohydrate 92.2g, of which sugars 91.5g; Fat 56g, of which saturates 33.7g; Cholesterol 11mg; Calcium 423mg; Fibre 1.5g; Sodium 208mg.

Honey and Banana Smoothie with Hot Chocolate Sauce

This is a delicious blend of honey and banana, served with a hot chocolate sauce.

Serves 2 generously

450g/1lb/2 cups mashed ripe banana
200ml/7fl oz/scant 1 cup natural (plain) yogurt
30ml/2 tbsp mild honey
350ml/12fl oz/1½ cups orange juice ice cubes, crushed

For the hot chocolate sauce

175g/6oz plain (semisweet) chocolate with more than 60 per cent cocoa solids
60ml/4 tbsp water
15ml/1 tbsp golden (light corn) syrup
15g/½oz/1 tbsp butter

1 First make the hot chocolate sauce. Break up the chocolate and put the pieces into a heatproof bowl placed over a pan of barely simmering water.

2 Leave undisturbed for 10 minutes until the chocolate has completely melted, then add the water, syrup and butter and stir until smooth. Keep warm over the hot water while you make the smoothie.

3 Place all the smoothie ingredients in a blender or food processor and blend until smooth. Pour into big, tall glasses, then pour in some chocolate sauce from a height and serve.

Cook's Tips

- *Pouring the chocolate sauce from a height cools the thin stream of sauce slightly on the way down, so that it thickens on contact with the cold smoothie. The sauce swirls around the glass to give a marbled effect, which is very attractive.*
- *The secret to a successful smoothie is to always serve them ice-cold. Whizzing them up with a handful of ice is the perfect way to ensure this. Keep an ice tray of frozen orange juice at the ready. It's a great way to add extra flavour.*

Grasshopper Coffee

This hot drink is named for the crème de menthe flavour suggestive of a green grasshopper colour.

Serves 2

dark and white chocolate 'after-dinner' style chocolate mints
50ml/2fl oz/¼ cup green crème de menthe
50ml/2fl oz/¼ cup coffee liqueur, such as Tia Maria or Kahlúa
350ml/12fl oz /1½ cups hot strong coffee
50ml/2fl oz/¼ cup whipping cream

1 Cut the dark and white chocolate mints diagonally in half.

2 Divide the two liqueurs equally between two tall, strong latte glasses. Combine well.

3 Fill each glass with the hot coffee and top them with whipped cream.

4 Decorate with the chocolate mint triangles, dividing the white and dark chocolate evenly between the drinks.

Cook's Tip

It is important to use strong coffee to prevent the drink from tasting watery or being too diluted by the liqueurs, though it should be weaker than espresso, which might be overpowering.

Variation

Another great use for crème de menthe is in a chocolatey alcoholic milkshake. You'll need a few scoops of mint chocolate chip ice cream, 120ml/4fl oz/½ cup milk, 30ml/2 tbsp crème de menthe, a sprig of fresh mint and 1 miniature or broken cream-filled chocolate sandwich cookie. In a food processor or blender, combine the ice cream, milk and crème de menthe. Whirl until smooth and pour into a chilled tall glass. Garnish with the broken cookie and a mint sprig.

Smoothie Energy 901kcal/3790kJ; Protein 13.2g; Carbohydrate 148.1g, of which sugars 142.2g; Fat 32.5g, of which saturates 19.4g; Cholesterol 23mg; Calcium 253mg; Fibre 4.9g; Sodium 176mg.
Grasshopper Coffee Energy 210kcal/868kJ; Protein 0.5g; Carbohydrate 6.4g, of which sugars 6.4g; Fat 14g, of which saturates 6.3g; Cholesterol 26mg; Calcium 19mg; Fibre 0g; Sodium 29mg.

Vanilla and Chocolate Caffè Latte

This luxurious vanilla and chocolate version of the classic coffee drink can be served at any time of the day topped with whipped cream, with cinnamon sticks to stir and flavour the drink. Caffè latte is a popular breakfast drink in Italy and France, and is now widely available elsewhere.

Serves 2

750ml/1 ¼ pints/3 cups milk
250ml/8fl oz/1 cup espresso or very strong coffee
45ml/3 tbsp vanilla sugar, plus extra to taste
115g/4oz dark (bittersweet) chocolate, grated
2 cinnamon sticks (optional)

1 Pour the milk into a small pan and bring to the boil, then remove from the heat.

2 Mix the espresso or very strong coffee with 475ml/16fl oz/2 cups of the boiled milk in a large heatproof jug (pitcher). Sweeten with vanilla sugar to taste.

3 Return the remaining boiled milk in the pan to the heat and add the 45ml/3 tbsp vanilla sugar. Stir constantly until dissolved. Bring to the boil, then reduce the heat.

4 Add the dark chocolate and continue to heat, stirring constantly until all the chocolate has melted and the mixture is smooth and glossy.

5 Pour the chocolate milk into the jug of coffee and whisk thoroughly. Serve in tall mugs or glasses. Top each serving with a swirl of whipped cream, and add cinnamon sticks, if you like, for stirring the drink.

Cook's Tip
Vanilla sugar is available from good food stores and large supermarkets, but it's easy to make your own: simply store a vanilla pod (bean) in a jar of sugar for a few weeks until the sugar has taken on the vanilla flavour.

New York Egg Cream

No eggs, no cream, just the best chocolate soda you will ever sip. This legendary drink is evocative of Old New York. No one knows why it is called egg cream but some say it was a witty way of describing richness at a time when no one could afford to put both expensive eggs and cream together in a drink.

Serves 1

45–60ml/3–4 tbsp good-quality chocolate syrup
120ml/4fl oz/½ cup chilled milk
175ml/6fl oz/¾ cup chilled carbonated water
unsweetened cocoa powder, to sprinkle

1 Carefully pour the chocolate syrup into the bottom of a tall glass.

2 Pour the chilled milk on to the chocolate syrup.

3 Pour the carbonated water into the glass, sip up any foam that rises to the top of the glass and continue to add the remaining water.

4 Dust with the cocoa powder and serve.

5 Stir the egg cream well before drinking.

Cook's Tips
• An authentic egg cream is made with an old-fashioned seltzer dispenser that you press and spritz.
• Chocolate syrup is available in supermarkets and food stores. It is a ready-to-use syrup, usually a combination of unsweetened cocoa powder, sugar or golden (light corn) syrup and various other flavourings. It is usually quite sweet and is most often used to flavour milk or as a dessert sauce. It cannot be substituted for melted chocolate in recipes. New Yorkers invariably use the chocolate syrup made by Fox's of Brooklyn called U-bet in their egg creams.

Caffè Latte Energy 543kcal/2290kJ; Protein 14.9g; Carbohydrate 76.5g, of which sugars 76g; Fat 22.1g, of which saturates 13.4g; Cholesterol 24mg; Calcium 451mg; Fibre 1.5g; Sodium 156mg.
Egg Cream Energy 302kcal/1266kJ; Protein 6.9g; Carbohydrate 32.9g, of which sugars 32.5g; Fat 16.9g, of which saturates 5.8g; Cholesterol 8mg; Calcium 202mg; Fibre 0.4g; Sodium 74mg.

Barbara

This cocktail recipe is variation on the classic White Russian (vodka, coffee liqueur and cream), but with a chocolatey flavour replacing the original coffee.

Makes 1 cocktail

1 measure/1½ tbsp vodka
1 measure/1½ tbsp white crème de cacao
½ measure/2 tsp double (heavy) cream
white chocolate, to decorate

Shake all the ingredients well with ice, and strain into a chilled cocktail glass. Grate white chocolate over the surface.

Cook's Tips

• *Endlessly useful in the cocktail repertoire, the world of chocolate-flavoured liqueurs begins with simple crème de cacao, which comes in two versions, brown or dark (which may also contain some vanilla flavouring) and white (which tends to be considerably sweeter). If the designation "Chouao" appears on the label, then the cocoa beans used have come from that particular district of the Venezuelan capital, Caracas.*
• *For all cocktail recipes, 1 measure should be taken as the standard cocktail measure, that is 25ml/1fl oz.*

Whiteout

A highly indulgent chocolate cream cocktail preparation which blends gin with sweet white crème de cacao. It tastes delicious and far more innocuous than it actually is.

Makes 1 cocktail

1½ measures/2 tbsp gin
1 measure/1½ tbsp white crème de cacao
1 measure/1½ tbsp double (heavy) cream
white chocolate, to decorate

Shake all the ingredients very well with ice to amalgamate the cream fully, and then strain into a chilled cocktail glass. Grate a small piece of white chocolate over the surface.

Arago

This delightful creamy chocolate- and banana-flavoured creation is quite irresistible.

Makes 1 cocktail

1½ measures/2 tbsp cognac
1 measure/1½ tbsp crème de banane
1 measure/1½ tbsp double (heavy) cream
grated dark (bittersweet) chocolate, to decorate

Shake all the ingredients well with ice, and strain into a chilled cocktail glass. Sprinkle the surface of the drink with grated dark chocolate.

Pompeii

Here is a spin on the formula for an Alexander cocktail (gin, crème de cacao and cream), but with the chocolate component given a sweeter, nutty edge.

Makes 1 cocktail

1 measure/1½ tbsp cognac
¾ measure/3 tsp crème de cacao
½ measure/2 tsp amaretto
1 measure/1½ tbsp double (heavy) cream
flaked almonds, to decorate

Shake all the ingredients well with ice and strain into a chilled cocktail glass. Sprinkle the surface with flaked almonds.

Cook's Tips

• *Use crème de cacao to boost the richness of your most chocolatey desserts, or add it to a cup of hot, strong coffee on a cold day for a quick chocolate fix.*
• *When using hot chocolate in a cocktail, it is always preferable to use good-quality unsweetened cocoa powder with a good, high proportion of real cacao solids in it. The alternative – drinking chocolate – is mostly sugar and has a much less concentrated flavour.*

Barbara Energy 201kcal/833kJ; Protein 0.2g; Carbohydrate 5.9g, of which sugars 5.9g; Fat 10.9g, of which saturates 4.3g; Cholesterol 18mg; Calcium 11mg; Fibre 0g; Sodium 25mg.
Whiteout Energy 305kcal/1262kJ; Protein 0.4g; Carbohydrate 6.1g, of which sugars 6.1g; Fat 17.3g, of which saturates 8.3g; Cholesterol 34mg; Calcium 17mg; Fibre 0g; Sodium 28mg.
Araga Energy 261kcal/1078kJ; Protein 0.4g; Carbohydrate 6.1g, of which sugars 6.1g; Fat 17.3g, of which saturates 8.3g; Cholesterol 34mg; Calcium 17mg; Fibre 0g; Sodium 28mg.
Pompeii Energy 271kcal/1121kJ; Protein 0.4g; Carbohydrate 8.6g, of which sugars 8.6g; Fat 16.2g, of which saturates 8.3g; Cholesterol 34mg; Calcium 16mg; Fibre 0g; Sodium 23mg.

Coffee and Chocolate Flip

Use only the freshest egg in this recipe, as it isn't cooked. The result is a smoothly frothy, intensely rich drink with a strong, beguiling coffee flavour. The chocolate element is in the garnish.

Makes 1 cocktail
1 egg
5ml/1tsp sugar
1 measure/1½ tbsp cognac
1 measure/1½ tbsp Kahlúa
5ml/1tsp dark-roast instant coffee granules
3 measures/4½ tbsp double (heavy) cream
unsweetened cocoa powder, to decorate

1 Separate the egg and lightly beat the white until frothy. In a separate bowl, beat the egg yolk with the sugar.

2 In a small pan, combine the brandy, Kahlúa, coffee and cream and warm over a very low heat. Allow the mixture to cool, then whisk it into the egg yolk.

3 Add the egg white to the egg and cream, and pour the mixture back and forth until it is smooth. Pour into a tall glass over crushed ice and sprinkle the top with cocoa powder.

Alhambra Royale

Perfect for relaxing with in front of a warm fire.

Makes 1 cocktail
250ml/8fl oz/1 cup hot chocolate
1 small piece orange rind
1½ measures/2 tbsp cognac
15ml/1 tbsp whipped cream
unsweetened cocoa powder, to decorate

Drop the orange rind into the hot chocolate. Heat the cognac in a metal ladle over a gas flame or over boiling water, and set it alight. Pour it, flaming, into the chocolate. Stir it in, and spoon a blob of whipped cream on to the surface of the drink. Sprinkle with cocoa powder.

Hollywood Nuts

Almond, chocolate and hazelnut are among the flavours in this cocktail.

Makes 1 cocktail
1 measure/1½ tbsp white rum
½ measure/2 tsp amaretto
½ measure/2 tsp brown crème de cacao
½ measure/2 tsp Frangelico
1 measure/1½ tbsp sparkling lemonade

Shake all but the last ingredient with ice and strain into a rocks glass half-filled with cracked ice. Add the lemonade and stir. Garnish with a slice of lemon.

Mistress

This is a long, creamy chocolate cocktail.

Makes 1 cocktail
1½ measures/2 tbsp gin
1 measure/1½ tbsp white crème de cacao
2 measures/3 tbsp pineapple juice
1 measure/1½ tbsp passion fruit juice
1 measure/1½ tbsp whipping cream
¼ measure/1 tsp Campari

Shake all but the last ingredient with ice and strain into a highball glass, half-filled with ice. Drizzle the Campari on top.

Blue Lady

This is a sweet, creamy cocktail that combines the flavours of two popular liqueurs, creating a most striking hue.

Makes 1 cocktail
1½ measures/2 tbsp blue curaçao
½ measure/2 tsp white crème de cacao
½ measure/2 tsp double (heavy) cream

Shake all the ingredients thoroughly with ice and strain into a chilled cocktail glass. Do not garnish.

Flip Energy 602kcal/2489kJ; Protein 7.5g; Carbohydrate 12.2g, of which sugars 12.2g; Fat 49.7g, of which saturates 26.6g; Cholesterol 293mg; Calcium 72mg; Fibre 0g; Sodium 109mg.
Alhambra Energy 361kcal/1512kJ; Protein 9.5g; Carbohydrate 27.9g, of which sugars 27.4g; Fat 15.1g, of which saturates 9.5g; Cholesterol 40mg; Calcium 300mg; Fibre 0g; Sodium 151mg.
Hollywood Nuts Energy 170kcal/706kJ; Protein 0g; Carbohydrate 7.2g, of which sugars 7.2g; Fat 3.9g, of which saturates 0g; Cholesterol 0mg; Calcium 6mg; Fibre 0g; Sodium 24mg.
Mistress Energy 300kcal/1249kJ; Protein 0.7g; Carbohydrate 14.3g, of which sugars 14.3g; Fat 14g, of which saturates 6.3g; Cholesterol 26mg; Calcium 25mg; Fibre 0g; Sodium 35mg.
Blue Lady Energy 201kcal/836kJ; Protein 0.2g; Carbohydrate 15.4g, of which sugars 15.4g; Fat 8.7g, of which saturates 4.2g; Cholesterol 17mg; Calcium 10mg; Fibre 0g; Sodium 18mg.

Piranha

This is one of those deceptive chocolate-flavoured cocktails that tastes relatively harmless, but in fact packs quite a punch, much like the predatory fish after which it is named.

Makes 1 cocktail

1½ measures/2 tbsp vodka
1 measure/1½ tbsp brown crème de cacao
1 measure/1½ tbsp ice-cold cola

Pour the alcohol into a rocks glass or short tumbler containing plenty of cracked ice and stir vigorously before adding the cola.

Brandy Alexander

One of the best chocolate-flavoured cocktails of them all, Brandy Alexander can be served at the end of a grand dinner with coffee, or as the first drink of the evening at a cocktail party, since the cream in it helps to line the stomach.

Makes 1 cocktail

1 measure/1½ tbsp cognac
1 measure/1½ tbsp brown crème de cacao
1 measure/1½ tbsp double (heavy) cream
grated dark (bittersweet) chocolate or nutmeg, to decorate

Shake the ingredients thoroughly with ice and strain into a tall cocktail glass. Scatter ground nutmeg, or grate a little whole nutmeg, on top. Alternatively, sprinkle with coarsely grated dark chocolate.

Cook's Tip
Creamy cocktails should generally be made with double (heavy) cream, as the single (light) version tends to be too runny.

Hammer Horror

Use the best vanilla ice cream you can find for this smooth cocktail, and preferably one that is made with whole egg and real vanilla, for extra richness.

Makes 1 cocktail

1 measure/1½ tbsp vodka
1 measure/1½ tbsp Kahlúa
60ml/4 tbsp vanilla ice cream
grated dark chocolate, to decorate

Add all the ingredients to a liquidizer with cracked ice, blend for a few seconds and then strain into a cocktail glass. Sprinkle the surface of the drink with grated dark chocolate.

Alexander the Great

This cocktail is another variation on the chocolate/coffee/cream combination. Related to the classic Brandy Alexander, this drink is reputed to have been invented by the late Hollywood singing star Nelson Eddy.

Makes 1 cocktail

1½ measure/2 tbsp vodka
½ measure/2 tsp Kahlúa
½ measure/2 tsp brown crème de cacao
½ measure/2 tsp double (heavy) cream

Shake all the ingredients well with plenty of ice, and strain into a cocktail glass. Add a couple of chocolate-coated coffee beans to the drink.

Cook's Tips
- *The liqueur components in Alexander the Great are Kahlúa and the brown version of chocolate liqueur. If your guests do not have such a sweet tooth, substitute Tia Maria and white crème de cacao.*
- *Chocolate-coated coffee beans are quite fashionable to serve on chocolate cocktails. They are naturally quite crunchy, but have the extra caffeine kick of the chocolate coating.*

Piranha Energy 174kcal/725kJ; Protein 0g; Carbohydrate 8.3g, of which sugars 8.3g; Fat 3.9g, of which saturates 0g; Cholesterol 0mg; Calcium 6mg; Fibre 0g; Sodium 24mg.
Brandy Alexander Energy 288kcal/1190kJ; Protein 0.6g; Carbohydrate 6.3g, of which sugars 6.3g; Fat 22.7g, of which saturates 11.7g; Cholesterol 48mg; Calcium 22mg; Fibre 0g; Sodium 30mg.
Hammer Horror Energy 243kcal/1012kJ; Protein 2.2g; Carbohydrate 17.6g, of which sugars 16.9g; Fat 9g, of which saturates 3.7g; Cholesterol 15mg; Calcium 65mg; Fibre 0g; Sodium 58mg.
Alexander the Great Energy 227kcal/938kJ; Protein 0.2g; Carbohydrate 5.9g, of which sugars 5.9g; Fat 10.6g, of which saturates 4.2g; Cholesterol 17mg; Calcium 11mg; Fibre 0g; Sodium 25mg.

Coffee Cognac Cooler

Topped with decorative chocolate curls, this drink is unabashedly decadent, and not for those who are counting calories. The recipe serves two, so you can both feel guilty together.

Makes 2 cocktails
250ml/8fl oz cold strong dark-roast coffee
80ml/3fl oz cognac
50ml/2fl oz coffee liqueur
50ml/2fl oz double (heavy) cream
10ml/2 tsp sugar
2 scoops coffee ice cream
chocolate curls or shavings, to decorate

1 Shake or blend all the ingredients except the ice cream together with plenty of crushed ice. Pour into tall cocktail glasses and gently add a scoop of ice cream to each.

2 Garnish with chocolate curls or shavings, and serve with a long-handled spoon. For more of a chocolate hit, pour a little melted chocolate on to a baking tray, allow it to cool and then chisel it carefully away in long curls with the point of a knife.

Savoy Hotel

It's a short step from London's Savoy Theatre to the American Bar in the hotel itself, where this delightful chocolate and brandy flavoured cocktail was created. It's a pousse-café or layered drink that requires a steady hand.

Makes 1 cocktail
1 measure/1½ tbsp brown crème de cacao
1 measure/1½ tbsp Bénédictine
1 measure/1½ tbsp cognac

Carefully pour each of the ingredients, in this order, over the back of a spoon into a liqueur glass or sherry schooner to create a multi-layered drink. Serve immediately, while the effect is intact.

Coffee-chocolate Soda

This is a fun, refreshing drink that tastes as good as it looks. The combination of chocolate ice cream and coffee-flavoured fizz makes for an unusually textured but thoroughly exciting cocktail. This recipe makes enough to serve two.

Makes 2 cocktails
250ml/8fl oz strong cold coffee
60ml/4 tbsp double (heavy) cream, or 30ml/2 tbsp evaporated milk (optional)
250ml/8fl oz cold soda water
2 scoops chocolate ice cream
chocolate-covered coffee beans, roughly chopped, to garnish

Pour the coffee into tall cocktail glasses. Add the cream or evaporated milk, if using. Add the soda water and stir. Gently place a scoop of ice cream into the mixture. Garnish with some of the roughly chopped chocolate-covered coffee beans. Serve with a long spoon or a straw.

Variation
Try chocolate mint ice cream and sprinkle with good-quality grated chocolate.

Captain Kidd

Brandy and dark rum make a heady, but very successful mix in a powerful cocktail, and this one is further enhanced by the addition of strong chocolate flavour. There are no non-alcoholic ingredients, you'll notice, so watch out.

Makes 1 cocktail
1½ measures/2 tbsp cognac
1 measure/1½ tbsp dark rum
1 measure/1½ tbsp brown crème de cacao

Shake well with ice, and strain into a chilled champagne saucer. Garnish with a physalis or a half-slice of orange.

Coffee Cognac Energy 298kcal/1237kJ; Protein 0.5g; Carbohydrate 13.9g, of which sugars 13.9g; Fat 13.5g, of which saturates 8.4g; Cholesterol 34mg; Calcium 16mg; Fibre 0g; Sodium 9mg.
Savoy Hotel Energy 192kcal/798kJ; Protein 0g; Carbohydrate 5.7g, of which sugars 5.7g; Fat 3.9g, of which saturates 0g; Cholesterol 0mg; Calcium 5mg; Fibre 0g; Sodium 22mg.
Soda Energy 255kcal/1057kJ; Protein 2.7g; Carbohydrate 12.4g, of which sugars 11.8g; Fat 21.3g, of which saturates 13.7g; Cholesterol 56mg; Calcium 75mg; Fibre 0g; Sodium 43mg.
Captain Kidd Energy 220kcal/912kJ; Protein 0g; Carbohydrate 5.7g, of which sugars 5.7g; Fat 3.9g, of which saturates 0g; Cholesterol 0mg; Calcium 5mg; Fibre 0g; Sodium 22mg.

Index